COLLECTIVE BARGAINING AND THE GIG ECONOMY

This open access book investigates the role of collective bargaining in the gig economy.

Despite the variety of situations covered by the term 'gig economy', collective agreements for employees and non-employees are being concluded in various countries, either at company or at branch level. Offline workers such as riders, food deliverers, drivers or providers of cleaning services are slowly gaining access to the series of negotiated rights that, in the past, were only available to employees.

Embedded in the EU legal framework, including the EU Commission's proposal for a Directive on improving working conditions in platform work and its Draft Guidelines on the application of EU competition law, both from December 2021, the chapters analyse recent high-profile decisions including Uber in France's Cour de Cassation, Glovo in the Tribunal Supremo, and Uber in the UK Supreme Court. They evaluate the bargaining agents in different Member States of the EU, to determine whether established actors are participating in the dynamics of the gig economy or if they are being substituted, totally or partially, by new agents. Interesting best practices are drawn from the comparison, also as regards the contents of collective bargaining, raising awareness in those countries that are being left behind in the dynamics of the gig economy.

The book collects the results of the COGENS (VS/2019/0084) research project, funded by the European Union, that gathered scholars and stakeholders from 17 countries. It will be an invaluable resource for scholars, trade unionists, employers' representatives and policy makers.

This book pertains to the results of the project 'COGENS: Collective Bargaining and the Gig Economy – New Perspectives' (VS/2019/0084), financed by the European Union. The opinions reflected in the text are those of the authors and not backed by the European Commission.

ACTION CO-FINANCED BY THE EUROPEAN UNION
VS/2019/0084

Collective Bargaining and the Gig Economy

A Traditional Tool for New Business Models

Edited by

José María Miranda Boto
and
Elisabeth Brameshuber

•HART•
OXFORD • LONDON • NEW YORK • NEW DELHI • SYDNEY

HART PUBLISHING

Bloomsbury Publishing Plc

Kemp House, Chawley Park, Cumnor Hill, Oxford, OX2 9PH, UK

1385 Broadway, New York, NY 10018, USA

29 Earlsfort Terrace, Dublin 2, Ireland

HART PUBLISHING, the Hart/Stag logo, BLOOMSBURY and the Diana logo are trademarks of Bloomsbury Publishing Plc

First published in Great Britain 2022

Open Access was funded by the European Commission.

A catalogue record for this book is available from the British Library.

A catalogue record for this book is available from the Library of Congress.

ISBN: HB: 978-1-50995-619-7
ePDF: 978-1-50995-621-0
ePub: 978-1-50995-620-3

Typeset by Compuscript Ltd, Shannon

To find out more about our authors and books visit www.hartpublishing.co.uk. Here you will find extracts, author information, details of forthcoming events and the option to sign up for our newsletters.

The authors dedicate this volume to their dear friend

MARIE-CÉCILE ESCANDE-VARNIOL

As a testimony of many years of fruitful collaboration, building teams and networks that go beyond the borders of Academia

PREFACE

This is a book that closes many months of research, started physically before the Covid-19 pandemic, and closed virtually when its end was, hopefully, closer. The Covid-19 pandemic has brought along a tremendous change in how we work, leading also to an increased demand for platform work. This is displayed by current figures: the size of the digital labour platform economy in the EU has grown almost fivefold from an estimated €3 billion in 2016 to about €14 billion in 2020 (C(2021) 4230 final, 5). According to the recent proposal of the Commission for a Directive on improving working conditions in platform work (COM(2021) 762 final), 'today, over 28 million people in the EU work through digital labour platforms. In 2025, their number is expected to have reached 43 million'.

COGENS was a research project led by the Universidad de Santiago de Compostela, the Wirtschaftsuniversität Wien and Astrées, with a team composed of researchers from 17 countries. It was co-financed by the European Union (VS/2019/0084). Within the framework of the project, its members started to debate the topic of collective bargaining in the gig economy in 2019. The two main axes of the research were subjects (both those who bargain and those who benefit from the bargaining process) and contents. The main activities of the project were two transnational seminars, held in Vienna and Lund, where a rich debate with stakeholders took place and helped the development of the research, culminating in a final conference, held in Santiago de Compostela, with a hybrid formula, in June 2021.

The COGENS project was integrated by the following researchers: Auriane Lamine (Belgium); Jakub Tomšej (Czech Republic); Judith Brockmann (Germany); José María Miranda Boto, Yolanda Maneiro Vázquez, Diana Santiago Iglesias, Guillermo Barrios Baudor and Daniel Pérez del Prado (Spain); Sylvaine Laulom, Marie-Cécile Escande-Varniol, Cécile Nicod and Christophe Teissier (France); Piera Loi (Italy); Tamás Gyulavári and Gábor Kártyás (Hungary); Luca Ratti (Luxembourg); Nicola Gundt (the Netherlands); Franz Marhold and Elisabeth Brameshuber (Austria); Łukasz Pisarczyk (Poland); Teresa Coelho Moreira (Portugal); Felicia Roşioru (Romania); Barbara Kresal (Slovenia); Jenny Julén Votinius (Sweden); Jeremias Adams-Prassl (United Kingdom); and Kübra Doğan Yenisey (Turkey). José María Miranda Boto and Elisabeth Brameshuber were in charge of the academic coordination of the team. Christophe Teissier, from Astrées, helped them in this task.

Within the project, particular focus was put on giving a voice to persons working in the gig economy, their service partners/employers and their respective representatives. This was effected by roundtable sessions in which, for example, the CEO of the largest food delivery company in Austria, the head of the department for social policy and health in the Austrian Economic Chambers, the Swedish Transport Workers' Union and the Swedish trade organisation for the self-employed participated. Professionals from institutions such as the International Labour Organization (ILO), the European Trade Union Institute for Research (ETUI) and the European Trade Union Federation (ETUC) also actively participated in the seminars by presenting and discussing, with academics and stakeholders, for example, of the Polish Solidarność, the French 'IRES – Sharers and workers network', the Riders' Union Bologna, the Hans Böckler Stiftung, the Spanish Unión General de Trabajadores and Comisiones Obreras, and the Agence Nationale pour l'Amélioration des Conditions de Travail.

The project's goal was to explore whether and if so, collective agreements could provide a means for guaranteeing (some) labour protection for persons working in the gig economy who are not classed as employees in the sense that the whole corpus of labour law applies. Unlike other research on the gig economy, this project thus took for granted that many persons working in the gig economy are not employees. It aimed at shedding some light on their (potential) collective labour rights. This entails, for example, the evaluation of the bargaining agents in different Member States, to check if the established actors are participating in the dynamics of the gig economy or if they are being substituted, totally or partially, by new agents. Interesting best practices can be drawn from the comparisons, raising awareness in those countries that are being left behind in the dynamics of the gig economy. Contents, of course, were studied too, in order to check the suitability of real collective bargaining in the gig economy. A first, theoretical approach revealed that 'digital' contents, specific issues relating to online work, for example, can be identified. Reality shows, though, that collective partners have also started to bargain on 'classical' issues, such as wages or paid holidays.

This book is the final distillation of the COGENS research project, with chapters moving between the poles of regulation *de lege lata* via interpretation of existing legal frameworks, regulation *de lege ferenda* and case analysis. These are exploratory papers, as collective bargaining is not a consolidated institution in the gig economy. Therefore, major parts of this book are dedicated, actually, to the convergence of possible regulations. Yet, part of the research also dealt with actual collective agreements in the gig economy, displayed by further chapters. Finally, theoretical speculation has left the ground to the study of real deals and the panorama is enriched with the verification of the proposed theoretical hypothesis.

The editors would like to express their gratitude to the authors of this book as well as the other members of the COGENS project for their in-depth, comprehensive but at the same time prospective analyses. This systematic examination of theoretical approaches to and actual practices of collective bargaining in this new field of economy can help and encourage academics and legal practitioners, as well as policymakers and other stakeholders to achieve a better understanding of the advantages of regulating labour relations via collective bargaining agreements.

Our especial thanks go to Roberta Bassi from Hart Publishing for her dedication and support in editing this book. Throughout the project, Tania Fernández Saborido helped in managing the logistics, for which we would like to thank her, too. The publication of this book would not have been possible without the administrative support of Jasmin Pieper, Universität Wien, and Lidia Gil Otero, Universidad de Santiago de Compostela.

José María Miranda Boto and Elisabeth Brameshuber
Vienna, October 2021

CONTENTS

PART II
ACTORS AND CONTENTS

LIST OF CONTRIBUTORS

José María Miranda Boto (editor) is Associate Professor of Labour Law at the Universidad de Santiago de Compostela and has acted as manager of the COGENS Project. He has published more than one hundred papers about Spanish and European Labour Law. He has been a guest professor at the universities of Lyon 2 and Vienna, and is the Secretary General of the Spanish Association of Labour and Social Security Law. He has also published two monographs about law in JRR Tolkien's Works.

Elisabeth Brameshuber (editor) is Professor of Labour and Social Security Law and Deputy Head of the Institute for Labour and Social Security Law, Universität Wien. In her research, besides collective bargaining in a changing world of work, she focuses on information and consultation rights, and fundamental rights and labour law, with recent publications on the European Pillar of Social Rights, amongst others. She is a member of the Austrian Federal Ministry of Labour's 'Rat Neue Arbeitswelten' (Council on the New World of Work).

Jeremias Adams-Prassl is Professor of Law at Magdalen College, Oxford. He is particularly interested in the future of work and innovation, with recent books including *Humans as a Service: the Promise and Perils of Work in the Gig Economy* (Oxford University Press 2018) and *Great Debates in EU Law* (MacMillan 2021). Since April 2021, he has led a five-year research project on 'Algorithms at Work', funded by the European Research Council and a 2020 Leverhulme Prize. He tweets at @JeremiasPrassl.

Judith Brockmann is Professor of Health Policy and Law at Hochschule für Angewandte Wissenschaften Hamburg. She studied law in Hamburg and Paris (Paris XI). Before joining HAW Hamburg, she was member of Hamburg University's law faculty for several years, after some years of being an independent lawyer in a Hamburg-based law firm. In her research, she focuses on interactions between labour law and social security law, also in a comparative law perspective, with a special focus on health issues. She is member of the European INLACRIS network and the Franco-German research group GEFACT.

Tamás Gyulavári is a Professor of Labour Law and Chair of Labour Law Department at Pazmány Peter Katolikus Egyetem, Budapest. He is editor of the *Hungarian Labour Law E-Journal* and has also been working in many EU projects in association with the Human European Consultancy, Leeds University,

Université Lyon 2, and Astrées. He was also an ILO expert in Albania (2012–16). He is member of the European Labour Law Network and the Academic Network of Experts on Disability.

Gábor Kártyás works as Associate Professor at the Labour Law Department of Pazmány Peter Katolikus Egyetem, Budapest. His main research fields are posted workers in EU law, temporary agency work, other multiparty employment relationships and working time. He has been involved in a number of international research projects, including the ETUI and Eurofound. Besides his academic activities he supports the labour law jurisdiction of the Supreme Court of Hungary (Kúria) as advocate general.

Marta Kozak-Maśnicka is a PhD student in the Department of Labour Law and Social Security at the Uniwersytet Warszawski. She is also a researcher at the Center for Research on the Law of Eastern Europe and Central Asia. Her scientific interests in labour law concentrate on the legal protection of whistleblowers in Europe and Poland, as well as platform work in the gig economy.

Barbara Kresal is Associate Professor of Labour Law and Social Security at the Univerza v Ljubljani and a researcher at the Inštitut za delo pri Pravni fakulteti v Ljubljani. She is a member of the European Committee of Social Rights. Her recent research focuses on non-standard forms of employment, precarious work, equal pay and non-discrimination, economic and social human rights, European Social Charter.

Sylvaine Laulom is Advocate General in the Social Chamber of the French Court of Cassation. Before she came into office at the Court in early 2019, she held a position as Professor of Private Law at Université Lumière Lyon 2. Her research interests are mainly European social law and national and comparative labour law. She directed and/or was involved in several research projects, in particular on collective bargaining in times of crisis, on discrimination, transnational collective bargaining, etc.

Piera Loi is Professor of Labour Law at Università di Cagliari. Director of the Master in Labour law and Industrial Relations in the private and public sector. Principal Investigator (2018–21) of the regional research group, Region of Sardinia, on 'Digital platforms work: risk and opportunities'. She is author of the 'Monograph on the Principle of Reasonableness and Proportionality in Labour Law' (Giappichelli 2016).

Yolanda Maneiro Vázquez is an Associate Professor of Labour and Social Security Law at Universidad de Santiago de Compostela. She is the co-manager of a research project granted by the Ministry of Science and Innovation (2018–22) on the case law of the European Court of Justice and its impact in Spain. Her publications include those on labour procedural law, fundamental rights and European Union social law. She is a mediator for the Galician System for the Extrajudicial Settlement of Labour Disputes.

Teresa Coelho Moreira is an Assistant Professor with Habilitation at Universidade do Minho – Escola de Direito, Braga. She is an integrated member of JusGov and coordinator of the Human Rights Research Group at the University of Minho Law School. She is also a collaborator in several postgraduate courses, master's and doctoral degrees at national and international level, and speaker at several national and international congresses. She has several publications at national and international level. She is a member of the Editorial Board of the several journals with peer review in Portugal, Spain, Italy, France, Brazil and Argentina.

Daniel Pérez del Prado (orcid.org/0000-0001-7106-6769) is an Associate Professor of Labour and Social Security Law at Universidad Carlos III de Madrid, PhD in Law and also an economist. He is author of four books and more than a hundred articles on social law but frequently analysed from an interdisciplinary perspective. He has had an intensive international activity, taking part in a number of research projects, developing research stays at some of the most prestigious universities and as an expert of the European Commission and the European Parliament.

Łukasz Pisarczyk is an Associate Professor in the Department of Labour Law at the Uniwersytet Warszawski and a visiting professor at the University of Silesia in Katowice (Uniwersytet Śląski w Katowicach); from 2016 to 2018 a member of the Codification Committee of Labour Law (Poland); a member of the editorial board of the journal *Monitor Prawa Pracy* (Monitor Labour Law); a member of the International Advisory Board of the *Italian Labour Law e-Journal*.

Luca Ratti is an Associate Professor of European and Comparative Labour Law at the Université du Luxembourg. He previously served as Senior Researcher and Adjunct Professor in Labour Law and Social Security at the University of Bologna, where he obtained his PhD. He was visiting post-doc at the University of Reading (UK). He is currently Principal Investigator in research projects funded by the European Commission and the Luxemburgish Fonds National de la Recherche (FNR).

Felicia Roşioru is Associate Professor of Labour Law and EU Employment Law at Universitatea Babes-Bolyai, Cluj-Napoca. She has been a visiting professor at Institut d'études du travail de Lyon, Université Lumière Lyon 2. Member of the COGENS, INLACRIS and NUTRA projects. Her research focuses, from a comparative perspective, on the concept of subordination, the status of intermediate categories, such as the economically dependent workers and the status and the collective rights of platform workers.

Jakub Tomšej is a teacher and researcher at the Department of Labour and Social Security Law at the Law Faculty of the Univerzita Karlova in Prague, specialising in labour and non-discrimination law. He has participated in several local and international research projects, and is an author or co-author of many books and papers. He acts as a Czech national expert in several professional networks, including the European Equality Law Network. He is also a practising lawyer in labour law.

Kübra Doğan Yenisey is Professor in Labour Law and Social Security Law at İstanbul Bilgi Üniversitesi and the General Secretary of the Turkish Association of Labour and Social Security Law. Having graduated from the Faculty of Law, Ankara University, she received her doctorate degree from the University of Geneva. She has authored and edited many books and numerous articles on individual and collective labour law. She is the founder director of the Comparative Labour and Social Security Law Research Center at İstanbul Bilgi University.

Introduction

JOSÉ MARÍA MIRANDA BOTO AND ELISABETH BRAMESHUBER

One of the main findings of the COGENS project is that at least in some countries, collective bargaining for gig workers is possible in theory or actually happens. In some cases, the law allows, apart from collective bargaining for employees, for collective bargaining for economically dependent employee-like workers.

The question is, though, whether collective bargaining agreements that are to be concluded for economically dependent employee-like workers, are in line with anti-trust law. The academic analysis carried out within the project revealed that a joint reading of paragraphs 42 and 33 of the Court of Justice of the European Union's judgment in *FNV Kunsten*[1] allows for an interpretation in favour of concluding collective agreements for 'service providers comparable to workers' without infringing EU anti-trust law. Yet, uncertainties remain as to which service providers are actually comparable.

Thus, competition law is regarded as one of the most serious obstacles on the path towards a new model of collective bargaining with an extended personal scope. The picture mapped in the project, though, and more specifically during the final conference and in this monograph, can serve as support in overcoming these obstacles, in particular within the Commission's initiative on collective bargaining for the self-employed and its respective Draft Guidelines, issued in December 2021 (C(2021) 8838 final).

Another key result is that a directive regulating platform work at EU level could establish that gig economy workers enjoy collective bargaining rights, as the Commission's second stage consultation on platform work points out, either in an article or a chapter. Although the Commission's proposal for a Directive on improving working conditions in platform work from December 2021 (C(2021) 762 final) does not state that all persons working in the platform economy have a right to collective bargaining, it remains to be seen whether the final Directive, if adopted, will nevertheless refer to such a right. There is no doubt that the European Union could legislate on collective labour law as mentioned in Article 153(1)(f) of the Treaty on the Functioning of the European Union (TFEU). The competence set forth in Article 153(1)(b) TFEU offers the legal basis necessary to carry out

[1] Case C-413/13 *FNV Kunsten Informatie en Media v Staat der Nederlanden* [2014] ECLI:EU:C:2014:2411.

this task if only working conditions are to be regulated, but the mention in Article 153(1)(f) TFEU of the 'representation and collective defence of the interests of workers and employers' gives a solid foundation for the development of collective labour law aspects.

This possible development would need to be, nonetheless, respectful of national competences and traditions. Directive 2002/14/EC offers a clear example for it, establishing a common floor that could be easily implemented in every Member State: the identification of specific workers' representatives must be left to national laws and practices. But the encouragement of specific rules for gig economy workers, such as the 'digitalisation' of electoral units or the creation of ways of allocating representation more easily to this type of worker are suitable contents for a supranational regulation.

As regards actors, traditional ones have proven to be the best placed to integrate traditional prerogatives and new technologies. New agents have, up until now, not succeeded in concluding collective agreements with the same effect as traditional ones. However, an analysis of reality shows that gig economy workers are sometimes reluctant to join traditional unions. Furthermore, the very unions were, at least at first, not ready to deal with the issue. In order to establish a strong model, the idea of 'Smart trade unions' should be brought to the debate, which might in the end even result in 'apps competing against apps': in a model of business based on digital reputations, both for workers and for companies, trade unions should adapt and make use of these new forms of communication.

Turning to the level of bargaining, two main results can be highlighted: first, the comparative analysis has shown that collective bargaining agreements in the gig economy exist at company (in the UK or in Denmark) as well as at branch level (in Austria or Spain). Yet, one of the main difficulties in promoting branch-level agreements seems to be that there is a conflict of interests on the employers' side, rather than a 'traditional' class conflict. It was reported that the position of platforms is often not receptive to collective bargaining. Nevertheless, in order to create a common floor of rights, branch-level agreements seem to be most appropriate.

As regards the contents of agreements in the gig economy, collective bargaining is actually, and should be used, as a tool to provide for detailed regulations. There are specific topics, for example, the regulation of the applied algorithms that are most specific to this sector. Yet, our research has also shown that traditional topics, such as remuneration and working time, are included in actual agreements. Since the necessities differ from sector to sector, tailor-made solutions agreed upon between management and labour seem to be more appropriate than general rules established by statutory law.

1

Collective Bargaining and the Gig Economy: Reality and Possibilities

JOSÉ MARÍA MIRANDA BOTO

I. A Variety of Situations

Whether a Kuhnian change of paradigms in business or simply a new way of performing traditional activities, the gig economy is a latent issue, and its regulation is extremely diverse in the Member States of the European Union (EU). Its very terminology is still the object of debate. The beatific initial designation of the 'sharing economy' is currently on the decline.[1] No one overlooks the fact that this terrain is an authentic hotbed of neo-Orwellian terminology, where under no circumstances are words haphazardly chosen.

The gig economy is not developed, of course, in the same way in the different Member States. Even if it is difficult to identify the real share of persons working under this formula, statistics show that there is a remarkable number of so-called 'gig workers' in some Member States, such as Germany, Italy and Spain. On the other hand, this phenomenon is practically non-existent in other States, for example in Poland, Romania and Hungary.

The activities implemented under the name 'gig economy' or 'platform economy' vary from each other; numerous divergent classifications exist. Nonetheless, the most straightforward classification includes, in one group, the so-called 'offline activities' that may be redirected to the idea of 'work on demand', and, in the other group, the so-called 'online activities' that may be tagged as 'crowdwork'.

Riders, drivers and domestic helpers are some of the most characteristic examples of the offline activities. They are usually at the centre of studies on the gig economy but are also at the core of the discussion when considering the collective dimension of labour law in the gig economy, as this book will do. The most remarkable new forms of collective expression can be found in these fields of

[1] Antonio Aloisi and Valerio de Stefano, *Il tuo capo è un algoritmo. Contro il lavoro disumano* (Laterza 2020) 104, for a very graphic synthesis: 'La lingua disonesta e lo spirito della condivisione: ciò che è mio è tuo' ('The dishonest language and the spirit of exchange: what is mine is yours').

activity. The first successful experiences of collective bargaining have taken place, actually, in these branches of activity. Why? The simplest explanation leads to their physical nature, being services that have existed for a long time, and which are now offered on the market under a new model of business, based on platforms and apps. Human proximity leads to the creation of community and that has been the road to a common expression of interests, connecting on-demand workers with traditional actors in the field of labour collective relations: trade unions.

On the other hand, the myriad of activities that can be classified as 'crowdwork' are more resistant to the development of this collective dimension of labour law. The collective representation of crowdworkers experiences the same problems previously detected concerning telework and collective labour relations. Isolation leads to the non-existence of collective voices, even though some practices, such as the 'Turker' community may be considered as milestones in the field of representation. In any case, the field of crowdwork and online activities is as yet an uncharted territory for labour law, the hidden face of the moon.

In recent years, the employment status of the people working through platforms has been a central issue in many countries and a regular field of study for scholars. Political and dogmatic positions have changed since the beginning of this kind of activity, from the defence of the advantages of this model of business,[2] to the need of a third status,[3] and to the full consideration as employees.[4] From this point of view, the role of the Labour Inspectorate and the courts has been decisive in many countries.

Nowadays, after some initial moments of misorientation about the new idea of subordination, there is a tide in the affairs of platforms that leads on to the consideration of these people as regular employees, as judgments in France, Italy, the Netherlands, Spain and the United Kingdom have shown. Jeremias Adams-Prassl, Sylvaine Laulom and Yolanda Maneiro Vázquez have written about that in this book. There are some other judgments, of course, in the opposite direction, but they can be identified as a minority. The position of the European Court of Justice, with diametrically opposed, but complementary positions in *Elite Taxi* and *Uber France*,[5] on the one hand, and *Yodel*,[6] on the other, constitutes a good synthesis of the panorama.

[2] Jesús Rafael Mercader Uguina, *El futuro del trabajo en la era de la digitalización y la robótica* (Tirant lo Blanch 2017).

[3] Adrián Todolí Signes, 'El impacto de la "Uber Economy" en las relaciones laborales: los efectos de las plataformas virtuales en el contrato de trabajo' [2015] *IUSLabor* 3.

[4] Anna Ginés i Fabrellas, *El trabajo en plataformas digitales. Nuevas formas de precariedad laboral* (Aranzadi, 2020).

[5] Case C-434/15 *Asociación Profesional Elite Taxi v Uber Systems Spain SL* [2017] ECLI:EU:C:2017:981; and Case C-320/16 *Uber France* [2018] ECLI:EU:C:2018:221, respectively. A comment of both in Yolanda Maneiro Vázquez, 'La jurisprudencia del Tribunal de Justicia en materia de economía de plataformas: a propósito de Uber' [2020] *Temas Laborales* 151.

[6] Case C-692/19 *B v Yodel Delivery Network Limited* [2020] ECLI:EU:C:2020:288.

It has taken more time, but legislators have also started to move. At the moment, the most advanced episode concerning the employment status of gig workers is the Spanish *Ley Rider*,[7] according to which a legal presumption exists as regards the application of labour law to delivery and distribution activities organised through a digital platform. This *Ley Rider* is a first small step towards the inclusion of gig economy workers in the general framework of labour regulation under the aegis of statutory law, but it has been saluted as a 'great advance' by Daniel Pérez del Prado in chapter eleven.

The consideration as employees of these persons will certainly lead in future to a development of the role of collective bargaining.[8] The phenomenon has already started, even in this period of legal uncertainty. It is true that the effective results are still very scarce, but the strength of facts has imposed itself. The variety of legal traditions regarding collective bargaining in the Member States is reflected in the variety of the Member States' approaches towards (not) regulating collective bargaining for persons working in the gig economy. But the first collective agreements have been effectively concluded, as we will see later, and they follow all the established, traditional patterns.

It is obvious that platform economy workers can only exercise their collective rights in so far as they are aware of their existence. Disputes will arise.[9] A first step must inevitably involve the organisation of the defence of those rights, primarily for information and consultation, for example. They are essential for social dialogue, a basic component of the European social model within the European Pillar framework. In the case of online tasks, this organisation becomes almost utopian due to the very nature of the activity. In the case of tasks where people do in fact have a shared physical presence, we will see that traditional forms of organisation are beginning to respond to the challenge.

Collective agreements could thus provide a means to include people who work in the context of the platform economy and, therefore, ensure a minimum level of protection, as reflected in the International Labour Organization (ILO) report on atypical employment.[10] Contrary to the recent evolution and decline in collective bargaining in certain Member States, the labour market challenges of the platform economy could lead to a revival of collective bargaining as a central regulatory instrument in these areas.[11] That road is yet to be taken, but as Tamás Gyulavári and Gábor Kártyás defend in chapter six, it is 'a must'.

[7] See: www.boe.es/diario_boe/txt.php?id=BOE-A-2021-7840.

[8] For another scenario, see Bernd Waas and Christina Hießl (eds), Collective Bargaining for Self-Employed Workers in Europe. Approaches to Reconcile Competition Law and Labour Rights (Wolters Kluwer 2021).

[9] For a panoramic vision, see Matthieu Vicente, 'Les conflits collectifs ayant pour support l'algorithme' in Patrice Adam, Martine Le Friant and Yasmine Tarasewicz (eds), *Intelligence artificielle, gestion algorithmique du personnel et droit du travail* (Dalloz 2020).

[10] *Non-standard employment around the world. Understanding challenges, shaping prospects* (ILO 2016).

[11] Jeremias Prassl, *Collective Voice in the Platform Economy: Challenges, Opportunities, Solutions* (ETUC 2018) 23: 'This is a crucial advantage of collective bargaining: the substantive norms can be shaped both to meet workers' needs and business operation requirements in a flexible and tailored way'.

II. A Variety of Sources, between Hard Law and Soft Law

It is clear, in any case, that collective bargaining cannot be the single source of regulation in the gig economy. It must be complementary, to a smaller or larger extent, to statutory law in most countries, depending on their traditions and practice, as Piera Loi shows in chapter two. The Spanish situation considering riders as employees is, at the moment, an exception. In most countries, no explicit piece of legislation exists as regards the legal status of gig economy workers.

In order to build a worthy regulation, constant communication between the different levels of law-making, not only at national level, but between European and international levels, is required. Online and cross-border activities of platforms bring with them the need for supranational legislation that settles a minimum floor and fosters national legislative interventions. And in this panorama, collective bargaining might find its place.

On the other hand, soft law is playing an alternative, remarkable role at the start of the collective regulation of working conditions in platforms. It has filled an initial gap in some countries, such as Germany via codes of conduct, as Judith Brockmann will show in chapter seven, and this could lead to interesting results. Finally, the role of public authorities, not necessarily through legislation, is of utmost importance in many countries and new ways are already being explored, in places such as Bologna, with the development of a local Charter.

Whatever the scope of possible legislation, it is clear that Member States and national social partners are going to be the main actors in this field. However, since the beginning of the COGENS research, the possibility of EU intervention in the gig economy has become more likely, and in February 2021 the European Commission launched a consultation on possible action addressing the challenges relating to working conditions in platform work. On 9 December 2021, when this book was already in proofs, the Commission announced its proposal for a Directive on improving working conditions in platform work.[12]

The legal basis that has been chosen for this Proposal is Article 153(1)(b) TFEU, working conditions. Collective bargaining is not the express purpose of this Proposal. It will apparently follow spontaneously with the establishment of the employment status of platform workers. Several recitals in the Proposal and some indications in the explanatory memorandum mention collective bargaining as a natural effect of the new situation. But there are very specific issues concerning collective bargaining and the gig economy that should be included in the final Directive.

Information and consultation rights concerning algorithmic management have been included in the Proposal. It is a first step, following the Spanish *Ley Rider*. But some others could follow. A directive could establish that gig economy workers enjoy collective bargaining rights and deal with their differences.

[12] COM(2021) 762 final.

There is no doubt that the EU could legislate on collective labour law as mentioned in Article 153(1)(f) TFEU. The mention of 'representation and collective defence of the interests of workers and employers' gives a solid foundation for the development of collective labour law aspects. Of course, this situation will imply the need for unanimity from the Council to pass a directive.

This possible development must, nonetheless, be extremely respectful of national competences and traditions. Directive 2002/14/EC offers a clear example for it, establishing a common floor that could be easily implemented in every Member State. The identification of the actual workers' representatives must be left to national laws and practices. But the encouragement of specific rules for gig economy workers, such as the 'digitalisation' of electoral units or the creation of ways of allocating representation more easily to this type of worker, are suitable subjects for supranational regulation.

In any case, the EU could have resorted to other more *audacious* avenues. Article 115 TFEU continues to allow, as it has done since 1957 when it was Article 100 of the Treaty establishing the European Community, 'the approximation of such laws, regulations or administrative provisions of the Member States as directly affect the establishment or functioning of the internal market'. Using this as a legal basis, the EU could approve a directive that creates a minimum level of rights for people working in the platform economy, regardless of their national legal categorisation. National competences would thus be respected, rights guaranteed, and there would be a supranational response to a supranational situation. In any case, these are my own theoretical considerations and I strongly suggest reading chapter three in this book by Luca Ratti to have as full a view of the possible role of the EU.

Another possible source of supranational regulation would be the Council of Europe, on the basis of the European Convention on Human Rights[13] or the European Social Charter.[14] The platform economy is beginning to be part of its concerns, as evidenced by Resolution 2312 (2019), 'The societal impact of the platform economy', of its Parliamentary Assembly.[15] It is true that the contents of the report are not particularly innovative and do not address collective aspects, but it contains an appreciable roadmap to future regulation in the labour field. It indicates a first step, and the Council has other possible avenues of expression.

Indeed, in a recent complaint brought before the European Committee of Social Rights, *Irish Congress of Trade Unions v Ireland*,[16] it was discussed whether

[13] Silvia Borelli and Daniel Dumont, 'Parlons des droits syndicaux des travailleurs tout court: Réflexions transversales à partir de la situation des travailleurs indépendants de plateformes' in Daniel Dumont, Auriane Lamine and Jean-Benoît Maisin (eds), *Le droit de négociation collective des travailleurs independent. Cadrages théoriques et études de cas* (Larcier 2020) 127–29.

[14] Carmen Salcedo Beltrán, 'Sinergias entre la OIT y los instrumentos internacionales de protección de los derechos sociales: estado actual y perspectivas' [2019] *Revista de Trabajo y Seguridad Social* CEF 434.

[15] assembly.coe.int/nw/xml/XRef/Xref-XML2HTML-en.asp?fileid=28299&lang=en.

[16] No 123/2016.

self-employed workers should have the right to bargain collectively through organisations that represent them. The basis for the complaint was that when labour providers do not have a substantial influence on the content of the contractual conditions, they should be given the possibility of improving the power imbalance through collective bargaining. The final decision established that there was no violation of the Charter. In a dissenting opinion, however, it was argued that the state must promote collective bargaining for all categories of workers. It thus remains to be seen what progression future complaints will follow, whether adhering to the majority opinion or changing the criteria and following the dissenting vote, in a contemporary imitation of Oliver Wendell Holmes. Barbara Kresal's contribution to this book (chapter four) is a must in this field.

Concerning soft law, a curious phenomenon can be observed in several countries, such as Italy, France and Germany, which is the appearance of documents or institutions in the realm of the platform economy that seek to influence it. In none of the cases are they collective bargaining instruments, but because of their originality, in search of a third way that is championed by some, some of them deserve to be examined. Here they will be presented shortly, but chapter seven by Judith Brockmann analyses the German sources with the depth they deserve.

The first in time among these documents was the Bologna Charter, the '*Carta dei diritti fondamentali dei lavoratori digitali nel contesto urbano*' of 2018, that had no effective legal value. It consists of 12 articles that are intended to promote safe and dignified employment, but at the same time it is compatible with the adaptability of the digital labour market, guaranteeing the improvement of the living and working conditions of service providers. Workers' representation and labour disputes are present in the Charter, but there is, however, no mention of collective bargaining. In any case, by recognising the two essential tools for negotiation – the identification of active subjects and the acceptance of pressure measures – the Bologna Charter created the right environment for a collective bargaining process to develop as a corollary of that recognition.

Germany has provided several examples in this catalogue of related performances, which have an added interest that involves an incursion into the field of crowdworking. First, there is the Code of Conduct 'Paid Crowdsourcing for the Better', signed by several companies, where a unilateral commitment is proclaimed on their part to respect and guarantee a 'Decalogue' of rights. It does not contain any mention of collective bargaining, but its contents approximate in a very important way to those that could be subject to it at a more advanced stage. Its most prominent result is the creation of a voluntary conflict resolution mechanism of its own, managed by the IG Metall Union. It only addresses individual conflicts, but to some extent it resembles very prominent outcomes of collective bargaining.

Also important is the Frankfurt Paper on Platform-Based Work, signed by seven trade union organisations from Austria, Germany, Denmark, Sweden and the United States, with a very considerable technical team of advisers. Among the essential points that it enumerates is first to respect the relevant collective agreements, but it also argues that, in a much more prominent way, it is necessary to insist on the right of workers to organise. A consequence of that right is the ability to negotiate and the declaration that platform operators are appropriate interlocutors to enter into negotiations. This last point is particularly relevant and may lead to successful outcomes in the future.

III. (Old) Trade Unions and New Agents

All these tools should lead to the creation of an environment that fosters the development of collective bargaining. In most countries, the existing legal framework for workers' representation and collective bargaining follows the logic of old patterns of work organisation. Thus, implementing collective rights for persons working in the gig economy proves to be rather difficult. A bargaining structure based on the single worksite and the single employer approach, taken together with the majority rule that exists in many Member States, entails structural difficulties in the search for solidarity among platform workers, and between platform workers and employees working at the same bargaining unit.

In this context, the actors established in the different national labour markets, ie, mainly trade unions, have been subjected to a curious initial paradox. On the one hand, they were already there, paraphrasing Augusto Monterroso's well-known short story *El dinosaurio*. Their organisational structures should have functioned as a first dam against the overflow of labour law channels by the gig economy. On the other hand, these same organisational structures have revealed themselves as one of the main obstacles when responding to the traditional models of structuring labour relations.[17] As has been noted, 'it does not seem to be the trade union and its typical performance that is at issue, but the kind of trade unions that manage the conflicts that already occur in the digital economy'.[18]

This is particularly true for those Member States where bargaining at company level prevails over bargaining at branch level. Without legislative intervention, in many countries such a decentralised model does not incentivise unions to support platform workers. Discussing platform workers' rights may even be an opportunity to rethink the existing bargaining models and, in some countries, to encourage industry-level collective bargaining, as Kübra Doğan Yenisey hints in chapter twelve of this book.

In this scenario, after nearly a decade of slow adaptation, old actors seem to be the best placed to integrate traditional prerogatives and new technologies. However, an analysis of reality shows that gig economy workers are sometimes

[17] From a Spanish point of view, Lidia Gil Otero, 'El doble canal de representación de los trabajadores ante la economía de plataformas' [2020] *Nueva revista española de derecho del trabajo* 228.

[18] Patricia Nieto Rojas, 'Acción colectiva en las plataformas digitales. ¿Sindicatos tradicionales y movimientos de base para representar idénticos intereses?' in *El futuro del trabajo: Cien años de la OIT – XXIX Congreso Anual de la Asociación Española de Derecho del Trabajo y de la Seguridad Social* (Ministerio de Trabajo, Migraciones y Seguridad Social 2019) 1525.

reluctant to join traditional unions. Furthermore, the very unions were, at least at first, not ready to cope with the issue. In order to establish a strong model, the idea of 'Smart trade unions' should be debated, as Felicia Roşioru does in chapter eight of this book, which might in the end even result in 'apps competing against apps'. By promoting debate, raising awareness and creating opinions using the very business model of the gig economy, gig workers could be reached more easily. In a model of business based on digital reputations, both for workers and for companies, this part of the activity of trade unions cannot be disregarded.

A perfect example of this can be found in the GMB–Hermes agreement, mentioned later. One of its clauses reads: 'Hermes's objective is to be known as a good company that also values those engaged on a contract for services for the valued contribution they make'. In many countries, this is not the usual clause that a reader expects in a collective agreement.

New agents bring along new ways of collective intervention, too. On the other hand, some practices have been denounced, as the creation of representative groups that are 'tutored' by platforms and break the dynamic of workers' representation. Yet, these new groups have never succeeded in concluding a collective agreement. They have brought new forms of expression of labour disputes, such as flash mobs, bike-riding demonstrations or blockades. They have indeed created some effects that call for attention.[19]

It is here that the difference between offline and online work is revealed again. Delivery people or drivers, in taking the best-known examples, can be seen physically, and something in common is born from coexistence: organisation. Trade unions can send their officials and perform their habitual tasks. Representation structures that parallel the traditional ones are arising in many countries, which pose a serious risk of competition to become the voice of workers.

Various factors can explain this situation. First, there are organisational difficulties derived from the limited stay of people in the company, which makes traditional representation structures unfeasible. It is easier for an electronic identity to last than the person who created it, in the manner of Pirate Roberts in *The Princess Bride*. The ease with which the platforms can remove people in a discretionary way contributes to this, without the identification yet occurring between such disconnections and anti-union behaviours, in the case of activists. That said, it is proven that there is a definite distrust of workers towards the unions on the suspicion that they intend to appropriate the conflict, whether or not this fear is justified.

Apart from that, it cannot be overlooked that the mentality and structure on the business side are also novel. First, because it is easy to notice that the platforms evade the classification of employer and do not want to assume the role of a negotiating subject. The only companies that can respond to the initial idyllic notion of the 'sharing economy' and that are usually presented as cooperatives do not need collective bargaining.

[19] Some examples in Aloisi and de Stefano (n 1) 183 ff.

As noted, in most of the countries where digital platforms arise, new movements of workers' organisations are emerging and also new forms of expression of collective disputes.[20] The emergence of these movements in a context where workers' organisations and their resistance activity have the advantage of using telecommunications, makes understanding the phenomenon more complex, since there are several actors who seek to capitalise on this.[21]

These are scenarios where the provision of work and the externalisation of the conflict that this entails can be easily visible. On the other hand, the obscurity of online work allows it to be easily described as the *far side of the moon*. The level of structural difficulty is the perception of who makes up the workforce, and the determination of the group that needs representation. Hence, in this area tools for community creation have emerged in advance of the mechanisms described for offline workers.

The best-known example of crowdworking is perhaps the Amazon Mechanical Turk. This already presents in its designation a remarkable ambiguity, since the original Turk was celebrated as the first automaton, but in reality, it hid a tiny man inside. This minimisation of the human was combated through external IT tools. It is in fact very appropriate that the pre-eminent position of the app was attacked through another computer programme. Connectivity brings collectivity.

The 'Turkopticon',[22] already in its version 2.0, was created jointly by the university world and the trade union world to allow workers to advertise and evaluate their employers and get in touch with each other. It is not, properly, a tool of representation for workers, and lacks any union content, but it is an interesting precedent for how new technologies can positively influence the protection of workers' rights. On the same platform, 'Turker Nation' appeared as an online forum where workers could contact each other. Some authors have seen it as the foundation on which future digital work centres can be built.[23]

Furthermore, the use of social networks in these areas is striking, since, in a way, it seems to return to the origins of the labour movement. Tools like Twitter have turned out to be virtual meeting places between disorganised workers, with pseudonyms to guarantee the anonymity of activists, infiltrations by employers, dissemination to try to get the attention of users and raise awareness of the problems, etc.

[20] Vanessa Cordero Gordillo, 'La huelga y otras medidas de acción colectiva en el ámbito de las plataformas digitales' in *El futuro del trabajo: Cien años de la OIT – XXIX Congreso Anual de la Asociación Española de Derecho del Trabajo y de la Seguridad Social* (Ministerio de Trabajo, Migraciones y Seguridad Social 2019).

[21] Francisco Trillo Párraga, 'Economía digitalizada y relaciones de trabajo' [2016] *Revista de Derecho Social* 76, 80.

[22] The best description is by its own creators, Lilly C Irani, and M Six Silberman, 'Turkopticon: Interrupting Worker Invisibility in Amazon Mechanical Turk', available at: crowdsourcing-class.org/readings/downloads/ethics/turkopticon.pdf.

[23] Kathryn Zyskowski and Kristy Milland, 'A Crowded Future: Working against Abstraction on Turker Nation' (2018) 4 *Catalyst: Feminism, Theory, Technoscience* 2: 'We argue that workers' labor belies conventional class classification, such as white-collar and blue-collar labor, and instead lays the groundwork for how to structure future digital workplaces'.

These are not, of course, tools relating to collective bargaining. But they are linked to its birth. Without the capacity of engaging in disputes and bringing out the workers' voice, it will never emerge. Collective bargaining is the solution to a problem and its exteriorisation is the first step to that goal. Whether traditional or innovative agents, technology is marking the path for workers' representation to enhance their capacities.

IV. Branch or Company-Level Agreements?

The most likely possibility as regards the future of bargaining in the gig economy is maintaining the current systems. Their efficacy though will greatly depend on the legal classification of platform workers. What remains is the dilemma of the bargaining level. Should agreements be concluded at company or at branch level? The answer to this question strongly depends on the strength of the respective negotiating agents.

The panorama of actual collective agreements shows that the first branch agreements concerning the gig economy, for example, the one for hotels and catering in Spain[24] or the one for logistics in Italy,[25] were concluded by trade unions and employers' organisations that did not take into account the specialities of this activity. They just enlarged their personal scope and absorbed the platform economy into the system.

Initially, in 2018, the last of them was agreed between the employers AGCI Servizi, Confcooperative Lavoro e Servizi and Legacoop Produzione e Servizi, and the Filt-Cgil, Fit-Cisl, Uiltrasporti trade unions to incorporate delivery people into the national collective agreement in the logistics sector. The agreement made specific mention of platform workers: '*anche attraverso l'utilizzo di tecnologie innovative (piattaforme, palmari, ecc)*'.[26] Thanks to this agreement, they were included in its scope, with a catalogue of specific rights.[27] The agreement concluded with a reference to second-level contracting as the appropriate area for development.

In the Spanish case, this decision had, theoretically, important consequences, as collective agreements of this type are compulsory for all employers and workers in its scope. Nonetheless, it is difficult to assess the actual success of this first step. Since 2019, except for error or omission from my part, only two cases have been brought to court and only in first instance courts.[28] It is true that the pandemic may have had an impact, but the number is astonishingly low, especially considering the usual rate of activity in Spanish labour courts.

[24] www.boe.es/boe/dias/2019/03/29/pdfs/BOE-A-2019-4645.pdf.

[25] www.politico.eu/wp-content/uploads/2020/09/Verbale-riders-18.7.2018.pdf.

[26] 'Including through the use of innovative technologies (platforms, palmtops, etc)'.

[27] For a sociological analysis, see Sergio Bologna and Sergio Curi, 'Relazioni industriali e servizi di logistica: uno studio preliminare' [2019] *Giornale di diritto del lavoro e di relazioni industriali* 161.

[28] *Juzgado de lo Social num.1 de Melilla* ECLI:ES:JSO:2020:6970; *Juzgado de lo Social num.3 de Oviedo* ECLI:ES:JSO:2020:6468.

We will come back later to the relevant contents of collective bargaining in those decisions. But the main point here is the absence of controversy, as in Sherlock Holmes' *The Adventure of Silver Blaze*: the dog did not bark.[29] Should we consider that the silence transmits a peaceful implementation of the working conditions included in the branch agreement by all the platforms? Or, on the other hand, is it the proof that this 'invasion' lacks any effect, as the platforms feel entitled to dismiss the compulsory application of the collective agreement? More time is needed to verify this issue.

The agreement between the Danish trade union 3F and Dansk Erhverv,[30] the Danish Chamber of Commerce, followed the old pattern concerning actors, too, but went a step further. It was bargained specifically for gig economy workers. At the beginning, only Just Eats workers were covered by the agreement. It was basically a company-level agreement with regard to its personal scope. However, it was then opened to other delivery companies. Thus, it can be considered the first real branch agreement concerning the gig economy in its own framework. Taking into account the whole scenario, it is easy to affirm that this solution will probably lead to greater success than the Italian and Spanish agreements referred to above, as it has more solid foundations.

In Austria, a branch level collective bargaining agreement was concluded for bicycle riders too, between traditional actors, the chambers of commerce, the Wirtschaftskammer, on the employer's side, and the Austrian trade union federation, the Österreichischen Gewerkschaftsbund, Gewerkschaft vida, on the other.[31] Its personal scope is limited to employees only, in line with traditional bargaining practices.

The contrast comes from an Italian national-level agreement for delivery of goods carried out by riders.[32] The bargaining agents were a new, specific employers' organisation, AssoDelivery, composed of platforms, and a traditional trade union, UGL, through its specific branch, UGL Rider. The personal scope was especially remarkable, as it included only self-employed riders. This agreement showed, at first sight, the capacity for adaptation and transformation of actors where there is will to bargain.

The agreement, however, was challenged in the courts by other trade unions, the most powerful ones on the Italian scene. In its ruling of 30 June 2021,[33] a Court in Bologna declared it 'obviously unlawful' ('*evidentemente illegittima*'), due to the lack of capacity of representation of the trade union. Collective bargaining, thus,

[29] On the possible judicial challenge of the agreement, that never took place, José María Miranda Boto, 'Negociación colectiva y economía de las plataformas: actores' [2019] *Revista de Derecho Social* 88.

[30] fagbladet3f.dk/artikel/nu-kan-danskere-bestille-takeaway-med-god-samvittighed.

[31] www.wko.at/service/kollektivvertrag/kollektivvertrag-fahrradboten-2020.html.

[32] olympus.uniurb.it/index.php?option=com_content&view=article&id=23625:rider1592020&catid=242&Itemid=139.

[33] sites.unimi.it/dati40/wp-content/uploads/2021/07/5-Tribunale-Bologna-PALLADINO-Nidil-ed-altri-c.-Deliveroo.pdf.

showed its *dark side* in this case. For a foreigner, it is remarkable how Bologna is the meeting point for a huge quantity of novelties relating to gig economy.

On the other hand, there are some company-level agreements, such as that in 2018 between the Danish trade union 3F and Hilfr,[34] concerning assistants who performed cleaning work in private households facilitated by the digital platform, or the one in the United Kingdom in 2019 between the GMB Union and Hermes, which provides delivery and collection services.[35] The pattern concerning workers' representation is the same. The traditional actor is successful in its traditional role when it can put pressure on the other bargaining agents. It is remarkable, by the way, that the Danish Confederation of Trade Unions has prepared a translation of the agreement, thus opening the way to innovation in other countries. Or hinting, perhaps, at the national origin of the majority of gig workers in the house cleaning branch in Denmark and their linguistic skills.

There is a remarkable innovation in both agreements, concerning their scope. According to the Hilfr text, 'freelancers automatically obtain employee status after 100 hours' work via the platform and are subsequently covered by this collective agreement'. In the GMB agreement, self-employed delivery people working under the direction of Hermes may voluntarily join the classification of 'self-employed plus', being in this way covered by the agreement, without being employees. As the United Kingdom has left the jurisdiction of the European Court of Justice, it is difficult to guess the articulation between this situation and the *FNV Kunsten* ruling.[36]

In Italy, the first company-level agreement was signed in 2019 by Filt Cgil, Fit Cisl and Uiltrasporti, for the social part, with the company Laconsegna Srl, based in Florence. Under this agreement, delivery people are recognised by the company as salaried workers and are subject to the national collective agreement in the logistics sector. At the moment of finishing this book, Spain joined this trend. An agreement has been signed (not yet published) between Just Eat and the main trade unions, CCOO and UGT. It establishes a minimum wage of €15,200 and makes a point about the right to digital disconnection. But its main importance lies in the fact that a platform has, for the first time, joined the *usual game*.

Whatever the level of bargaining, clear and direct conclusions can be extracted. In the very few collective agreements that have been concluded in the field of the gig economy, traditional trade unions have been the main actors, following traditional rules. They have no rivals, and their position of monopoly has not yet been challenged. And it is very probable that it never will be.

[34] www2.3f.dk/~/media/files/mainsite/forside/fagforening/privat%20service/overenskomster/hilfr%20collective%20agreement%202018.pdf.

[35] www.gmb.org.uk/sites/default/files/Hermes%20Partnership%20%26%20Procedure%20Agreement%201%20with%20GMB.pdf.

[36] Case C-413/13 *FNV Kunsten Informatie en Media v Staat der Nederlanden* [2014] ECLI:EU:C:2014:2411.

Finally, the role of employers' organisations is the opaquest of all. It no longer responds to a class conflict, but to a conflict of interests, as traditional companies do not share their position and outlook with the new platforms. According to many stakeholders, the position of platforms is not receptive to collective bargaining, but the Italian case shows that there are exceptions to this.

V. The Contents of Collective Bargaining in the Gig Economy

There is a remarkable consensus among academics and stakeholders that the issue of the contents of collective bargaining should be left to the social partners. No specific legal regulation is deemed necessary in this field. Each national development should follow its traditions and their practices.

The analysis of the actual contents of collective bargaining in the gig economy provides us with a very diverse answer. The scarce number of collective agreements allows a thorough examination and the construction of a model theory. The main classification that has been elaborated in the COGENS research consists of abstract, general and specific contents.

The first group refers to the situation when gig economy workers were incorporated into existing branch agreements, such as in Spain concerning hotels and catering, or the Italian logistics' agreement. In the first case, the collective agreement did not include any specific material rule concerning gig workers; they have just enlarged their personal scope.

In the Italian and Austrian cases mentioned above, there are relevant contents, of course, such as remuneration, work schedules, part-time work, training, personal protection equipment and third-party liability insurance. But none of them could be identified as being specifically designed or bargained for gig workers. There are no characteristic traits of the activity in the agreement. The analysis of these contents, thus, lacks any special interest in order to build a model of specific bargaining for platforms.

The second group of contents in our classification includes traditional categories of regulation that have a special dimension in the gig economy. They include remuneration and working time as the main examples: issues that have been always present in the labour market, as indicated in the first group, but present nowadays remarkable characteristics, such as the role of the app in their determination.

The first company-level agreement, signed by the Danish trade union 3F and Hilfr Aps, is the perfect example of this situation, as it covers all the traditional issues. Concerning wages, it contains, for example, the following rule: 'Via the platform, the employee can set his/her individual wage. Meanwhile, it can never be lower than the wage stipulated in this collective agreement'. Similar and even more detailed contents can be found in the Italian national-level agreement.

They are not innovative clauses, but they are the visible expression of the possible space for collective bargaining agreements in the field of the gig economy. In the same agreements, moreover, there are rules concerning the new, technological aspects of the termination of the employment contract: 'Deletion or other depersonalisation of the employee's profile on the platform shall be considered as dismissal', according to the Danish agreement. Similar contents can also be found in the Italian national-level agreement. It is easy to perceive that this agreement is adapting well-established structures.

The majority of platforms, actually, provide the platform with a wide right to suspend the worker or to terminate cooperation, typically without having an obligation to give reasons or under relatively vague criteria only (eg, referring to rating without stating the acceptable level) and without a notice period. Collective bargaining may thus be a useful tool in the protection of workers, modulating these wide powers.

The Hermes agreement follows its own path, as it is dedicated to the organisation of collective mechanisms of information, consultation and bargaining. No attention is paid in it to the *digital* aspects of the provision of services. It has, however, a very remarkable content, as it challenges the *loneliness* of platform workers already pointed out. According to the agreement, the trade union is entitled to hold 'recruitment days eight times a year', with the collaboration of the company. It is, clearly, a bid for the missing proximity that can help to strengthen the bonds between deliverers and reinforce their collective voice under the sway of the trade union.

The third group of contents is the more 'exploratory' one and has not yet provided any real outcome. It is the field where collective bargaining can be a tool of innovation, dealing with issues that so far have not been a traditional concern. That is the reason for the 'specific' denomination that is proposed here: rights that mainly concern platform workers.

This kind of *digital* content will probably find its place in future collective bargaining, as some of the issues cross the borders of the gig economy. We are used, for example, to ratings concerning platform workers and their performance. But who cannot deny the possibility of some *Black Mirror*-inspired future, where all human activities are subject to evaluation?

The recent French Décret nº 2021-952,[37] for example, has established a regulation on platform workers' data and individual access to them. Workers' ratings and their control, in a further step, could also be regulated by collective agreements. The negotiation and supervision of the algorithm employed by the platform, or the regime of workers' ratings is the most remarkable of these possibilities.

The Spanish legislation had opened previously a possible way of collective development, as the *Ley Rider* has included the right of the workers' representatives 'to be informed by the company of the parameters, rules and instructions on which algorithms or artificial intelligence systems are based, that affect decision-making

[37] www.legifrance.gouv.fr/jorf/id/JORFTEXT000043799996.

that may have an impact on working conditions, access to and maintenance of employment, including profiling'. It is, once again, a first, limited step, as it refers to information rights and not collective bargaining. But the gate has been opened for further regulations, as the algorithm has entered the Labour Code.

Out of the gig economy field, indeed, there is already a presence of algorithms in a collective agreement. In Spain, the new branch agreement for financial credit institutions (note, not banks)[38] has included a clause (article 35.5) on 'rights in the face of artificial intelligence'. In it, there is a right for workers 'not to be subject to decisions based solely and exclusively on automated variables'. The contents of the algorithm will not be bargained, but its effects will be controlled.

In any case, the right to demand transparency in the decisions and outcomes of AI systems as well as the underlying algorithms must be guaranteed, establishing the right to appeal decisions made by algorithms, and having it reviewed by a human being. Through collective agreements reached by social partners, the parties could address both data input into automated hiring systems and promotion of employees, for example, and employees' control over the afterlife of the data created by these systems.

Social partners in all sectors could act as spearheads on this issue. In the 'Green Paper on the Future of Work in Portugal',[39] for example, one of the lines for reflection is to

> encourage, in particular, the regulation of the use of algorithms in the context of collective bargaining, involving the social partners and ensuring the treatment of the matter at the level of collective agreements, in order to ensure an adequate use of AI and to reflect the needs specific to each sector.

Also, collective agreements could reinforce principles that minimise the new risks associated with the autonomous behaviour of AI, establishing requirements to ensure the protection of privacy and personal data, equality and non-discrimination, ethics, transparency and the explicability of systems based on algorithms, both in terms of the selection of job candidates, and of the execution of the employment contract and the inspection of the worker's professional activity. Furthermore, collective agreements could regulate the consultation of the employees' unions on the implementation, development and deployment of AI systems. Teresa Coelho Moreira, in chapter nine, analyses all these possibilities.

VI. A Short Conclusion

The COGENS research has shown that nowadays collective bargaining exists for workers in the gig economy in the Member States, although differences exist as

[38] boe.es/boe/dias/2021/10/15/pdfs/BOE-A-2021-16788.pdf.

[39] www.portugal.gov.pt/download-ficheiros/ficheiro.aspx?v=%3d%3dBQAAAB%2bLCAAAAAAABAAzNLQwMQMAqSscTAUAAAA%3d.

regards the personal scope of the agreements, the actors involved, the contents regulated and the effects of the bargaining agreements.

Since gig economy and especially crowdworking are transnational issues, a response from the EU seems most appropriate. Of course, the EU's intervention needs to be in accordance with national law and industrial relations practices. Yet, the Treaties offer possibilities to regulate on collective labour law issues.

At national level, traditional actors have managed to conclude collective agreements in the field of the gig economy. Although European social partners seem to be reluctant as regards their role of regulating collective bargaining, it seems that trade unions have taken up the challenge of regulating collective bargaining in the gig economy. New actors have not yet lived up to their promises. Our research has shown, too, that agreements were concluded at company level by single employers as well as at branch level mainly by traditional employers' associations. Yet, in order to create a common floor of rights, branch level agreements seem to be most appropriate.

As regards the contents of collective bargaining agreements in the gig economy, collective bargaining should be used as a tool to provide detailed regulations. There are specific topics, for example, the regulation of the applied algorithms that are most specific to this sector. Thus, a tailor-made solution agreed upon between management and labour seems to be more appropriate than general rules established by statutory law.

PART I

The Sources of a Possible Regulation

2

The Boundaries between Collective Agreements and Statutory Legislation in the Gig Economy

PIERA LOI

I. The Regulatory Dilemma in Digital Platform Work: Statutory Legislation, Collective Agreements or Case Law?

The aim of this chapter is to analyse the interactions between different sources of regulation in digital platform work, between collective agreements, statutory legislation, case law and other sources of regulation, from a comparative point of view. How have the boundaries between regulatory sources changed due to the expansion of digital platform work? Is there a common trend to be highlighted or in each national legal system have the traditional regulatory patterns been followed? Particularly, how has collective bargaining, as a regulatory source, changed its relationship with other regulatory sources like statutory legislation and case law? One of the possible perspectives is to consider if statutory legislation can still be defined as an auxiliary source of regulation for collective actors, and if collective agreements can be still conceived as residual regulatory sources. Another perspective is to evaluate if collective agreements should be considered as the preferable regulatory sources and whether statutory legislation should limit its role to the definition of fundamental rights.

Notwithstanding the fragmented framework emerging from the comparative analysis on the regulatory trends in European Union (EU) Member States as far as digital platform work is concerned, we can anticipate the major common trends: the first is the legislators' aphasia; the second is the judicial activism on classification of platform workers; the third is the attempt of collective bargaining of expanding its traditional scope of application beyond subordination. These three common trends (with some exceptions) are important signals of the regulatory force of collective agreements in digital platform work, notwithstanding the obstacles due to the isolation of workers, the lack of unionisation and the reduction of unions' representation.[1] This first analysis will surely be reviewed after the adoption of the recent proposal of a Directive on improving working conditions in Platform work[2] since the Directive will necessarily produce more legal regulation at national level.

Another phenomenon, which is worth highlighting, is the appearance of complementary regulatory sources, beyond statutory legislation, collective agreements and case law, in the form of codes of conduct, unions' charters or city charters involving non-traditional institutions and actors. Anticipating our concluding remarks we can say that the rich and composite net of regulatory sources which is emerging, is nothing but the result of the complexity and ever-changing nature of the phenomenon of digital platform work and the role of AI needing to be regulated.

The comparative research[3] shows that labour law in different legal systems has developed through a fruitful relationship and interdependence between statutory law and other residual law-making powers like collective agreements, to which the regulatory functions have been delegated, in order either to resolve complex interests conflicts or to respond to flexibility needs. On the other hand in some legal systems, characterised by a legal abstentionism, statutory legislation has traditionally been considered as the residual regulatory power in regulating the employment relationship. The British 'collective laissez-faire' in which the regulation has traditionally proceeded autonomously of the state,[4] but also the tradition of Nordic countries to consider statutory legislation as the residual regulatory source in the employment relationship[5] can be considered the most relevant examples. Nevertheless, in many legal systems collective agreements have always been considered as resources for the regulatory needs, and also at supranational level, as in the EU, collective bargaining is considered a fundamental resource, notwithstanding its limits,[6] due to their degree of effectiveness, flexibility and adaptability.

The traditional complexity and plurality of labour law sources, the interaction of law, collective agreements, case law in national legal systems, have been influenced in many ways by the enactment of European legislation and by the presence of collective actors also at European level. In other words, the system

[1] Kurt Vandaele, *Will trade unions survive in the platform economy? Emerging patterns of platform workers' collective voice and representation in Europe* (ETUI 2018) 15.

[2] EU Commission, 'Proposal for a Directive on Improving Working Conditions in Platform Work' (Brussels, 9 December 2021) COM(2021) 762 final.

[3] Bob Hepple and Bruno Veneziani (eds), *The Transformation of Labour Law in Europe: A Comparative Study of 15 Countries 1945–2004* (Hart Publishing 2009).

[4] Ruth Dukes, 'Otto Kahn-Freund and Collective Laissez-Faire: An Edifice without a Keystone?' (2009) 72 *MLR* 220.

[5] See Jonas Malmberg, 'The Collective Agreement as an Instrument for Regulation of Wages and Employment Conditions' (2002) 43 *Scandinavian Studies in Law* 190.

[6] As underlined by the seminal work of Antonio Lo Faro, *Funzioni e finzioni della contrattazione collettiva comunitaria. La contrattazione collettiva come risorsa dell'ordinamento giuridico comunitario* (Giuffrè 1999).

of labour law sources aimed at regulating socio and economic phenomena, has reached a higher level of complexity, due to national and supranational interference. Surprisingly, the complexity of the regulatory mechanisms and the complex interactions in the multilevel layers of regulation have left unregulated many aspects of the working relationship either due to its transnational features, or to the difficulties in finding the employer, that is the subject responsible for the fundamental obligations, or again due to the nature of the work performed using digital platforms. Whether it is just a lack of effectiveness of the existing apparatus of labour law rules or a true regulatory void, in the case of work performed by digital platforms, we must admit that there is a need for regulation and that the regulatory dilemma is to define which regulatory source would be more suitable or which combination of sources (and at what level) would be more acceptable.

In this complex picture of layers of regulatory sources, especially in a multilevel system of legal sources, we should not forget the regulatory role of case law.

It is well known that one of the myths of the legal thought of the nineteenth century, at least in civil law countries, is the completeness of law, composed of abstract legal norms applied through a rational and logical process. The idea that legal orders are rational and logical systems where both judges and scholars when applying the legal norm to the single case perform a quasi-scientific activity composed of logical processes, has been deeply influenced by Friedrich von Savigny, founder of the so-called German Historical School, convinced that legal orders are characterised by an intrinsic rationality and, in these systems, the judge in applying and interpreting the law, using logic and a quasi-scientific method, is simply reconstructing the intrinsic meaning of the law already in existence from the beginning. These theories are expressed in other terms by the Montesquieu principles of the separation of powers (legislative, executive and judiciary) and definitely reinforce the idea that the judge is nothing but the mouth of the law (*la bouche de la loi*).[7]

Also, Kelsen states that every legal system is inherently complete in the sense that there is no legal question for which it provides no answer, no legal problem for which it has no solution.[8] These theses are nonetheless considered rather dubious[9] and not corresponding to the reality of legal orders suffering from their inherent incompleteness[10] or their difficulties in regulating social and economic phenomena whose complexity produce, as a result, from one side the loss of effectiveness

[7] Charles de Secondat de Montesquieu, *De l'esprit des lois* (1748), available at: www.ecole-alsacienne.org/CDI/pdf/1400/14055_MONT.pdf.

[8] Hans Kelsen, *Pure Theory of Law* (University of California Press 1967).

[9] Eugenio Bulygin et al, *Essays in Legal Philosophy* (Oxford University Press 2015).

[10] For a discussion on the incompleteness of law in the different families of legal orders, see Katharina Pistor and Chenggang Xu, *Incomplete Law: A Conceptual and Analytical Framework – And its Application to the Evolution of Financial Market Regulation* (2003) 35 *New York University Journal of International Law & Politics* 931.

of legal norms, and from the other the risk of colonisation of reality, which is an effect of the juridification of social spheres.[11]

No legal scholar, today, would describe a legal system as complete or the judge role as being *'la bouche de la loi'*, or would define the legal interpretation as a merely logical and scientific operation, denying any creative function of the case law. On the contrary, case law, driven by a judicial activism, has also proven to be a regulatory resource in civil law legal systems. This judicial activism has been particularly intense in digital platform work litigation on workers' classification and, from this point of view, case law has been shown to be an essential source of regulation in the absence of other sources.

II. The Aphasia of Legislators in Regulating Digital Platform Work

Starting from the general regulatory crisis of the law in the welfare states as highlighted by Habermas,[12] we would like to analyse the reasons for the general aphasia of the law on digital platform work, making some hypotheses about the reasons why national legislators are reluctant to intervene in this issue.

One of the reasons could be the complexity and the rapid pace of change in digital platform work. It suffices to mention the discussion about the role of algorithms in shaping the working relationship, which implies, when the boss is an algorithm,[13] the wider discussion on the problem of identifying models of liability of autonomous software agents, considered as mathematically formalised information flows, capable of autonomous actions and entailing a massive loss of control for human actors. One of the major challenges that labour law sources have to face in regulating digital platform work is precisely the massive presence in the employment relationship of automated decision processes by algorithms, which need enormous quantities of data and are changing the structure of labour markets.[14] Particularly when the working activity is performed entirely online, the working activity consists in the production by the worker of a huge amount of data processed by a server and used by the employer to organise the whole production system. But even for the other category of digital platform, in which services are performed in the real world, the working activity consists in the production by the worker of a huge amount of data, used by the platform's algorithms to exercise

[11] Jürgen Habermas, 'Law as Medium and Law as Institution' in Gunther Teubner (ed), *Dilemmas of Law in the Welfare State* (De Gruyter 2020).

[12] ibid.

[13] Jeremias Adams-Prassl, 'What If Your Boss Was an Algorithm? Economic Incentives, Legal Challenges, and the Rise of Artificial Intelligence at Work' (2019) 41 *Comparative Labor Law & Policy Journal* 123.

[14] See Christophe Degryse, *Digitalisation of the economy and its impact on labour markets* (ETUI 2016).

the organisation, direction and control of managerial prerogatives, exactly as is happening in the manufacturing sector.

When the working activity consists of producing data, the first difficulty is to deal with the issue of data's intangibility and to define data's location: 'the problem is not that data is located nowhere, but that it may be located anywhere, and at least parts of it may be located nearly everywhere'.[15] Most of the time the dispersion of data is a security choice made by enterprises that could choose, instead of storing each data on a single machine or set of machines, to distribute all data across many computers in different locations and replicate the data over multiple systems, to avoid a single point of failure. When the working activity is performed entirely online, the difficulty of defining data location implies, among others, the question of defining the applicable labour law rule, on the basis of the place where the work is performed, in cases where the employment relationships have transnational features. Undoubtedly, the datafication processes in the employment relationship raise unprecedent questions which still remain unsolved by the law, for example, how to evaluate, and possibly remunerate, data production when this is not the object of the exchange in the employment relationship. Let us think about the case of digital platform work, that the EU Commission defines as an 'on-location labour platform' referring to a digital labour platform which only or mostly intermediates services performed in the physical world, for example, ride-hailing, food delivery, household tasks like cleaning, plumbing, caring:[16] in all these cases the remuneration which the parties to the contract have agreed upon, is for the service performed in the physical world (the food delivery or the ride-hailing) and not for the huge amount of data produced by the worker via an app, which are essential for the same organisation of the production activity. In this case other regulatory sources, like collective agreements, are better suited to regulate the issue of data remuneration to reduce the exposure of workers to unprecedent risks, due to the datafication processes which reinforce the imbalance of powers inside the digital working place.[17]

As Teubner explains: 'algorithms from the digital world, robots, software agents with a high level of intelligence and the ability to learn … generate new kinds of undreamt dangers for humans'.[18] Contract law and liability law are engaged in defining a new legal status for the autonomous digital information systems, because of the increasing number of 'accidents' occurring without anyone being responsible for them. The solution of giving autonomous software agents an independent legal status and recognising them with artificial personhood, even if

[15] Kristen E Eichensehr, 'Data Extraterritoriality' (2017) 95 *Texas Law Review* 145.

[16] Commission, 'First Phase Consultation of Social Partners Under Article 154 TFEU on Possible Action Addressing the Challenges Related to Working Conditions in Platform Work' (Consultation Document) C(2021) 1127 final, 5.

[17] Emanuele Dagnino and Ilaria Armaroli, 'A Seat at the Table: Negotiating Data Processing in the Workplace: A National Case Study and Comparative Insights' (2019) 41 *Comparative Labor Law & Policy Journal* 173.

[18] Gunther Teubner, 'Digital Personhood? The Status of Autonomous Software Agents in Private Law' (2018) *Ancilla Iuris* 107, 108.

under certain conditions, is a way of avoiding liability gaps that will expand in the future. The lack of consensus on these issues and the lack of responsibility is also linked to the fact that legal doctrine uses traditional conceptual instruments when referring to the new digital subjects.[19]

Besides that we should always be aware that machines do not act in their own interests but in the interests of humans or organisations, especially enterprises, but in the future we cannot exclude that algorithms will act in their self-interest.[20] Accordingly, the interactions of digital and human actions will be more frequent than the action of algorithms in isolation. With the increasing use of artificial intelligence and the development of artificial neural networks, one could also ask the question whether defining a new legal status for the autonomous digital information systems 'is a sufficient legal response to highly sophisticated machine learning techniques employed in decision making that successfully emulate or even enhance human cognitive abilities?'[21]

We have tried to sketch some of the problems raised by the introduction of digital technologies and algorithms in general and in particular in employment relationships. Is it really a new social and economic phenomenon needing new regulation? Or does the existing set of rules in each legal system simply need a process of adaptation?

If the use of digital technologies in workplaces is a new phenomenon, the first question to be tackled is whether legal orders, and especially statutory labour law sources, are per se flexible enough to regulate it. One could argue, as a matter of fact, that the existing set of rules simply needs a process of adaptation or, on the contrary, that due to the radical changes introduced by digital technologies in workplaces it is essential to adopt new legal sources. When asking whether new legislation is needed or not, we should also ask what are the residual law-making powers to which the regulatory function could be delegated in order to complete the process of regulation or to avoid some of the pitfalls of new legislation? No less important, among the set of questions that should be investigated, is the one relating to the relationship between the different sources of regulation – law, collective agreements, case law and the individual contract of employment – and how the digitalisation and the introduction of AI in the workplace could alter these relationships or if other sources of regulation could emerge.

III. Can We Still Speak about Auxiliary Legislation?

When comparative labour lawyers have to depict a comparative analysis of the relationships between statutory legislation and collective bargaining it is crucial

[19] ibid, 112.

[20] ibid, 114.

[21] Argyro Karanasiou and Dimitris A Pinotsis, 'Towards a Legal Definition of Machine Intelligence: The Argument for Artificial Personhood in the Age of Deep Learning' [2017] *ICAL* 119.

not to forget the lessons of Hugo Sinzheimer, Otto Kahn-Freund and Gino Giugni. Sinzheimer's idea of an economic constitution (*Wirtschaftverfassung*) meant robust state intervention to help collective subjects (unions and employers' associations) to regulate the economy, trying to overcome the imbalance between capital and labour.[22] Following Sinzheimer's ideas, Otto Kahn-Freund believed that one of the most important functions of labour law legislation was

> seeking to promote collective bargaining, to ensure the observance of collective agreements, to define and to delineate the freedom of organisation and the freedom to strike, and the right to promote union interests at the level of the plant or enterprise.[23]

He called such legislation 'auxiliary' in contrast to 'regulatory' legislation, although sometimes its effect could be to restrain rather than to advance collective bargaining. The same view was shared by Gino Giugni who actively contributed to the enactment of the Workers' Statute (Statuto dei lavoratori) a clear example of legislation having an auxiliary function aimed at creating the conditions for autonomous regulatory activities by collective actors.[24] Although these ideas have been declining in different ways in many EU legal orders it should be investigated how, in the case of digital platform work, the statutory legislation has in some cases ceased to perform an auxiliary function for collective actors and collective agreements and, on the contrary, has been an obstacle.

We should underline that changes in the auxiliary function of statutory legislation produce important effects on the boundaries between the two sources of regulation (statutory legislation and collective agreements) and in that regard Kahn-Freund highlighted the fact that 'cultural, economic, geographic, historical and political factors determine the borderline of legislation and collective bargaining … and their significance and mutual relation sometimes change very rapidly'. The case of digital platform work seems really to fit with Kahn-Freund's analysis since it is a phenomenon whose fast pace is capable of modifying the borderline and the mutual relations between legislation and collective bargaining. Nonetheless, it would not be sufficient to use the case of digital platform work to explain how the boundaries between statutory legislation and collective agreement have changed. Other phenomena have anticipated such changes. The scheme of auxiliary legislation described by Kahn-Freund has taken different forms in national legal orders due to differences in industrial relations systems, but even in those systems where the traditional auxiliary function of legislation was mature, deep changes occurred because of dramatic events like the economic and financial crisis of 2008.

When we talk about 'auxiliary legislation' the legislation's function, as Kahn-Freund reminds us, is not to settle wages, hours or other conditions of

[22] See Ruth Dukes, 'Hugo Sinzheimer and the Constitutional Function of Labour Law' in Guy Davidov and Brian Langile (eds), *The Idea of Labour Law* (Oxford University Press 2011) 62.

[23] Paul Davies and Mark Freedland, *Kahn-Freund's Labour and the Law*, 3rd edn (Stevens & Sons 1983) 53.

[24] Gino Giugni, *Diritto Sindacale* (Cacucci 2014).

employment, but to 'make rules for their settlement, chiefly by the collective parties themselves, and for the enforcement of the terms they have settled. It establishes "rules of the game"'. The description of the legislation's function as regulating 'the rules of the game' that other self-regulatory mechanisms should perform, is also at the core of the reflexive and procedural theories of law,[25] in which statutory legislation's function is a procedural one, aiming at defining actors and procedures that should be followed by collective actors and collective bargaining. As Barnard and Deakin say,

> the preferred mode of intervention is for the law to underpin and encourage autonomous processes of adjustment, in particular by supporting mechanisms of group representation and participation, rather than to intervene by imposing particular distributive outcomes. This type of approach finds a concrete manifestation in legislation which seeks, in various ways, to devolve rule-making powers to self-regulatory processes.[26]

The regulatory crisis of modern legal systems, due to a more and more complex societal framework, expressed by the pluralisation of regulatory sources as a reaction to complexity by autonomous social spheres, can either be seen as a resource or as a menace to legal systems. The question we would like to raise is whether and how the traditional auxiliary function of legislation has changed in regulating digital platform work. Digital platform work is an expression of wider phenomena, like globalisation and digital innovation involving society as a whole, which put into question the same capacity of legislation to regulate these phenomena either for the limited scope of application of national legislation when we deal with a transnational dimension, or for the speed and changing nature of the phenomena.

Describing the role of statutory legislation regulating digital platform work in EU Member States and in some overseas countries we should, first, highlight the common trend of a scarce intervention of statutory legislation on the issue. We will see in the next paragraph some examples of statutory legislation in EU Member States, but it is important to underline the fact that the limited activism of legislators has finally produced serious obstacles to other regulatory sources like collective agreements. Can we still consider the law is performing an auxiliary function for collective agreements in regulating digital platform work? Which obstacles to collective bargaining could come from the law?

When we analyse how statutory legislation could hinder collective bargaining in digital platform work, one of the most relevant obstacles is represented by the question of classification of digital platform workers. Digital platform workers

[25] Gunther Teubner, 'Substantive and Reflexive Elements in Modern Law' (1983) 17 *Law and Society Review* 239; Ralf Rogowski and Ton Wilthagen, *Reflexive Labour Law* (Kluwer 1994).

[26] Catherine Barnard and Simon Deakin, 'Market access and regulatory competition' in Catherine Barnard and Joanne Scott (eds), *The Law of the Single Market: Unpacking the Premises* (Hart Publishing 2002) 219–20.

classified as independent workers could be excluded from collective bargaining rights by competition legal rules. In a certain number of EU Member States, collective agreements can be concluded by unions representing employees only (Denmark, Austria, France, Belgium, Hungary) whereas in other EU Member States unions also representing economically dependent independent contractors, can conclude collective agreements (Germany, the Netherlands, Italy). In this case at national[27] or European level[28] the claim of a violation of competition rules by collective agreements signed by unions representing independent contractors, is a indeed a relevant obstacle for regulating digital platform work through collective agreements. Although it should be said that the same EU institutions have taken another direction on the issue of collective bargaining of independent contractors, adopting initiatives aimed at overcoming the obstacle of Article 101(1) of the Treaty on the Functioning of the European Union (TFEU) which prohibits agreements between undertakings that restrict competition[29] in order to guarantee protections to the gig economy workers.

Another way in which statutory legislation can represent a hurdle for collective bargaining in digital platform work is the introduction of representativeness thresholds for the validity of collective agreements. One example is the collective agreement signed on 17 September 2020, between Assodelivery (an Italian employers' association of digital platforms delivering food) and the UGL (Union) regulating working conditions of independent couriers. The Bologna Tribunal[30] has considered the collective agreement not valid since it has been signed by a union not a representative at national level, as required by Law no 128/2019 regulating the couriers' status and their basic labour law rights. Measuring representativeness for digital platform workers could risk, in this case, excluding digital platform workers, from the scope of application of collective agreements and from collective representation.[31]

IV. Is New Legislation Needed? Different Approaches of Statutory Legislation on Digital Platform Work

All legal orders face the same dilemmas in regulating digital platform work: from one side, legislation seems to be an instrument incapable of following the rapid changes of economic reality; from the other side, collective agreements

[27] See the Danish case of the collective agreements signed between the platform Hilfr and the United Federation of Danish Workers (3F) in 2018 considered as conflicting with competition law by the Danish Competition Authority (2020).

[28] Case C-413/13 *FNV Kunsten Informatie en Media v Staat der Nederlanden* [2014] ECLI:EU:C:2014:2411.

[29] See Commission, 'Collective bargaining agreements for self-employed – scope of application of EU competition rules' (Inception Impact Assessment) Ares(2021)102652.

[30] Tribunale di Bologna, 30 June 2021.

[31] Vandaele (n 1).

seem to suffer serious problems of the representativeness of the category of workers to which they should apply. The case law at first seemed to be the only regulatory source capable of answering the needs of protection for the digital platforms labour force, guaranteeing them recognition of labour rights and visibility.[32]

Whether new legislation is needed or not, it should be decided on the basis of an analysis of the advantages and pitfalls of legal regulation and at the same time we should also ask which are the residual law-making powers that could avoid some of the pitfalls of new legislation on digital platform work (in particular collective agreements and case law). At the same time, it should be decided what model of legislation should be implemented: the alternatives seems to be on the one hand, to adopt specific statutory legislation for work performed via app or digital platforms, detailed and tailored to the cases to be regulated. In this case, at least two main risks should be highlighted: the necessity of frequent updating of this legislation, due to the rapid changes in the issues regulated, and the risk of hyper regulation that could end up in the colonisation of the reality as preconised by Habermas. On the other hand, the model of legislation that should be implemented should be based on general principles, defining basic labour and social security rights to be recognised for platform workers, and leaving the residual regulatory space to collective agreements.

Any model of legislation – based on general principles, defining basic labour and social security rights to be recognised for platform workers – should first deal with the question, surely still unresolved and quite new not only for labour lawyers but also for private law lawyers and constitutional lawyers – of the legal responsibility of digital agents.[33] This issue is also particularly important with a view to reconstructing the parties of a collective agreement for digital platform workers. The basic idea would be to first anchor legal responsibility for digital agents to the capacity of taking decisions: there is a necessary connection between the capacity of taking autonomous or semi-autonomous decisions and responsibility.[34] Digital agents, like digital platforms, 'do not act as self-interested action units, but always in interaction with people for whose pursuit of interests they are used',[35] and from the economic point of view their relations with the enterprise using them could be reconstructed as a principal–agent relationship in which the agent is dependent but autonomous.[36] But if we come to the

[32] Valerio De Stefano, 'The Rise of the "Just-in-Time Workforce": On-Demand Work, Crowdwork and Labour Protection in the "Gig-Economy"' (2016) 37 *Comparative Labor Law & Policy Journal* 471, 480.

[33] Teubner, 'Digital Personhood?' (n 18) 109.

[34] European Parliament, 'European Parliament resolution of 16 February 2017 with recommendations to the Commission on Civil Law Rules on Robotics' (16 February 2017) P8_TA(2017)0051.

[35] Teubner, 'Digital Personhood?' (n 18) 114.

[36] Michael C Jensen and William H Meckling, 'Theory of the Firm: Managerial Behavior, Agency Costs and Ownership Structure' (1976) 3 *Journal of Financial Economics* 305, 306.

fundamental questions of who is the employer[37] and who is responsible for the decisions taken autonomously by the algorithms of the platform, at least we should admit that these digital subjects take decisions, affecting workers independently from their classification, that should be controlled or negotiated by collective agents. The main idea that we would like to discuss is then that at least a new general principle in new statutory legislation should be introduced, legitimising digital collective agents to negotiate with the algorithms.

Some theoretical approaches seem to prefer legislative abstentionism on digital platform work, with a different set of justifications. The first is that digital platform workers have to be considered like all non-standard workers in general;[38] this means that the existing labour laws can be applied to digital platform workers by a simple process of adaptation. Another approach advances the idea that the gig economy is nothing new and is just a modern form of 'Taylorism',[39] whereas others think that more traditional schemes like agency work can be applied to digital platform work.[40] In all those cases it seems that many scholars propose to respond to the questions raised by digital technologies with traditional conceptual instruments, no new legislation is needed and the existing set of legal rules simply needs a process of adaptation.

Although case law in all legal systems was trapped between legal categories often inadequate to adapt to the new forms of work, the theoretical approach adopted by some Supreme Courts was on the one hand to classify digital platform workers as employees in order to guarantee the protections of labour law.[41] With the same aim of guaranteeing the labour law protections, other Supreme Courts have tried to overcome the binary division between independent work and subordination affirming that, there is no sense in asking if these forms of working relationship in an economic reality which is continuously and rapidly being modified, can be classified as subordinate work or that of an independent contractor, whereas it is better from a prevention perspective (to avoid the abuses of bogus self-employment) and from a remedial perspective (to guarantee an equivalent protection of subordinate work to economically dependent workers) to go beyond the categories of subordinate and independent work (the Italian Supreme Court in this case has classified them as hetero-organised workers).[42]

It seems, nonetheless, that there are reasons for adopting new legislation on digital platform work, seen as a new phenomenon needing new regulation.

[37] Jeremias Adams-Prassl and Martin Risak, 'Uber, Taskrabbit, & Co: Platforms as Employers? Rethinking the Legal Analysis of Crowdwork' (2016) 37 *Comparative Labor Law & Policy Journal* 604.

[38] De Stefano (n 32) 480.

[39] Phoebe V Moore, *The Quantified Self in Precarity: Work, Technology and What Counts* (Routledge 2018) 211.

[40] Michele Faioli, 'La gig economy è un processo di matchmaking nel mercato del lavoro' (2017) 2 *Rivista Giuridica del Lavoro e della previdenza sociale* 111.

[41] See the French Cour de cassation, 4 March 2020, no 374 *Uber*; and the Spanish Tribunal Supremo, 25 September 2020, no 805/2020 *Glovo*.

[42] See the Italian Corte di cassazione 24 January 2020, n. 1163/2020, Foodora, paras 25–27.

An interesting case is the Spanish Real Decreto-ley 9/2021 (11 May 2021) modifying the Estatuto de los trabajadores in order to guarantee labour rights to people delivering food in the framework of digital platform work. Where is the novelty? In the introduction of the Real Decreto-Ley it is said: 'La aplicación de estos medios tecnológicos ha introducido elementos novedosos en las relaciones laborales'. The novelty is indicated in the 'métodos de cálculo matemáticos o algoritmo'. It is precisely the introduction of algorithms in the employment relationship which represents the innovation needing a new regulation for the Spanish legislator. We should not underestimate that the regulatory choice in this case is justified by the need for guaranteeing labour protections to digital platform workers (in particular those delivering food) like the right to be informed about the functioning of algorithms which take decisions affecting workers.

Other rationales can be found in the (few) cases of activation by national legislators adopting new statutory legislation on digital platform work. One of the most important is the need to overcome the uncertainties of case law in applying traditional labour law categories, in litigation on digital platform workers' classification. How to overcome the famous question of District Judge Vince Chabria, describing the difficulty a jury will face in discerning whether drivers for the service Lyft are employees or independent contractors ('handed a square peg and asked to choose between two round holes').[43] One technique could be the introduction, through statutory legislation, of legal presumptions on digital platform workers' status, in order to avoid misclassification of digital platform workers.[44] Interestingly, the Real Decreto-ley 9/2021 introduced in the Spanish system a legal presumption of subordination for digital platform workers in the food delivery sector. A similar legal presumption of subordination for digital platform workers in the transport service sector has been introduced in Portugal by Lei no 45/2018 on transport services through digital platforms (article 10, paragraph 10, Lei no 45/2018).

The same kind of technique is used by the California Bill (AB5) approved by the California Assembly in 2019,[45] which introduced a severe ABC test to ascertain the status of independent contractors. Although it does not introduce a legal presumption, this piece of legislation tries to limit the relevance of free will in classifying workers, with relevant consequences for digital platform workers often misclassified as independent contractors.

Also the Italian case of Law no 128 of 2 November 2019 can be considered an attempt through legislation to reduce the misclassification risks for digital platform workers: although it does not introduce a legal presumption of subordination, this statutory legislation applies to digital platform workers delivering food the same labour law protection as employees if they are classified as

[43] *Cotter v Lyft, Inc* 13-cv-04065-VC (ND Cal, 2015).

[44] Miriam A Cherry, 'Beyond Misclassification: The Digital Transformation of Work' (2016) 37 *Comparative Labor Law & Policy Journal* 577.

[45] California Assembly Bill AB-5 of 19 September 2019 codifying the *Dynamex Operations West, Inc v Superior Court*, 4 Cal 5th 903 (2018).

hetero-organised workers (an intermediate category of independent workers considered as economically dependent because of their insertion in an organised activity). The same Law no 128 of 2019 (amending D Lgs 81/2015 article 47 bis ff) also recognises, at the same time, basic labour law protections for genuinely independent couriers. Among them are: a written contract containing a right to be informed of their rights, interests and security; a minimum wage set by collective agreements signed by most of the representative unions and employers associations at sectoral level; 10 per cent compensation for night working, working on public holidays; a non-discrimination right in access to and exclusion from the digital platform; personal data protection; insurance for accidents at work and professional illnesses.

This kind of legislation should, in principle, reduce the misclassification litigation, but what is more important is that it also goes towards the definition of a set of basic labour law rights for independent workers in digital platform work and, what is more relevant, can function as a trigger for collective bargaining; either because it delegates explicitly the regulatory function to collective agreements for independent couriers (as in the Italian case) or because through the legal presumption of subordination it automatically legitimates collective bargaining.

The choice of granting basic rights, especially collective rights, also to independent digital platform workers, seems to be the direction taken by the French legislation: the Loi d'orientation des mobilités of 24 December 2019, introduced in the French Labour Code the principle of the social responsibility of digital platforms (articles L.7341-1–L.7342-11 Labour Code), and article 60 of Law No 2016-1088 of 8 August 2016 (Regarding Labour, Modernising Labour Relations, and Securing Career Tracks) introduced a separate category of the self-employed working for online platforms, granting them the right to constitute and to join a trade union and an obligation to providing vocational training for independent digital platform workers. It should be verified, anyway, if the right to constitute a trade union and to join it is sufficient to guarantee the right to collective bargaining, or if the competition law rules will, once again, be an obstacle.

V. Should Residual Law-Making Power be Left to Collective Bargaining?

The rather scarce, but significant, interventions of statutory legislation leave open the question of which source of regulation should fill the regulatory gaps in digital platform work.

Surely legal categories and classification litigation are some of the main threats to unionisation. All legal orders face the same regulatory dilemmas in regulating digital platform work: the law seems to be a regulatory instrument incapable of following the rapid changes in reality and the case law is trapped between legal categories often inadequate to adapt to the new forms of work. At the same time, collective agreements are regulatory sources flexible enough to answer the regulatory needs and seem the most promising tool 'in an attempt to increase wages, reduce constant surveillance, restrain the pervasive command power, improve working conditions' but the list of hurdles for digital platform workers exercising collective rights and collective bargaining is a long one.[46] How can all these hurdles be eliminated, and which legislation or which collective agreement should be applied to digital platform work having in most cases a transnational dimension? The EU Commission takes as granted the cross-border nature of digital platform work and the fact that digital labour platforms are internet-based and, in many cases, transnational. That is why legislative action at EU level is considered 'the most appropriate means to ensure adequate protection of people working through platforms and avoid fragmentation of the single market'.[47] One of the most important issues to be ascertained is, from this point of view, the redefinition of the scope of application of collective agreements to platform workers classified as self-employed. Notwithstanding the fact that scholars claim wide recognition of the right to collective bargaining for any worker, independently from his or her classification,[48] in some countries the right to collective bargaining is still granted exclusively to employees and, as a consequence, collective agreements signed by unions representing independent workers can conflict with competition law. The same set of questions raised at EU level about the clashes between self-employed collective agreements and competition law is common in legal systems outside the EU.[49]

The picture of national legal and collective sources regulating digital platform work appears very fragmented so far; that is why the EU institutions are worried about the fact that fragmented national regulation of digital platform work might 'have a stifling effect on the employment, competitiveness and innovation potential of platform work' and at the same time, still in the light of market objectives, leaving the issue of digital platform work unregulated at EU level 'can lead to unfair competition' and moreover 'EU-level action to improve working conditions in platform work may help create a more level playing field between digital labour platforms and other forms of business'.[50] Initiatives at EU level, aimed at harmonising the working conditions of digital platform workers, will certainly

[46] Antonio Aloisi, 'Negotiating the digital transformation of work: non-standard workers' voice, collective rights and mobilisation practices in the platform economy' (2019) 3 EUI Working Papers, available at: cadmus.eui.eu/bitstream/handle/1814/63264/MWP_Aloisi_2019_03.pdf?sequence=1, 2.

[47] Commission, 'First Phase Consultation of Social Partners Under Article 154 TFEU on Possible Action Addressing the Challenges Related to Working Conditions in Platform Work' (n 16) 26.

[48] Nicola Countouris and Valerio De Stefano, *New Trade Union Strategies for New Forms of Employment* (ETUC 2019).

[49] See the Australian case Tess Hardy and Shae McCrystal, 'Bargaining in a Vacuum? An Examination of the Proposed Class Exemption for Collective Bargaining for Small Businesses' (2020) 42 *Sydney Law Review* 311.

[50] Commission, 'First Phase Consultation of Social Partners Under Article 154 TFEU on Possible Action Addressing the Challenges Related to Working Conditions in Platform Work' (n 16) 26.

reduce the risks on law shopping as far as the social protections granted to digital platform workers are concerned, and the fact that social partners at EU level have signed a framework agreement on digitalisation is an important step in that direction.[51] European initiatives aimed at harmonising the working conditions of digital platform workers would be important but, as the EU Commission admits, the dimension of digital platform is not European, and as some research suggests, if we look at the division of digital gig work, a high percentage of online platform workers is located in non-EU countries where labour costs and working conditions are lower than in EU countries.[52] Therefore, the risks of law shopping in the case of digital platforms are still very high.

It is not only legislation but also case law which plays an important role in sustaining collective bargaining as a regulatory source. Case law auxiliary function can be seen in litigation on the classification of digital platform workers: qualifying digital platform workers as employees certainly enlarges the scope of application of collective agreements. In reality, the auxiliary function of case law can be even more explicit: the Court of Appeal of Turin (in 2019) said that the collective agreement applicable to define the wages of Foodora riders (classified as hetero-organised workers) is the Sectoral Collective Agreement of Transport and Logistic.[53] At supranational level, the judicial attitude towards collective agreement for digital platform workers is manyfold: on the one hand, the Court of Justice of the European Union has declared that when service providers are classified as genuinely self-employed, the collective agreements that their representative organisations conclude would fall within the scope of Article 101 TFEU, with a possible violation of competition law rules, unless they are bogus self-employed.[54] On the other hand, the European Committee of Social Rights in its conclusions on Complaint No 123/2016 *Irish Congress of Trade Unions v Ireland*, recognised the right to collective bargaining for self-employed workers, under Article 6, paragraphs 2 and 4 of the European Social Charter, on the basis of the vulnerability of the self-employed and the necessity to rebalance the imbalance of power inside the working relationship. In relation to the possible conflicts with competition law, the Committee concluded that it

> does not consider that permitting the self-employed workers in question to bargain collectively and conclude collective agreements, including in respect of remuneration, would have an impact on competition in trade that would be significantly different from the impact on such competition of collective agreements concluded solely in respect of dependent workers (employees).[55]

[51] EU Social Partners, *Framework Agreement on Digitalisation* (ETUC, Business Europe, CEEP, SME United 2020), available at: www.etuc.org/system/files/document/file2020-06/Final%2022%2006%2020_Agreement%20on%20Digitalisation%202020.pdf.

[52] Vili Lehdonvirta, 'Where are online workers located? The international division of digital gig work' (Oxford Internet Institute 2017), available at: www.oii.ox.ac.uk/blog/where-are-online-workers-located-the-international-division-of-digital-gig-work/.

[53] Court of Appeal of Turin, 4 February 2019, no 26/2019, 23.

[54] *FNV Kunsten* (n 28).

[55] European Committee of Social Rights, *Irish Congress of Trade Unions (ICTU) v Ireland* (8 August 2016) C 123/2016, Case No 1, 100.

In some cases the bargaining activities and collective actions are led by quasi-unions or independent unions like the Independent Workers' Union of Great Britain in the UK Deliveroo case.[56] In this case the High Court did not recognise the right to bargain collectively to Deliveroo riders since they were not classified as workers having access to the fundamental right to bargain collectively recognised by Article 11 of the European Convention on Human Rights. An attempt to find a way out seems to the collective agreement signed by another independent union in the UK, the GMB, which signed a collective agreement with Hermes Parcelnet Ltd recognising the couriers' right to choose a particular status of self-employed plus, giving them the right to holiday pay (pro-rata up to 28 days) and individually negotiated pay rates that allow couriers to earn at least £8.55 per hour over the year.

In other cases, traditional unions incorporate gig workers' collective interests in sectoral collective bargaining, as in Italy where the sectoral collective agreement in the transport and logistics sector (2018/2019), signed between the three main union confederations and the Sectoral Employers' Association, regulate the contract of employment of workers delivering food for the main delivery platforms. The same happens in Spain where the sectoral collective agreement of Hosteleria, signed in 2019, regulates the couriers' delivering food activities.

Whereas in other cases public authorities enter in the arena of collective representation. In Italy, a quasi-union of couriers (delivering food) signed in 2018 with Bologna's mayor, the 'Urban Charter of fundamental couriers' rights' defined minimum and equitable hourly wages (comparable to wages set by sectoral collective agreements); dismissal with due notice; health and security insurance; freedom of association; and protection of privacy. It was agreed that this Charter should be incorporated into other collective agreements signed by the Union and food delivery platforms in Bologna, so it could be an useful fertile ground for collective bargaining.

Surely an attempt to find new forms of collective representation, involving new and old collective actors,[57] is the Frankfurt Paper on Platform-Based Work, signed in 2016, by a number of trade Unions from different EU Member States with the aim of defining industrial relations fundamental principles in the platform based work? The importance of this Paper is not only linked to the contents, but to the variety of actors involved that are platform operators, clients, policymakers, workers and worker organisations. From this point of view the Frankfurt Paper suggests the importance of involving a plurality of actors in order to enlarge the panel of stakeholders that could regulate digital platform work. Nonetheless, following the suggestions of some scholars that digital platforms should be considered

[56] ibid.

[57] Austrian Chambers of Labour (Arbeiterkammer); Austrian Trade Union Federation (ÖGB); Danish Union of Commercial and Clerical Workers (HK); German Metalworkers'Union (IG Metall); International Brotherhood of Teamsters Local 117; Service Employees International Union; Unionen.

as employers,[58] we should examine whether traditional schemes of collective bargaining levels (sector, multi-sector or enterprise level) can still be used. Any possible answer needs to consider the different real situations and the difficulties of building a collective interest and a '*demos*' behind the collective bargaining activity. Often digital platforms operate at national level, thus national level bargaining should be considered as a possible option in order to avoid decentralisation of collective bargaining and trying to reconstruct solidarity between workers.

It seems that, notwithstanding the fact that alternative regulatory sources of digital platform work are emerging, produced by different subjects, in some case in the form of charters, proclaimed either by private subjects, like the digital platforms in the framework of their social responsibility – as in the French case of Art L 7342-9 Code du Travail – or by public institutions like the city of Bologna, cannot be seen as alternative sources to collective agreements, but on the contrary as sources of regulation that could help collective agreements to expand their scope of application.

From this short analysis we can conclude that collective bargaining in digital platform work, notwithstanding the variety of relationships with statutory legislation, still needs the auxiliary function of the law. It seems that the most serious question at stake is a legislative intervention, first at EU level, eliminating the conflicts of collective bargaining for self-employed and competition law rules. As underlined by some scholars,[59] eliminating the preclusion of collective bargaining to the self-employed, especially in digital platform work, implies a paradigm shift that could rebuild a 'sane' relationship between the two main regulatory sources (collective agreement and statutory legislation).

[58] See Jeremias Prassl, *The Concept of the Employer* (Oxford University Press 2015); Prassl and Risak (n 37) 619.

[59] Silvia Rainone and Nicola Countouris, 'Collective bargaining and self-employed workers. The need for a paradigm shift' (2021) 11 *ETUI Policy Brief* 4.

3

A Long Road Towards the Regulation of Platform Work in the EU

LUCA RATTI

I. Introduction

The regulation of work performed through online platforms – often referred to as 'platform work' – constitutes probably the most challenging task for regulators in the current socio-economic landscape. Given the characteristics of platform work, including the fact that platforms are often located in countries different from where the person actually performs her tasks, law-makers proved to be cautious in introducing specific rules applicable exclusively to platform workers. Domestic legal systems, depending on how widespread is platform work and how adaptable is labour regulation, mostly responded through case law to the emerging needs of platform workers, who increasingly suffered from insecure working conditions and the precarity depending therefrom.

National responses have been variably commented and systematised in literature, and prompted the European Union (EU) legislator to multiply the initiatives to regulate. Since February 2021, the EU Commission has explored the possibility to regulate platform work at EU level. Aiming to respect Member States' autonomy and the principles of subsidiarity and proportionality, in December 2021 the Commission tabled a proposal for a directive on platform work.

This chapter provides an overview of existing instruments – including soft law initiatives – and first assesses the recent EU Commission's roadmap towards the enactment of a directive regulating platform work. It starts by recalling the novelty of platform work as the object of legal research, an element to keep in mind while questioning which regulatory response is more desirable (section II). It then analyses the latest judicial developments in the field, which call for an intervention of the legislator – particularly at EU level – to settle at least some of the many regulatory issues raised by the performance of platform work across all Member States (section III). Attention is further given to the two rounds of public consultations launched by the EU Commission which culminated in the elaboration of a directive on platform work on the basis of Article 153(3) of the Treaty on the Functioning of the European Union (TFEU) (section IV). The proposal came as a consequence of the unwillingness of EU social partners to carry on negotiations on the working conditions of platform workers (section V). The final section (section VI) of this chapter concludes the analysis by assessing the proposed directive against the two main forms of platform work, namely crowd-work and work on-demand via app. It argues that treating different types of work in the same manner would risk over-homogenising the legal framework applicable to platform work.

II. Three Ages of the Study of Platform Work: Time to Regulate?

While delving into the brief history of platform work, one could be surprised to discover its real novelty.

In the *Cambridge Handbook of the Law of the Sharing Economy*, Aurélien Acquier recalls that the giants of the platform economy around the world (including Airbnb, Uber and Lyft) were all founded as of 2008.[1] Not only is the emergence of the sharing economy a very recent phenomenon, but so is the very idea behind the expression 'gig economy', meant at the beginning to serve as a proxy for a wide array of new forms of work provision.[2] Hence, the *infancy* of platform work. Against such novelties, organisational economists and labour lawyers correctly defined platform capitalism as a new form of putting-out,[3] which challenged from the very outset the Coasean boundaries of the firm.[4]

At a later stage came the *adolescence*. Scholars articulated their analysis trying to define platform work as their object of study, albeit in a general and incomplete way. They did so by using some identifiers, which in turn showed the emergence of a proper dichotomy. A commonly accepted taxonomy was eventually proposed in the 2018 Eurofound report on *Work on Demand*, which clearly distinguished between work on-demand via app, on the one hand, and crowd-work on the other.[5]

At last came *adulthood*. Labour courts' case law started to develop a proper set of arguments to classify platform work according to existing legal principles. Common features began to emerge across the many forms of platform work – for

[1] Aurélien Acquier, 'Uberization Meets Organizational Theory: Platform Capitalism and the Rebirth of the Putting-Out System' in Nestor M Davidson, Michèle Finck and John J Infranca (eds), *Cambridge Handbook of the Law of the Sharing Economy* (Cambridge University Press 2019) 13–14.

[2] Valerio De Stefano, 'The Rise of the "Just-in-Time Workforce": On-Demand Work, Crowdwork and Labour Protection in the "Gig-Economy"' (2016) 37 *Comparative Labor Law & Policy Journal* 471.

[3] Matthew Finkin, 'Beclouded Work, Beclouded Workers in Historical Perspective' (2016) 37 *Comparative Labor Law & Policy Journal* 603.

[4] Julia Tomassetti, 'Does Uber Redefine the Firm? The Postindustrial Corporation and Advanced Information Technology' (2016) 34 *Hofstra Labor & Employment Law Journal* 1.

[5] Eurofound, *Work on Demand: Recurrence, Effects and Challenges* (Publications Office of the European Union 2018).

example, the fact that all of them are platform-based jobs, that they address an indefinite plethora of individuals, that they promote at least in principle the freedom to accept and refuse tasks, etc. Yet, other characteristics remained distinctive of only some forms of platform work.

An overall consideration of both common and distinctive characteristics – which also reflect emerging needs of protection – made clear that case law could not accommodate all the variations typical of platform work in existing legal frameworks and showed that regulation is needed. As revealed by a 2019 European Trade Union Institute (ETUI) study, whereas Member States are intervening to regulate specific aspects of platform work, much more needs to be done to accomplish effective protection for workers.[6]

This pleads in favour of an EU intervention, taking into consideration the range of fields that Articles 151 and 153 TFEU put at the core of EU social policy. Moreover, the regulation at Member State level risks being underproportioned vis-a-vis the amplitude of the phenomenon itself. Regulating a phenomenon such as platform work which is currently in its adulthood means, for the EU, encompassing as many facets of the subject as possible, while granting an efficient response in regulatory terms.

III. Partial Responses from EU Initiatives

Several legal initiatives put in place by the EU in the past years have contributed to establishing few legal principles applicable to the performance of work through online platforms. The legal questions considered in the well-known cases such as *Uber Spain*,[7] *Uber France*[8] and *Yodel Delivery*[9] were left partially unravelled and continued to articulate in parallel with a number of EU law instruments.

The attention of EU institutions to the legal issues stemming from online platforms in the internal market started in 2015 with the Communication on a Digital Single Market Strategy.[10] The Communication aimed at ensuring that transparency, users' data protection, inter-platform movement and prevention of illegal contents were respected.

The Digital Single Market Strategy resulted in two intertwined documents: the Communication on Online Platforms and the Digital Single Market – Opportunities and Challenges for Europe[11] and the Communication on the European Agenda

[6] Isabelle Daugareilh, Christophe Degryse and Philippe Pochet, *The Platform Economy and Social Law: Key Issues in Comparative Perspective* (ETUI 2019).

[7] Case C-434/15 *Asociación Profesional Elite Taxi v Uber Systems Spain SL* [2017] ECLI:EU:C:2017:981.

[8] Case C-320/16 *Uber France* [2018] ECLI:EU:C:2018:221.

[9] Case C-692/19 *B v Yodel Delivery Network Ltd* [2020] ECLI:EU:C:2020:288.

[10] European Commission, 'A Digital Single Market Strategy for Europe' (Communication) COM(2015) 192 final.

[11] Commission, 'Online Platforms and the Digital Single Market Opportunities and Challenges for Europe' (Communication) COM (2016) 0288 final.

for Collaborative Economy.[12] The latter document urged Member States to 'assess the adequacy of their national employment rules considering the different needs of workers and self-employed people in the digital world as well as the innovative nature of collaborative business models' as well as to 'provide guidance on the applicability of their national employment rules in light of labour patterns in the collaborative economy'.[13] The reaction from the EU Parliament further called for an intervention by the EU Commission to resolve the many uncertainties of the regulation of work performed via online platforms.[14]

The issue was raised during the formulation of the 20 Guiding Principles forming the European Pillar of Social Rights. In its final version, the Pillar contained some relevant principles which explicitly or implicitly address the regulation of platform work.

Principle 4 on 'active support to employment' applies to 'everyone' and provides that everyone has 'the right to timely and tailor-made assistance to improve employment or self-employment prospects'.

Principle 5 on 'secure and adaptable working conditions' provides that 'innovative forms of work that ensure quality working conditions shall be fostered' (letter c) and that 'employment relationships that lead to precarious working conditions shall be prevented (including by prohibiting abuse of atypical contracts)' (letter d).

Principle 12 on 'social protection' refers not only to subordinate employees, but extends it to the self-employed, 'regardless of the type and duration of their employment relationship'.

As importantly highlighted in the subsequent Commission Staff Working Document monitoring the implementation of the Pillar,[15] its goal is to

> support a renewed process of convergence towards better working and living conditions across Europe. It is about delivering new and more effective rights for citizens, addressing emerging social challenges and the changing world of work in light of, in particular, emerging types of employment deriving from new technologies and the digital revolution.[16]

The ability of the Pillar to effectively set up ready-to-use principles informing EU social policy may be questioned on technical grounds.[17] Yet, the 'shadow' of the

12 Commission, 'A European Agenda for Collaborative Economy' (Communication) COM (2016) 356 final.

13 ibid, 13.

14 European Parliament, 'European Agenda for the Collaborative Economy. European Parliament resolution of 15 June 2017 on a European Agenda for the collaborative economy' (15 June 2017) P8_TA(2017)0271.

15 Commission, 'Monitoring the implementation of the European Pillar of Social Rights' (Communication) COM (2018) 130 final.

16 ibid, 2.

17 Frank Hendrickx, 'European Labour Law and the Millennium Shift: From Post to Pillar' in Frank Hendrickx and Valerio De Stefano (eds), *Game Changers in Labour Law: Shaping the Future of Work* (Wolters Kluwer 2018).

Pillar went far beyond expectations and covered both legal instruments already in place and new legislative proposals, showing an overall intention to label all social policy-related initiatives with the Pillar's imprint.[18]

The year 2019 saw the enactment of two important legal instruments, which did not aim to encompass the specificities of platform work, but whose propositions may nonetheless help platform workers to have some basic rights granted.

The first was Directive 2019/1152 on transparent and predictable working conditions,[19] which repealed the 'Cinderella Directive' (91/533). It aims to promote transparent and stable employment that guarantees adaptability to the labour market. While substantially confirming the previous Directive's material scope (see especially Article 4), Directive 2019/1152 expands its personal scope to cover 'every worker in the Union who has an employment contract or employment relationship as defined by the law, collective agreements or practice in force in each Member State with consideration to the case-law of the Court of Justice' (Article 2). As correctly observed, this definition reflects the 'tensions between the Europeanist pursuit of the Commission's proposal and the national will of the Member States, represented in the Council, to maintain control over their labour regulation systems'.[20] A narrow interpretation may result in having platform workers left outside the scope of the Directive, at least given the current state of domestic legislation and of the Court of Justice of the European Union (CJEU) jurisprudence. While the original formulation of the Directive's personal scope explicitly included platform workers,[21] its final version may result in undermining its very ambition.[22]

As argued elsewhere, the definition of worker contained in Article 1(2) of Directive 2019/1152 may include those who work under disguised contractual forms, whose independency is merely notional (Recital (8)).[23] Moreover, the constant use of the *effet utile* principle by the CJEU may result in a broader application of Directive 2019/1152 which takes into account the evolving concept of a

[18] Sacha Garben, 'The European Pillar of Social Rights: An Assessment of its Meaning and Significance' (2019) 21 *Cambridge Yearbook of European Legal Studies* 101, 106.

[19] Council Directive (EU) 2019/1152 of 20 June 2019 on transparent and predictable working conditions in the European Union [2019] OJ L186.

[20] José María Miranda Boto, 'Much Ado about Anything? The New Directive (EU) 2019/1152 on Transparent and Predictable Working Conditions in the European Union' in Franz Marhold et al (eds), *Arbeits- und Sozialrecht für Europa. Festschrift für Maximilian Fuchs* (Nomos 2020) 157.

[21] Commission, 'Commission Staff Working Document Impact Assessment Accompanying the Document Proposal for a Directive the European Parliament and of the Council of 20 June 2019 on transparent and predictable working conditions in the European Union' (Staff Working Document) SWD (2017) 478 final.

[22] Bartłomiej Bednarowicz, 'Delivering on the European Pillar of Social Rights: The New Directive on Transparent and Predictable Working Conditions in the European Union' (2019) 48 *Industrial Law Journal* 604, 613.

[23] Luca Ratti, 'Crowdwork and Work On-Demand in the European Legal Framework: Promises and Expectations' in Maria Teresa Carinci and Filip Dorssemont (eds), *Platform Work in Europe. Towards Harmonisation?* (Intersentia 2021) 203.

'worker' under EU law.[24] It remains that both the preambles and some provisions in the body of the Directive (Article 11, Directive 2019/1152, Complementary measures for on-demand contracts) point to the inclusion of casual work arrangements, asking Member States to

> take one or more of the following measures to prevent abusive practices: (a) limitations to the use and duration of on-demand or similar employment contracts; (b) a rebuttable presumption of the existence of an employment contract with a minimum amount of paid hours based on the average hours worked during a given period; (c) other equivalent measures that ensure effective prevention of abusive practices.

The second legislative initiative of the late Juncker Commission was Council Recommendation (2019/C 387/01) of 8 November 2019 on access to social protection for workers and the self-employed. Built on the premise that people working on a status different from that of a typical subordinate employee deserved to benefit from proper social protections,[25] the Commission had initially planned to issue a Directive on the basis of Articles 153(1)(c), 151 and 352 TFEU. Its guiding principles should have been: (a) ensuring similar social protection rights for similar work; (b) tying social protection rights to individuals and making them transferable; (c) making social protection rights and related information transparent; and (d) simplifying administrative requirements.[26] The process ended up with a soft law instrument – a Recommendation – the only result achievable after the serious criticism received from the Council. The Recommendation's stipulations now feature rather generic definitions (eg, Article 7(a) on 'type of employment relationships') and make constant reference to domestic legislation (eg, Article 8 mentioning the 'voluntary application to the self-employed'), which eventually risks leaving the most vulnerable work relationships (especially those performed through online platforms) 'trapped' in precarity.[27]

Considering the above, it is easy to conclude that until recently the regulation of platform work remained highly controversial and unsatisfactory. The need to respect the principles of subsidiarity and proportionality (Article 5 TEU) eventually contributed to weaken the position of the EU Commission vis-a-vis its Member States. Furthermore, the state of both the domestic and European case law in the field left unresolved a number of crucial issues, *in primis* that of the

[24] See Commission, *Report Expert Group: Transposition of Directive (EU) 2019/1152 on transparent and predictable working conditions in the European Union* (Publications Office of the European Union 2021).

[25] This was initially at the core of the Commission's action. See Commission, *Access to Social Protection for All Forms of Employment: Assessing the Options For a Possible EU Initiative* (Publications Office of the European Union 2018).

[26] Commission, 'Consultation Document of 26.4. 2017. First phase consultation of Social Partners under Article 154 TFEU on a possible action addressing the challenges of access to social protection for people in all forms of employment in the framework of the European Pillar of Social Rights' COM (2017) 2610 final.

[27] Ane Aranguiz and Bartłomiej Bednarowitz, 'Adapt or Perish: Recent Developments on Social Protection in the EU under a Gig Deal of Pressure' (2018) 9 *European Labour Law Journal* 329, 345.

legal qualification of the different forms of platform work, often dependent on the concrete circumstances of the single case.[28]

The lack of political consensus over a clear legislative intervention further amplified platforms' ability to benefit from judicial uncertainty and often avoid being subject to labour law's protective rules.

IV. A Preliminary Assessment of the Current EU Commission's Roadmap to Regulate Platform Work

The 'bits-and-pieces' approach taken by the EU legislative institutions in the past years was eventually altered once the von der Leyen Commission took office. Initially through political statements, and more concretely with a specific legislative action during its first months of mandate, the current Commission clearly manifested its intention to legislate in the field of platform work.

A. The First-Phase Consultation

In February 2021, the Commission launched a first-phase consultation with the EU social partners on a possible action addressing the challenges related to working conditions in platform work.[29]

The consultation followed the procedure laid down by Article 154 TFEU, pursuant to which social partners are asked to give their opinion on the opportunity to take legislative action in the field. Several important topics were discussed at the first stage, including platform workers' employment status, working conditions and access to social protection. Of specific relevance in the context of the COGENS book project, the first-phase consultation document expressly addressed access to collective representation and bargaining, and the cross-border dimension of platform work. On collective representation, the document made access to collective bargaining conditional on the employment status of people working through platforms, while leaving aside the interaction with EU competition law, targeted by an ad hoc consultation with social partners.[30]

[28] Valerio De Stefano et al, 'Platform Work and the Employment Relationship' (2021) ILO Working Paper.

[29] Commission, 'First Phase Consultation of Social Partners Under Article 154 TFEU on Possible Action Addressing the Challenges Related to Working Conditions in Platform Work' (Consultation Document) C(2021) 1127 final.

[30] Commission, 'Collective Bargaining Agreements for Self-Employed – Scope of Application of EU Competition Rules', available at: www.ec.europa.eu/info/law/better-regulation/have-your-say/initiatives/12483-Collective-bargaining-agreements-for-self-employed-scope-of-application-EU-competition-rules_en.

In particular, the first-phase consultation document aimed to

> consult the social partners on collective bargaining aspects in platform work that go beyond the competition law dimension. Taking due account of the autonomy of social partners and in line with national practices, such aspects could for example support social partners' coverage of platform work, facilitate contacts between people working through platforms, and promote social dialogue, also to cater to new technological developments and the impact these may have on the world of work.[31]

One of the fields that the same document expressly mentions is algorithmic management and the way collective agreements may regulate it. Building on examples of collective agreements which already include some managerial prerogatives within the list of matters to be negotiated with employees' representatives, collective agreements should be given more space by EU law. This can be done in the form of promotion and recognition of collectively agreed solutions to accommodate the novelties brought about by the massive use of technologies in the management of platform workers, including data protection and AI management.[32]

On the cross-border dimension of platform work, the first-phase consultation document is less straightforward. It simply mentions that the global nature of online platforms that intermediate work 'potentially poses challenges to the application of EU law relating to freedom of movement (of workers and of services), jurisdiction and applicable law (Brussels Ia and Rome I regulations) and social security coordination'.[33] Particularly concerning social security, the mismanagement of social security benefits could impact the sustainability of national public budgets.[34] Therefore, the main challenge remains determining the country where contributions are to be paid.

The first-phase consultation document received attention from the media, politicians, academics and especially from social partners at the European level. BusinessEurope warned the Commission of the risk of adopting a one-size-fits-all approach to govern the many forms of platform work. It contended that Member States are best placed to regulate, and that existing EU law instruments require effective implementation and enforcement.[35] The European Trade Union Confederation (ETUC), on the contrary, reacted positively to the first consultation. While acknowledging that a basic distinction between on-location labour

[31] See (n 29) 20.

[32] Valerio De Stefano, '"Negotiating the Algorithm": Automation, Artificial Intelligence and Labour Protection' (2019) 41 *Comparative Labor Law & Policy Journal* 15.

[33] See (n 29) 16–17.

[34] Here the Consultation Document cites the Report prepared for the European Commission by Grega Strban (coordinator), Dolores Carrascosa Bermejo, Paul Schoukens and Ivana Vukorep, *Social security coordination and non-standard forms of employment and self-employment: Interrelation, challenges and prospects* (2020) (Luxembourg, Publications Office of the European Union).

[35] BusinessEurope, 'Consultation Response to the First phase social partner consultation on possible action addressing the challenges related to working conditions in platform work' (2021), available at: www.businesseurope.eu/sites/buseur/files/media/position_papers/social/2021-04-06_platform_work_-_final_response_1st-phase_consultation_.pdf.

platforms and online labour platforms should remain, it also insisted that the distinction

> cannot imply that workers active in some type of platform company continue to be denied their labour and social rights. It can only help identifying additional challenges and issues that must be tackled over and beyond the minimum level of rights.

The ETUC further argued in favour of introducing a rebuttable presumption of employment status and a reversal of the burden of proof to the employer in cases establishing the employment relationship.[36] The main message coming from the first-phase consultation, however, was that neither side was willing to enter negotiations according to Article 155 TFEU.

B. The Second-Phase Consultation

In June 2021 the Commission launched a second consultation to further question the EU social partners regarding the direction of a possible legislative intervention in the field.[37]

The analysis of the second document elaborates on three main components: (a) challenges; (b) existing regulatory gaps; and (c) policy proposals.

(a) Some regulatory challenges are presented in the document as pivotal for articulating EU rules on platform work.[38]

The first is the lack of clarity on the employment status of platform workers. The Commission provides evidence of the high risk of misclassification, mainly relying on the diversified case law across EU Member States. The starting point of any discussion, however, is that the classification as self-employed is highly unsatisfactory and exacerbates litigation in the field.[39]

A second challenge is identified in algorithmic management. The consultation document highlights that the many stages of an employment relationship are nowadays permeated by algorithms, from recruitment to surveillance, from supervision to termination. This calls for increased transparency and accessible information is of paramount importance, since the lack of information may lead to undermining the very functioning of social dialogue and collective representation.[40]

[36] ETUC, 'ETUC Reply to the First Phase Consultation of Social Partners under Article 154 TFEU on Possible Action Addressing the Challenges Related to Working Conditions in Platform Work' (1 April 2021), available at: www.etuc.org/en/document/etuc-reply-first-phase-consultation-social-partners-under-article-154-tfeu-possible-0.

[37] Commission, 'Second-Phase Consultation of Social Partners Under Article 154 TFEU on Possible Action Addressing the Challenges Related to Working Conditions in Platform Work' (Consultation Document) C(2021) 4230 final.

[38] ibid, 5–13.

[39] Andrew Stewart and Shae McCrystal, 'Labour Regulation and the Great Divide: Does the Gig Economy Require a New Category of Worker?' (2019) 32 *Australian Journal of Labour Law* 4.

[40] Valerio De Stefano and Simon Taes, 'Algorithmic Management and Collective Bargaining' (2021) 10 *Foresight Brief*, available at: www.etui.org/sites/default/files/2021-05/Algorithmic%20management%20and%20collective%20bargaining-web-2021.pdf.

The third challenge highlighted in the consultation document deals with the cross-border nature typical of platform work. This point proves to be the most controversial. On the one hand, it implies a clear classification of the status of platform workers functional also to the collection of social security contributions and, on the other, replicates the practical impossibility to capture the performance of online work as if it was carried out in a given workplace.

(b) As for regulatory gaps,[41] the Commission correctly mentions that a number of existing legal instruments already cover workers. Yet, only some of them include the self-employed in their personal scope (eg, anti-discrimination directives). As the previous analysis has shown (above section III), EU rules already in force (including soft law such as the Recommendation on social protection for all forms of employment) are unable to meet the emerging needs of platform workers and would require the adaptation of an extensive circumstantial interpretation.

(c) The most promising part of the second-phase consultation document consists of the policy proposals that the Commission put on the table,[42] aimed at stimulating social partners' discussion and finally get into more complex negotiations.

A first concrete proposal is to address misclassification in employment status. This can be done by introducing a rebuttable presumption of an employment relationship between the person performing work and the platform, by merely shifting the burden of proof (*rectius*, allowing claimants to provide prima facie evidence of their status), or introducing an administrative procedure which may certify the exact qualification of the relationship.

A second proposal aims to address the main issues stemming from the massive use of algorithmic management. It includes improving information, guaranteeing 'timely and justified human oversight' over the performance, ensuring 'appropriate channels for redress', reinforcing the involvement of social partners in their information and consultation rights, promoting ratings portability, and excluding automatic termination or equivalent practices via algorithms.

A third proposal is meant to tackle the cross-border nature of platform work, and suggests considering 'either a register of, or transparency obligations for, platforms', as well as to identify people performing through platforms in order to ensure the portability of their social security rights.

Finally, the consultation document recognises the importance of collective actors in ensuring compliance with the rules and supports the collective representation of people performing via platforms. This may also include the removal of legal obstacles to collective bargaining for platform workers from an EU competition law perspective.[43]

[41] See Commission Consultation Document, 'Second-Phase Consultation' (n 37) 13–15.

[42] ibid, 19–25.

[43] On which see extensively Ioannis Lianos, Nicola Countouris and Valerio De Stefano, 'Re-thinking the competition law/labour law interaction: Promoting a fairer labour market' (2019) 10 *European Labour Law Journal* 291. See also BusinessEurope, 'EC public consultation on collective bargaining agreements for self-employed – scope of application EU competition rules' (20 May 2021),

In September 2021, the chances that an agreement on platform work would be concluded at EU level appeared to be very small. The ETUC issued a reasoned opinion responding to the second-phase consultation, where it conveyed some clear messages.[44] First, platform workers should not be considered as a special category of workers, thus the idea of introducing third-way classifications should be rejected. Second, while platforms may take different forms 'there is nothing structurally novel about "work through platforms" (in its many manifestations) that would prevent existing general labour law principles and in relevant cases collective agreements to regulate this social phenomenon'.[45] Third, a rebuttable presumption of employment relationship should be introduced, with the reversal of the burden of proof, as well as the protection of new rights for platform workers relating to algorithmic management and safety at work. The ETUC highlighted the importance for the EU to 'encourage Member States and social partners to stimulate social dialogue in platform work and to support capacity building in this context', which 'is yet one more argument in favour of the liability of platform companies as employers'. Only by recognising platforms as employers would workers' representatives be entitled to and effectively engaged in collective actions, including negotiating collective agreements.[46]

The political momentum to take action in the field of platform work was further stressed in a Resolution adopted by the European Parliament, emphasising the importance to guarantee that people working for digital labour platforms have the same level of social protection as standard comparable workers.[47]

C. The Proposal for a Directive on the Working Conditions of Platform Workers

Eventually, on 9 December 2021, the Commission tabled a Proposal for a Directive on improving working conditions in platform work.[48]

According to its explanatory memorandum,[49] the proposed directive is based on three main objectives: (1) to ensure that people working through platforms

available at: www.businesseurope.eu/sites/buseur/files/media/position_papers/social/2021-05-21_self-employed_collective_bargaining_-_reply_to_consultation.pdf.

[44] ETUC, 'ETUC reply to the Second phase consultation of social partners under Article 154 TFEU on possible action addressing the challenges related to working conditions in platform work' (10 September 2021), available at: www.etuc.org/en/document/etuc-reply-second-phase-consultation-social-partners-under-article-154-tfeu-possible.

[45] ibid.

[46] ibid.

[47] European Parliament, 'European Parliament Resolution of 16 September 2021 on fair working conditions, rights and social protection for platform workers – new forms of employment linked to digital development (2019/2186(INI))' (16 September 2021) P9_TA(2021)0385.

[48] COM(2021) 762 final.

[49] Explanatory Memorandum to the Proposal for a Directive of the European Parliament and of the Council on improving working conditions in platform work (COM(2021) 762 final).

have – or can obtain – the correct employment status in light of their actual relationship with the digital labour platform and gain access to the applicable labour and social protection rights; (2) to ensure fairness, transparency and accountability in algorithmic management in the platform work context; and (3) to enhance transparency, traceability and awareness of developments in platform work and improve enforcement of the applicable rules for all people working through platforms, including those operating across borders.

As mentioned in the Directive's Impact assessment, 'as a result of actions to address the risk of misclassification, between 1.72 million and 4.1 million people are expected to be reclassified as workers (circa 2.35 million on-location and 1.75 million online considering the higher estimation figures)'.[50] The Directive's Recitals stress the importance of digital labour platforms 'in matching the demand for the service with the supply of labour by an individual who has a contractual relationship with the digital labour platform and who is available to perform a specific task, and can include other activities such as processing payments'.[51]

Article 2(1) defines a 'digital labour platform' as

> any natural or legal person providing a commercial service which meets all of the following requirements:
>
> (a) it is provided, at least in part, at a distance through electronic means, such as a website or a mobile application;
>
> (b) it is provided at the request of a recipient of the service;
>
> (c) it involves, as a necessary and essential component, the organisation of work performed by individuals, irrespective of whether that work is performed online or in a certain location.

An innovative aspect of the Directive concerns its personal scope of application, which includes not only 'platform workers' who have an employment contract or relationship, but also 'persons performing platform work', meaning a broader set of individuals, including genuine self-employed. While the distinction is determined by the criteria and procedures laid down in Articles 3, 4 and 5 of the Directive, a substantial floor of rights is recognised for all individuals performing platform work.

Of the articulated text – comprised of 54 Recitals and 24 Articles – we will here focus on the Directive's ability to address the complexity of platform work. Considering its main forms, namely crowdwork (online) and work on-demand via app (on-site), three main aspects deserve attention.

First, Article 4(1) introduces a legal presumption whenever a digital labour platform 'controls, within the meaning of paragraph 2, the performance of work'. Controlling the performance of work is meant by:

> (a) effectively determining, or setting upper limits for the level of remuneration;

[50] Commission staff working document accompanying the Proposal for a directive of the European Parliament and of the Council on improving working conditions in platform work (SWD(2021) 396).

[51] ibid, Recital 18

(b) requiring the person performing platform work to respect specific binding rules with regard to appearance, conduct towards the recipient of the service or performance of the work;
(c) supervising the performance of work or verifying the quality of the results of the work including by electronic means;
(d) effectively restricting the freedom, including through sanctions, to organise one's work, in particular the discretion to choose one's working hours or periods of absence, to accept or to refuse tasks or to use subcontractors or substitutes;
(e) effectively restricting the possibility to build a client base or to perform work for any third party.

When two of the listed situations occur, the relationship between the digital labour platform and the individual is presumed to be an employment relationship. Such a presumption is not absolute, since Article 5 entitles any of the parties to rebut it in legal or administrative proceedings and places the burden of proof on digital labour platforms (Article 5(2)).

The presumption builds on existing experiences at national level and reflects the need to introduce more legal certainty, which would also facilitate enforcement by judicial and administrative authorities.[52] By favouring the qualification of platform workers as employees, the legal presumption further supports trade unions in their collective representation and bargaining, exempting the relevant collective agreements from competition law rules.

The approach taken by the proposed directive reflects an idea of a legal presumption as a bureaucratic process run by the authorities entitled to qualify employment relationships. The list of criteria provided by Article 4(2) departs from existing presumptions based on general legal concepts (such as carrying out an activity 'on behalf and within the scope of the organisation and management of another': Article 8(1) of the Spanish Estatuto de los Trabajadores)[53] or on the non-recurrence of certain situations (such as the presumption of self-employment provided by Article L. 8222-1 of the French Code du Travail),[54] or on the mere passing of time (such as the Dutch presumption as per Article 7:610a of the Civil Code).[55] As argued by Kullmann,[56] it remains to be seen how strict the CJEU's scrutiny of the limits of EU internal market freedoms deriving from the legal presumption of platform work will be, given the loose criteria established in the case of *Commission v France*.[57]

[52] Miriam Kullmann, '"Platformisation" of Work: An EU Perspective on Introducing a Legal Presumption' [2021] *European Labour Law Journal.*

[53] Manuel Carlos Palomenque López and Manuel Alvarez de la Rosa, *Derecho del Trabajo* (Editorial Universitaria Ramón Areces 2021) 549.

[54] Gilles Auzero, Dirk Baugard and Emmanuel Dockès, *Droit du travail* (Dalloz 2022) 277.

[55] Guus Heerma van Voss, 'The Concept of "Employee": The Position in the Netherlands' in Bernd Waas and Guus Heerma van Voss (eds), *Restatement of Labour Law in Europe. Vol I. The Concept of Employee* (Hart Publishing 2017) 499, 500.

[56] See (n 52).

[57] Case C-255/04 *Commission v France* [2006] ECLI:EU:C:2006:401.

A second nucleus of provisions which unquestionably innovates the EU legal landscape concerns Chapter III on algorithmic management. Of particular interest are Article 6, which introduces information duties including platform workers, their representatives and labour authorities as addressees; Article 7, which obliges platforms to regularly monitor the effects of automated decisions on the safety and health of platform workers; and Article 8, which requires platforms to provide an explanation and, if necessary, a timely review, of any decision affecting platform worker's working conditions, without prejudice to existing protections against dismissals (Article 8(4)).

A third important aspect, where the proposed directive is however less incisive in formulating a coherent set of rules, concerns the provisions on collective bargaining and collective representation of the interests of platform workers. The issue emerges here and there in the text (for instance, in Articles 6(4), 9(1), 9(3), 12(1) and 12(3)), and more directly in Article 14, which grants the 'representatives of persons performing platform work' having a 'legitimate interest' the right to 'engage in any judicial or administrative procedure to enforce any of the rights or obligations arising from this Directive'.

The above-mentioned aspects of the proposed directive show that the objective is to enable a large number of persons performing platform work to qualify as workers, as far as work on-demand via app is concerned. It seems less evident where the work activities are carried out entirely online and the labour platform's control is less intrusive – at least in theory – of the individuals' freedom to autonomously organise their work. In the same way, many of the rights recognised for the representatives of persons performing platform work may be less effective when it comes to crowdwork tasks. More adherent to the crowdwork model is the Directive's clear commitment to regulating algorithmic management, including human review of significant decisions, which may apply indifferently to online and on-location work performances.

D. The Commission's Guidelines on Collective Bargaining for Solo Self-Employed Persons

Concomitantly with the proposed directive on the working conditions of platform workers, the EU Commission initiated a consultation procedure on a draft Communication containing 'Guidelines on the application of EU competition law to collective agreements regarding the working conditions of solo self-employed persons'.[58]

[58] Commission, Approval of the content of a draft for a Communication from the Commission 'Guidelines on the application of EU competition law to collective agreements regarding the working conditions of solo self-employed persons' (2021), available at: ec.europa.eu/commission/presscorner/detail/en/ip_21_6620.

While such guidelines are not intended to become an integral part of the directive on platform work, they will surely serve as a useful complement to its provisions.

What is here of interest (more details in Brameshuber, chapter fourteen in this volume) is that the consultation guidelines apply to any form of collective negotiation concerning solo self-employed persons in matters such as 'remuneration, working time and working patterns, holidays, leave', etc.[59] The regulatory strategy expressed by the guidelines implies their binding nature only with regard to the EU Commission, in its role to ensure compliance with Article 101 TFEU. Whenever solo self-employed persons are considered to be 'in a situation comparable to that of workers, their collective agreements should be considered to fall outside the scope of Article 101 TFEU regardless of whether they would fulfil the criteria for being false self-employed persons'.[60]

The Commission proposes considering as being in a 'comparable situation' three types of individuals: (a) economically dependent solo self-employed persons, meaning those who earn at least 50 per cent of their annual work-related income from a single counterparty;[61] (b) solo self-employed persons working 'side-by-side' with workers, even if they do not qualify as workers under the applicable domestic rules; and (c) solo self-employed persons working through digital labour platforms.

It is in particular this last category which demonstrates the importance of also including in the exemption from Article 101 TFEU persons performing via platforms as defined by the above-mentioned Directive. Irrespective of their classification as 'platform workers', such persons may nonetheless benefit from having their working conditions defined by collective agreements without any interference from the same EU Commission.

V. The Collective Self-Regulation of Platform Work: EU Social Partners Lagging Behind

Labour law historians taught us that the main achievements in the early stages of the second Industrial Revolution were intrinsically a consequence of the collective (re)action aimed at demands for more legal protections and to get basic labour rights recognised.

In the (convoluted) journey – expertly described by Antoine Jacobs[62] – which brought the collective self-regulation of work from 'repression' to 'toleration' and finally to 'recognition', a crucial role was played by the virtuous combination

[59] ibid, para 16.
[60] ibid, para 21.
[61] ibid, para 25.
[62] Antoine Jacobs, 'Collective Self-Regulation' in Bob Hepple (ed), *The Making of Labour Law in Europe: A Comparative Study Of Nine Countries Up To 1945* (Hart Publishing 1986) 196.

between concrete actions by social partners and ambitious legal reforms.[63] Reforms were made possible by the introduction of legal instruments aimed at supporting and nurturing the system of collective self-regulation of work. Particularly important was constitutional coverage, as that provided by the Weimar Constitution, and the creation of legal institutions and instruments to make collective self-regulation possible and enforceable.[64]

What we can now see on platform work is that social partners at national and even local level are taking the initiative, by imaging alternative forms of cooperation or even by organising industrial action and signing collective agreements.[65] Both are done in a regulatory vacuum and have placed excessive responsibilities on the social partners themselves, as well as on the judiciary. Lacking specific rules to adequately respond to platform workers' needs, labour courts at all levels have adapted existing rules.[66] The results of judicial scrutiny are all but consistent and point to the need for the legislator to take into account the most pressing regulatory issues, some of which have already been considered by the EU Commission's initiative.

In contrast, dissimilar momentum is recorded amongst social partners at EU level. Albeit invited by the Commission in its two-stage consultation process, social partners did not demonstrate the willingness to negotiate on the rights of platform workers.

On the one side of the spectrum, employers reiterated that any regulation would undermine competitiveness. Therefore, a spontaneous development of social dialogue at national level would suffice.[67] On the other side, trade unions made clear that, while being 'always ready to enter into dialogue with employers on how to improve working conditions', mere voluntary instruments (eg, codes of conduct, charters or labels that have already been introduced in some Member States) would simply delay legislative action and must therefore be repudiated. The ETUC, for instance, insisted that an EU Directive would be the only way to achieve in a reasonable time the protections needed by platform workers.[68]

[63] Jacobs (ibid 232) included in 'repression' the prosecution of trade unions and particularly of industrial action happening in almost all legal systems from late medieval times until the end of the nineteenth century. 'Toleration' meant the affirmation of a certain liberty to conclude collective agreements and even to manifest and strike, in a scenario of abstention of state powers in the field, thus resulting in an immunity rather than a state's support. Finally, 'recognition' identified the positive actions by public authorities and/or amongst social partners.

[64] Antoine Jacobs, 'Collective Labour Relations' in Bob Hepple and Bruno Veneziani (eds), *The Transformation of Labour Law in Europe: A Comparative Study of 15 Countries 1945–2004* (Hart Publishing 2009) 203.

[65] See Judith Bröckmann, ch 7 in this volume.

[66] See extensively, Jeremias Adams-Prassl, Sylvaine Laulom and Yolanda Maneiro Vázquez, ch 5 in this volume.

[67] BusinessEurope, 'Consultation Response to the First phase social partner consultation' (n 35).

[68] 'ETUC, reply to the Second phase consultation' (n 44).

In assessing this hesitation, some attention should be drawn to the (increasingly) controversial understanding of collective autonomy in the EU legal framework. The recent case of *EPSU v Commission*,[69] clearly demonstrates that even when an agreement is found amongst social partners at EU level, the Commission retains a wide margin of discretion not only to run formal checks (such as that on the representativity of signatory parties pursuant to *UEAPME v Council*),[70] but to decide whether the merit of the agreement is in line with the EU's aims and priorities. According to the CJEU:

> Article 155(2) TFEU confers on that institution a specific power which, although it can be exercised only following a joint request by management and labour, is, once such a request has been made, similar to the general power of initiative laid down in Article 17(2) TEU for the adoption of legislative acts, since the existence of a Commission proposal is a precondition for the adoption of a decision by the Council under that provision. That specific power falls within the scope of the role assigned to the Commission in Article 17(1) TEU, which consists in the present context in determining, in the light of the general interest of the European Union, whether it is appropriate to submit a proposal to the Council on the basis of an agreement between management and labour, for the purpose of its implementation at EU level.[71]

Another element to consider is the strict approach taken by EU and domestic competition authorities vis-a-vis some collective agreements. One of the most innovative – the Danish Hilfr-3F collective agreement concluded in April 2018 – introduced a number of entitlements for workers performing cleaning services via the platform, including their status, hourly rates and some paid holiday and pension rights.[72] Soon after, the Danish Competition Authority targeted the agreement asking for the removal of the provisions regarding hourly rates, seen as 'price floors' contrary to internal competition amongst undertakings. This step made the platform remove the remuneration schemes from the agreement.[73] The matter was of concern to trade unions, which saw it as a 'severe setback on the spread of collective bargaining with platform companies'.[74]

VI. Conclusion: *sectari rivulos*?

A conclusive point remains unaddressed by the Commission's legislative initiative and seems underestimated also at doctrinal level: should online platforms, and

[69] Case C-928/19 *EPSU v Commission* [2021] ECLI:EU:C:2021:656.

[70] Case T-135/96 *UEAPME v Council* [1998] ECLI:EU:T:1998:128.

[71] *EPSU* (n 69) para 47.

[72] Anna Ilsøe, 'The Hilfr Agreement – Negotiating the Platform Economy in Denmark' (2020) FAOS Research Paper 176.

[73] Danish Competition and Consumer Authority, 'Commitment Decision on the Use of a Minimum Hourly Fee' (26 August 2020), available at: www.en.kfst.dk/nyheder/kfst/english/decisions/20200826-commitment-decision-on-the-use-of-a-minimum-hourly-fee-hilfr/.

[74] 'ETUC Reply to the First Phase Consultation' (n 36).

platform work accordingly, be distinguished according to the nature of the work performed? As a consequence, should the rules on work on-demand be separated from those on crowdwork and other online work arrangements?

It is argued elsewhere that fundamental differences exist, which is an element to be considered while regulating.[75] Comparative studies have underlined the irreconcilable dissimilarity (at least) between the two main forms of platform work,[76] while economic considerations may bring further elements of complexity, such as distinctions based on the level of skills required to perform the tasks via the online platform.[77]

According to the same consultation documents accompanying the Commission's initiative, 'on-location labour platform' refers to a digital labour platform which only or mostly intermediates services performed in the physical world, for example, ride-hailing, food delivery, household tasks (cleaning, plumbing, caring), while 'online labour platform' refers to a digital labour platform which only or mostly intermediates services performed in the online world, for example, AI training, image tagging, design projects, translations and editing work, software development.[78]

It is understandable that the position taken by trade unions at EU level is that any regulation on platform work should encompass all forms thereof, the heterogeneity argument not fitting with trade unions' requests.[79] Yet, we may nonetheless consider the risks relating to an underestimation of the persistent differences between the various business models of platform work.

Assessing the state of litigation in the field, we can observe that the vast majority of cases decided on platform workers deal in fact with workers on-demand who are mostly riders and drivers.[80] Very few cases deal with crowdworkers,[81] an element

[75] Luca Ratti, 'Online Platforms and Crowdwork in Europe: A Two-step Approach to Expanding Agency Work Provisions?' (2017) 38 *Comparative Labor Law & Policy Journal* 477.

[76] Harald Hauben, Marta Kahancová and Anna Manoudi, *European Centre of Expertise in the field of labour law, employment and labour market policies: Thematic Review 2021 on Platform Work* (Publications Office of the European Union 2021) 6; Harald Hauben, Karolien Lenaerts and Willem Waeyaert, 'The Platform Economy and Precarious Work; Publication for The Committee on Employment and Social Affairs, Policy Department for Economic, Scientific and Quality of Life Policies' (2020), available at: www.europarl.europa.eu/RegData/etudes/STUD/2020/652734/IPOL_STU(2020)652734_EN.pdf; Maria Cesira Urzí Brancati, Annarosa Pesole and Enrique Fernández-Macias, *New Evidence on Plat-Form Workers in Europe: Results from the Second COLLEEM Survey* (Publications Office of the European Union 2020).

[77] Zachary Kilhoffer et al, *Study to Gather Evidence on the Working Conditions of Platform Workers* (Publications Office of the European Union 2019), available at: www.ceps.eu/wp-content/uploads/2020/03/KE-01-20-054-EN-N.pdf.

[78] ibid.

[79] 'ETUC reply to the Second phase consultation' (n 44).

[80] Christina Hießl, 'Case Law on the Classification of Platform Workers: Cross-European Comparative Analysis and Tentative Conclusions' *Comparative Labor Law & Policy Journal* (forthcoming)

[81] For an interesting case where the worker performed both on-location and online tasks, see the decision by the German Supreme Court: BAG 1.12.2020, 9 AZR 102/20, ECLI:DE:BAG:2020:011220.U.9AZR102.20.0, available at: www.rechtsprechung-im-internet.de/jportal/portal/t/19ke/page/bsjrsprod.psml?pid=Dokumentanzeige&showdoccase=1&js_peid=Trefferliste&documentnumbe

which may derive from their inability to get access to justice, probably hindered by the cross-border character and the overseas location of most crowdwork platforms and/or from the micro-nature of crowdwork tasks that generate lower revenues and consequently less remunerative litigation.

The main characteristics of the job performed by crowdworkers, on the one hand, and workers on-demand on the other, relate to different features such as the virtual or rather non-virtual nature of work, the global or rather local execution of it, the different methods of adjudication, the bid-based or rather defined rate of payment, the complexity of tasks and control over the performance, and the general or rather specialised nature of online platforms themselves.

The history of labour law and industrial relations may serve as a good basis for further reflection on this dichotomy. While the very first 'indications of labour law are found some time after the process of industrialisation had begun', regulatory changes were prompted by the activism of workers' organisations throughout the nineteenth century.[82] 'Workers' at that time meant especially 'labourers', ie, manual workers. The importance of labourers well before the emergence of a new class of working people made it possible for collective agreements and social laws to start protecting health and safety, and providing minimum standards, such as minimum remuneration rates and maximum working hours.[83] Later on, in the history of labour law emerged the need to specifically regulate employees' work, and there came the distinction between blue-collar and white-collar workers, a distinction finally repealed in recent times in some European countries.[84] Albeit increasingly blurred, the boundaries between the two categories of workers are still reflected in some pieces of legislation (eg, occupational health and safety) as well as collective bargaining agreements.

It would be entirely fictitious to simply transpose that distinction in the field of platform work. Furthermore, one may tend to stick to the Latin adage *melius est petere fontes quam sectari rivulos*, and then resisting the temptation to dissect too much reality, for the sake of clarity and consistency of any legal intervention in the field.

Nonetheless, some elements of reflection may lead to conclude that the dichotomy between work on-demand via app (on-location) and crowdwork (online) should be carefully considered while assessing the current Proposal for a Directive on platform work. The Directive's provisions, in fact, leave unresolved some regulatory conundrums arising from the ubiquitous character of crowdwork, including its typical cross-border nature.

r=1&numberofresults=10908&fromdoctodoc=yes&doc.id=KARE600061600&doc.part=L&doc.price=0.0&doc.hl=1#focuspoint.

[82] Bob Hepple, 'Introduction' in Bob Hepple (ed), *The Making of Labour Law in Europe* (Hart Publishing, 1986) 14, 22.

[83] Jaques Le Goff, *Du silence à la parole: Une histoire du droit du travail des années 1830 à nos jours* (PUR 2019) 117.

[84] In some countries the 'statut unique' was introduced very recently (2009 in Luxembourg; 2014 in Belgium), while in other countries it was already achieved in the 20th century (eg, Italy).

First, on the status of platform workers, the EU Commission's proposal introduces a rebuttable presumption of subordination (chapter II) and internal procedures aimed at increasing information and transparency (chapter III). The criteria listed to guide labour inspectorates and judges' qualification of work performed through platforms are hardly referrable to crowdworkers. Amongst such criteria (Article 4), for instance, crowdwork platforms typically do not require 'the person performing platform work to respect specific binding rules with regard to appearance, conduct towards the recipient of the service or performance of the work' (letter (b)), and neither do they effectively restrict 'the freedom, including through sanctions, to organise one's work, in particular the discretion to choose one's working hours or periods of absence, to accept or to refuse tasks or to use subcontractors or substitutes' (letter (d)) nor typically restrict 'the possibility to build a client base or to perform work for any third party' (letter (e)). Given the very functioning of the presumption introduced by Article 4, it seems therefore that most crowdworkers will find it hard to see their status assimilated to an employment relationship, thus failing to enjoy the rights recognised for workers by EU and national legislation.

A second aspect deserves attention. The cross-border nature of online work activities is not explicitly addressed by the proposed directive. The common practice by most crowdwork platforms, to include in the 'terms of service' specific clauses for the choice of applicable law and jurisdiction, may well be overturned by the application of Article 8, Rome I Regulation. Its concrete functioning, however, is entirely dependent on the ability to identify the place where the work was 'habitually carried out'. From a platform worker's perspective, determining the habitual place of work is still controversial.[85] Considering that oftentimes platform work (particularly crowdwork) is merely a secondary source of income and involves a shorter working time than the main worker's occupation,[86] the identification of the habitual place of work is virtually impossible. But even from an online platform perspective, the idea of applying to each and every crowdworker a distinct set of legal rules depending not on the type of work, but rather on exogenous factors such as the worker's place of residence, makes clear that any all-purpose solution would encounter critical implementation issues.

Against this background, scholars have elaborated on possible strategies to overcome the extraterritoriality of crowdwork. One proposal argues mirroring existing regulations on specific types of work performed in mobile contexts, such as road transport or at sea. This sectorial option would have the advantage of being backed not only by international laws and treaties, but by a dedicated set

[85] The case law of the CJEU demonstrates that some highly mobile workers pose serious issues to its identification. See Eva van Ooij, 'Highly mobile workers challenging Regulation 883/ 2004: Pushing borders or opening Pandora's box?' (2020) 27 *Maastricht Journal of European and Comparative Law* 573, 581–83.

[86] See *European Centre of Expertise* (n 76).

of principles provided by the ILO Maritime Labour Convention 2006.[87] Another scholarly proposal refers to the current General Data Protection Regulation (GDPR) to argue for a number of indicators which may trigger the application of EU law.[88] While in a GDPR context, such indicators refer to offering multiple languages, offering payment in euros, using domain names of Member States, or offering local testimonials, in a platform work context we may think of criteria able to reveal the EU-based nature of the work performed (eg, the fact the final recipient is based in an EU Member State) in order to trigger the application of EU rules.

Policy questions relating to the global nature of crowdwork evidently do not have cut-and-dried answers. Nonetheless, the fact that the proposed directive seems to apply to the prototype of a 'rider' or 'driver' carrying out their activity through a 'digital labour platform' as defined by Article 2(1) remains controversial. The same rules and procedures laid down for 'persons performing platform work' (Article 2(1)(3)) perfectly cover work performed 'in a certain location' (Article 2(1)(c)) but are less adaptable to work performed 'online'. The position of crowdworkers vis-a-vis digital platforms remains therefore partly unaddressed by the proposed directive, which risks leaving behind large groups of persons and thus fails to achieve the very declared objective to reclassify 1.5 million online workers.

Underestimating the many differences between the forms of platform work – as the proposed text of the directive seems to be doing – not only misses the opportunity to tailor EU rules, but ignores the embryonic forms of collective representation and collective bargaining that in the two fields of work on-demand via app (on-location) and crowdwork (online) already exist.

[87] Miriam A Cherry, 'Beyond Misclassification: The Digital Transformation of Work' (2016) 37 *Comparative Labor Law & Policy Journal* 577, 584, 596; Miriam A Cherry and Winifred R Poster, 'Crowdwork, Corporate Social Responsibility, and Fair Labor Practices' in F Xavier Olleros and Majlinda Zhegu (eds), *Research Handbook on Digital Transformations* (Edward Elgar Publishing 2016) 307.

[88] Miriam A Cherry, 'A Global System of Work, A Global System of Regulation? Crowdwork and Conflicts of Law' (2019) 44 *Tulane Law Review* 48, 50.

4

Collective Bargaining for Platform Workers and the European Social Charter

BARBARA KRESAL*

I. Introduction

This chapter aims to shed light on the issue of collective bargaining in the gig economy from the perspective of the European Social Charter. The initial question is therefore: what can the European Social Charter contribute to this discussion? The answer is: the human rights perspective. The right to collective bargaining is a human right. It is enshrined in Article 6 of the European Social Charter:

> With a view to ensuring the effective exercise of the right to bargain collectively, the Parties undertake … to promote, where necessary and appropriate, machinery for voluntary negotiations between employers or employers' organisations and workers' organisations, with a view to the regulation of terms and conditions of employment by means of collective agreements (paragraph 2 of Article 6 of the Charter).

It is worth noting that paragraph 1 of Article 6 of the Charter is devoted to the promotion of joint consultations, paragraph 3 to conciliation and voluntary arbitration for settlement of labour disputes, and most important, paragraph 4 of Article 6 of the Charter explicitly guarantees the right to collective action, including the right to strike. In addition to Article 6 on the right to collective bargaining, Article 5 of the Charter should be mentioned which guarantees the right to organise.

The right to collective bargaining, together with the right to strike, both enshrined in Article 6 of the Charter, and the right to organise, enshrined in Article 5 of the Charter, are strongly interrelated issues, inseparable, fundamental collective labour rights. There can be no effective collective bargaining without the right to strike or collective action more broadly. On the other hand, the right to

* Opinions expressed in this article are those of the author and do not represent the official position of the European Committee of Social Rights or the Council of Europe.

collective bargaining is an essential element of and inextricably linked to the right to organise. At the same time, collective bargaining represents an essential basis for the realisation of other fundamental labour rights guaranteed by the Charter, namely the right to just conditions of work (Article 2), to safe and healthy working conditions (Article 3), the right to fair remuneration (Article 4) and so on, not to explicitly mention all of them.[1] Collective labour rights, ie, the right to organise, to bargain collectively, together with the right to strike and collective action, function as a correction to the imbalance of power between employers and workers, between capital and labour, and enable the fulfilment of all other labour rights, thus supporting the realisation of the concept of decent work in practice. Without collective representation and trade union activities, collective bargaining and the right to strike, workers would merely be weak individuals competing with each other for jobs/gigs by offering their labour under the conditions in which fair remuneration and the overall concept of decent work is seriously threatened or even impossible. And this is equally or even more true for platform workers.

There are other relevant international – universal and regional – treaties that guarantee the right to collective bargaining as a human right, fundamental right, fundamental labour right. Article 8 of the International Covenant on Economic, Social and Cultural Rights is relevant, as well as ILO Conventions, in particular 87 and 98,[2] and 151 and 154. Collective bargaining is also protected under Article 11 of the European Convention on Human Rights which guarantees freedom of assembly and association.[3] Last but not least, Article 28 of the Charter of Fundamental Rights of the European Union (CFREU) recognises the right of collective bargaining and action.[4] There is a lot of relevant international and supranational material in this area; the chapter will focus on the European Social Charter.

[1] In this sense, see, eg, European Committee of Social Rights, *Swedish Trade Union Confederation (LO) and Swedish Confederation of Professional Employees (TCO) v Sweden* (3 July 2013) C 85/2012, Decision on admissibility and the merits, para 109: 'From a general point of view, the Committee considers that the exercise of the right to bargain collectively and the right to collective action, guaranteed by Article 6 §§2 and 4 of the Charter, represents an essential basis for the fulfilment of other fundamental rights guaranteed by the Charter'.

[2] Two of eight ILO fundamental conventions which cover subjects that are considered fundamental principles and rights at work, among them the freedom of association and the effective recognition of the right to collective bargaining (ILO Declaration on Fundamental Principles and Rights at Work, adopted by the International Labour Conference 86th Session, 18 June 1998).

[3] Although not explicitly mentioned in Article 11 of the ECHR, the right to bargain collectively is covered by this provision which clearly stems from the case law of the ECtHR, since the landmark judgment in *Demir and Baykara v Turkey* App no 34503/97 (ECtHR, 12 November 2008). For more on historical development and dynamic interpretation of Article 11 with respect to the trade union rights, collective bargaining and the right to strike, see eg, Antoine Jacobs, 'Article 11: The Right to Bargain Collectively' in Filip Dorssemont, Klaus Lörcher and Isabelle Schömann (eds), *The European Convention on Human Rights and the Employment Relation* (Hart Publishing 2013); Filip Dorssemont, 'The Right to Take Collective Action under Article 11 ECHR' in Filip Dorssemont, Klaus Lörcher and Isabelle Schömann (eds), *The European Convention on Human Rights and the Employment Relation* (Hart Publishing 2013); Keith D Ewing and John Hendy, 'The Dramatic Implications of Demir and Baykara' (2010) 39 *Industrial Law Journal* 2.

[4] Art 28 of the CFREU stipulates: 'Workers and employers, or their respective organisations, have … the right to negotiate and conclude collective agreements … and … to take collective action …, including

II. The European Social Charter

The European Social Charter is the Council of Europe's most comprehensive instrument on economic and social human rights: rights that are essential and indispensable for people in their daily lives, for each individual throughout their life; rights that give substance to the concept of human dignity. It is often referred to as the counterpart, the sister treaty of the European Convention on Human Rights and as the Social Constitution of Europe.[5] In its revised version of 1996, the Charter guarantees 31 economic and social human rights, also known as fundamental social rights.[6]

The European Social Charter is a living instrument that responds to current problems in (European) societies by guaranteeing human rights in the most important areas of people's daily lives and collective labour rights are among them. Through the interpretation of its provisions by the European Committee of Social Rights (ECSR), the Charter and the rights it guarantees can also respond to the changing world of work and address current challenges in this area. One of these challenges is certainly the increase in non-standard work and in particular the increase in platform work.

With regard to Article 6, § 2, in which the right to collective bargaining is enshrined, the distinction between the original and revised versions of the Charter is not relevant, as the text of Article 6 has not been changed and is the same in both versions. Of the 43 States Parties bound by the Charter, either the 1961 Charter or the revised Charter, 41 are bound by Article 6, § 2.[7] It is worth noting that all EU

strike action'. For a detailed analysis see, eg, Filip Dorssemont and Marco Rocca, 'Article 28 – Right of Collective Bargaining and Action' in Filip Dorssemont et al (eds), *The Charter of Fundamental Rights of the European Union and the Employment Relation* (Hart Publishing 2019); Bernard Ryan, 'The Charter and Collective Labour Law' in Tamara K Hervey and Jeff Kenner (eds), *Economic and Social Rights under the EU Charter of Fundamental Rights: A Legal Perspective* (Hart Publishing 2003) in particular 81–84.

[5] See, eg, Oliver De Schutter, *The European Social Charter: A Social Constitution for Europe /La Charte sociale européenne: une constitution sociale pour l'Europe* (Bruylant 2010); Niklas Bruun, Klaus Lörcher and Isabelle Schöman (eds), *The European Social Charter and the Employment Relation* (Hart Publishing 2017); Gráinne De Búrca and Bruno De Witte, *Social Rights in Europe* (Oxford University Press 2005); DJ Harris, 'A Fresh Impetus for the European Social Charter' (1992) 41 *International & Comparative Law Review* 659; Karin Lukas, *The Revised European Social Charter – An Article by Article Commentary* (Edward Elgar 2021) and many others.

[6] The European Social Charter was adopted in Turin in 1961, the 1988 Additional Protocol added four rights, the 1991 Amending Protocol (Turin Protocol) has considerably improved the regular reporting system and the 1995 Additional Protocol introduced the collective complaints procedure. In 1996, the Revised European Social Charter was adopted, updated and upgraded with additional rights, which should gradually replace the original 1961 Charter. Today, 36 countries are bound by the revised Charter (in 2021, Spain and Germany ratified the revised Charter), while seven countries are still bound by the 1961 Charter (Croatia, Czech Republic, Denmark, Iceland, Luxembourg, Poland and the United Kingdom). The European Social Charter, in its original or revised version, is thus binding on 43 out of 47 Member States of the Council of Europe (only Monaco, San Marino, Liechtenstein and Switzerland have not ratified the Charter). Updated information on ratifications at: www.coe.int/en/web/european-social-charter/signatures-ratifications.

[7] Only Andorra and Turkey have not accepted Article 6 §2.

Member States have accepted and are thus bound by Article 6, § 2 of the Charter and, therefore, have to respect it.

What does this mean for platform workers and for the gig economy? Again, the answer is clear: platform workers must not be denied the right to collective bargaining, a human right guaranteed by the European Social Charter. As a fundamental right, guaranteed by the Charter and other legally binding human rights instruments, the right to collective bargaining must also be effectively guaranteed to platform workers.

Collective labour rights, including the right to collective bargaining, are fundamental rights, human rights protected by constitutional, European and international law, and must be interpreted in line with their fundamental, human rights character and with their aim and purpose in mind.[8] Historically, the recognition of trade union rights, such as the freedom to form and join trade unions, collective bargaining and concluding collective agreements as well as the recognition of the right to strike supporting effective collective bargaining, have been among the most important milestones in the development of labour law, decent working and living conditions, and thus the potential for the realisation of the concept of human dignity in practice.[9] The interpretation concerning the right to collective bargaining and its implementation in practice must take into account changes in the world of work and adequately address current challenges, such as, for example, platform work.

III. Platform Work

There have already been some attempts in various countries to regulate platform work in legislation and by soft law mechanisms,[10] relevant case law is developing,[11] and there are also activities in this respect at EU level.[12] There is

[8] Barbara Kresal, 'Slovenia' in Bernd Waas and Christina Hießl (eds), *Collective Bargaining for Self-Employed Workers in Europe. Approaches to Reconcile Competition Law and Labour Rights* (Wolters Kluwer 2021).

[9] Katarina Kresal Šoltes, 'Nestandardne oblike dela in kolektivne pogodbe [Non-standard work and collective agreements]' (2018) 18(2–3) *Delavci in delodajalci* 265.

[10] See the chapters of this volume written by Piera Loi (ch 2 on the boundaries between the collective agreements and statutory legislation); by Daniel Pérez del Prado (ch 11 on the Spanish Perspective); and by Judith Brockmann (ch 7). For a detailed overview, see also, Valerio De Stefano et al, 'Platform Work and the Employment Relationship' ILO Working Paper (ILO Publications 2021).

[11] See the chapter of this volume written by Jeremias Adams-Prassl, Sylvaine Laulom and Yolanda Maneiro Vázquez (ch 5 on comparative experiences from Europe's Supreme Courts). See also: Christina Hießl, 'Case Law on the Classification of Platform Workers: Cross-European Comparative Analysis and Tentative Conclusions' (2021) *Comparative Labor Law & Policy Journal* (forthcoming), available at: papers.ssrn.com/sol3/papers.cfm?abstract_id=3839603; De Stefano et al (n 10).

[12] See the chapter of this volume written by Luca Ratti (ch 3 on the EU normative patchwork). See also: Valerio De Stefano and Antonio Aloisi, *European legal framework for 'digital labour platforms'* (Publications Office of the European Union 2018); Tamás Gyulavári, 'Collective rights of platform workers: The role of EU law' (2020) 27 *Maastricht Journal of European and Comparative Law* 406;

a legislative initiative at EU level on improving the working conditions of platform workers and in June 2021, the second-stage consultation of European social partners on this issue was launched.[13] The limited access of platform workers to collective representation and collective bargaining has been identified as one of the key challenges in platform work in this initiative (in addition to the following challenges: the employment status of platform workers is unclear and many platform workers are misclassified as self-employed; automated decision-making by algorithms can be discriminatory, non-transparent etc; the cross-border nature of platform work).

Another EU-level initiative relevant for the issues discussed aims to overcome legal uncertainty as regards the non-applicability of EU competition law in the case of the collective bargaining of the self-employed. According to the Commission, its purpose is to ensure that EU competition law does not stand in the way of collective agreements that aim to improve the working conditions of the self-employed in a weak position.[14] This problem has already been dealt with extensively in the labour law literature.[15]

Martin Risak, *Fair working conditions for platform workers – Possible regulatory approaches at the EU level* (Friedrich Ebert Stiftung/International Policy Analysis 2018); Martin Gruber-Risak and Christian Berger, 'Platform Work' (2021) 3 *Policy Brief* 1; Leïla Chaibi, 'A proposal to legislate for the rights of platform workers' (*Social Europe*, 16 November 2020), available at: socialeurope.eu/a-proposal-to-legislate-for-the-rights-of-platform-workers, etc.

[13] Commission, 'Second-Phase Consultation of Social Partners Under Article 154 TFEU on Possible Action Addressing the Challenges Related to Working Conditions in Platform Work' (Consultation Document) C(2021) 4230 final; general information available at: ec.europa.eu/commission/presscorner/detail/en/IP_21_2944. See also: ETUC, 'ETUC Resolution on the protection of the rights of non-standard workers and workers in platform companies (including the self-employed)' (28 October 2020), available at: www.etuc.org/en/document/etuc-resolution-protection-rights-non-standard-workers-and-workers-platform-companies#_ftn2; and ETUC, 'ETUC reply to the Second phase consultation of social partners under Article 154 TFEU on possible action addressing the challenges related to working conditions in platform work' (10 September 2021), available at: www.etuc.org/en/document/etuc-reply-second-phase-consultation-social-partners-under-article-154-tfeu-possible.

[14] Commission, 'Collective bargaining agreements for self-employed – scope of application EU competition rules' (2021), available at: ec.europa.eu/info/law/better-regulation/have-your-say/initiatives/12483-Collective-bargaining-agreements-for-self-employed-scope-of-application-EU-competition-rules_en.

[15] Just to mention some of them, eg, Bernd Waas and Christina Hießl, *Collective Bargaining for Self-Employed Workers. Approaches to Reconcile Competition Law and Labour Rights* (Wolters Kluwer 2021); Silvia Rainone and Nicola Countouris, 'Collective bargaining and self-employed workers. The need for a paradigm shift' (2021) 11 *ETUI Policy Brief* 4; Ioannis Lianos, Nicola Countouris and Valerio De Stefano, 'Re-thinking the competition law/labour law interaction: Promoting a fairer labour market' (2019) 10 *European Labour Law Journal* 291; Michael Doherty and Valentina Franca, 'Solving the "Gig-saw"? Collective rights and platform work' (2020) 49 *Industrial Law Journal* 352; Maria José Schmidt-Kessen et al, '"I'll call my Union", said the driver – Collective bargaining of gig workers under EU competition rules' (2021) 2 *Europaraettslig Tidskrift* 237; Giorgio Monti, 'Collective labour agreements and EU competition law: five reconfigurations' [2021] *European Competition Journal*, available at: www.tandfonline.com/doi/full/10.1080/17441056.2021.1930452; Dagmar Schiek and Andrea Gideon, 'Outsmarting the gig-economy through collective bargaining – EU competition law as a barrier?' (2018) 32(2–3) *International Review of Law, Computers & Technology* 275.

There is also much labour law literature dealing with platform work in general and collective bargaining in the platform economy in particular.[16] The central question is of course their employment status. Without going into detail, as this is not the subject of this chapter, it is nevertheless useful to emphasise that the fact that work is organised through digital platforms should not be a decisive factor for denying an employee's status and labour rights to platform workers, taking into account the principle of primacy of facts in the assessment of whether an employment relationship exists or not in a particular case of platform work.[17] The unclear employment status of platform workers and the problem of misclassification is definitely one of the core problems in the area of platform work.

Platform work should not be perceived and treated as a completely new, specific non-standard form of employment, even less as a specific form of self-employment. Platform work is merely a specific organisation of work, with the use of modern technology. It raises certain specific issues that need to be regulated, but at the same time, existing labour law rules and existing legally binding human rights can and should also apply in the area of platform work.

It is also worth noting that platform work is very diverse. Platform workers are not a homogeneous group and there is a high degree of individualisation, isolation, fragmentation of work, fluctuations and so on. Many platform workers are not unionised. The most visible part of platform work, ie, riders (food delivery platforms) and taxi drivers (Uber etc) attract the most attention, to some extent also cleaners and other domestic work, but this area is already much more invisible; moreover, there are other types of work organised through digital labour platforms where the work is performed locally (so-called on-location platform work). Even more invisible and far from public attention is platform work which is performed entirely virtually (so-called online platform work) and is quite often associated with even worse working conditions, greater isolation and the lack of a collective voice for these workers.

The employment status of many platform workers is still quite unclear; there are differences between countries and case law is developing very rapidly. There

[16] See, eg, De Stefano et al (n 10); Jeremias Prassl, *Humans as a Service: The Promise and Perils of Work in the Gig Economy* (Oxford University Press 2018); Jeremias Adams-Prassl and Martin Risak, 'Uber, Taskrabbit, & Co: Platforms as Employers? Rethinking the Legal Analysis of Crowdwork' (2016) 37 *Comparative Labor Law & Policy Journal* 619; Sangeet Paul Choudary, *The Architecture of digital labour platforms: Policy recommendations on platform design for worker well-being* (International Labour Office 2018); ILO, 'Job Quality in the Platform Economy' (20 February 2018), available at: www.ilo.org/wcmsp5/groups/public/---dgreports/---cabinet/documents/publication/wcms_618167.pdf; Annarosa Pesole et al, *Platform Workers in Europe: Evidence from the COLLEEM Survey* (Publications Office of the European Union 2018); MC Urzí Brancati, A Pesole and E Fernandez Macias, *New Evidence on Plat-Form Workers in Europe: Results from the Second COLLEEM Survey* (Publications Office of the European Union 2020); Michael Doherty, 'Trade unions and the Gig Economy' in Frank Hendrickx and Valerio De Stefano, *Game Changers in Labour Law: Shaping the Future of Work* (Wolters Kluwer 2018); Nolwenn Allaire et al, *Covering risks for platform workers in the digital age* (Science Po 2019).

[17] A specific organisation of work through digital platforms should instead be adequately taken into account when assessing various criteria/indicators for the existence of the employment relationship in accordance with the principle of primacy of facts, which should be adapted to specific characteristics of platform work and adequately interpreted.

are more and more judgments of national courts confirming that platform workers are workers/employees and should be afforded labour law protection, but there are also judgments stating that they are self-employed.[18] The fact is that in practice most of them still work as self-employed, often under very precarious working conditions. They face legal and practical obstacles when trying to enforce their rights.

There are various legal and practical obstacles for effective realisation of their right to collective bargaining in practice. Collective bargaining requires, first, at least two parties, ie, actors (on the employers' and workers' sides) with the ability and will to promote and defend their interests through collective negotiations and, second, an adequate legal framework that recognises the right to collective bargaining and promotes collective bargaining for all workers, whereby legal rules (in all legal areas, including competition law) and their interpretation and application in practice, must be in conformity with the requirements stemming from the legally binding human rights treaties, including the Charter.

What are the requirements with respect to the right to collective bargaining under the European Social Charter?

IV. The Right to Collective Bargaining as a Human Right

As a starting point, it is useful to clarify that from a human rights perspective, the formal status of platform workers within the national legal system should not be a decisive factor and the right of platform workers to collective bargaining should be recognised irrespective of whether they are employees or self-employed workers (or have some other intermediate status).[19]

The case law of the ECSR, the supervisory body under the European Social Charter, can be helpful in supporting this standpoint.

It must be clearly emphasised, however, that the specific issue of collective bargaining in the platform economy has not yet been directly addressed by the ECSR. To date, the ECSR has not had the opportunity to deal with this issue, ie, the right of platform workers to collective bargaining. Actually, there has been no decision yet within the collective complaints procedure specifically on platform workers; within the reporting system, platform work was addressed in Conclusions 2020, under Article 1, § 2 (the right of workers to earn their living in an occupation freely entered upon) and it will be addressed in Conclusions 2021,

[18] See, eg, Hießl (n 11); and De Stefano et al (n 10).

[19] This does not imply that employment status is not important. First and foremost the problem of misclassification and bogus self-employment status of many platform workers should be resolved. However, from the human rights perspective as regards the right to collective bargaining, the employment status is not decisive. In order to answer the question whether platform workers have the right to collective bargaining or not, it is not necessary to resolve the question whether a platform worker is an employee or not.

this time under Article 12 (the right to social security). It is also worth noting that in Conclusions 2018, the Committee posed a general question on Article 6, § 2 concerning self-employed workers and collective bargaining which will be part of the reporting cycle 2022.

Although there is no ECSR case law specifically dealing with collective bargaining in the gig economy, the ECSR case law is of relevance and should be taken into account when discussing this issue. Of particular interest in this regard is the ECSR decision of 12 September 2018 (*ICTU v Ireland*)[20] which is presented in more detail in the next section of this chapter.

There is no doubt that platform workers who are employees and perform work under a contract of employment have the right to collective bargaining as well as all other labour rights. The problem arises when platform workers perform work as self-employed. Even if platform workers are considered self-employed, they should not be denied the right to collective bargaining.

The ECSR case law is clear:

> Although the Charter with one exception (Article 19§10) does not state whether its employment-related provisions apply to the self-employed, … the Committee has constantly held that in principle the provisions of Part II of the Charter apply to the self-employed except where the context requires that they be limited to employed persons. No such context obtains in a generalised way for Article 6§2.[21]

A similar approach has been taken by the International Labour Organization (ILO). The ILO Committee on Freedom of Association emphasised with respect to freedom of association, whose essential element is the right to bargain collectively,[22] that

> the criterion for determining the person covered by that right, therefore, is not based on the existence of an employment relationship, which is often non-existent, for example, in the case of agricultural workers, self-employed workers in general or those who practice liberal professions, who should nevertheless enjoy the right to organise.[23]

[20] European Committee of Social Rights, *Irish Congress of Trade Unions (ICTU) v Ireland* (12 September 2018) C 123/2016, Decision on the merits.

[21] ibid, para 35.

[22] ILO, *Freedom of Association: Compilation of decisions of the Freedom of Association Committee*, 6th edn (International Labour Office 2018) 231, para 1232: 'The right to bargain freely with employers with respect to conditions of work constitutes an essential element in freedom of association, and trade unions should have the right, through collective bargaining or other lawful means, to seek to improve the living and working conditions of those whom the trade unions represent'. (See also, ILO, *Freedom of Association: Digest of decisions and principles of the Freedom of Association Committee of the Governing Body of the ILO*, 5th edn (International Labour Office 2006) para 881; ILO, '344th Report of the Committee on Freedom of Association' (2007), Case No 2467, para 570 and Case No 2460, para 995; ILO, '346th Report of the Committee on Freedom of Association' (2007), Case No 2488, para 1353; ILO, '350th Report of the Committee on Freedom of Association' (2008), Case No 2602, para 676; ILO, '351st Report of the Committee on Freedom of Association' (2009), Case No 2581, para 1335; ILO, '354th Report of the Committee on Freedom of Association' (2009), Case No 2684, para 831 and Case No. 2581, para 1111.)

[23] ILO, *Compilation* (2018) (n 22) 70, para 387 (see also the ILO, *Digest* (2006) (n 22) para 254; ILO, 'Interim Report – Report No 342' (2006), Case No 2423, para 479; ILO, '359th Report of the Committee on Freedom of Association' (2011), Case No 2602, para 365, Case No 2786, para 453; ILO, '360th Report', Case No 2757, para 990).

This important principle of a broad personal scope of fundamental labour rights,[24] including the right to collective bargaining, was recently confirmed, for example, in the Report of the Global Commission on the Future of Work:

> We therefore emphasise the need for the universal ratification and application of all the fundamental ILO Conventions. All workers – including the self-employed and those in the informal economy – and employers must enjoy freedom of association and the effective recognition of the right to collective bargaining.[25]

V. *ICTU v Ireland*

Various categories of workers deemed self-employed were denied the right to bargain collectively. The case concerned the decision of the Irish Competition Authority prohibiting self-employed workers (voice-over actors, musicians, freelance journalists)[26] from concluding collective agreements setting out minimum rates of pay and other working conditions, with an argument that this would amount to a breach of competition law. The complainant organisation, the Irish Congress of Trade Unions (ICTU) alleged that this decision by the Competition Authority amounted to a violation of Article 6 of the European Social Charter.

In its preliminary considerations, the ECSR stressed that 'the world of work is changing rapidly and fundamentally with a proliferation of contractual arrangements, often with the express aim of avoiding contracts of employment under labour law, of shifting risk from the labour engager to the labour provider' and that 'this has resulted in an increasing number of workers falling outside the definition of a dependent employee, including low-paid workers or service providers who are de facto "dependent" on one or more labour engagers'.[27] According to the ECSR, these developments must be taken into account when determining the scope of Article 6, § 2 in respect of self-employed workers.[28]

[24] In this sense see also Nicola Countouris and Valerio De Stefano, 'The Labour Law Framework: Self-Employed and Their Right to Bargain Collectively' in Bernd Waas and Christina Hießl (eds), *Collective Bargaining for Self-Employed Workers in Europe. Approaches to Reconcile Competition Law and Labour Rights* (Wolters Kluwer 2021) 5; Valerio De Stefano, 'Not as simple as it seems: The ILO and the personal scope of international labour standards' (2021) 16 *International Labour Review* 387.

[25] Report of the Global Commission on the Future of Work – ILO, *Work for a Brighter Future* (International Labour Office 2019) 43.

[26] As already mentioned above, the case does not concern platform workers. Since many platform workers are (at least formally) self-employed, the situation is comparable to the one dealt with in this case in which the voice-over actors, musicians and freelance journalists were also self-employed persons.

[27] *ICTU v Ireland* (n 20) para 37.

[28] ibid.

The ECSR emphasised that self-employed workers should enjoy the right to bargain collectively through organisations that represent them, including in respect of remuneration for services provided and that restrictions with respect to this right are only permitted in accordance with Article G of the Charter.[29] This means that restrictions on the right to collective bargaining (eg, for the self-employed) must pass the proportionality test to be acceptable. Only such restrictions are permitted which are provided by law, pursue a legitimate aim and are necessary in a democratic society. According to the ECSR, 'nothing in the wording of Article 6 of the Charter entitles States Parties to impose restrictions on the right to bargain collectively of particular categories of workers',[30] and therefore only restrictions in accordance with Article G are acceptable.

In my view it is important to point out that since the right to collective bargaining is a human right, it should be treated as such in all areas of law; collective bargaining for the self-employed should not be merely 'allowed as an exception' in competition law, but should be recognised as a fundamental right that could only be limited exceptionally under a strict proportionality test.[31]

In its preliminary considerations, the ECSR explained that for the assessment in the instant case, it was not necessary to make an exact analysis of the status of self-employed and to elaborate a general definition of how self-employed workers are covered by Article 6, § 2. The Committee considered it necessary and sufficient to point out that

> even without developing the precise circumstances under which categories of self-employed workers fall under the personal scope of Article 6§2, an outright ban on collective bargaining of all self-employed workers would be excessive as it would run counter to the object and purpose of this provision.[32]

Another important clarification can be found in preliminary considerations which concern the distinction between the worker/employee and the self-employed. The ECSR explained that 'in establishing the type of collective bargaining that is protected by the Charter, it is not sufficient to rely on distinctions between worker and self-employed, the decisive criterion is rather whether there is an imbalance of power between the providers and engagers of labour' and that 'where providers of labour have no substantial influence on the content of contractual conditions, they must be given the possibility of improving the power imbalance through collective bargaining'.[33]

Since the categories of self-employed workers in question were denied collective bargaining with respect to their remuneration, the Committee considered that such a situation 'amounted to a ban on collective bargaining'.

[29] ibid, para 95.
[30] ibid, para 36.
[31] See also Countouris and De Stefano (n 24) 16: 'we think that reversing the existing approach that considers collective bargaining an exception to competition law principles is essential'.
[32] *ICTU v Ireland* (n 20) paras 36 and 40.
[33] ibid, para 38.

An important argument made by the ECSR when checking the proportionality was that the categories of persons included in the notion of 'undertaking' were over-inclusive.[34] The ECSR also indicated several criteria to be used when determining whether a person can be considered as genuine independent self-employed. For the self-employed workers in question (such as voice-over actors, certain musicians and freelance journalists) the ECSR considered it evident that 'they cannot predominantly be characterized as genuine independent self-employed meeting all or most of criteria such as having several clients, having the authority to hire staff, and having the authority to make important strategic decisions about how to run the business' and that '(t)he self-employed workers concerned here are obviously not in a position to influence their conditions of pay once they have been denied the right to bargain collectively'.[35] In addition, the ECSR explained that it

> does not consider that permitting the self-employed workers in question to bargain collectively and conclude collective agreements, including in respect of remuneration, would have an impact on competition in trade that would be significantly different from the impact on such competition of collective agreements concluded solely in respect of dependent workers (employees).[36]

The ECSR's decision in *ICTU v Ireland* sets important general principles with respect to the right to collective bargaining for self-employed workers and clarifies that self-employed workers are covered by Article 6, § 2 of the Charter and should in principle enjoy the right to collective bargaining. However, in this case, the ECSR held that there was a violation prior to the amendments of 2017 to the Irish legislation at stake, but that these amendments (which entered into force before the decision of the ECSR was reached) brought the situation into conformity with the Charter and therefore decided that there was no violation of Article 6, § 2.

In my view, collective bargaining is a particularly important collective labour right and should be effectively guaranteed in practice to all workers, including self-employed workers who are not independent contractors/undertakings; it should not be subjected to competition authorities and be dependent on their decisions. All States Parties should refrain from restricting the right to collective bargaining and from impeding its effective implementation in practice. They should promote collective bargaining for all categories of workers, including self-employed workers who are in need of such protection.[37]

[34] ibid, para 98: 'Although the restriction was provided for by law and could be said to pursue a legitimate aim of ensuring effective and undistorted competition in trade with a view to protecting the rights and freedoms of others, the Committee considers that the ban was excessive and therefore not necessary in a democratic society in that the categories of persons included in the notion of "undertaking" were over-inclusive'.

[35] ibid, para 99.

[36] ibid, para 100.

[37] See also the Joint separate opinion of P Stangos and B Kresal in which they emphasise that collective bargaining should be effectively guaranteed to all categories of self-employed workers and promoted, and that amendments to the Irish legislation at stake were not sufficient to bring the challenged Irish

VI. The Right to Collective Bargaining in the Platform Economy: Obligation to Recognise, Respect and Promote

The obligation to promote collective bargaining is particularly relevant for platform workers. In addition to legal obstacles, there are numerous practical obstacles for effective collective bargaining of platform workers in practice. Many platform workers are not unionised; quite often, they do not even know each other; isolation, individualisation, fragmentation and fluctuations are common features of platform work, and so on.

Already in its first conclusions in 1969 the Committee of Independent Experts stressed that 'according to Article 6§2, domestic law must recognise that employers' and workers' organisations may regulate their relations by collective agreement' and that 'if necessary and useful, ie in particular if the spontaneous development of collective bargaining is not sufficient, positive measures should be taken to facilitate and encourage the conclusion of collective agreements'.[38] The Committee also emphasised that collective bargaining should remain free and voluntary.[39]

In practice, there have been some cases of spontaneous development of collective bargaining in the platform economy. However, it seems that this is not sufficient and that more effort should be put into discussions on possible positive measures which could promote, facilitate and encourage collective bargaining for platform workers.

The perspective and focus in discussions on platform work should be changed. Doubts regarding whether platform workers have the right to collective bargaining or not should be resolved. From a human rights perspective, it is clear that the right to collective bargaining should be guaranteed to all workers, including platform workers, irrespective of their employment status. Competition law should be interpreted accordingly, taking into account legally binding human rights treaties, including the Charter. Discussions should focus on the question how to promote effective and fruitful collective bargaining in the platform economy.

legislation in line with the requirements of Article 6 § 2 of the Charter, therefore not just situation prior to the amendments of 2017, but also the situation after the amendments of 2017 amounted to a violation of Article 6§2 of the Charter. Legal regulation which puts the right to collective bargaining of certain categories of self-employed workers in the hands of the executive and makes the realisation of this right entirely dependent and conditional on a prior decision of executive power (Minister's Order authorising an exemption) is a serious barrier and can result in refraining potential self-employed workers from their collective engagement and collective bargaining. Such restriction of their right to collective bargaining cannot be justified and is excessive. According to the Joint separate opinion, such type of regulation (which leaves room for all sorts of subjective interpretation by the executive) is at variance with the measures to 'promote' collective bargaining required by Article 6 §2 of the Charter and hence in breach of that provision.

[38] Conclusions I (1969), Statement of Interpretation on Article 6§2.

[39] ibid.

There are many issues in the area of platform work that could be negotiated upon and regulated by collective agreements at all levels.[40]

VII. Conclusion

The European Social Charter, the Council of Europe's human rights treaty, guarantees the right to collective bargaining which is, together with the right to collective action, including the right to strike, enshrined in Article 6, and the right to organise which is enshrined in Article 5. These are fundamental collective labour rights.

The ECSR has not yet explicitly addressed the issue of collective bargaining for platform workers. Nevertheless, its case law on the right to collective bargaining is of relevance for the correct understanding of this right in the platform economy.

It is important that a human rights perspective is not overlooked when discussing the issue of collective bargaining for platform workers.

Given the fundamental rights/human rights character of the right to collective bargaining, being recognised as such in constitutional, European and international law, including in the European Social Charter, this right has to be effectively guaranteed to platform workers who are in need of such protection, and irrespective of their employment status, be they employees, self-employed or in any other 'third', intermediate category.

This does not imply that the employment status of platform workers is not important. First and foremost, the problem of misclassification and the bogus self-employment status of many platform workers should be resolved. However, this is not relevant and should not be a decisive factor in recognising the right to collective bargaining for platform workers, as all platform workers irrespective of their employment status should enjoy collective labour rights, including the right to collective bargaining.

[40] See the chapters in part II of this volume.

5

The Role of National Courts in Protecting Platform Workers: A Comparative Analysis

JEREMIAS ADAMS-PRASSL, SYLVAINE LAULOM AND YOLANDA MANEIRO VÁZQUEZ

I. Introduction

Recent years have seen a stark increase in litigation brought by workers and trade unions against gig economy platforms. In this chapter, we discuss a series of recent high-profile decisions –*Take Eat Easy*[1] and *Uber*[2] in France's Court of Cassation, *Glovo* in the Spanish Supreme Court,[3] and *Uber* in the UK Supreme Court.[4] We contextualise each decision, before exploring their implications from a comparative perspective across a range of salient areas, including similarities and differences in legal approaches and fact finding, policy responses and enforcement, and the broader implications for the gig economy business model in our respective jurisdictions – including consequences for both individual rights and the collective representation of gig workers.

Discussion is structured as follows. Section II sets out the national context and relevant legal provisions in French, Spanish and UK law, sequenced to reflect the dates of the most recent decisions (March 2020, September 2020 and February 2021, respectively). Section III then explores each ruling in depth, analysing its doctrinal and practical relevance for each legal order. Section IV turns to providing broader perspectives, exploring the distinct political and operator responses in different markets. Section V concludes with a series of concluding comparative remarks.

[1] Soc, 28 November 2018, n°17-20.079, FP-P+B+R+I.
[2] Soc, 4 mars 2020, n° 19-13.316, FP-P+B+R+I.
[3] Judgment n° 805/2020, rec 4746/2019.
[4] *Uber BV v Aslam* [2021] UKSC 5.

II. National Contexts

The precise details of gig economy platforms' business model vary widely depending on national and local circumstances, and continues to change and evolve. There are nonetheless a number of core features behind increasingly sophisticated business models, beginning with the availability of a large supply of workers who can easily be matched with consumer demand. This digital intermediation of work can take a number of forms, including in particular the provision of transportation and delivery services. Algorithms take into account a wide range of relevant factors, from the quality of previous work and current availability to geographic location, and optimise the quality of each match – before charging a small fee for the service. Platforms' role goes far beyond mere matchmaking, however. Instead, they offer Digital Work Intermediation: in order to deliver tightly curated products and services to customers, gig economy operators actively shape the entire transaction through close control over their workers – while insisting that they are self-employed, independent providers of services.

This model has given rise to significant complexity in policy debates and litigation. In this section, we set the scene by exploring the very distinct legal and political contexts against which the ensuing decisions need to be understood.

A. France

The Supreme French Civil Court, the Court of Cassation, has already issued two important decisions regarding the reclassification of the employment relationship between platform work and workers. One concerns a delivery driver (*Take Eat Easy* case)[5] and the other an Uber driver (*Uber* case).[6] Others are expected in the near future.

France belongs to those countries where there is a binary distinction between self-employed and employees with employment rights only afforded to employees.[7] Even before the development of digital platforms, the need to adopt a third category and/or evolving the case law definition of employee have been the subject of recurrent debates among scholars. These debates have intensified with the

[5] Soc, 28 November 2018, n°17-20.079, FP-P+B+R+I.

[6] Soc, 4 mars 2020, n° 19-13.316, FP-P+B+R+I. See the English translation of the decision on the website of the Court: www.courdecassation.fr/getattacheddoc/5fca56cd0a790c1ec36ddc07/1daeef98447aad7f497cd80e4c1e75dc.

[7] This presentation must be tempered. There is a specific and old section of the Labour code (Part 7) devoted to specific professions: journalists, artists, models, caregivers, home workers, employees of building, attendants and nursing assistants, some managers of businesses. All these professions have in common that subordination could be difficult to characterise. The legislator aimed to extend the legal regime of the subordinate employees to these workers for a certain and variable extent. Journalists are, for example, entirely assimilated as employees and enjoy some additional advantages, whereas only protections concerning salary, dismissal and working time have been granted to managers of food franchises.

installation in France of numerous work platforms. Very quickly, reports,[8] articles and proposals multiplied. As a French author wrote in 2018:

> Rarely has a subject generated so much analysis in such a short period of time. Many institutional reports and doctrinal writings have examined the 'challenges' posed to labour law by 'platform capitalism'.
>
> There are always two underlying questions: 1° Are all platform workers truly self-employed? In other words: is it not possible to attribute the status of employee to some of them? 2° Don't those whose self-employed status is indisputable deserve to benefit from some special guarantees, if only because of the close dependence they have on the platform?[9]

As a result, the first legislation was enacted in August 2016. Law n°2016-1088, 8 August 2016 (the Labour Act), includes provisions dedicated to some platform workers and gives them some individual and collective rights. However, these provisions apply to '*independent*' platform workers[10] and therefore leaves the question of the qualification of their employment relationship intact.

Platform workers, mainly riders and drivers, then went to court to request that their contracts be reclassified as employment contracts. The lower courts were divided on the issue of reclassification, but the majority of them were reluctant to recognise the existence of an employment relationship for platform workers.[11] In this context, the decisions of the Court of Cassation were highly anticipated.

B. Spain

The Supreme Court judgment (STS) of 25 September 2020[12] put an end to the debate in Spain on the nature – employee or self-employed – of the relationship between delivery drivers (riders) and the digital platforms for which they provide their services. Since the first judgments on this issue were handed down, the different courts have failed to reach an agreement regarding such a relationship: most of them considered this relationship to be an employment relationship,[13]

[8] See the first reports on this issue: B Mettling, *Transformation numérique et vie au travail*, Rapport à l'attention de M El Khomri, Ministre du Travail, sept 2015, available at: (travail-emploi.gouv.fr/IMG/pdf/rapport_mettling_-transformation_numerique_vie_au_travail.pdf); IGAS, *Les plateformes collaboratives, l'emploi et la protection sociale*, mai 2016, available at: www.igas.gouv.fr/IMG/pdf/2015-121R.pdf; Rapport annuel du Conseil d'Etat, Puissance publique et plateformes numériques: accompagner 'l'ubérisation', 13 juillet 2017, available at: www.ladocumentationfrancaise.fr/var/storage/rapports-publics/174000714.pdf.

[9] A Fabre, 'Les travailleurs des plateformes sont-ils des salariés? Premières réponses frileuses des juges français' [2018] *Droit Social* 547.

[10] The Labour Act gives them the right to strike and the right to create, adhere to and represent their collective interests through trade unions (Art L 7342-5 and L 7342-6 of the Labour code).

[11] Fabre (n 9).

[12] Judgment n° 805/2020, rec 4746/2019.

[13] Among them, in relation to the company Glovo: judgments of 21 February 2020 (rec 5613/2019): 7 May 2020 (rec 6774/2019) and 12 May 2020 (rec 5613/2019). STSJ Madrid 27 November 2019

while others, on the other hand, confirmed the nature of these delivery drivers as economically dependent self-employed workers.[14]

STS 25 September 2020 is of extraordinary importance for the employment situation of riders working for platforms such as Glovo or Deliveroo, and it is also easily applied to other delivery drivers of similar platforms, such as UberEats, Amazon or Uber drivers. However, its application to activities carried out in the service of other types of platforms, such as translators, lawyers, etc, has not yet been analysed. In any case, the ruling offers sufficient clues to verify, in each case, whether these new forms of service provision by platforms meet the requirements to decide if their workers can be considered as employees or not.[15]

It is necessary to underline the difficulties that the applicants have had to overcome on their way to the Supreme Court. This Court has been the only one able to give a general and uniform answer on this issue. In all these cases, the claims for recognition as employees have been brought by individual workers because of the termination of their contracts (their 'disconnection' from the platform). Given the functioning of the Spanish dismissal procedural system, the reward that these workers could obtain, in the form of severance pay, hardly compensates for the inconvenience derived from the long judicial process to which they were subjected. This is due to the low length of service of most of these riders, which is a decisive element in the calculation of severance pay. It is very likely that in the attempt to reach an agreement prior to the trial (prior conciliation procedure) required by Spanish procedural law, these workers could have received financial compensation higher than the legal indemnity in exchange for accepting the termination of their contract and not bringing the claim before the labour courts. Thus, these lawsuits have, above all, a symbolic value, as they have allowed the Supreme Court to provide a general solution for all riders who find themselves in a similar situation. But it has also been the trigger for legal reform that, through Law 12/2021 of 28 September (Law 12/2021),[16] has modified the Spanish Workers' Statute (Estatuto de los Trabajadores, ET) to recognise them as employees.

Throughout this process, the Labour Inspectorate has played a key role in response to the complaints lodged by several trade unions regarding the situation of riders providing services on certain platforms, especially Glovo and Deliveroo.

(rec 588/2019), 18 December 2019 (rec 714/2019) and 3 February 2020 (rec 749/2019); STSJ Asturias 25 July 2019 (rec 1143/2019). Regarding Deliveroo, judgments of the TSJ Madrid 17 January 2020 (rec 1323/2019) and STSJ Cataluña 16 July 2020 (rec 5997/2019).

[14] STSJ Madrid 19 September 2019 (rec 195/2019) regarding the company Glovo, origin of the STS of 25 September 2020 discussed here.

[15] In this sense, Diego Álvarez Alonso and Carolina Martínez Moreno, 'Trabajo y plataformas: primera sentencia del Tribunal Supremo a propósito de un repartidor de Glovo' (2020) 72 *Trabajo y Derecho*.

[16] Law 12/2021 of 28 September amending the revised text of the Law on the Workers' Statute, approved by the Law on the Workers' Statute, approved by Royal Legislative Decree 2/2015, of 23 October, in order to guarantee the labour rights of those dedicated to delivery in the field of digital platforms.

C. United Kingdom

The *Uber* ruling in the United Kingdom is but the latest step in a series of broader policy debates surrounding fragmenting labour markets. While the gig economy is sometimes perceived as a unique or distinct phenomenon, the legal challenges involved are similar to those which have been litigated for over a decade in the context of so-called 'zero-hours' contract arrangements, where employers do not guarantee workers any set number of shifts or other work engagements.[17]

At the heart of the ensuing legal debates is worker status, by now a well-established intermediate category beyond the traditional 'binary' divide between employees (working under a contract of service and thus entitled to the full range of employee-protective norms), and independent contractors (self-employed under contracts for services beyond the scope of employment law). 'Employees', working under a contract of service or employment,[18] come within the full scope of protective measures once relevant qualifying periods have been met, including notably unfair dismissal protection.

'Worker' status is an additional category, in extensive use since the late 1990s, with entitlements including working time and national minimum wage protection. Workers are defined as employees as well as those working under

> any other contract … whereby the individual undertakes to do or perform personally any work or services for another party to the contract whose status is not by virtue of the contract that of a client or customer of any profession or business undertaking carried on by the individual.[19]

Materially identical definitions apply under specific regimes which are often at the (substantive) centre of zero-hours and gig-economy litigation, including notably the National Minimum Wage Act 1998[20] and the Working Time Regulations.[21]

A government-sponsored 'review of modern working practices' in 2017 recommended that the UK 'should retain the current three-tier approach to employment status as it remains relevant in the modern labour market, but rename as "dependent contractors" the category of people who are eligible for worker rights but who are not employees'.[22] This change, however, has not been adopted to date.

In litigation, questions surrounding worker status have occupied the courts for nearly two decades,[23] with issues ranging from the appropriate criteria to

[17] Abi Adams and Jeremias-Prassl, 'Zero-Hours Work in the United Kingdom' (2018) ILO Working Paper, Conditions of Work and Employment Series 101.

[18] s 230(1) Employment Rights Act 1996 (ERA).

[19] s 230(3)(b) ERA.

[20] s 54(3)(b).

[21] SI 1998/1833, reg 2(1).

[22] Department for Business, Energy & Industrial Strategy, *Good Work: The Taylor Review of Modern Working Practices* (London 2017) 35.

[23] Beginning with *Byrne Bros v Baird* [2002] ICR 667 (EAT) in which Recorder Underhill QC (as he then was) held that 'Drawing the distinction in any particular case will involve all or most of the same considerations as arise in drawing the distinction between a contract of service and a contract for services – but with the boundary pushed further in the putative worker's favour' ([17(5)]).

its relationship with employee status and other statutory categories.[24] In addition to numerous claims at first instance and the appeal courts,[25] questions surrounding worker status have also faced the Supreme Court in high-profile cases including *Clyde & Co LLP v Bates van Winkelhof*[26] and *Smith v Pimlico Plumbers*.[27]

III. The Rulings

Despite this broad diversity in context and legal background, the overarching similarity between the last instance rulings in France, Spain and the United Kingdom is striking: the senior courts consistently found that despite platforms' protestations to the contrary, drivers and/or riders could not be classified as independent contractors, beyond the scope of employment law. Upon closer inspection, however, a number of distinctions also become apparent – unsurprisingly, perhaps, given the fact that the legal construction of employment relations is understood in distinct ways in each jurisdiction.

A. France

As alluded to, above, there are two rulings which fall to be discussed in the French context.

i. *The* Take Eat Easy *Ruling*

The facts of the first case involved Take Eat Easy, a company that used a digital platform and an app to connect partner restaurants, customers ordering food through the platform and delivery riders. One of the delivery riders, after two road accidents, initiated proceedings before the Labour Court to seek the reclassification of his contractual relationship as an employer–employee relationship. The Paris Court of Appeals dismissed his claim, but the Court of Cassation ultimately ruled otherwise.

The Court of Cassation first recalled that,

> the existence of an employment relationship does neither depend on the will expressed by the parties nor on the designation that the parties have given to their agreement; it depends on the factual circumstances in which the workers exercise their activity.

[24] Notably the definition of workers in s 83(2) of the Equality Act 2010: *Jivraj v Hashwani* [2011] UKSC 40.

[25] See J Prassl, 'Who is a Worker?' (2017) 133 *Law Quarterly Review* 366 (Case Note).

[26] *Clyde & Co LLP v Bates van Winkelhof* [2014] UKSC 32.

[27] *Pimlico Plumbers* [2018] USC 29, [18].

This principle of the unavailability of the qualification of the employment contract is not new. Its current wording is taken from a previous judgment, the *Labbane* case, which concerned a taxi driver.[28]

The Court of Cassation then recalled that the relationship of subordination, which is the determining factor under French law to assess whether a work relationship is an employer–employee relationship, is characterised by the powers of direction, control and sanction. In the case at hand, the existence of such a relationship of subordination was duly established for the Labour Chamber of the Court of Cassation.

The Court of Cassation noted from the findings of the trial judges that 'the app included a geo-tracking system which enabled the company to monitor the delivery rider's position in real time and to record the total number of kilometres travelled', which likely characterised a power of direction and control by Take Eat Easy. The Court then noted the existence of a power of sanction, revealed through a system of bonuses and penalties (use of the English word 'strikes' in the company's internal jargon) attributed to the worker in case he or she failed to fulfil his or her contractual obligations. According to the Dean of the Labour Chamber of the Court of Cassation, Jean-Guy Huglo, this system of sanctions prevails as the determining criterion and reveals alone the relationship of subordination, to the extent that it enables the platform operator to unilaterally terminate the contract, just like for a dismissal.[29]

As such, the elements relied upon by the Paris Court of Appeals to reject the reclassification of the services agreement as an employment contract – for example, in particular the fact that the worker remained free to choose his or her working days, the number of working days and the time slots during which he or she wished to work, and that he or she was not bound by any exclusivity or non-compete covenant – were irrelevant.

Under these circumstances, the worker was placed under the subordination of the platform operator Take Eat Easy, which means that he was in fact an employee.

ii. The Uber *Ruling*

The *Take Eat Easy* case did not resolve all the issues at stake, in particular because it could only apply to platforms operating in a similar manner. Shortly thereafter, a new case, involving the most famous platform, Uber, was brought before the Court of Cassation, and gave the Court the opportunity to clarify the solution resulting from the *Take Eat Easy* decision.

After a driver's account was permanently closed by Uber BV, the driver brought the case before the industrial tribunal calling for the contractual relations to be

[28] Soc, 19 nov 2000, n° 98-40572, Bull V, 2000, n° 437, Also see Cass Ass Plén 4 mars 1983, n° 81-11647, Bull 1983, Ass Plén, n° 4.

[29] Interview with the Dean of the Social Chamber, Jean-Guy Huglo, 'Take Eat Easy: une application classique du lien de subordination' *Semaine Sociale Lamy*, 2018, n° 1842–43, 3.

reclassified as a contract of employment. The Paris Court of Appeals found that the taxi driver was bound by a contract of employment.

The Court of Cassation first recalled the classical definition of the notion of subordination that is 'characterised by the performance of a job under the authority of an employer who has the power to give orders and instructions, to oversee performance thereof, and to sanction the subordinate for any breaches'. The Court then referred to a previous case, the *Société Générale* ruling,[30] according to which 'working within an organised service may constitute an indication of subordination in cases where the employer unilaterally determines the terms and conditions of performing the job'. The Court also characterised self-employed work by the following elements: the possibility of building up one's own clientele, the freedom to set one's own tariffs, the freedom to set the terms and conditions for providing the service.

The Court goes on to analyse the various elements that make it possible to characterise the existence of an employment contract.

(1) The driver has joined a transport service created and entirely organised by that company, a service which exists only thanks to this platform, through the use of which the driver does not constitute a proprietary clientele, does not freely set his fares or determine the terms and conditions for conducting his/her transportation business.
(2) The driver is required to follow a particular route which he is not free to choose and for which fares adjustments are applied if the driver does not follow that route.
(3) The final destination of the journey is sometimes not known to the driver, who is not really free to choose, as a self-employed driver would, the journey which befits him/her or not.
(4) The company has the right to temporarily disconnect the driver from its application as of three refusals of rides and the driver may lose access to his account in the event that an order cancellation rate is exceeded or in case of reports of 'problematic behaviour'.

The Court of Cassation therefore approved the Court of Appeals for having deducted from all these elements the performance of work under the authority of an employer who has the power to give orders and instructions, to oversee performance thereof and to sanction breaches, and for having ruled that the driver's self-employed status was therefore fictitious:

> In this case, the existence of a relationship of subordination when the ride-hailing driver connects to the Uber application is thus recognized, the Court of Cassation having ruled out taking into consideration the fact that the driver has no obligation to connect and that no sanction exists in the event of the absence of connections for any length of time (unlike what existed in the Take Eat Easy application).[31]

[30] Soc, 13 nov 1996, n° 94-13, 187, Bull V, n° 386.
[31] See the explanatory note to the *Uber* ruling by the Court.

Three elements emerge from this decision and the documents published by the Court and accompanying the decision.[32] First, the Court presents its ruling as a classic application of its traditional case law on contracts of employment. Scholars who have commented on the decision also highlight the classicism of the solution. In other words, the Court of Cassation did not need to change its definition of the employment contract to recognise that platform workers are indeed employees. This would be somewhat paradoxical when one considers the debates that preceded the *Uber* ruling. In reality, this classism of the solution is not at all paradoxical but rather shows the prevalence of the discourse of certain platforms that have tried to convince, against the reality of working conditions, that platform workers are independent.

Second, the importance of EU law in the Court's reasoning must be stressed. The existence of an autonomous notion of worker, within the meaning of Directives 2003/88 on working time and 89/391 on health and safety at work, means that the French definition must remain similar to the European one. Otherwise, two notions of worker would have to coexist, which cannot be desirable. The analysis of the Uber platform as a transportation service set up and entirely organised by Uber BV can also be seen as a transposition of the *Elite Taxi* ruling of the European Court.[33] The *Allonby* case[34] also justified the position of the Court not to take into account the freedom of the driver to connect to and disconnect from the platform. According to the Dean of the Social Chamber of the Court,

> the meaning of our decision is that drivers are only in a subordinate relationship when they are connected. This issue has already been decided by the ECJ in the Allonby judgment of 13 January 2004 in respect of a temporary teacher in the UK which was claimed to be independent. The ECJ states that the fact that a person has a right to refuse an assignment is not relevant in assessing the existence of a subordinate relationship. The fact that the driver is free to determine the hours of his activity does not negate the findings of fact that, during his hours of activity for the platform, he is under a relationship of subordination.

Third, the reclassification of the employment contract is based on two essential elements: the work takes place within a service entirely organised by the platform, which has the power to sanction. These sanctions are different from classic contractual sanctions, and it is because they are specific that the contract is reclassified.

B. Spain

The STS highlights the essential characteristics that a service relationship must have in order to be considered an employment relationship. To this end, the classic

[32] See also the interview with the Dean of the Social Chamber, Jean-Guy Huglo, *Semaine Sociale Lamy* (16 mars 2020) 1899.

[33] Case C-434/15 *Asociación Profesional Elite Taxi v Uber Systems Spain SL* [2017] ECLI:EU:C:2017:981.

[34] Case C-256/01 *Debra Allonby v Accrington & Rossendale College and Others* [2004] ECLI:EU:C:2004:18.

concept of dependence should be adapted to the new realities of work on platforms. It is considered as an 'abstract concept that manifests itself differently depending on the activity', especially when, as in this case, the work provided for a platform is assessed.[35] The Supreme Court indicates the difficulties in deciding whether or not the characteristics of an employment relationship are present in doubtful cases. Thus, there is a need to examine the evidence, both favourable and unfavourable, in order to make a decision 'in each specific case' based on 'the totality of the concurrent circumstances'.

Therefore, platform workers require a case-by-case assessment. First, according to the Supreme Court, the ideas of *ajenidad*[36] and dependence 'are the essential elements defining the employment contract'. They are not immutable concepts, but flexible, in order to allow their adaptation to the new social realities of the time in which the rules are to be applied. Second, dependence has become more flexible, especially through digital control systems.[37]

To demonstrate how these two requirements have been relaxed, the Spanish Supreme Court used two important decisions of the European Court of Justice (ECJ). On the one hand, *Allonby* of 13 January 2004, in relation to teachers. There, the ECJ recognised that the power of teachers to refuse a particular service does not preclude recognition of their employment relationship. On the other hand, *Elite Taxi* of 20 December 2017, concerning drivers at the service of the Uber platform. It recognised the concurrence of these two characteristics: the *ajenidad*, due to the relevance of the app as an essential means of provision; and the dependence, due to the 'decisive influence' of Uber on the conditions of the provision of services carried out by the drivers (fixing the maximum price, control over the quality of vehicles and the behaviour of the drivers, disciplinary powers).

In summary, according to the Spanish Courts, these are prima facie indicators of economic *dependence*:

- Scoring system through the final customer's assessment (already qualified as evidence in STS 29 December 1999).
- GPS geolocation and kilometre logging: permanent monitoring system.
- Control through the application of compliance with specific delivery instructions (deadline, prohibition of corporate logos, form of addressing the end user, etc).

[35] On this question, see, Jeremias Adams-Prassl, 'What If Your Boss Was an Algorithm? Economic Incentives, Legal Challenges, and the Rise of Artificial Intelligence at Work' (2019) 41 *Comparative Labor Law & Policy Journal* 123.

[36] This is a Spanish word which is hard to translate. It refers to the idea of profits and risks in an employment relationship appertaining to the employer.

[37] See Anna Ginés i Fabrellas, 'Algorithms as subordination. The role of technology in classifying workers in the platform economy', XIII European Regional Congress of the International Society for Labour and Social Security Law: Work and Employment in the Digital Era: Legal Challenges (Lisbon, 5–7 May 2021).

- Credit card in the name of Glovo for the purchase of products by the user. If necessary, Glovo will advance the rider 100 euros.
- Final compensation for the time spent at the collection point waiting for the order.
- Specification in the contract of 13 causes for its termination due to breach by the worker (disciplinary power). Some of these correspond literally to those provided for in Article 54 ET, the general regulation of the issue.
- The information necessary to operate the system is exclusively in the hands of Glovo (member shops, order).

Concerning *ajenidad*, the Supreme Court judgment distinguishes five types:

- In services: Glovo makes all commercial decisions (prices, payment, methods, remuneration, invoicing, etc).
- On the risks: Glovo risks a much higher amount of money in its business than the rider who makes the delivery.
- In the profits: Glovo takes ownership of the result which benefits the company.
- In the means: a difference should be established concerning the ownership of the company's means: the platform's (without which the activity cannot be provided) and those of the delivery drivers – mobile phone and bicycle have infinitely lower value.
- On the brand: the delivery person is obliged to provide the service under a third-party's brand (Glovo).

Thus, Glovo is not an intermediary that merely establishes contact between the delivery persona and the end customer. It *coordinates and organises the service through the platform's management algorithm*.[38] Some of the aspects covered by it are the following:

- Coordination of delivery times, prohibition of corporate logos, how to address the customer.
- Customer rating of delivery drivers (essential for order allocation and final remuneration).
- Constant geolocation of the rider (real-time service compliance monitoring).
- The rider and the customer cannot perform or obtain the service outside the platform. For this reason, riders have very limited autonomy that only affects 'secondary issues', such as the choice of the means of transport used for delivery (bicycle, motorbike, car), the smartphone used to receive orders and delivery information, or the route chosen for delivery.

[38] Álvarez Alonso and Martínez Moreno (n 15) 7: 'without all this contribution from the company, this economic activity cannot be carried out, and it is clear that delivery drivers lack the infrastructure or capacity to carry it out on their own … it is even a little ridiculous to attribute to them the status of self-employed entrepreneurs simply on the basis of the use of a bicycle their own'.

- The 'brand image', completely standardised, provided by the company and with the company's characteristic logos and colours, which makes it recognisable for the client, in such a way that the worker himself becomes the image of the company.[39]

C. United Kingdom

The employment status of Uber drivers was the first gig economy decision to reach the UK Supreme Court. The company's business model requires little explanation, and has become an archetype of the organisation of platform-mediated work.[40] Two important aspects of the factual matrix before the Court should nonetheless be highlighted: first, the sheer number of individuals working for the company: '[a]t the time of the employment tribunal hearing in 2016, there were about 30,000 Uber drivers operating in the London area and 40,000 in the UK as a whole'.[41]

Second, the carefully crafted complex contractual structures which underpin the transport provision. The language of 'Partner Terms' and 'Services Agreement[s]' is not surprising in and of itself. What is more perplexing, on the other hand, is the fact that the contractual arrangements then refer to drivers as 'Customers' and passengers as 'Users'. Under this setup, Uber purports

> to provide electronic services … to the driver, which include access to the Uber app and payment services, and the driver agrees to provide transportation services to passengers …. The agreement states that Customer acknowledges and agrees that Uber BV does not provide transportation services and that, where Customer accepts a User's request for transportation services made through the Uber app, Customer is responsible for providing those transportation services and, by doing so, 'creates a legal and direct business relationship between Customer and the User, to which neither Uber [BV] nor any of its Affiliates in the Territory is a party'.[42]

Further complex arrangements regulate the relationship between different corporate entities on Uber's side, including a Dutch parent company (Uber BV), operator of the Uber app, and UK subsidiaries (Uber London Ltd and Uber Britannia Ltd), which hold the relevant private hire licences in London and the rest of the country, respectively.[43]

i. Litigation History

The *Uber* litigation spanned a period of five years. In 2016, a group of Uber drivers led by Yaseen Aslam and James Farrar brought a number of claims, including for

[39] ibid, 13–14.

[40] J Prassl, *Humans as a Service: The Promise and Perils of Work in the Gig Economy* (Oxford University Press 2018) ch 1. See also *Uber BV v Aslam* (n 4) [6]–[21].

[41] *Uber BV v Aslam* (n 4) [5]. The numbers have continued to grow over the last five years.

[42] ibid, [24].

[43] ibid, [3], [30]–[33].

failure to pay the National Minimum Wage and grant paid annual leave, against the platform. In a first instance judgment handed down that autumn, Employment Judge Snelson at the London Central Employment Tribunal was unequivocal in finding that claimant drivers were workers, rather than independent contractors. The language in *Aslam, Farrar v Uber* was unusually pointed. The Tribunal, the Judge noted, were

> struck by the remarkable lengths to which Uber has gone in order to compel agreement with its (perhaps we should say its lawyers') description of itself and with its analysis of the legal relationships between the two companies, the drivers and the passengers. Any organisation (a) running an enterprise at the heart of which is the function of carrying people in motor cars … (c) requiring drivers and passengers to agree, as a matter of contract, that it does not provide transportation services … and (d) resorting in its documentation to fictions, twisted language and even brand new terminology, merits, we think, a degree of scepticism. Reflecting on [the platform's] general case, and on the grimly loyal evidence of [Uber Manager] Ms Bertram in particular, we cannot help being reminded of Queen Gertrude's most celebrated line:
>
> 'The lady doth protest too much, methinks'.[44]

A detailed analysis of the facts before the Tribunal led to the conclusion that Uber's extensive contractual documentation did not reflect the reality of its relationship with the drivers, and were therefore to be disregarded. 'This is, we think, an excellent illustration of the phenomenon of which Elias J warned in the *Kalwak* case of "armies of lawyers" contriving documents in their clients' interests which simply misrepresent the true rights and obligations on both sides'.[45]

In November 2017, the Employment Tribunal's decision was fully vindicated in a carefully argued decision denying Uber's appeal. Her Honour Judge Eady QC, sitting in the London Employment Appeal Tribunal, upheld the first instance decision, confirming the drivers' worker status. While more measured in terms of language, her substantive finding on the question of worker status was unequivocal. Uber's appeal had focused on the argument that in the absence of direct contractual relationships as set up in its terms and conditions, the business model could be explained in its entirety as the result of regulatory requirements, including in particular Transport for London's Private Hire Licensing regime.[46] In rejecting these arguments, HHJ Eady returned to the key question at stake:

> The issue at the heart of the appeal can be simply put: when the drivers are working, who are they working for? The ET's answer to this question was that there was a contract between ULL and the drivers whereby the drivers personally undertook work for ULL as part of its business of providing transportation services to passengers in the London area.[47]

[44] *Aslam and Farrar v Uber* Case No 2202550/2015 (London Employment Tribunal) [87] (citations omitted). The decision was made available at: www.judiciary.gov.uk/wp-content/uploads/2016/10/aslam-and-farrar-v-uber-reasons-20161028.pdf.

[45] ibid [96] (citations omitted).

[46] *Uber BV v Aslam and Others* UKEAT 0056/17, [32] ff.

[47] ibid, [103].

Following extensive scrutiny of Uber's challenges to the Tribunal's judgment, the EAT was 'satisfied the ET did not err either in its approach or in its conclusions … [and was therefore] entitled to conclude there was a [worker] contract between [Uber] and the drivers'.[48]

Just over a year later, in December 2018, the majority of the Court of Appeal arrived at a similar conclusion in rejecting Uber's further appeal. The Master of the Rolls, Sir Terence Etherton, and Bean LJ found that the Employment Tribunal was 'not only entitled, but correct, to find that each of the Claimant drivers was working for [Uber] as a "limb (b) worker"'.[49]

At this point in the litigation, the company's focus had firmly turned to the relationship between its written contractual arrangement (which it argued conclusively settled the question as to worker status) and the facts as determined by the Employment Tribunal. Adopting a nuanced position to determining the contractual position, and carefully highlighting relevant factors in support of both sides' arguments, the majority adopted a broad reading of the Supreme Court's '*Autoclenz*' sham contracting doctrine:

> We consider that the extended meaning of 'sham' endorsed in *Autoclenz* provides the common law with ample flexibility to address the convoluted, complex and artificial contractual arrangements, no doubt formulated by a battery of lawyers, unilaterally drawn up and dictated by Uber to tens of thousands of drivers and passengers, not one of whom is in a position to correct or otherwise resist the contractual language. As to the reality, not only do we see no reason to disagree with the factual conclusions of the ET as to the working relationship between Uber and the drivers, but we consider that the ET was plainly correct.[50]

Underhill LJ, on the other hand, disagreed with the approach adopted by his colleagues. Expressing a general reticence to depart from the contractual terms set out, above, His Lordship instead gave precedence to the intricate set of arrangements put in place by the company: 'standing back so as to be able to see the wood as well as the trees, it still seems to me that the relationship argued for by Uber is neither unrealistic nor artificial. On the contrary, it is in accordance with a well-recognised model for relationships in the private hire car business'.[51]

ii In the Supreme Court

The stage was thus set for the Supreme Court. In a decision handed down on 19 February 2021, seven Justices unanimously rejected Uber's final appeal, and fully vindicated the Employment Tribunal's findings both as to employment status and the applicability of the working time regime.

[48] ibid, [116].
[49] *Uber BV and others v Aslam and others* [2018] EWCA Civ 2748 [71].
[50] ibid, [105].
[51] ibid, [146].

Following a detailed analysis of the relevant facts, statutory provisions and litigation history, Lord Leggatt, with whom all the Justices agreed, first turned to the core of submissions made on Uber's behalf, *viz* whether drivers were 'performing services solely for and under contracts made with passengers through the agency of Uber London', rather than working for the platform.[52] Having rejected Uber's arguments as to the importance of the private hire licensing regime and its role as a booking agent on 'ordinary principles of the law of contract and agency',[53] His Lordship turned to the central question: in determining worker status, is the interpretation of the parties' written agreements an appropriate starting point?[54]

The answer to this question required a detailed examination of the Supreme Court's previous decision in *Autoclenz v Belcher*,[55] in which Lord Clarke had suggested that 'The question in every case is … what was the true agreement between the parties'.[56] Employment contracts could not be treated in the same way as ordinary commercial agreements, not least because the 'relative bargaining power of the parties must be taken into account'.[57]

Given that inequality of bargaining power can be a feature of contractual relations in various contexts, however, Lord Leggatt set out to explore more fully the 'theoretical justification for [the *Autoclenz*] approach'. The critical distinction, His Lordship suggested, could be found in the fact that 'the rights asserted by the claimants were not contractual rights but were created by legislation. Thus, … the primary question was one of statutory interpretation, not contractual interpretation'.[58]

The appropriate approach was thus 'to have regard to the purpose of a particular provision and to interpret its language, so far as possible, in the way which best gives effect to that purpose'.[59] In the context of employment legislation, that meant the protection of vulnerable workers. Given their subordination to employer control, 'such relations cannot safely be left to contractual regulation'.[60] To do otherwise 'would reinstate the mischief which the legislation was enacted to prevent'. Indeed, the

> efficacy of [employment law] protection would be seriously undermined if the putative employer could by the way in which the relationship is characterised in the written contract determine, even prima facie, whether or not the other party is to be classified as a worker. Laws such as the National Minimum Wage Act were manifestly enacted to

[52] *Uber BV v Aslam* (n 4) [42].
[53] ibid, [45].
[54] ibid, [57].
[55] *Autoclenz v Belcher* [2011] UKSC 41.
[56] ibid, [29].
[57] ibid, [21], [35].
[58] *Uber BV v Aslam* (n 4) [69].
[59] ibid, [70].
[60] ibid, [75].

> protect those whom Parliament considers to be in need of protection and not just those who are designated by their employer as qualifying for it.[61]

Taking the contractual documentation at face value, or even as the starting point in the classification exercise, in other words, 'would in effect … accord Uber power to determine for itself whether or not the legislation designed to protect workers will apply to its drivers'.[62] This had long been recognised by Parliament, not least in specifically voiding any clauses purporting to contract out of the Employment Rights Act and other employment legislation.[63]

How, then, should the worker test be applied? It is necessary for tribunals

> both to view the facts realistically and to keep in mind the purpose of the legislation … The greater the extent of … control [exercised by the putative employer over the work or services performed by the individual concerned], the stronger the case for classifying the individual as a 'worker' who is employed under a 'worker's contract'.[64]

This approach, Lord Leggatt noted, was also in line with the jurisprudence of the Court of Justice.[65]

On the facts of the case, five elements of Uber's business model were highlighted as particularly salient for the question of worker status: (1) the power to set rates and determine the percentage of Uber's 'service fee'; (2) full control over contractual terms and conditions; (3) information asymmetries created by the app to exercise tight algorithmic control once a driver is logged on; (4) a 'significant degree of control over the way in which drivers deliver their services'; and (5) tight restrictions on communications between drivers and passengers.[66] The fact that drivers could choose flexibly when to work, on the other hand, was not incompatible with worker status:

> [I]t is well established and not disputed by Uber that the fact that an individual is entirely free to work or not, and owes no contractual obligation to the person for whom the work is performed when not working, does not preclude a finding that the individual is a worker, or indeed an employee, at the times when he or she is working.[67]

The Tribunal was thus 'entitled to find that the claimant drivers were "workers" who worked for Uber London under "worker's contracts" within the meaning of the statutory definition. Indeed, that was, in [His Lordship's] opinion, the only conclusion which the tribunal could reasonably have reached'.[68] Similarly, insofar as the question of during which periods Uber drivers were working was concerned,

[61] ibid, [76].
[62] ibid, [77].
[63] ibid, [79].
[64] ibid, [87].
[65] ibid, [88], citing Case C-610/18 *FMB Ltd v Raad van bestuur van de Sociale verzekeringsbank* [2020] EU:C:2020:565, paras 60–61.
[66] *Uber BV v Aslam* (n 4) [94]–[101].
[67] ibid, [91].
[68] ibid, [119].

given that the 'app was designed to operate coercively' to ensure compliance with 'an obligation to accept a minimum amount of work', the Tribunal's finding was that working time included all periods when the app was switched on and drivers were ready and willing to accept trips.[69]

IV. Reverberations

Given the high profile of the respondent gig economy employers, the decisions thus discussed quickly attracted significant international and domestic media attention. In this section, we turn to the longer-term implications, both in terms of operators' responses to the judgments, and the broader political and legal responses developments which ensued.

A. France

The *Uber* decision of the Court of Cassation was highly publicised by the Court itself at both national and international levels. For the first time, the Court decided to publish the decision simultaneously in English and Spanish, accompanied by a press release and an explanatory note, which were themselves translated into these two languages. In addition to a pedagogical desire to explain the decision, its translation certainly testifies the French Court's desire to actively contribute to the debates on an international scale.

Beyond the immediate solution given to a specific dispute, the *Uber* ruling did not put an end to the debates on the qualification of the employment relationship between a worker and a platform work. First, the reclassification of the contract depends on the specific conditions of work organisation within each platform. It is very well known that platforms work have very different operating methods and may change their operation as the courts recognise employment contracts. Second, contrary to what one might have thought, the *Uber* ruling, although well known, did not lead to a wave of requests for reclassification on the part of Uber drivers or other platform workers. Neither did it lead to an organised action seeking for the reclassification. Actions for reclassification have remained fairly isolated and in most cases only occur after the contract has ended. Finally, when workers have taken their case to court, the lower courts have not necessarily followed the position of the Court of Cassation. Indeed, new cases are currently pending before the Court of Cassation, one again concerning an Uber driver, another concerning a very different type of platform work. The Court should thus be led to be precise in its jurisprudence.

[69] ibid, [129], [123].

Finally, the legal context of the decisions has also changed since the first *Take Eat Easy* decision. Contrary to other countries, the legal response has not been the creation of a third category of workers. Since the Labour Act in 2016, the government's assumption is that platform workers are self-employed. This assumption has two consequences. The first is that the need for specific protections for these workers is not denied, but the legislator intends to grant these protections only to self-employed workers. The second is that the *Take Eat Easy* and *Uber* decisions have not exactly fallen into the pattern of analysis proposed by the legislative interventions. Indeed, in 2019 the legislator devised a response to the Court's case law, which was thwarted by the Constitutional Council. The Mobility Act (LOM Act)[70] introduced provisions applicable to platforms engaged in car transport and delivery of goods by motor or non-motor vehicles. Platforms are encouraged to establish voluntary codes of practice defining rights and obligations towards platform workers. In exchange, the draft bill stated that the drawing up of a code of practice and compliance with the commitments made in connection with the listed topics could not characterise the existence of a subordination link (and therefore the existence of an employment contract) between the platform and the workers. However, the Constitutional Council declared this provision unconstitutional as it is up to the judge to reclassify the relationship between the worker and the platform as an employment contract whenever such relationship is in fact characterised by the existence of a subordination link.[71] The decision of the Constitutional Council confirms the major role that judges can play in the legal organisation of platform work. It was also taken into account by the Court of Cassation in its *Uber* ruling. Explaining the decision, the Dean of the Social Chamber explained that the criterion of the subordination link was 'sanctuarised' by the Constitutional Council. Therefore, the Court of Cassation had to stick to its traditional definition of the employment contract.[72] The LOM Act also granted to self-employed workers, riders and drivers some other individual rights like the right to disconnect without risk of being sanctioned and the right to refuse a ride.[73] These rights are important as they can help to strengthen the independence of these workers and avoid the requalification of their contracts. In April 2021, an ordinance was adopted aiming at establishing a collective representation of self-employed workers in two sectors (drivers and riders).[74] The text is incomplete and further provisions are to be adopted soon.

To conclude, it is undeniable that the Court's decisions have played a role both in the current debates on the status of platform workers and in the legislative responses that are helping to shape the initial features of a regime for certain

[70] Act 2019-1428, 24 December 2019.

[71] Decision DC n° 2019-794 of the Constitutional Council, 20 December 2019.

[72] Huglo, above (n 32).

[73] Art L 1326-4 of the Transport Code.

[74] Ordinance n° 2021-484 of 21 April to establish representation for platform workers and Draft law ratifying Ordinance n° 2021-484 and empowering the Government to complete by ordinance the rules organising social dialogue with platforms.

platform workers, including the legal recognition of collective rights. The reclassification of the employment relationship between the worker and the platform as an employment contract could have put an end to the debate. If there is an employment contract, labour law must apply and these workers should then benefit from all the collective rights granted to employees. However, as we have indicated the individual actions of a few workers have not led to an increase in court cases. The reasons for not going to a tribunal are not easily identifiable. One reason may be the lack of collective organisation to support this action and/or the absence of collective demands for it in France. The idea that platform workers want protections but not an employment contract is very widespread in France. One thing is certain: while recourse to the courts may make it possible to strengthen the position of platform workers, it cannot replace effective recognition of collective rights for these workers.

B. Spain

For the purposes of this chapter, concerning the functioning of collective bargaining in the platform economy, the most interesting consequence is undoubtedly the enactment of Law 12/2021, specifically the information obligation included in the new section (d) of article 64.4 ET.[75]

Article 64.4 ET describes in detail the right of the works council – and, of the staff delegates in companies with fewer than 50 workers – to be informed and to know certain company information that particularly affects the working conditions and remuneration of the workers in the company. Thus, workers' representatives will have the right to know and be informed about the company's balance sheet and profit and loss account, employment contract and termination of employment models, sanctions imposed on workers for very serious misconduct, among other issues. The new paragraph (d) establishes the following:

> Article 64.4 ET: The works council shall have the right to be informed by the company 'at appropriate intervals in each case' of 'the parameters, rules and instructions on which algorithms or artificial intelligence systems are based that affect decision-making that may have an impact on working conditions, access to and maintenance of employment, including profiling'.

The following elements can be drawn from this new mandate:

1. The company has an obligation to inform the works council. The rule is clear on the subjects bound by this obligation, which, in return, is configured as a right for the workers' representatives.
2. Although the wording of the paragraph is not very specific, it does provide information on three key elements: who the subjects of the obligation are;

[75] Lidia Gil Otero, 'El doble canal de representación de los trabajadores ante la economía de plataformas' (2020) 228 *Nueva revista española de derecho del trabajo* 31.

> when the obligation arises; what the content of the information is. Who: the company (obligation) and the workers' representatives (right). When: at the intervals specified in Article 64.4. ET: 'at the appropriate intervals in each case'. This is an indeterminate legal concept that must be specified by the parties concerned, possibly through collective bargaining. The rule specifies that the information must be periodic. However, in this case, unlike in other employment conditions, the legislator has not set a minimum period (eg, information on the right to equal treatment and equal opportunities must be provided 'at least annually', Article 64.3 ET). Therefore, it is up to the parties to determine whether the information is to be provided at regular intervals or whether, on the contrary, it is only necessary to provide such information when there is a change in the algorithm that could affect the conditions indicated.

What is to be reported: the parameters, rules and instructions on which artificial intelligence algorithms or systems are based. The information is restricted, and it could be said that it is specific to those – parameters, rules and instructions – that affect decision-making that may have an impact on working conditions, access to and maintenance of employment, including profiling. The information must include that which may affect decision-making both by the employer and by the worker himself. Thus it is known, as the STS 25 September 2020 itself points out, that this algorithm conditions determining aspects of the working conditions, such as the specific time slots of carrying out their activity in turn determine the volume of orders that the worker will receive and these in turn, determine the salary, and, ultimately, the score of qualification that is decisive for maintaining the employment.

A no less relevant issue concerns the quality and quantity of information to be provided by the company about the algorithm. This is a strictly technical element which, in its strictest terms, may be difficult to understand for those who do not have specific training in this area. For this reason, the question arises as to how the employer is going to provide this information. Article 64.4 ET provides an interesting indication on information in general, when it defines that 'information means the transmission of information by the employer to the works council, so that it is aware of a specific issue and can proceed with examination'. Consequently, and in view of this definition, it will not be sufficient for the employer to display the algorithm or its composition, but the information provided about it must be adequate for the workers' representatives to be aware of the possibilities of the algorithm to influence 'working conditions, access to and maintenance of employment, including profiling' (article 64.4.(d) ET). Depending on the type of activity carried out by the platform, it would be appropriate for the parties to negotiate what specific information and on what terms should be provided to works' representatives.

Paragraph 6 also specifies that

> the information shall be provided by the employer to the works council, subject to any specific provisions in each case, at such time, in such manner and with such content as are appropriate to enable the employees' representatives to examine it properly and, where necessary, to prepare the consultation and the report.

The following paragraph specifies that

> in such a way as to enable the employees' representatives, on the basis of the information received, to meet with the employer, to obtain a reasoned reply to any report and to be able to compare their views or opinions.

Even though the new regulation has added the aforementioned section (d), this should not be seen as an element that is alien to the rest of the elements of which the workers' representatives must be informed, as indicated in the other sections of Article 64 ET. In fact, it is very likely that this algorithm will affect or have repercussions, in one way or another, on the company's final balance sheet or profit and loss account (section 4.a)), on the sanctions that may be imposed on workers (section 4.c)),or may lead to significant changes in terms of work organisation and employment contracts in the company (section 5).

C. United Kingdom

The Supreme Court's decision has already been the subject of extensive academic commentary, both in terms of its implications for labour law,[76] and the political economy of labour market regulation more broadly.[77] The company's immediate response was an attempt to confine the ruling to a narrow set of claimants and facts. In a statement on 19 February 2021, Jamie Heywood, Uber's Regional General Manager for Northern and Eastern Europe, suggested that the company would

> respect the Court's decision which focussed on a small number of drivers who used the Uber app in 2016. Since then we have made some significant changes to our business, guided by drivers every step of the way. These include giving even more control over how they earn and providing new protections like free insurance in case of sickness or injury. We are committed to doing more and will now consult with every active driver across the UK to understand the changes they want to see.[78]

The company was proposing, in other words, to continue with its self-employment business model as before the ruling, thus denying the vast majority of workers access to the fundamental rights set out in Lord Leggatt's speech. Any further

[76] See notably, Alan Bogg and Michael Ford, 'The death of contract in determining employment status' (2021) 137 *LQR* 392; D Brodie, 'Confronting the Gig Economy' (2021) 2 *Jur Rev* 102; Joe Atkinson and Hitesh Dhorajiwala, 'The Future of Employment, Purposive Interpretation and the Role of Contract after *Uber*' (2021) *MLR*, available at: doi.org/10.1111/1468-2230.12693; Zoe Adams, 'One Step Forwards For Employment Status, Still Some Way To Go: The Supreme Court's Decision in *Uber v Aslam* Under Scrutiny' (2021) 80 *Cambridge Law Journal* 221.

[77] J Adams-Prassl and D Coyle, 'Uber and Beyond: Policy implications for the UK' (Bennett Institute for Public Policy, University of Cambridge, March 2021), available at: www.bennettinstitute.cam.ac.uk/publications/uber-and-beyond-policy-implications-uk/.

[78] M-A Russon, 'Uber Drivers are Workers not Self-Employed, Supreme Court Rules' (*BBC News*, 19 February 2021), available at: www.bbc.co.uk/news/business-56123668.

status discussions would require renewed rounds of law suits, potentially locking the company and its drivers into never-ending cycles of costly and complex litigation.

It therefore came as a surprise when just a month later, Uber's CEO Dara Khosrowshahi took to the pages of the London *Evening Standard* to promise that the company was 'turning the page on driver rights'. Noting that Uber 'could have continued to dispute drivers' rights to [employment law] protections in court' he announced that 'Beginning today, Uber drivers in the UK will be treated as workers', and expressed his 'hope [that] our competitors, who are engaged in their own legal battles, will rethink their approach and join us in taking this step'.[79]

The recognition of workers' rights was not limited to the individual dimension. On 26 May 26 2021, the GMB (a major transport trade union) announced that it would formally be recognised by Uber, allowing for the collective representation of up to 70,000 drivers in the UK. The agreement covers a wide range of topics, including

- National earnings principles: including Uber's National Living Wage guarantee and holiday pay.
- Pension: including how to encourage drivers to enrol and contribute.
- Discretionary benefits: including free AXA insurance for sickness and injury, and Uber's driver loyalty programme.
- Health, safety and wellbeing: to ensure that drivers are safe when working on the app, including personal safety, road safety and driver well-being.
- Account deactivations: GMB will play a role representing drivers if they lose access to the Uber app.
- Representation: GMB and Uber leadership will meet quarterly to discuss driver issues and concerns.
- Organising drivers: Uber has agreed access rights for GMB representatives at driver hubs to enable them to meet and support drivers.[80]

V. Concluding Reflections

Amongst a vast heterogeneity of business models, one common factor unites nearly all gig economy platforms' business models: they are premised on the systematic denial of workers' employment status. As discussion in this chapter has shown, this assertion has been resolutely rejected by last instance courts in all jurisdictions surveyed: the highest appellate courts in France, Spain and the United Kingdom have sent a clear message that gig economy workers cannot be excluded from the scope of employment-protective norms.

[79] Dara Khosrowshahi, 'Uber chief executive Dara Khosrowshahi says "we're turning the page on driver rights"' *Evening Standard* (17 March 2021), available at: www.standard.co.uk/comment/comment/uber-chief-executive-dara-khosrowhahi-drivers-rights-turning-page-b924529.html.

[80] *GMB News*, 'Uber and GMB strike historic union deal for 70,000 UK drivers' (26 May 2021), available at: gmb.org.uk/news/uber-and-gmb-strike-historic-union-deal-70000-uk-drivers.

And yet, as the ensuing discussion has shown, some fundamental differences remain. They are to some extent driven by underlying distinctions in the applicable legal regimes (such as, eg, a divide between binary versus tripartite structures for employment status). Larger factors, however, are similarly at play, including (but not limited to) differences in political and legislative discourse in the run-up to each decision, the varying roles of state and private enforcement, and the political and legal response from platform operators.

These distinctions serve as an important reminder of the importance – and inherent limits – of relying on judicial enforcement as an overall strategy in ensuring fair and decent working conditions – not least in considering the importance of recent litigation in galvanising collective action and social partnership.

6

Why Collective Bargaining is a 'Must' for Platform Workers and How to Achieve it

TAMÁS GYULAVÁRI AND GÁBOR KÁRTYÁS

I. Introduction

The chapter maps and evaluates the possible role of collective bargaining in the regulation of platform workers' working conditions. Due to its flexibility and ability for quick reaction, autonomous regulation by the two sides of industry would have significant potential to elaborate a legal framework on the new phenomenon of platform work.

In this context, section II summarises the merits of collective bargaining and analyses how these could be used by platform workers and their employers. The hierarchy of labour law sources is a key issue in this context, thus, section III will highlight the potential solutions of adjusting collective agreements and other labour law sources in this regard. Section IV will use working time as an example to elucidate dogmatic and practical problems in the way of collective sources of employment. Some collective agreements concluded in the platform economy have already addressed the issue of working time. These first empirical examples will also be analysed. Since European Union (EU) law and policy is widely expected to give impetus to collective bargaining in this new sector, therefore, section V will confront declared social objectives with present competition law obstacles. We will highlight the flaws that come from a strategy of using old recipes for new problems. Finally in section VI, the Hungarian legal system will be used as an example to identify the difficulties at national level in an Eastern European context. Overall, we will outline the potential objectives and the blocking factors in collective bargaining as a suitable tool to improve working conditions in the sharing economy.

II. The Merits of Collective Bargaining

In the second decade of the twenty-first century, the right to bargain collectively is enshrined in a remarkable set of global[1] and European level international agreements,[2] and it is also included in the constitutions of the majority of EU Member States. Its significance cannot be debated, yet, the question is how to adopt and enforce such a right within the digital workplace. While acknowledging the practical and legal challenges of collective bargaining in the platform economy, in this section we concentrate on the practical merits of collective negotiations. A short overview of its basic functions may well illustrate why collective bargaining is essential for the parties in the platform economy.

First, the main objective of collective bargaining is to countervail the inequality between the worker and the employer inherent in the employment relationship by enabling the workers to form 'collective power'. In Otto Kahn-Freund's classical words, 'As a power countervailing management the trade unions are much more effective than the law has ever been or will ever be'.[3] Bargaining on a collective level can introduce adequate protective measures against an overemphasis on employer-oriented flexibility and means a more transparent and formal standard-setting process than individual negotiations.[4] In this way, working conditions are fixed by the power relationship between the 'collectivity of workers' and the employer(s).[5]

Guy Davidov described the inequality in the parties' bargaining power as democratic deficits within the employment relationship which can be corrected by collective bargaining. On the one hand, collective agreements set out various rules and procedures the employer must follow, thus, it leads to less arbitrary managerial decisions. On the other hand, collective bargaining is a forum for employees to let their voice to be heard, and to participate in the decision-making processes that will affect them.[6] Such basic functions shall be relied upon by all persons who work in a subordinate relationship.[7] The worldwide phenomenon of

[1] See especially the ILO Declaration on Fundamental Principles and Rights at Work, ILO Right to Organise and Collective Bargaining Convention 1949 No 98 (adopted 1 July 1949, entered into force 18 July 1951) 96 UNTS 257; and ILO Collective Bargaining Convention 1981 No 154 (adopted 3 June 1981, entered into force 11 August 1983) 1331 UNTS 267.

[2] Council of Europe, European Social Charter (Revised) (adopted 3 May 1996, entered into force 1 July 1999) ETS 163 (ESC), Art 6; Charter of Fundamental Rights of the European Union [2000] OJ C364/12 (CFREU), Art 28.

[3] Otto Kahn-Freund, *Labour and the Law* (Stevens & Sons 1978) 6, 10.

[4] Anneke Goudswaard et al, 'Organisation of working time: Implications for productivity and working conditions. Overview Report' (Eurofound, 11 August 2013), available at: www.eurofound.europa.eu/sites/default/files/ef_publication/field_ef_document/ef1250en.pdf, 23–25.

[5] Marco Rocca, *Posting of Workers and Collective Labour Law: There and Back Again* (Intersentia 2015) 98.

[6] Guy Davidov, 'Collective Bargaining Law: Purpose and Scope' (2004) 20 *International Journal of Comparative Labour Law and Industrial Relations* 81, 83–85.

[7] See also the ECJ's reasoning on collective bargaining and false self-employed persons. Case C-413/13 *FNV Kunsten Informatie en Media v Staat der Nederlanden* [2014] ECLI:EU:C:2014:2411, paras 38–42.

litigations around the employee status of platform workers shows that this form of employment is not without subordination.

Second, setting the working conditions in a collective agreement enhances stability in the workplace, and makes easier the settlement of labour and industrial disputes. Collective bargaining tries to take working conditions out of competition, making it so that such conditions are not fixed following the interplay between supply and demand of labour.[8] Collectively agreed terms create a transparent and stable framework for employment and may not be challenged later in an industrial action (peace obligation).[9] Research shows that employers covered by collective agreements have lower fluctuation among employees, higher information flows coming from employees and increased firm-specific investments (especially in workers' training), which can all lead to more efficiency.[10] Collective bargaining is important in the reduction of uncertainty, which confronts both employees and management.[11] Following these principles, a transparent and stable working environment could be mutually advantageous for platforms and their workers too.

As the third basic function, as opposed to legislation, the parties of collective bargaining have much better knowledge of the priorities of the workplace or sector and thus the bargaining process educes better and quicker reactions to rapidly changing market requirements.[12] Consequently, this regulatory technique is the most flexible and most specific solution as it allows employment rules to be designed by those who will be subject to the regulations and who will apply (and also comply with) them. Collective bargaining, as a rule-making process, is based on joint decision-making between independent organisations. Through such joint authorship of the rules, negotiating parties accept joint responsibility for the implementation and renewal of rules.[13] Through collective bargaining the provisions of labour law can be adapted to the needs of the given sector, region, profession, as well as of the specific employer organisation and of the collective of employees working there. In labour law, as seen above, the individualisation of the legal framework of employment shall not be relied on for the individual agreement of the employer and the employee, as this would not result in a fair deal due to the asymmetry of power between the parties. Such individualisation shall be carried out on a collective level (see also below, section III).

Moreover, self-regulation by collective agreements may not only set the details not regulated by law or fill in the legislative gaps, but in most jurisdictions parties can even deviate from the law by their collective agreement, however, in general,

[8] Rocca (n 5) 98.

[9] See Art 6(4) of the European Social Charter.

[10] Davidov (n 6) 91–94.

[11] Commission, *Report of the High level group on industrial relations and change in the European Union* (Office for Official Publications of the European Communities 2002) 25.

[12] Edoardo Ales, 'The Regulatory Function of Collective Agreements in the Light of Its Relationship with Statutory Instruments and Individual Rights: A Multilevel Approach' in Tamás Gyulavári and Emanuele Menegatti (eds), *The Sources of Labour Law* (Kluwer Law International 2020) 69.

[13] Commission, *Report of the High level group on industrial relations* (n 11) 25.

but with a growing number of exceptions, only in favour of the employee.[14] These features may make collective bargaining a silver bullet for the platform economy. There is literally no part of labour law that is not challenged by the special structure and operation of platforms: from data protection and privacy, through non-discrimination and working time, to workplace health and safety, or collective rights. Up to the beginning of the 2020s, national legislation rarely made any initiatives to regulate these issues.[15] Also, given the huge variety of the different platforms,[16] it is of the utmost importance that parties can adjust the legal framework to their specific needs by collective agreements.

The above-mentioned benefits can be further enhanced, if collective bargaining takes place at a higher level, and the agreement covers a wider range of employers. Traditionally, the benefit of sectoral (wage) bargaining has been that they have provided a level playing field for employers by preventing undercutting through lower standards by domestic competitors. Short of government regulation, it may create the basis for joint employer investment in training, research and a 'good' industrial climate.[17] Consequently, an agreement that covers all platforms in a given sector can eliminate competition in working conditions and may still leave room for company-level agreements to set the specificities of the different platforms.

Considering the above, both platforms and workers would miss an efficient tool to regulate employment, if collective bargaining – due to practical or legal reasons – is not an option in the platform economy. Collective bargaining's basic functions include in particular the improvement of working conditions, balancing labour market inequalities, and taking working conditions such as wages out of competition. Uniformity of working conditions within the different sectors limits competitive pricing among entrepreneurs and competition among workers in the labour market.[18] These crucial roles are equally important for platform workers. In addition, filling legislative gaps would also have special relevance in platform work due to scarce or lacking special regulation.

[14] Tamás Gyulavári and Emanuele Menegatti, 'Introduction: Recent Trends in the Hierarchy of Labour Law Sources' in Tamás Gyulavári and Emanuele Menegatti (eds), *The Sources of Labour Law* (Kluwer Law International 2020) 6–7.

[15] As an exception, see Italian Decree no 101/2019 which introduced new provisions for the social protection of self-employed platform workers in the delivery sector. Thomas Haipeter and Feliciano Iudicone, 'New Social Initiatives on Cloud – and Gigwork – Germany and Italy Compared' (2020) 2 *Hungarian Labour Law E-Journal*, available at: www.ias.jak.ppke.hu/letolt/2020_2_a/03_ThHaipeter_FIudicione_hllj_uj_2020_2.pdf 17, 37–38. Also, in February 2021, the European Commission started a consultation process on possible action addressing the challenges relating to working conditions in platform work, C(2021) 4230 final and SWD (2021) 143 final.

[16] Jeremias Adams-Prassl and Martin Risak, 'Uber, Taskrabbit, & Co: Platforms as Employers? Rethinking the Legal Analysis of Crowdwork' (2016) 37 *Comparative Labor Law & Policy Journal* 604, 619.

[17] Commission, *Report of the High level group on industrial relations* (n 11) 27.

[18] Emanuele Menegatti, 'The Impact of the European Union Economic Governance on the Hierarchy of National Labour Law Sources' in Tamás Gyulavári and Emanuele Menegatti (eds), *The Sources of Labour Law* (Kluwer Law International 2020) 119.

III. Relationship between Collective Agreements and the Other Labour Law Sources

As seen above, company level and also higher-level collective agreements may fulfil a set of functions in regulating employment. These regulatory functions must be performed in a complex system of labour law sources.[19] This issue has not come to the forefront of the platform work discussion so far. Therefore, it may be meaningful to stress that collective agreements must comply with existing and constantly evolving national rules (principles) of the hierarchy of labour law sources. The provisions of collective agreements do not stand alone, but must be enforced only when they are in line with the national rules on such a hierarchy of sources, which may differ from country to country. As a result, collective agreements must have a clearly regulated relationship with the following labour law sources: international standards, statutory law, other collective agreements, agreement of the parties (primarily but not only the contract of employment), unilateral by-laws (regularly called 'terms and conditions') of the employer.

The relationship between statutory law and collective agreements became a fundamental topic of employment regulation in the last century. As a result of legal developments, the principle of 'in favour' has universally settled the relationship of statutory provisions and collective agreements. Therefore, collective agreements can improve working conditions by having better rules than the law. International standards are implemented in most national jurisdictions predominantly through statutory law, so they are part of this prospect. This hierarchy principle of allowing only '*in melius* derogations' (only in favour of employees) has proved to be successful and also dominant all over the world. Nevertheless, the last decades have brought about more and more exceptions from this regulatory model in several countries, for instance in the field of working time.[20] As a result, statutory norms have slowly mutated from a 'single rule' to a 'double-barrelled' model. As of now, employment provisions are of two kinds: allowing or prohibiting *in peius* derogations (to the disadvantage of employees) from the law for collective agreements.

This hierarchy raises the topical dilemma of whether certain provisions of collective agreements will allow worsening statutory standards for collective agreements (or not). Such legal provisions would allow legislation to extend certain employment protections to platform workers, for instance on organisation of working time, but collective agreements could exclude their application. This may be a potentially useful solution in the case of platform workers (not such a bad thing), but merely in a very limited circle of rights, when, for example, the peculiarities of the given sector or employer fully justify such a (decisive) loosening of

[19] This issue has also been analysed by the author in: Tamás Gyulavári, 'Floor of rights for platform workers' in Tamás Gyulavári and Emanuele Menegatti (eds), *Decent Work in the Digital Age: European and Comparative Perspectives* (Hart Publishing, forthcoming).

[20] Gyulavári and Menegatti, 'Introduction: Recent Trends' (n 14) 7.

statutory standards. Nonetheless, this is a purely legislative matter which must be addressed in the course of regulating platform work by statutory law (if and when it happens).

The parallel operation of different (lower and higher) levels of collective agreements also brings up regulatory questions regarding their relationship. The principle of favour was the undeniable pattern in their legal relationships up to recent times, but decentralisation of collective bargaining in the highly protective (continental) European systems recently cracked this traditional order.[21] This development is severely damaging in relation to platform work, since sector-level agreements may prevail over company level in terms of efficiency and adequacy.

Moving on to individual agreements, it is not surprising that agreements of the parties, particularly employment contracts, have traditionally been severely restricted in their derogations in labour law regulation. They are, in fact, almost exclusively confined to bettering labour standards in the labour market, both in relation to statutory law and collective agreements. This logical relationship of contract, law and collective agreement comes from the weaker position of employees, who are unable to achieve a fair deal with employers. This paradigm is principally suitable in the platform economy due to the extremely unbalanced bargaining powers of platforms and their workers. As a consequence, the more favourable rule should be applied without exception between the employment contract on the one hand, and statutory law or collective agreements on the other.

Due to the almost non-existent specific regulation in statutory and collective instruments on platform work, unilateral terms and conditions (platform statutes) of digital platforms set the basic conditions of work, including pay. Since terms and conditions, one-sidedly dictated by the platform, are the central and almost exclusive source of rights and obligations of the parties for the moment, their place in the hierarchy of labour law sources is a key issue. This flawed situation may be remedied in various ways. First, the unlimited regulatory freedom of platforms should be restricted in statutory law by defining the possible topics and minimum contents of unilateral by-laws. Second, the principle of favourable derogations should be applied between unilateral statutes and statutory laws, or collective agreements, without exceptions. This strict hierarchy should be expressly regulated in statutory law. Altogether these changes would guarantee that unilateral company rules (terms and conditions) are fully in line with statutory minimum standards, and are used solely to improve the working conditions of platform workers, or to implement legal requirements to the specific company, but without decreasing the level of protection.

[21] See, for instance: Massimo Pallini, 'Italian Industrial Relations: Toward a Strongly Decentralized Collective Bargaining' (2016) 38 *Comparative Labor Law & Policy Journal* 1, 2; Paul Marginson, 'Coordinated bargaining in Europe: From incremental corrosion to frontal assault?' (2015) 21 *European Journal of Industrial Relations* 97, 99; Udo Rehfeldt and Catherine Vincent, 'The decentralisation of collective bargaining in France: an escalating process' in Salvo Leonardi and Roberto Pedersini (eds), *Multi-employer bargaining under pressure: Decentralisation trends in five European countries* (ETUI 2018) 151.

IV. The Example of Working Time: A Popular Topic of Bargaining

Working time, perhaps second only to wages, is the working condition that has the most direct impact on the day-to-day lives of workers. The number of hours worked and the way in which they are organised can significantly affect not only the quality of work, but life outside the workplace. Working time is also critical for enterprises. Hours of work and their organisation are important in determining productivity, and whether an enterprise is profitable and sustainable.[22] The fundamental protections offered by the rules of working time cannot be put aside in digital work environments. However, it shall not mean that all traditional legal institutions can apply without adjustment. Probably the main idea of applying working time regulations to platform workers is that adjustment shall not be understood as opt out: technical reasons alone cannot justify the non-application of working time guarantees. Against this background the most convenient way to reconcile the needs of a given sector or specific form of employment and working time regulations is collective bargaining. This concept is neither unfamiliar in the working time Conventions of the International Labour Organization (ILO), nor in the EU Working Time Directive.

The relevant ILO Conventions set the basic protective measures and collective bargaining is promoted to reach an agreement on terms and conditions of employment that are more favourable than those already established by law.[23] Several instruments set out the requirement to consult the organisations of employers and workers concerned if it is intended to exclude some categories of workers from their scope. Others require consultation of workers' and employers' organisations for the introduction of permanent or temporary exceptions to the protective measures set in the relevant instrument.[24] However, it is not possible to set aside the standards prescribed by the ILO Conventions in a collective agreement.

In EU labour law it is the Working Time Directive[25] which illustrates best how EU law builds on the flexible transmission of directives into national law by collective agreements.[26] Article 18 allows derogations from the articles on daily rest, breaks, weekly rest period, length of night work and reference periods by means of collective agreements. Importantly, such derogations are open not only for agreements of universal application, but for 'agreements concluded between the two

[22] International Labour Organization (ILO), *Ensuring decent working time for the future. General Survey concerning working-time instruments* (International Labour Office 2018) 2.

[23] ibid, 287–88.

[24] ibid, 276–77.

[25] Council Directive 2003/88/EC of 4 November 2003 concerning certain aspects of the organisation of working time OJ L299/9.

[26] Keith D Ewing, 'The Death of Social Europe' (2015) 26 *King's Law Journal* 76, 81. Some argue that such broad authorisations to deviate from the Directive raise questions about the degree of union representation of the workers and the extent of the coverage of such agreements. This is all the more

sides of industry at a lower level'.[27] Nonetheless, the Directive prescribes that such derogations shall be allowed on condition that equivalent compensating rest periods are granted to the workers concerned or, in exceptional cases where it is not possible for objective reasons to grant such periods, the workers concerned are afforded appropriate protection. Thus, the standards set by EU law may be varied at national level by a private process of collective bargaining.[28] Besides this general provision on derogations in collective agreements, the Directive expressly refers to the possible regulatory role of collective agreements in various cases.[29] Moreover, the details of rest breaks shall be defined primarily in collective agreements and national legislation may regulate it only if the bargaining was not successful.[30] Note, that the Directive also offers flexibility by various exceptions for sectors of activity or particular type of employment to which the application of the main rules would be inappropriate or simply unworkable.[31] These exceptions are necessary to guarantee flexibility but shall not deprive employees of the adequate protections.[32]

Yet, there is only limited case law on how to interpret the mentioned clauses on possible derogations in collective agreements. In the *Accordo* case, the Court of Justice of the European Union (CJEU) emphasised the importance of legal certainty as regards the rules derogating from EU law.[33] In *Jaeger*, the Court stated that derogations must be interpreted strictly.[34] As regards 'equivalent compensating rest periods', the Court – taking the Directive's aim as a starting point – set the requirement that such rest periods must follow on immediately[35] and it is only in entirely exceptional circumstances that the Directive enables other appropriate protection instead of compensatory rest.[36] The case law suggests that collective agreements making use of the derogation clauses will be subject to strict scrutiny if the question of their legal compliance with the Directive's requirements is questioned in a future case. However, the door is wide open for the parties to adjust EU level working-time requirements to their specific circumstances by way of collective bargaining.

problematic as the Directive itself does not define the relevant level where the bargaining shall take place. Catherine Barnard, *EC Employment Law*, 2nd edn (Oxford University Press 2012) 414.

[27] Ales (n 12), 48.

[28] Ewing (n 26) 81–82.

[29] As regards the definition of night worker and work involving special hazards or heavy physical or mental strain, the limits of weekly working time, the reference periods for the calculation of length of night work and the possible derogations to certain activities or sectors, see WTD Arts 2(4)(ii), 8 (b), 6 (a), 16 (c), 17(2).

[30] Brian Bercusson, *European Labour Law*, 2nd edn (Cambridge University Press 2009) 299.

[31] Philippa Watson, *EU Social and Employment Law*, 2nd edn (Oxford University Press 2014) 257.

[32] ACL Davies, *EU Labour Law* (Elgar European Law 2012) 203.

[33] Case C-227/09 *Antonino Accardo and Others v Comune di Torino* [2010] ECLI:EU:C:2010:624, para 55.

[34] Case C-151/02 *Landeshauptstadt Kiel v Norbert Jaeger* [2003] ECLI:EU:C:2003:437, para 89.

[35] ibid, para 94.

[36] ibid, para 98.; see also, Case C-428/09 *Union syndicale Solidaires Isère v Premier ministre and Others* [2010] ECLI:EU:C:2010:612, para 55.

A. Examples: Working Time in Collective Agreements in the Platform Economy

Empirical evidence shows that working-time rules set by collective agreements for platforms is not just a theoretical issue. There are various techniques used in practice to regulate working time in the platform economy by collective agreements. In the following, we summarise the main examples.

The first solution is to include platform workers in the traditional framework of social dialogue, and extend the scope of existing collective bargaining agreements to gig workers.[37] An example is the food delivery and hostelry branch level collective agreement in Spain, which was amended in 2019 to cover also 'the delivery service of elaborated or prepared meals and drinks' on foot or in any type of vehicle that does not require administrative authorisation, as a provision of the establishment's own service or on behalf of another company, including digital platforms or through them.[38] The same strategy was followed by some traditional trade unions in Italy who successfully bargained with different platforms to recognise food delivery riders as employees and thus bring them under the scope of the relevant sector-level collective agreement.[39] The advantage of this method is that the parties can use the long-standing framework of traditional bargaining processes, and they can also build on already existing achievements in terms of the content of the collective agreements. However, the simple adoption of the working conditions tailored for a different employment setting might miss answering the specificities of the platform economy. Furthermore, as these traditional collective agreements apply only to employees, gig workers working outside the employment relationship are not covered.

A similar aim was targeted, but reached by a different method, in the first ever collective agreement in the platform economy. The Danish company Hilfr (offering cleaning services) and the trade union 3F agreed in August 2018, that after 100 hours of work a worker automatically becomes a 'Super Hilfr' (unless he or she objects), and thus has the status of an employee. As employees, they accrue rights to pensions, holiday entitlements and sick pay.[40] In this case the employment of

[37] José María Miranda Boto, 'Collective Bargaining and the Gig Economy: Actors' (2020) 2 *Hungarian Labour Law E-Journal*, available at: hllj.hu/letolt/2020_2_a/02_MirandaBoto_hllj_uj_2020_2.pdf, 6–10.

[38] COGENS, 'Collective Bargaining and the Gig Economy – New Perspectives', available at: cogens2019.eu/.

[39] Eurofound, 'Collective agreement between Just Eat, trade union CGIL, CISL and UIL Trasporti and workers in Italy' (23 July 2021), available at: www.eurofound.europa.eu/data/platform-economy/initiatives/collective-agreement-between-just-eat-trade-union-cgil-cisl-and-uil-trasporti-and-workers-in-italy; Eurofound, 'Collective agreement between LaConsegna and FILT-CGIL, FIT-CISL and UIL Trasporti of Florence' (23 July 2021), available at: www.eurofound.europa.eu/data/platform-economy/initiatives/collective-agreement-between-laconsegna-and-filt-cgil-fit-cisl-and-uil-trasporti-of-florence.

[40] Kristin Jesnes, Anna Ilsøe and Marianne J Hotvedt, 'Collective agreements for platform workers? Examples from the Nordic countries' [2019] *Nordic future of work Brief* 3, 3.

gig workers is not entirely placed under the reach of labour law, but the agreement itself sets the criteria to switch from freelancer to employee. Some working-time protections apply after the worker advances to employee status.

In the Nordic countries there are also cases where platform workers fall under the scope of a collective agreement which apply to another form of atypical employment. Some platform companies hire workers on marginal part-time employment contracts, which makes it possible for the workers to be covered by existing collective agreements without this being in conflict with competition law. An illustration of this is the case of *Bzzt* in Sweden. The company provides personal transport services by moped. Their agreement with the Swedish Transport Workers' Union allows Bzzt drivers to be covered by the Taxi Agreement, which gives the workers access to the same standards as traditional taxi drivers. Some other Nordic platform companies register as temporary employment agencies, and the workers are then covered by collective agreements on temporary agency work. The cases of Chabber in Denmark (employing waiters, bartenders and kitchen assistants) and Insta-jobs (a platform for students and different categories of high-skilled workers) and Gigstr (platform for low-skilled gigs) in Sweden are examples of this.[41] Again, a possible drawback is that joining an already existing agreement does not mean that gig workers' (like moped drivers') specific interests are represented. Also, only a minority of gig workers are employed under these special contracts (marginal part-time or agency work). Moreover, collective bargaining for agency workers has its own challenges – mainly stemming from the shared employer position of agencies and user companies – which might also impede the effective bargaining for gig workers.[42]

There are also examples, where collective agreements expressly target platform workers. In Italy, the parties signing the sector-level collective agreement for logistics, freight transport and shipping agreed in July 2018 on the special terms applicable to distribution of goods with cycles, mopeds and motorcycles (riders) that take place in an urban environment, also through the use of innovative technologies (platforms, palmtops, etc). Albeit the agreement applies only to employees, its content was elaborated to answer the needs of platform work. The agreement sets the measure of weekly working time (39 hours and 48 hours including overtime) and the basic requirements of work-time schedules (the weekly working time can be distributed up to a maximum of six days and can be adjusted over a period of four weeks). The duration of the part-time service cannot be less than 10 hours per week with a minimum daily service of two hours. The increase in the duration of the work performance as well as the change in the work location must be communicated with a notice of at least 11 hours. The parties also acknowledge the varying characteristics of the different platforms, and call

[41] ibid, 2.

[42] James Arrowsmith, *Temporary agency work and collective bargaining in the EU* (European Foundation for the Improvement of Living and Working Conditions 2008).

for the adoption of 'second-level' collective agreements applicable to the specific companies.[43]

As for other examples of 'platform economy specific bargaining', in February 2021, 3F and the Danish Chamber of Commerce (Dansk Erhverv) reached a nationwide collective agreement for food delivery riders. The agreement sets the normal weekly working time as minimum of eight hours and up to 37 hours, with overtime allowed up to 44 hours in total.[44] In Austria, from 2020 a new collective agreement applicable to bicycle couriers (only employees) contains a 40-hour week and the option to work only four days a week. It also stipulates additional holiday and Christmas remunerations.[45] In September 2019, Foodora and the United Federation of Trade Unions in Norway concluded an agreement, which introduced night compensation for work after midnight and extra pay in winter.[46]

These agreements are only the first steps in elaborating the necessary working-time rules for platform work in collective agreements. As seen above, their content is so far limited to the introduction of some basic protective measures like the maximum and/or minimum level of weekly working time. Whilst traditional topics such as hours, wages and holiday arrangements continue to play a significant role, it is also important to keep in mind the specificities of platform-based work and include these in negotiations.[47] Nonetheless, some special provisions appear, like the stipulation of special periods when a higher remuneration is due. Apparently these agreements do not make use of the broad authorisation of the Working Time Directive to derogate from some statutory provisions and substitute them with innovative solutions designed for the special character of platform work, which still offer adequate protection to the workers. However, one should not overlook the dates of these first agreements: it was only two or three years ago when these ground-breaking achievements appeared, and it is quite likely that the number and content of such platform economy specific agreements will quickly improve in future.

Although the barriers of collective bargaining for the self-employed are well known, we have already witnessed the first attempts to apply a collective agreement for gig workers working outside the employment relationship. In 2019, the GMB Union and the delivery company Hermes signed a collective bargaining

[43] COGENS (n 38).

[44] Eurofound, 'The Danish trade union 3F' (9 April 2021), available at: www.eurofound.europa.eu/data/platform-economy/initiatives/the-danish-trade-union-3f.

[45] Eurofound, 'Collective agreement for bicycle couriers in Austria' (9 April 2021), available at: www.eurofound.europa.eu/data/platform-economy/initiatives/collective-agreement-for-bicycle-couriers-in-austria.

[46] Eurofound, 'Collective agreement between Foodora and the United Federation of Trade Unions (Fellesforbundet)' (9 April 2021), available at: www.eurofound.europa.eu/data/platform-economy/initiatives/collective-agreement-between-foodora-and-the-united-federation-of-trade-unions-fellesforbundet.

[47] Jeremias Prassl, *Collective Voice in the Platform Economy: Challenges, Opportunities, Solutions* (ETUC 2018) 22.

agreement in the UK for self-employed couriers in the platform economy. The agreement introduced the right to paid holiday for delivery workers without an employment contract, showing that even a traditional labour law institution might be compatible with self-employment.[48] Another interesting attempt to apply a collective agreement to the self-employed food delivery workers took place in Italy. Albeit the agreement was rejected in September 2020 by the Italian Ministry of Labour and denounced by the three nationally representative unions, its content very much resembles some of the specific working-time issues in the gig economy, especially for non-employee riders. The agreement sets out a system of supplementary allowances for night work, holidays and negative weather conditions and an hourly incentive of €7 for the first four months from the launch of the service in a new city, even in the absence of offers of work. The parties agreed to organise training for riders with particular reference to road safety and food transport safety. The agreement also offered a certain number of days and hours for riders who are trade union leaders.[49] These stipulations point out some sector-specific priorities as regards working time.[50]

V. Objectives and Obstacles in EU Law

As has been argued, collective agreements should be allowed and promoted in national legal systems for the broadest possible circle of workers to exploit all their potential benefits. We may suppose that all international labour standards promote such developments. However, EU law is somewhat problematic in this regard. Although it emphasises at its highest levels the importance of collective bargaining, at the same time EU primary law also created and still promotes serious obstacles to competition law in the face of the limited personal scope of such bargaining.

Prima facie, EU law is very much promoting collective bargaining with a wide personal scope based on the worker concept. As for the case law of the European Court of Justice, the *Albany*[51] and *Laval* judgments[52] have emphasised the role

[48] Eurofound, 'GMB Union and Hermes' (9 April 2021), available at: www.eurofound.europa.eu/data/platform-economy/initiatives/gmb-union-and-hermes.

[49] Eurofound, 'Collective agreement between AssoDelivery and UGL' (23 July 2021), available at: www.eurofound.europa.eu/data/platform-economy/initiatives/collective-agreement-between-assodelivery-and-ugl.

[50] It is worth noting that Italian Decree no 101/2019 introduced new provisions of social protection for the self-employed delivery platform workers. Although this is a legislative instrument, it also enhances collective bargaining in the sector. As regards working time, it prescribes that the agreements must contain clauses to remunerate night work, weekend and holiday work, and work during unfavourable weather conditions, which must be at least 10% higher than the standard pay. Eurofound, 'Social protection for self-employed delivery platform workers' (9 April 2021), available at: www.eurofound.europa.eu/data/platform-economy/initiatives/social-protection-for-self-employed-delivery-platform-workers.

[51] Case *C-67/96 Albany International BV v Stichting Bedrijfspensioenfonds Textielindustrie* [1999] ECLI:EU:C:1999:430, paras 53–58.

of fundamental rights in the EU, such as freedom of assembly and collective bargaining between employers and workers. Beyond CJEU case law, EU primary law also underlined the importance of collective bargaining in several instruments. According to Article 152 of the Treaty on the Functioning of the European Union (TFEU), the Union recognises and promotes the role of the social partners and facilitates dialogue between them. Article 28 of the Charter of Fundamental Rights of the European Union (CFREU) also speaks of 'workers and employers, or their respective organisations', when it guarantees the right 'to negotiate and conclude collective agreements'. Furthermore, the European Pillar of Social Rights states that social partners 'shall be encouraged to negotiate and conclude collective agreements in matters relevant to them, while respecting their autonomy and the right to collective action'.[53]

It does not follow from these provisions that the right to collective bargaining should be narrowly interpreted, covering only employees.[54] EU labour law and respective CJEU case law tend to accept that the right to collective bargaining may extend beyond the national category of employees. The above-mentioned legal texts all refer to workers and their respective organisations, which leads us to the labour law literature on the EU concept of worker, in particular regarding the right to collective bargaining.[55] However, it is still unclear and widely debated in EU labour law and also in labour law literature, where the right to collective bargaining ends in terms of its personal scope.[56] The old task comes in a new role, since it is not an employment relationship calling for a definition and judiciary test, but this time genuine self-employment that should be defined. This definition and test would bring about the clear demarcation of the right to conclude a collective agreement (among other legal issues).

And here comes the central problem, as EU competition law instruments, primarily Article 101 TFEU, are founded on a far more simplified personal scope divided into the two strict groups of employees and undertakings. However, the clear lines between hierarchical labour relations versus actions among business actors (undertakings) supplying goods to serve consumer demand have become blurred. The dogmatic basis of such a distinction in personal scope has served, that

[52] Case C-341/05 *Laval un Partneri Ltd v Svenska Byggnadsarbetareförbundet and Others* [2007] ECLI:EU:C:2007:809, para 91.

[53] ec.europa.eu/info/sites/default/files/social-summit-european-pillar-social-rights-booklet_en.pdf, Right/Principle Nr 08 Social dialogue and involvement of workers.

[54] Although the European Pillar of Social Rights implies potential EU law and national limitations to the right to collective bargaining and actions.

[55] See, for instance: Martin Risak and Thomas Dullinger, *The concept of 'worker' in EU law. Status quo and potential for change* (ETUI aisbl 2018); Emanuele Menegatti, 'Taking EU Labour Law Beyond the Employment Contract: The Role Played by the European Court of Justice' (2019) 11 *European Labour Law Journal* 26.

[56] See, eg: Mark Freedland and Nicola Countouris, 'Some Reflections on the "Personal Scope" of Collective Labour Law' (2017) 46 *Industrial Law Journal* 52; Marco Biasi, '"We Will All Laugh at Gilded Butterflies". The Shadow of Antitrust Law on the Collective Negotiation of Fair Fees for Self-Employed Workers' (2018) 9 *European Labour Law Journal* 354.

genuine undertakings, bearing financial risks in the market, would be banned to prevent, restrict or distort competition within the internal market.

For labour lawyers it has become quite clear in recent years, that the ban on collective bargaining should not include those formally classified as non-employees. The hardship comes from the clear definition of the personal scope of this right and the way it is limited. There have been several proposals[57] and initiatives by the European Commission[58] to overcome this stalemate. Nevertheless, the present legal situation in EU law is far from satisfactory as national provisions ensuring the right to collective bargaining for self-employed workers may be challenged before the European Court of Justice. This may happen in the case of (new) laws adopted in Member States, but also in consequence of legal disputes on existing practices (as in the *Albany*,[59] *Becu*[60] cases etc).

As the examples analysed in section IV.A show, these EU law constraints do not stop collective negotiations with digital platforms, but EU law is far from the wide perception of collective negotiations envisaged by Article 28 CFREU. We must take the *FNV Kunsten* decision as the last word so far in this story, whereby not only the right to collective bargaining is restricted, but the right to be covered by the scope of collective agreements at any level.[61] In the following section, we will show the impediments of collective bargaining with platforms at national level through the Hungarian example.

VI. Impediments at National Level: The Hungarian Experience

Hungary can be characterised as a typical Eastern European collective labour law system with weak social partners, low collective bargaining coverage (around 20 per cent) and practically non-existent sectoral-level negotiations. So, collective agreements play a minimal role in employment regulation, if at all, it exists

[57] In particular: Ioannis Lianos, Nicola Countouris and Valerio De Stefano, 'Re-thinking the competition law/labour law interaction: Promoting a fairer labour market' (2019) 10 *European Labour Law Journal* 291; Tamás Gyulavári, 'Collective rights of platform workers: The role of EU law' (2020) 27 *Maastricht Journal of European and Comparative Law* 406; Michael Doherty and Valentina Fránca, 'Solving the "Gig-saw"? Collective rights and platform work' (2020) 49 *Industrial Law Journal* 352; Prassl (n 47).

[58] Commission, 'First Phase Consultation of Social Partners Under Article 154 TFEU on Possible Action Addressing the Challenges Related to Working Conditions in Platform Work' (Consultation Document) C(2021) 1127 final; Commission 'Second-Phase Consultation of Social Partners Under Article 154 TFEU on Possible Action Addressing the Challenges Related to Working Conditions in Platform Work' (Consultation Document) C(2021) 4230 final; European Parliament, 'European Parliament Resolution of 16 September 2021 on fair working conditions, rights and social protection for platform workers – new forms of employment linked to digital development (2019/2186(INI))' (16 September 2021) P9_TA(2021)0385.

[59] *Albany* (n 51).

[60] Case C-22/98 *Jean Claude Becu and Others* [1999] ECLI:EU:C:1999:419.

[61] *FNV Kunsten* (n 7).

merely at (large) company level.[62] As for the other side of the story, the share of Hungarian platform work is low in a Western European,[63] but remarkable in a regional (Eastern European) comparison. According to the ETUI Survey, internet work is most widespread in Poland and Slovakia, while platform work is most frequent in Hungary.[64] So the country features a pre-matured collective bargaining system with a rapidly growing, but moderately sized platform industry.

The working conditions of platform workers is certainly defined by their legal status, as Hungarian employment law is a clear binary model based on the classical principle of 'all or no protection'. Therefore, platform workers may either be employees in a typical or atypical employment relationship under the Labour Code (with all employment protection), or self-employed entrepreneurs under the Civil Code (without any employment protection). The latter (self-employment) may be performed in several forms, such as a natural person, individual entrepreneur, or company member. Self-employed persons always contract through a civil law service contract, which does not involve any employment protection.[65] Since platforms and their workers go equally for the cheapest employment solution with the lowest taxes and social security contributions, thus, they almost exclusively opt for the cheaper self-employment. Although there are no statistics in this regard, practice shows that platform workers are dominantly self-employed workers. And the labour law situation described above, in our view, is also typical for other countries in Eastern Europe.

Within the above outlined national labour law framework, collective agreements simply cannot have a significant part in shaping the working conditions of platform workers. Most importantly, it is only an employee who can be covered by a collective agreement, since 'the scope of collective agreements may cover … rights and obligations arising out of or in connection with employment relationships'.[66] So a platform worker may fall under the scope of a collective agreement, at any level, if she is an employee. If platform workers are self-employed, they are automatically excluded from the right to be covered by a collective agreement, also at sector level.

As for employee representation, collective agreements are concluded primarily by trade unions. Trade unions are associations (under civil law),[67] so

[62] Tamás Gyulavári, 'Chasing the Holy Grail? Stumbling Collective Bargaining in Eastern Europe and the Hungarian Experiment' in Sylvaine Laulom (ed), *Collective Bargaining Developments in Times of Crisis* (Kluwer Law International 2017).

[63] Agnieszka Piasna and Jan Drahokoupil, *Digital labour in Central and Eastern Europe: Evidence from the ETUI Internet and Platform Work Survey* (ETUI 2019) 6.

[64] Csaba Makó, Miklós Illéssy and Saeed Nosratabadi, 'Emerging Platform Work in Europe: Hungary in Cross-country Comparison' (2020) 5(2) *European Journal of Workplace Innovation*, available at: journal.uia.no/index.php/EJWI/issue/view/91 147, 157-158; Piasna and Drahokoupil (n 63) 18.

[65] Makó, Illéssy and Nosratabadi (n 64) 162–65; Tamás Gyulavári, 'Internetes munka a magyar jogban – Tiltás helyett szabályozás?' (2018) 3 *Pro Futuro*, available at: ojs.lib.unideb.hu/profuturo/article/view/2903/2902, 83.

[66] Art 277(1)a) of the Labour Code (Act 1 of 2012).

[67] Act 5 of 2013 on the Civil Code and Act 175 of 2011 on civil organisations.

any non-employee platform worker may freely be a member. According to the definition in the Labour Code, 'trade union shall mean all organizations of workers whose primary function is the enhancement and protection of employees' interests related to their employment relationship'.[68] So trade union membership is open for platform workers, but trade unions represent 'primarily' the social and economic interests of employees. It is debatable, therefore, whether 'secondarily' they are also allowed to represent self-employed workers. But this right clearly does not extend to the right to conclude a collective agreement with a personal scope extending to them.

Sector-level agreements hardly exist despite some rare exceptions[69] and legislative efforts.[70] This results in a deformed structure, concentrated on company level, which is remarkably different from the dominant European collective bargaining model. There is an extension mechanism of the scope of collective agreements;[71] however, the scope of the extended collective agreement may cover only employees, exactly as at company level.[72] Therefore, sector-level and extended collective agreements presently cannot play any role in the regulation of platform work (beyond covered employees).

Apart from trade unions, works councils, elected by employees, may also conclude 'normative works agreements', which may in fact replace collective agreements if the employer is not covered by a collective agreement, and there is no trade union at the employer with entitlement to conclude a collective agreement.[73] But even this quasi-collective agreement may cover only employees. Unfortunately, there is no data on the number of such quasi collective (works) agreements, but their role is most probably very limited in the entire labour market.

As a whole, the Hungarian system of collective agreements is unable to affect the working conditions of platform workers. This evaluation may be underpinned by several factors and arguments. Above all, the entire collective bargaining system is fading away and struggling with fundamental structural problems. If there is any collective bargaining, it is present in large companies at workplace level. Sector-level agreements and extended collective agreements play a marginal role.

Collective agreement coverage has traditionally been low since its birth in 1992,[74] compared with the 'old' EU Member States. However, even this moderate coverage has been diminishing since the adoption of the new Labour Code

[68] Art 270(2)a) of the Labour Code.

[69] There are some sector-level collective agreements from time to time, for instance in electricity supply (see: www.vd.hu/villamosenergia-ipari-agazati-kollektiv-szerzodesek_29939).

[70] See, in particular, Act 74 of 2009 on sectoral dialogue committees and medium level social dialogue.

[71] Extension of collective agreements is regulated by Arts 15–18 of Act 74 of 2009.

[72] Art 15 of Act 74 of 2009.

[73] Art 268(1) of the Labour Code.

[74] Act 22 of 1992 on the Labour Code introduced the new employment regulation after the political changes in 1990.

in 2012, resulting in the present circa 20 per cent coverage. Moreover, about 15 per cent of all workers fall outside the scope of the Labour Code (as non-employees). Since only employees may be covered by a collective agreement, thus, even fewer than 20 per cent of all workers are covered by any collective agreement. So platform work cannot be protected by collective agreements, and the extension of the right would not mean a great change due to the weaknesses of the whole system of collective bargaining. Therefore, statutory law will play the dominant role in regulation of platform workers' working conditions if legislation undertakes this project (at all).[75] As a final positive remark, this does not mean that reforms in EU and Hungarian labour law could not lead to some changes in the present framework.

VII. Conclusions: Objectives and Obstacles

We presented the arguments that show why collective agreements are useful regulatory tools in regulating working conditions in the labour market in general, and for platform workers especially. They may better the working conditions of vulnerable workers, balance competition within the labour market and fill legislative gaps. So collective negotiations between platforms and their workers, both at company and sector level, have several advantages.

However, this process is impeded by various legal constraints. At EU level, antitrust rules require the exclusion of undertakings from the right to conclude a collective agreement and to be covered by one. Since the demarcation line between employee and undertaking is far from clear and exact, the exclusion of all non-employees is the present competition law practice. Many proposals are on the table, but presently the right to collective bargaining is not ensured for self-employed platform workers.

This limitation in EU law has a negative effect on national labour laws, although these also mostly follow the binary model, providing all or no protection for platform workers. In addition, the weak system of collective bargaining is often also an obstacle in itself. Still, despite all the pitfalls and barriers, there are companies and workers negotiating on the working conditions in the platform economy with significant first achievements. The next step labour law shall take at both the EU and national level is to clear the unnecessary legal obstacles in the way of these autonomous processes.

[75] There has not been any legislative activity in this field.

7

Voluntary Commitments as Alternative Instruments for Standard-Setting? The Example of the German 'Code of Conduct – Paid Crowdsourcing for the Better'

JUDITH BROCKMANN

I. Introduction

The changing labour environment of the gig economy[1] has challenged traditional instruments of labour law regulation and industrial relations.[2] As the right to conclude collective bargaining agreements and their application are often limited to employees, soft law may seem an alternative solution to set minimum standards. One example of such a soft law instrument is the German Code of Conduct – Paid Crowdsourcing for the Better,[3] which will be presented in this chapter, and which resulted from negotiations between employers.

Since soft law has limited normative power, it is rightly argued that it cannot substitute for collective bargaining. However, such alternative forms of rule-making may contribute to ameliorate working conditions. Soft law rules are more easily applicable as they do not depend on the qualification of the individual contract and the legal status of workers. So, they may be used even if collective bargaining agreements are legally limited to employees or are not applicable for other reasons.

[1] Linda Nierling, Bettina-Johanna Krings and Leon Küstermann, *The Landscape of Crowd Work in Germany: An overview of the scientific and public discourse* (Karlsruher Institut für Technologie 2020).

[2] Antonio Aloisi, 'Negotiating the digital transformation of work: non-standard workers' voice, collective rights and mobilisation practices in the platform economy' (2019) 3 EUI Working Papers, available at: cadmus.eui.eu/bitstream/handle/1814/63264/MWP_Aloisi_2019_03.pdf?sequence=1; Georg Jäger et al, 'Crowdworking: working with or against the crowd?' (2019) 14 *Journal of Economic Interaction and Coordination* 761.

[3] Crowdsourcing: crowdsourcing-code.com.

After taking a look at the elaboration of the Code of Conduct and its context, a brief presentation of the content of the German Code of Conduct will follow. It will be analysed focusing on three aspects: (1) the lack of a legally binding nature; (2) its scope and its applicability; and (3) the access to rights and enforcement mechanisms.

As the German example of the Ombuds Office shows, trade unions and employers may even set up alternative conflict resolution mechanisms, facilitating and ameliorating the access to rights of crowdworkers as well as potentially preparing the field for future collective bargaining. The negotiation and the involvement in alternative conflict resolution bodies also raise the visibility of the trade unions among crowdworkers, possibly incentivising them to organise. Finally, the content of soft law such as the German Code of Conduct may also influence legislative initiatives to set minimum standards for platform work.

II. The Code of Conduct in the View of Initiatives on Crowdwork in Germany

The elaboration of the Code of Conduct may be seen in the general context of the development of platform work. The German government has monitored the development of platform work from an early stage,[4] however, the government and the legislator have been reluctant to regulate on the issues arising from platform work.[5] So, dealing with legal issues arising in the context of platform work has been left to the actors in the field,[6] and – only recently – to the courts.[7] Over the last years, several initiatives concerning crowdwork can be noticed in Germany, in particular on the trade union side. They have led to the establishment of informal cooperation between stakeholders on the platforms side and trade unions.[8]

[4] Federal Ministry of Labour and Social Affairs, *Re-Imagining Work. Green Paper Work 4.0* (Federal Ministry of Labour and Social Affairs 2015) 15; Federal Ministry of Labour and Social Affairs, *Re-Imagining Work, White Paper Work 4.0* (Federal Ministry of Labour and Social Affairs 2017) 55 ff and passim.

[5] Johannes Kiess, 'The gig economy and social partnership in Germany: towards a German Model 4.0?' (SNIS Project, 2017), available at: snis.ch/projects/gig-economy-and-its-implications-for-social-dialogue-and-workers-protection/.

[6] See also Hannah Johnston and Chris Land-Kazlauskas, *Organizing On-Demand: Representation, Voice, and Collective Bargaining in the Gig Economy* (International Labour Office 2019).

[7] BAG 1.12.2020, 9 AZR 102/20, ECLI:DE:BAG:2020:011220.U.9AZR102.20.0: www.rechtsprechung-im-internet.de/jportal/portal/t/19ke/page/bsjrsprod.psml?pid=Dokumentanzeige&showdoccase=1&js_peid=Trefferliste&documentnumber=1&numberofresults=10908&fromdoctodoc=yes&doc.id=KARE600061600&doc.part=L&doc.price=0.0&doc.hl=1#focuspoint.

[8] See Thomas Haipeter and Feliciano Iudicone, 'New Social Initiatives on Cloud – and Gigwork – Germany and Italy Compared' (2020) 2 *Hungarian Labour Law E-Journal*, available at: www.ias.jak.ppke.hu/letolt/2020_2_a/03_ThHaipeter_FIudicone_hllj_uj_2020_2.pdf 17 for a detailed analysis.

A. The Frankfurt Paper on Platform-Based Work

Here, 'The Frankfurt Paper on Platform-Based Work'[9] should be mentioned. The declaration consists in proposals for platform operators, clients, policymakers, workers and worker organisations to discuss social aspects of platform work. Within the topics are the social and economic consequences of platform work and the role of trade unions. Also, it calls to evaluate and discuss

> the possibilities for a 'co-operative turn' in labor-management relations in the 'platform economy,' in which workers, clients, platform operators, investors, policy makers, and worker organisations work together to improve outcomes for all stakeholders; and potential recommendations for platform operators, clients, policy makers, researchers and research funders, and other actors in the platform economy.[10]

Conceptualised by a group of trade unions and worker organisations, ie, the Arbeiterkammer (Austrian Chamber of Labour), the Österreichischer Gewerkschaftsbund – ÖGB (Austrian Trade Union Federation), HK Denmark (Danish Union of Commercial and Clerical Workers), Industriegewerkschaft Metall – IG Metall (German Metalworkers Union), International Brotherhood of Teamsters Local 117 (Washington State, USA), Service Employees International Union – SEIU (USA); Unionen (Swedish Trade Union) and expert advice, it was elaborated after a first international workshop in April 2016[11] and adopted on 6 December 2016.

The declaration may be considered as a call for cooperation with interested platforms to develop decent labour conditions. It reads (in extracts):

> We propose therefore that the growth of platform-based work presents a *novel opportunity for the development of a 'co-operative turn' in labor-management relations*. The 'traditional' conflictual processes of labor-management relations have secured crucial rights for workers over the years and will continue to be important. *But insofar as platform operators understand that their own long-term well-being, and that of society at large, is bound up with the ability of workers – regardless of legal status – to secure good work, future labor-management interactions may be organized around interests deeply shared by all parties*. This possibility offers the hope of great gains for all parties.[12]

Some core issues in the declaration are:

- The respect for the right of crowdworkers to organise.
- Salaries corresponding to minimum or collective agreement wages applicable in the crowdworker's location.

[9] Fair Crowd Work, 'The Frankfurt Declaration on Platform-Based Work', available at: faircrowd.work/unions-for-crowdworkers/frankfurt-declaration.

[10] ibid.

[11] Nierling, Krings and Küstermann (n 1) 50.

[12] Fair Crowd Work (n 9) 10 (emphasis added).

- The possibility to earn an adequate income within the time frame of a full-time position.
- The guarantee for crowdworkers of access to social protection independently of their employment status.
- The respect of national law and international principles.
- Cooperation with stakeholders at both local and national level.
- Information on the employment status of crowdworkers.
- Transparency regarding the business model of platforms.

The Frankfurt declaration can be considered as a reaction to challenges for social partnership and collective bargaining in the gig economy currently being broadly discussed.

B. Challenges for Social Partnership and Collective Bargaining in the Gig Economy

Some of the characteristics of the gig economy challenge the traditional models, modes and instruments of industrial relations and social partnership and collective bargaining in particular. Without claiming to be exhaustive, some of them are recalled below.[13]

Identifying, organising and representing collective interests of crowdworkers is more difficult than in the 'analogue' world. Workers tend to work on their own rather than in teams. Typically, they do not even have a common working place where they regularly meet. While 'on-demand' app workers may meet each other physically by accident or intentionally (eg, riders or drivers), this is not the case for crowdworkers carrying out activities exclusively online that do not require contact with each other. This is especially true when the crowd is global. So, there might be little or no coherence as a 'collective'. These circumstances do not promote the expression and organisation of collective interests. Traditional trade union work and membership recruitment is not suited to this working environment, one reason being that their starting point is usually the workplace, which plays a central role. Trade unions are on their way, and need to adapt their activities and collective action to the gig economy. As a matter of fact, currently, the large majority of crowdworkers is not unionised.[14]

[13] See, in detail, Antonio Aloisi, 'A Thematic Working Paper for the Annual Conference of the European Centre of Expertise (ECE) in the field of labour law, employment and labour market policies: Exploring ways to improve working conditions of platform workers: The role of EU labour law' (European Union 2019), available at: www.researchgate.net/publication/340548183_Platform_Work_in_the_EU_Lessons_learned_legal_developments_and_challenges_ahead; Dominik Leist, Christina Hießl and Monika Schlachter, 'Plattformökonomie – eine Literaturauswertung' (Bundesministerium für Arbeit und Soziales 2017), available at: nbn-resolving.org/ urn:nbn:de:0168-ssoar-55486-2.

[14] Jeremias Prassl, *Collective Voice in the Platform Economy: Challenges, Opportunities, Solutions* (ETUC 2018) 14 ff; Thomas Haipeter, 'Don't Gig Up, German Case Study Report' (Don't Gig Up 2019),

Challenges are also related to their employment status. In many national legal systems, the employment status of platform workers is not explicitly regulated and they are often qualified as self-employed rather than employees in a labour law governed relationship.[15] As many legal systems reserve the right to conclude collective agreements for employees in a labour relationship, there is little incentive to collectively bargain in favour of platform workers. If the legal framework allows for collective bargaining for the self-employed, the question of possible representation (who is bargaining?) and meeting the conditions for the conclusion of agreements existing in some national legal orders, for example, the representativeness criterion, need to be answered to promote collective bargaining in the gig economy. These questions are partly addressed in the Member States and currently discussed on a European Union level.[16]

Another challenge for collective bargaining and the conclusion of agreements is the transnational (if not global) character of working relationships in the gig economy, in particular when it comes to online performed (crowd) work. Transnational situations challenge the conclusion of collective bargaining agreements.[17] This does not only concern the determination of the applicable law.[18] Examples from the 'analogue era' show that the conclusion of transnational agreements is possible and beneficial for all parties involved. However, these examples also show that strong representation of collective interests is needed to overcome any obstacles to collective bargaining and to generate sufficient negotiating pressure. These usually thrive on the good cooperation of established social partners, which is (still) lacking in the gig economy.

C. The Elaboration of the Code of Conduct

The Code of Conduct in its actual shape has been elaborated by crowdsourcing platforms together with representatives and experts of the German trade union IG Metall and the support of the Deutscher Crowdsourcing Verband eV (DCV). They built upon the basis of a firm-level code of conduct, introduced by the platform Testbirds in 2015.[19] Testbirds then invited other platforms to join the

available at: www.dontgigup.eu/wp-content/uploads/2020/05/Casestudy_DE.pdf; Haipeter and Iudicone (n 8).

[15] See Harald Hauben, Marta Kahancová and Anna Manoudi, *European Centre of Expertise in the field of labour law, employment and labour market policies: Thematic Review 2021 on Platform Work* (Publications Office of the European Union 2021) for a comprehensive overview.

[16] See Luca Ratti's contribution (ch 3) in this volume.

[17] See Gregor Thüsing, 'International Framework Agreements: Rechtliche Grenzen und praktischer Nutzen' (2010) 63 *Recht der Arbeit* 78.

[18] On these problems see also Commission, 'First Phase Consultation of Social Partners Under Article 154 TFEU on Possible Action Addressing the Challenges Related to Working Conditions in Platform Work' (Consultation Document) C(2021) 1127 final, 16 f.

[19] Sahil Deva and Veronika Wasza, 'Testbirds – Software testing solutions in the crowdsourcing industry' in Werner Wobbe, Elva Bova and Catalin Dragomirescu-Gaina (eds), *The digital economy and the single market* (FEBS 2017) 62 et seq.

initiative and started collaborating with IG Metall. In 2017, a revised version of the Code of Conduct was published. Initially it was signed by five platforms, some resigned and others have joined since then. One of the most important achievements of this revised version is the provision of an Ombuds Office.

III. The Code of Conduct: A Brief Presentation

A. The Content

The Code of Conduct contains statements on the 'Objective and Purpose', the 'Area of Application'[20] and sets out 10 substantive principles. Its content will be briefly described in the following section.

The Code of Conduct is conceived as a 'self-imposed guideline for prominent crowdsourcing companies' that 'will be continuously developed and improved'. It aims to 'create a basis for a trusting and fair cooperation between service providers, clients and crowdworkers, supplementary to current legislation'.

The scope of the Code of Conduct is limited to the members who 'commit to follow the indicated principles and to promote them within their company as well as with collaborating parties'. The text underlines that it is a 'voluntary and self-regulated' instrument. The signatory members commit to 'constant exchange with politics, science and other social groups such as unions or associations'. It is open for new platforms to join.

The Code of Conduct endows 10 principles, addressing the following topics and issues.

1. Tasks in conformance with the law: platforms commit in particular not to offer jobs that contain illegal, discriminating, fraudulent, demagogic, violent or anti-constitutional content as well as to respect regulations regarding age limitations.
2. Clarification on legal situations: platforms commit 'to inform the crowdworkers about the legal regulations in general and tax regulations in particular, connected to crowdworking'. If they are not allowed to do so under national law, 'they inform the crowdworkers that they have to take care of the legal matters themselves'.
3. Fair payment: all subscribers commit to pay a fair and appropriate wage. The Code of Conduct also contains general guidelines on calculating wages considering, for example, 'task complexity, necessary qualifications, local dependence and wage standards as well as predicted expenditure of time'. Transparent communication is required concerning the possible wage in the case of the satisfactory execution of the task as well as the payment conditions.

[20] All citations in the following section, except indicated otherwise, refer to the Code of Conduct: crowdsourcing-code.com.

4. Motivating and good work: platforms commit to 'providing a user-friendly and intuitive platform to navigate, as well as direct possibilities to request support'. The Code of Conduct gives examples for measures that 'shall be taken to meet the expectations of crowdworkers regarding motivating and fulfilling work', including training opportunities for crowdworkers registered on the platform.
5. Respectful interaction: the platforms commit to core values such as reliability, trust, honesty, openness and mutual respect. They stress their importance in the triangle relationship between clients, crowdworkers and platforms as 'intermediar[ies]' between them.
6. Clear tasks and reasonable timing: the platforms engage in transparent descriptions of the tasks, including time and content, respecting the interests of both clients and crowdworkers.
7. Freedom and flexibility: crowdworkers working with subscribers of the Code of Conduct choose to accept or refuse offered tasks. 'The refusal … should not lead to negative consequences and no pressure should be applied by the platform providers'.
8. Constructive feedback and open communication: the Code of Conduct stresses the importance of good communication, prompt feedback, assistance and technical support. The platforms engage to encourage communication between crowdworkers and implement technical features to promote it 'provided it is helping the execution of the project and is technically possible'.
9. Regulated approval process and rework: the Code of Conduct provides for transparent approval processes and preliminary information of the crowdworker on the procedures. In general, the 'denial of projects must be justified and based on the project description' and 'the possibility of reworking must be given unless the project specifications do not allow for it'. The Code of Conduct also provides for the appointment of a so-called Ombuds Office.
10. Data protection and privacy: one of the most important principles provides for the '[r]espect for and protection of the crowdworkers' privacy', including personal data or contact information. They may not be revealed to third parties without written consent. This also applies to information concerning the clients. Platforms should act under confidentiality.

Principle 9 of the Code of Conduct in its latest version states that 'every platform commits to set a fair and neutral complaint process for crowdworkers. If the crowdworker and the platform could not come to an agreement, the Ombuds Office which has been established for this purpose, can be called upon'. The Ombuds Office was appointed in November 2017. In September 2018, the latest rules of procedure (the Rules) were published, and are available both in German and English.[21]

[21] ombudsstelle.crowdwork-igmetall.de/rules.html; ombudsstelle.crowdwork-igmetall.de/en.html.

The Rules provide that the five members of the Ombuds Office are appointed for one year by the signatories of the Code of Conduct as follows:

- One neutral Chair.
- One representative of the German Crowdsourcing Association (Deutscher Crowdsourcing Verband eV)
- One representative of the German Confederation of Trade Unions (Deutscher Gewerkschaftsbund) or one of its member unions.
- One representative from one of the platforms that has signed the Code of Conduct.
- One worker that is registered on one of the platforms that has signed the Code of Conduct.

The administration of the Ombuds Office is operated by the German trade union IG Metall. The starting point of the procedure is adapted to the working environment: complaints can be introduced via email (§ 4(3) of the Rules), they may be filed via an internet form, equally available in German and English.[22]

The Ombuds Office has a double competence. On the one hand, it mediates disputes that arise between workers and platforms that are signatories to the Code of Conduct (§2(1) of the Rules). The Rules provide a clause of subsidiarity. The parties who require legal protection may only call upon the Ombuds Office once other extra-legal bilateral attempts to resolve the situation are unsuccessfully exhausted (§ 2(2) and § 4(1) of the Rules).

On the other hand, the Ombuds Office monitors respect of the Code of Conduct in general. Signatories of the Code of Conduct, a registered worker, IG Metall or the DCV may appeal to the Ombuds Office indicating that a platform inappropriately proclaims that it adheres to the Code of Conduct (§ 4(2) of the Rules) because it has violated the Code of Conduct multiple times and should no longer be entitled to claim that it adheres to the Code of Conduct. In such cases, the Ombuds Office will decide whether the right to claim adherence to the Code of Conduct is to be revoked (§ 2(2) of the Rules).

Attention shall be drawn to some procedural particularities. The Rules provide that the duration of a procedure should not exceed a period of three month (§ 7(1) of the Rules). The procedure itself is free of cost, and every party supports their own costs. Section 7(2) of the Rules provides – especially when dealing with individual complaints of platform workers – a 'low-cost process', preferring video conferencing over in-person meetings.

If the worker filing the complaint lives in a country other than Germany, a representative from a trade union based in that country may join the Ombuds Office process in an advisory capacity, if the worker wishes (§ 3(4) of the Rules).

[22] ombudsstelle.crowdwork-igmetall.de/en.html.

The Ombuds Office publishes annual reports on its activities.[23] Until today, it has dealt with more than 40 cases. It should be stressed, that the Ombuds Office has used its annual report to publish basic legal opinions on the interpretation of the principles of the Code of Conduct that arose on the occasion of disputes.[24] The reports also show that the Ombuds Office has proposed structural changes to platforms to avoid disputes, on the occasion of the individual proceedings. In particular, it recommended in several cases to establish worker advisory boards to which workers could turn with suggestions for improvements regarding the platform's work processes and functionality.[25]

B. Signatory Parties

Obviously, joining the Code of Conduct is totally voluntary. Even though elaborated in collaboration with the trade union IG Metall, it is set up as a voluntary engagement by the platforms and not signed by the trade union. Originally, five platforms signed the Code of Conduct, others joined quickly in 2017. Meanwhile, two platforms have resigned from the Code of Conduct, and two new platforms joined in 2019.[26] Today, it is applied by nine platforms.

The group of signatories[27] is very diverse, in many aspects: the platforms offer all sorts of micro-tasks from data collection to testing, but also highly specialised creative tasks in design, text production or translation. They offer on-location work on demand or pure online, virtual crowdwork, so tasks are executed either locally or globally. Business activities are run on very different levels: either limited to national or regional level or worldwide. All sorts of legal business models can be found. Also, the platforms' company sizes differ, both in terms of turnover figures and registered platform workers. Most, but not all signatory platforms are German-based.[28] In total, the number of registered crowdworkers can be estimated at two million.[29]

[23] Ombuds Office, *Annual reports on the activities in 2017 to 2018* (Frankfurt 2019) and *2019* (Frankfurt 2020), available at: ombudsstelle.crowdwork-igmetall.de/en.html.

[24] Ombuds Office, *Report of the activities of the Ombuds Office of the Code of Conduct for Paid Crowdsourcing, 2019* (2020), available at: ombudsstelle.crowdwork-igmetall.de/pdf/Ombuds_Office_for_paid_Crowdsourcing_Report_2019_EN.pdf, 2 ff.

[25] Ombuds Office, *Report of the activities of the Ombuds Office of the Code of Conduct for Paid Crowdsourcing, 2017–2018* (2019), available at: ombudsstelle.crowdwork-igmetall.de/pdf/Ombuds_Office_for_paid_Crowdsourcing_Report_2017_2018_EN.pdf, 2.

[26] Robert Fuss, 'Textbroker und Jovoto treten dem "Code of Conduct" für Crowdworking bei' (Fair Work Crowd, 5 July 2019), available at: faircrowd.work/de/2019/07/05/textbroker-und-jovoto-treten-dem-code-of-conduct-fuer-crowdworking-bei/.

[27] Testbirds; Clickworker; Content.de; Crowdguru; Streetspotr; AppJobber; Digivante; Jovoto; TextBroker; crowdsourcing-code.com.

[28] Information is drawn from the websites of the platforms: www.testbirds.com/company/about-us/company-history/; www.clickworker.com/about-us/; www.content.de; www.crowdguru.de/en/about-us/; streetspotr.com; en.appjobber.com; www.digivante.com/about-us/; www.jovoto.com/about; www.textbroker.co.uk/about-textbroker.

[29] Nierling, Krings and Küstermann (n 1) 49.

C. Old and New Issues

Considering the content of the Code of Conduct in comparison to 'traditional' collective agreements, it is noticeable that numerous conventional topics are dealt with. Admittedly, this is done much less concretely than in collective agreements. The commitment to compliance with legal regulations hardly seems innovative. Transparency obligations (Principle 2) are recognised in labour law, but in terms of civil law contracts with self-employed workers they may be regarded as an *acquis*. Payment and wages (Principle 3) are classical issues. Other topics such as motivating and good work (Principle 4), respectful interaction (Principle 5) and feedback and open communication (Principle 8) are not traditional. However, they concern and establish rather a certain culture in the contractual – and working – relationship, than legally important working conditions or social protection. Thus, they may be suitable for promoting a more worker-friendly environment in the gig economy.[30] Clear tasks and reasonable timing (Principle 6) evoke working time as a traditional issue. Even though the Code of Conduct does not mention limits to working time, it requires at least clear task definition and reasonable time planning, giving the crowdworkers enough time to fulfil their tasks. Principle 7 on 'freedom and flexibility' is a reaction to the specific situation of platform work. It requires, in particular, that the refusal of offered tasks should not lead to any negative consequences and that no pressure should be applied by the platforms. With regard to the reported practices of many platforms, this principle potentially leads to better working conditions. Principle 9 concerning regulated and transparent approval processes and rework can be considered to deal with new issues. The approval process, the acceptance and denial of work provided by platform workers is particularly important. This is also true for the possibilities of reworking with a platform. Data protection and privacy, addressed in Principle 10, are not genuinely new issues, but they are of increased importance in the gig economy. However, a worker's rights concerning the algorithms used by the platforms, an issue that may be considered to be crucial,[31] is not mentioned in the Code of Conduct.

IV. Legal Analysis

In the following section, selected legal aspects shall be discussed. The – lack of – legally binding force, the scope and applicability, and contribution of the Code of Conduct to facilitate the access to rights seem of particular interest.

[30] Andrea Suchanek, 'Nutzen und Kosten von Verhaltensregeln aus unternehmensethischer Sicht' (2011) 1 *Neue Zeitschrift für Arbeitsrecht – Beilage* 3, 4.

[31] See Valerio De Stefano, '"Negotiating the Algorithm": Automation, Artificial Intelligence and Labour Protection' (2019) 41 *Comparative Labor Law & Policy Journal* 15.

A. Legally Binding Nature

Voluntary agreements have no legally binding force as such. This is one of the characteristics of soft law. In this perspective, they cannot be regarded as alternatives to collective bargaining agreements and cannot replace them. Their limited legal value does not allow for a level of protection or guarantees, comparable to collective bargaining agreements. Obviously, soft law instruments such as the Code of Conduct cannot guarantee that platform workers enjoy the same level of social protection as so-called 'standard workers'.[32] However, besides the moral incentive for platforms to observe the voluntary engagement, there might be different legal mechanisms that render the Code of Conduct binding.

The first approach only concerns the platforms/subscribers themselves. This is because, unlike charters at the company level, mutual control is created through joint, cross-company engagement. This is institutionalised by the Code of Conduct through the competence given to the Ombuds Office. It makes compliance with the Code of Conduct controllable. Compliance with the principles is surely voluntary, but not arbitrary. And in this way, platforms that do not comply with the Code of Conduct can be excluded, in which case they lose the right to invoke the Code of Conduct and use the adherence as a competitive advantage. Some national legal systems may provide special legal instruments such as unilateral commitments of the employer that might be applicable. In other cases, where the binding nature of the agreement cannot be based on labour law, it has to be found in common civil law.

One approach could be to argue that the Code of Conduct becomes part of the terms of the contract. This would theoretically allow for the platform worker to sue for its enforcement. This seems problematic, because the terms of the Code of Conduct remain too general and are not sufficiently detailed. This is characteristic of this kind of voluntary agreement, as it is not limited to one platform, but conceived in very general terms to fit all different kinds of business models, tasks and sizes of platforms.[33] Without further concretisation, the principles established in the Code of Conduct can hardly be considered enforceable.

Another way to conceptualise the legally binding nature would be to consider the Code of Conduct to be one of the bases, or at least an important consideration in the contract. The non-observance of the Code of Conduct can then be regarded as a breach of the principle of good faith. It depends on the national law applicable to the contract whether such a situation would grant the crowdworker a right to claim the application of the rules of the Code of Conduct or rather lead to a claim for damages. In the latter case, of course, damage would have to exist in the first place, and be proven.

[32] On this political claim, see European Parliament, 'European Parliament Resolution of 16 September 2021 on fair working conditions, rights and social protection for platform workers – new forms of employment linked to digital development (2019/2186(INI))' (16 September 2021) P9_TA(2021)0385.

[33] See above, section III.B.

To guarantee the enforcement of the principles set up by the Code of Conduct, independently of the Ombuds Office, it is necessary to transpose them into the contract between the platforms and the crowdworkers.[34] This is typically done by the general terms and conditions. The Code of Conduct itself does not expressively provide for a monitoring procedure of the general terms and conditions of the signatory parties. However, they may be controlled by the Ombuds Office if a claim is introduced indicating that a platform inappropriately proclaims that it adheres to the Code of Conduct (§ 4(2) of the Rules). In this regard, the platform reviews established by the faircrowd.work initiative,[35] rating the working conditions on platforms, including the general terms and conditions, may be very useful.[36]

B. Scope and Applicability

When it comes to the scope of the Code of Conduct its limits are obvious. It is as far from a possible *erga omnes* effect that collective agreements can have under certain conditions as is conceivable. On the platform side it only concerns subscribers, currently nine of them. Even if this might be a considerable share of the most popular platforms in Germany,[37] it is of course only a tiny proportion of the platforms that are present on the national, let alone global market.[38] So even if the Code of Conduct might have an impact on standards in certain small segments of the market, it is far from influencing the competition between platforms even on the national market. It can be doubted that platforms gain a considerable competitive edge from subscribing to the Code of Conduct.

On the other hand, one of the advantages is that the principles are to be applied to all workers registered on a platform. Compared with national legal systems where the binding force of collective agreements may be limited to employees in a labour relationship or trade union members, as is the case in Germany, this may be an advantage. Soft law instruments, such as the Code of Conduct or charters can more easily cover different phenomena of work and labour relationships in the gig economy, not distinguishing between 'work on-demand via app' or 'crowdwork',[39]

[34] On the necessity of transposing national regulation to promote enforcement of soft law, see Eva Kocher, 'Unternehmerische Selbstverpflichtungen im Wettbewerb – Die Transformation von "soft law" in "hard law" durch das Wettbewerbsrecht' [2005] *GRUR – Gewerblicher Rechtsschutz und Urheberrecht* 647 passim.

[35] Markus Ellmer et al, *Platform workers centre stage!* (Hans Boeckler Foundation 2019) 42 ff.

[36] Fair Crowd Work: faircrowd.work.

[37] Catherine Bettina Baethge et al, *Plattformarbeit in Deutschland. Freie und flexible Arbeit ohne soziale Sicherung* (Bertelsmann Stiftung 2019) 14.

[38] Fairwork, *Work in the Planetary Labour Market: Fairwork Cloudwork Ratings 2021* (Fairwork 2021), available at: fair.work/wp-content/uploads/sites/131/2021/06/Fairwork-cloudwork-2021-report.pdf. See also, Michele Cantarella and Chiara Strozzi, 'Workers in the crowd: the labor market impact of the online platform economy' (2021) *Industrial and Corporate Change 2021* 1.

[39] Luca Ratti, 'Online Platforms and Crowdwork in Europe: A Two-step Approach to Expanding Agency Work Provisions?' (2017) 38 *Comparative Labor Law & Policy Journal* 477; Luca Ratti,

'on-location labour platform' and 'online labour platform'.[40] However, in combination with the lack of legally binding force, the (personal) scope of application shows a clear weakness and disadvantage of the Code of Conduct compared with traditional collective agreements.[41]

This is all the more true for the lack of – necessary – participation of the social partners and of workers' representatives in particular. Surely, in a situation characterised by a relatively low rate of unionisation amongst platform workers and legal uncertainty regarding the representation of platform workers' collective interests, the Code of conduct may appear as a suitable solution? In the actual case of the German Code of Conduct, it was an opportunity for the platform companies on the one hand, and for the trade unions on the other, to cooperate. Thus, the implication of trade unions is not at all a (legal) condition for the elaboration of this kind of soft law instrument, characterised by the unilateral nature of the agreement. However, it may be an instrument to build up social partnership in the gig economy.

Finally, one considerable advantage is the independence of the Code of Conduct from the applicable national rule. The legal mechanism of a voluntary commitment overcomes the difficulties regarding transnational collective agreements. But these advantages cannot overcome the lack of participation of the workers and the missing representation of their interests. One of the most important functions of collective bargaining, namely to balance differences in bargaining power and conflicting interests, cannot be fulfilled by such alternative instruments.

C. Access to Rights

It can be discussed whether and how the appointment of the Ombuds Office facilitates or hinders the access of the crowdworkers to rights.

The lack of legally binding force is undoubtedly one of the considerable weaknesses of the Code of Conduct, compared with traditional collective agreements. The fact that the voluntary agreements are not binding and enforceable in detail is a weakness in comparison to collective agreements. That alone makes access to rights more difficult.[42]

'Crowdwork and Work On-Demand in the European Legal Framework: Promises and Expectations' in Maria Teresa Carinci and Filip Dorssemont (eds), *Platform Work in Europe. Towards Harmonisation?* (Intersentia 2021) 203.

[40] Zachary Kilhoffer et al, *Study to Gather Evidence on the Working Conditions of Platform Workers* (Publications Office of the European Union 2020), available at: www.ceps.eu/wp-content/uploads/2020/03/KE-01-20-054-EN-N.pdf.

[41] For a general appreciation on the effectiveness of soft law and unilateral voluntary engagements, see Wolfgang Däubler, 'Soft law und kollektives Arbeitsrecht – Wittenberg-Prozess – Verhaltensrichtlinien von Unternehmen – Ehrenkodex für Betriebsräte' (2011) 1 *Neue Zeitschrift für Arbeitsrecht – Beilage* 42, 44 ff.

[42] Eva Kocher, 'Barrieren der Mobilisierung von Arbeitsrecht – Oder: Lässt sich Fairness erzwingen?' (2012) 1 *Juridikum* 63; Eva Kocher, 'Unternehmen als Adressaten des Arbeitsrechts: Die Bedeutung

However, the Code of Conduct's alternative dispute resolution instrument,[43] the Ombuds Office, can be regarded as a considerable achievement in this respect.

The Code of Conduct requiring a previous attempt to settle the dispute prior to filing a complaint does not seem to be a considerable obstacle to access to the Ombuds Office. On the contrary, it is in accordance with the general principle of good faith to raise claims first against the contracting party. Moreover, this is also appropriate for reasons of efficiency and procedural economy. Crucially, the Code of Conduct clearly states that the possibility of appealing to the Ombudsman does not restrict access to the state courts. So, it is to be regarded as an additional option for crowdworkers without creating any disadvantage for them.

And the way the procedure is designed decidedly lowers potential barriers to access to dispute resolution. First, this results from the possibility of submitting applications by email or via an internet form. Second, the possibility of conducting the procedure either in German or in English also facilitates access to this type of conflict resolution. Third, according to § 7(1) of the Rules, the procedure before the Ombuds Office is free of charge. As the parties have to cover their own costs, the Ombuds Office is required to seek inexpensive arrangements during the procedures. So, there are no noteworthy bureaucratic or administrative or linguistic or financial[44] barriers.[45]

Finally, a procedural particularity has to be stressed: in a case where the claimant lives in a country other than Germany, § 3(4) of the Rules provides that a representative from a trade union based in that country may join the Ombuds Office in an advisory capacity if the worker wishes. This provision is obviously conceived to facilitate the access to the procedure and is protective of the concerned crowdworker's rights.

The reports and results of the procedures before the Ombuds Office speak for themselves: in the large majority of cases, the mediation of the Ombuds Office succeeded, helping the parties to find consensual solutions for their disputes, without the need of a formal decision.[46] So it might be regarded as an instrument that creates a space for meetings and discussions which effectively leads to alternative, ie, extra-judicial, dispute resolution.

der rechtlichen Erzwingbarkeit durch externe Akteurinnen und Akteure' in Dorothea Alewell (ed), *Rechtstatsachen und Rechtswirkungen im Arbeits- und Sozialrecht* (Rainer Hampp Verlag 2019).

[43] The Ombuds Office is a hybrid instrument that uses elements of conciliation and arbitration, see Sara Araujo, Barbara Safradin and Laura Brito, *Comparative Report on Labour conflicts and access to justice: the impact of alternative dispute resolution* (ETHOS Consortium 2020), available at: eg.uc.pt/bitstream/10316/87017/1/Comparative%20Report%20on%20Labour%20conflicts%20and%20access%20to%20justice.pdf, 17 f.

[44] See Eusebi Colàs-Neila and Estela Yélamos-Bayarri, *Access to Justice: A Literature Review on Labour Courts in Europe and Latin America* (ILO 2020) 20 f.

[45] On the importance of these factors for accessibility in particular in transnational situations see Araujo, Safradin and Brito (n 43) 40 ff.

[46] Ombuds Office, *Annual Reports 2018, 2019*.

V. Conclusions and Perspectives

The Code of Conduct is an 'alternative' soft law instrument that may promote the respect of certain principles regarding the contractual relations between platforms and platform workers and their working conditions. The independence of the applicable (national) law and benchmarking effects may be considered as strengths. Furthermore, the independence of the legal status of the crowdworker makes unilateral engagements easy to use.

However, the unilateral character is a major weakness of codes of conduct in general compared with collective agreements. They cannot contribute to the rebalancing of powers between employers and workers by negotiating labour conditions. To fulfil this function, collective actors (old or new ones)[47] are needed.[48]

Even if a voluntary and unilateral engagement does not create enforceable individual rights, it may ameliorate the crowdworker's legal situation. The introduction of alternative dispute resolution instruments such as the German Ombuds Office may be considered to facilitate access to justice; although it does not influence on the access to justice understood as state jurisdiction, but creates a low-threshold offer to enforce their individual interests even in the absence of individual rights.

Alternative unilateral and voluntary engagements cannot be a substitute for collective agreements. They are no 'remedy' to legal obstacles concerning collective bargaining in favour of platform workers. However, they may prepare the ground for collective bargaining and, if platforms and trade unions agree to cooperate, build up mutual trust and help build social partnership. From this perspective, they should not be regarded as an alternative but rather as transitional measures on the way to collective bargaining in the gig economy. So, despite all the shortcomings, 'The Ombuds Office can be regarded as a good example of how corporatism, an idea at the heart of the German welfare state and labour relations, can look when facing the challenges of new forms of work'[49] – at least for the time being.

[47] José María Miranda Boto, 'Collective Bargaining and the Gig Economy: Actors' (2020) 2 *Hungarian Labour Law E-Journal*, available at: hllj.hu/letolt/2020_2_a/02_MirandaBoto_hllj_uj_2020_2.pdf, 1.

[48] See Ayad Al-Ani and Stefan Stumpp, 'Rebalancing interests and power structures on crowdworking platforms' (2016) 5(2) *Internet Policy Review* 1 passim.

[49] Nierling, Krings and Küstermann (n 1) 51.

PART II

Actors and Contents

8

The 'Smart' Trade Union: New Strategies for a Digitalised Labour Market

FELICIA ROŞIORU

I. Introduction

Trade unions face new challenges in the 4.0 labour market: changed working patterns, limited human interaction, automation and globalisation are probably just some strong obstacles to their traditional role. In this context, trade unions have tried innovative ways to reach all workers by 'beating platforms at their own game', that is by using the same means as platforms do (digital tools such as social media, websites, trade union apps and platforms' ratings and reviews). The question still remains whether there can be genuine collective bargaining without employers, as platforms are (still) not willing to play this role and taking into account that it is a contentious question whether platform workers enjoy the right to strike.

The 4.0 labour market has definitely changed the world of work, by changing working patterns: there is no single workplace, nor community of workers, among other aspects. In many cases, fundamental rights seem to have been deleted and protection of human work and dignity was left out of the digital world, governed by automated rules and algorithmic management. Efficiency is the keyword and intensive management practices usually apply to 'compliant' humans who perform repetitive and rather unskilled tasks under automated control. Labour rights were reset in many cases in a sort of a 'no man's land', where very few rights apply to platform workers. In a sort of a history repeated, topics and institutions consolidated about a century ago come back to the surface with a new, 'digital' aspect.

In this context, trade unions have to face new obstacles, including limited human interaction, automation and often transnational dimension of the work performed. Such factual obstacles are doubled by the existing legislative framework in some Member States, as well as by the existing European Union (EU) rules on competition, that have turned into 'legal' obstacles to the collective representation of platform workers. Trade unions' activity is often hindered by the lack of community of platform workers, geographically dispersed in a borderless world of work, characterised by high worker turnover. As the staging is new, the 'old', traditional actors had to 'update' their strategies: a digital world requires digital means and a 'smart' industry requires 'smart' actions. New actors have emerged, engaging in different initiatives in order to gain protection for platform workers.

In some European countries, trade unions have rapidly adapted to this context and used different strategies, such as linking groups of self-employed workers to the institutional unions (structurally: Norway, the Netherlands, Switzerland, Germany; or just informally: Belgium, France); or to independent unions (United Kingdom, Germany). In other cases, the actors in the national struggle are groups of self-employed workers (Italy, Spain, Finland), sometimes supported by trade unions. There is a huge silence in other countries, particularly in Eastern Europe, where trade unions are less active and follow the rather traditional approach of representing the majority (full-time employees with open-ended contracts), even if platform work is rapidly spreading.

In this chapter we highlight the 'updated' role of trade unions and the strategies used in order to effectively represent the rights and interests of platform workers. There are 'new labour patterns', 'new actors' and 'new roles', but by 'undressing' platform work – that is, by removing the 'smart' aspect relating to the use of apps and the internet – we get to the old story of a person performing work under the control of, and for the benefit of, another, in exchange for remuneration. In this new world of platform work, the main role of trade unions remains the traditional one – representing the workers' interests and negotiating on their behalf and for their protection. In particular in countries with a long bargaining tradition, trade unions have managed to represent and defend rights and interests of certain categories of platform workers through collective bargaining. However, in Industry 4.0, trade unions have often had to reinvent themselves, to become 'smart', attractive and accessible to platform workers with various sociological profiles, in the same way as the new patterns of work.

The strategies used by trade unions for that purpose are diverse, as well as their involvement in recruiting and representing location-based platform workers and crowdworkers. We highlight some results of our research, focusing on the 'smart', innovative strategies used by trade unions in some countries in order to reach all workers and raise awareness by 'beating platforms at their own game', that is by using the same means as platforms do. We highlight, from the very beginning, that while there is fervent trade union activity in some European states (especially Spain, Italy, Sweden, Denmark, the Netherlands, the UK and Germany), where the phenomenon of platform work is older, there are basically no initiatives in many EU Member States, especially in Eastern European countries.[1]

Given the particularities of online workers ('crowdworkers') and of location-based workers via the app, who are dispersed and often working under time

[1] Digital Platform Observatory: digitalplatformobservatory.org/.

constraints, an 'online community' has to be built in order to give such workers a collective voice, to defend their interests and to fight precariousness. Even if, initially, the online presence of trade unions (on YouTube, Facebook, Twitter) was rather limited, their use of digital tools has progressively developed (*faircrowd.work* or *turespuestasindical.es* or different trade union apps[2] are just some examples). The trade unions' strategy to 'think outside the box' includes the use of social media as the main communication, coordination channel (such as WhatsApp) and/or the main organisation and publication instrument (such as Facebook or Twitter). A genuine bargaining power depends largely on visibility; in this context, trade unions and riders' associations draw public attention to the situation of platform workers, especially of bike couriers (such as Bongo Cat 4 Couriers). 'Beating platforms at their own game' strategies include the use of trade union apps and of platforms' ratings and reviews. The strategies must be diverse, as there is a diversity of work performed on different types of platforms, with different business models. The question still remains whether these strategies can lead to genuine collective bargaining, as many platforms are (still) not willing to play the role of employer, and without the right to strike.

II. Overview of the Obstacles to the Collective Representation of Platform Workers

Trade unions face different obstacles when it comes to the collective representation of platform workers. General obstacles relate to the legal ability of trade unions to represent platform workers, usually classified as self-employed, as well as to obstacles in organising them (from recruitment to interests' reconciliation and effective representation), as the workforce is highly fragmented. Other obstacles are specific to crowdworkers, such as the lack of visibility and the transnational dimension of their work.

Factual obstacles also hinder the collective representation of platform workers, as it requires a community whose interests should be defended, the willingness to have a common voice and the structural power for bargaining and defence. Platform workers are fragmented, performing task-based work, in isolation and with a high worker turnover, entailing a lack of community, as well as of organisational and material resources. They often lack visibility, with the notable exception of the delivery sector,[3] leading to difficulties for trade unions in identifying and recruiting them. Platform workers also face difficulties in bringing the employer to the negotiating table. In this context, in order to play their traditional roles, trade

[2] Unite the Union: www.unitetheunion.org/why-join/your-union-on-your-mobile/. Similar apps are used by trade unions in Australia or Canada.

[3] Kurt Vandaele, Agnieszka Piasna and Jan Drahokoupil, '"Algorithm breakers" are not a different "species": attitudes towards trade unions of Deliveroo riders in Belgium' (ETUI 2019) 10.

unions had to 'think outside the box', to raise awareness and to recruit such workers. The traditional leaflets and trade union newsletters distributed among workers in the undertaking are useless, as platform workers are dispersed and difficult to reach through traditional means; 'smart' strategies were necessary. Social media, as well as other digital tools, prove to be great communication and coordination channels, as well as powerful organisation and publication instruments (such as Facebook, Twitter, WhatsApp etc). Leaflets can now be distributed online; workers can easily be consulted; information and messages rapidly spread among users. For people working online or using digital tools, trade unions should also be at a 'click' distance, in the same space where workers are and/or answering to their daily routine of using social networking sites.

There is, however, a vicious circle, as the question remains whether a trade union might have a genuine interest in recruiting platform workers if they only have the legal capacity to represent and defend employees. And, of course, at a second stage, it is difficult to find the proper social partner in order to negotiate rights for the self-employed. Therefore, we shall briefly highlight the legal obstacles and the strategies – 'traditional' or 'smart' – that were adopted in order to overcome them.

A. Legal Obstacles to the Collective Representation of Platform Workers

One of the most important obstacles to the 'typical' form of collective representation of platform workers is the law itself, as in many EU countries the right to form or to join a trade union is recognised only for employees. Accordingly, an important part of trade unions' strategies – in those countries where they could be highlighted – was rather traditional, consisting in offering support to location-based platform workers (where signs of control on behalf of the platform can be proven) to address the courts in order to be reclassified as employees (as was the case of bike couriers working for Deliveroo, Foodora, Take Eat Easy and of Uber drivers, in Spain, France, Italy, the Netherlands and the UK, for example).[4] Thus, challenging misclassification is a part of the trade unions' strategy to represent platform workers, leading to full protection in terms of labour law. However, not all platform workers are genuinely misclassified.

Another important traditional trade union strategy was linked to concluding collective bargaining agreements (in Denmark, Sweden, Italy, the UK) or establishing works councils (in Austria and Germany) for certain categories of platform workers. In some other cases, such workers were included in the national

[4] See especially, in this volume, ch 5 by Jeremias Adams-Prassl, Sylvaine Laulom and Yolanda Maneiro Vázquez.

agreement in the logistics sector (in Italy) or in the State Labour Agreement for the hospitality sector (in Spain).[5]

National legislation tends to limit the right of self-employed workers to form or to join a trade union and, in particular, the right to collective bargaining and to collective action, disregarding the fact that they are fundamental rights. Only in 12 European states (Austria, Belgium, Denmark, France, Germany, Italy, Netherlands, Serbia, Spain, Sweden, the UK and, recently, Ireland) can collective bargaining or 'some other form of union involvement' be used or has effectively been used to negotiate terms and conditions of work for self-employed workers.[6] Non-dependent and semi-dependent workers usually enjoy the 'ordinary' freedom of association, different from the freedom to form or join trade unions, and may create 'civil law' associations. Collective agreements cannot be concluded by such associations on their behalf; any agreement being applicable only *inter partes*. Consequently, there are important limits to the collective representation of self-employed workers in general, of platform workers in particular.[7] On the other hand, even in those countries where trade unions have the legal ability to conclude collective agreements on behalf of the workers who are not formally classified as employees, such agreements might fall under the rules on competition. According to the Court of Justice of the European Union, even if self-employed workers perform the same activities as employees, they are service providers and are, in principle, 'undertakings' within the meaning of the European rules on competition, because they offer services for remuneration in a given market. Consequently, when a trade union represents self-employed workers, carries out negotiations on behalf of such workers and concludes a collective agreement, it does not act as a social partner, but as an association of undertakings.[8] However, the Court leaves the door open for collective bargaining agreements for 'service providers comparable to workers'. In June 2020, the European Commission addressed the issue of collective bargaining for the self-employed, so there is hope for an effective right for such workers to conclude collective agreements.

For the time being, platform workers do not usually formally enjoy, in national legislation, the right to strike and the guarantees (including against dismissal)

[5] See Commission, 'Second-Phase Consultation of Social Partners Under Article 154 TFEU on Possible Action Addressing the Challenges Related to Working Conditions in Platform Work' (Analytical Document) SWD(2021) 143 final, 105. See Commission 'Second-Phase Consultation of Social Partners Under Article 154 TFEU on Possible Action Addressing the Challenges Related to Working Conditions in Platform Work' (Consultation Document) C(2021) 4230 final.

[6] Lionel Fulton, *Trade unions protecting self-employed workers* (ETUC 2018) 11. It does not contain data on seven EU Member States: Croatia, Cyprus, Greece, Luxembourg, Malta, Portugal and Romania. In Romania, according to Law no 62/2011, trade unionism and collective bargaining are recognised only for employees.

[7] Ricardo Rodríguez Contreras and Claude Emmanuel Triomphe (eds), *The impact of new forms of labour on industrial relations and the evolution of labour law in the European Union* (European Parliament, 2008) 112.

[8] Case C-413/13 *FNV Kunsten Informatie en Media v Staat der Nederlanden* [2014] ECLI:EU:C:2014:2411, para 30. See in more detail the contribution by Brameshuber in this volume (ch 14), pages 229 et seq and pages 245 et seq especially on the European Commission's Initiative on Collective Bargaining Agreements for the Self-Employed and its Respective Draft Guidelines.

that are associated with it. In some countries, like the UK, bike couriers had the opportunity to take direct action without having to respect the legal strike constraints, as they do not apply to 'independent contractors'.[9] However, the lack of legal constraints was associated with the lack of legal guarantees, allowing platforms to simply disconnect and replace 'troublemaking' couriers through digital management methods. A coordinated collective action is a 'challenging task' for location-based platform workers, as the algorithmic management would automatically set higher rates, encouraging occasional workers to log in.[10]

In addition to the legal boundaries, the rules enacted by trade unions and/or their attitudes (at least in the initial stages of platform work) made it more difficult or even impossible in some cases for the self-employed to join unions.[11] Trade unions in Romania and Hungary, for example, show no intention to organise and represent the self-employed, nor to defend platform workers. However, as new forms of work have developed in the context of the digital economy, trade unions have reconsidered – in some countries – their position on organising the self-employed.[12] The precarity of platform workers represented an additional incentive in tackling the legal obstacles to their effective representation and defence of their interests.

Trade unions' strategies to tackle the legal obstacles to collective bargaining were also rather traditional and not exclusively platform-work related, relying mainly on the fact that the freedom of association (and its specific right to collective bargaining and to collective action) are fundamental human rights. They are recognised by international and European conventions and bodies both for employees and self-employed workers, although in practice such workers usually show lower levels of involvement in union membership and activism. Solemnly included in the Philadelphia Declaration of 1944 concerning the aims and purposes of the International Labour Organization (ILO), freedom of association was reaffirmed, together with the effective recognition of the right to collective bargaining, in the ILO Declaration on Fundamental Principles and Rights at Work (1998). The self-employed are not specifically excluded from ILO Convention 87[13] and, in order to respect Convention 98, competition law should not prevent the self-employed from concluding collective agreements.[14] Self-employed workers or those under civil law contracts enjoy the right to establish and join organisations

[9] Kurt Vandaele, *Will trade unions survive in the platform economy? Emerging patterns of platform workers' collective voice and representation in Europe* (ETUI 2018) 15.

[10] ibid.

[11] Lei Delsen, 'European trade unions and the flexible workforce' (2007) 21 *Industrial Relations Journal* 260.

[12] Fulton (n 6) 10.

[13] ILO Freedom of Association and Protection of the Right to Organise Convention 1948 No 87 (adopted 9 July 1948, entered into force 4 July 1950) 68 UNTS 17, Art 2.

[14] ILO, *Report of the Committee of Experts on the Application of Conventions and Recommendations. Report III (Part 1A)* (International Labour Office 2013) 144–45.

of their own choosing within the meaning of Convention 87,[15] regardless of the existence of an employment relationship.[16] The right to collective bargaining is general in scope and it should also cover organisations representing self-employed and temporary workers, as well as outsourced or contract workers.[17]

Besides the recognition of the freedom of association both by the European Convention on Human Rights and the Revised European Social Charter, the Parliamentary Assembly of the Council of Europe has stated, in the context of globalisation and of the economic crisis, that social dialogue is a traditional inherent part of European socio-economic processes. Undermining and limiting collective bargaining leads to growing inequalities and negative effects on working and employment conditions, on European economies and democracy.[18]

The European Committee of Social Rights, when interpreting the provisions of the European Social Charter, highlighted the insufficiency of the distinction between worker and self-employed, 'in establishing the type of collective bargaining that is protected by the Charter'.[19] The world of work is changing rapidly and an increasing number of workers fall outside the definition of employee, as a dependent provider of work. The category of self-employed includes a growing number of low-paid workers or service providers who are de facto 'dependent' on one or more labour engagers.[20] Collective mechanisms in the field of work are justified by the weak position of employees in establishing the terms and conditions of their contract, but also many self-employed workers are in a dependent, precarious position and have no substantial influence on the content of contractual conditions. This interpretation is in line with the case law of Court of Justice of the European Union on collective agreements, the anti-cartel regulations being considered inapplicable to collective agreements in order to overcome the lack of individual bargaining power. The Committee has concluded that, when assessing the scope of the right to collective bargaining, 'the decisive criterion is rather whether there is an imbalance of power between the providers and engagers of labour' and not the legal status of the person performing work.[21] The ILO Committee on Freedom of Association has also highlighted that the employment relationship is often non-existent and should not be used as the criterion for determining the persons covered by the right to establish and join organisations.[22]

[15] ILO Committee on Freedom of Association, Recommendation of 03/2012 case n 2888 Poland.

[16] ILO, *Freedom of Association. Compilation of decisions of the Committee on Freedom of Association*, 6th edn (International Labour Office 2018) 70.

[17] International Labour Conference, *Giving globalization a human face. General Survey on the fundamental Conventions concerning rights at work in light of the ILO Declaration on Social Justice for a Fair Globalization. Report III (Part 1B)* (International Labour Office 2012) 85–86.

[18] Council of Europe (Resolution 2033) 'Protection of the right to bargain collectively, including the right to strike' (28 January 2015) para 3.

[19] European Committee of Social Rights, *Irish Congress of Trade Unions (ICTU) v Ireland* (8 August 2016) C 123/2016, Case No 1, para 38.

[20] ibid, paras 36–37.

[21] ibid, para 38.

[22] ILO, *Freedom of Association* (n 16) 70.

The right to bargain collectively and to collective action are the foundations for the fulfilment of other social fundamental rights, such as those relating to participation in the determination and improvement of the working conditions and environment, fair conditions of work, safe and healthy working conditions, fair remuneration, protection in cases of termination of employment, dignity at work, information and consultation in collective redundancy procedures.[23]

B. Factual Obstacles to the Collective Representation of Platform Workers

Some of the most important factual obstacles to the collective representation of platform workers are linked to their lack of community and of visibility, limiting the trade unions' possibility to identify and recruit such workers. Other important obstacles relate to difficulties in identifying the employer and/or the unwillingness of the digital labour platforms to involve in collective bargaining, to join existing employers' associations or to establish their own associations, as well as in the lack of organisational and material resources of platform workers.

Platform workers have specific, sometimes conflicting interests; the alleged independence in the activity they perform, often combined with the easy access and the fact that they see it as being only occasional, renders collective representation of such workers rather difficult. As there is no single workplace, most often platform workers do not know each other.

Normally, trade unions encounter difficulties in finding and recruiting platform workers, as they do not wear distinctive signs, with the major exception of bike couriers. Such couriers or riders wear helmets, fluorescent jackets and the lunchbox with the company logos, rendering them visible and allowing them to recognise each other. Having this advantage, bike couriers represent the major exception to the weak structural power of on-demand workers and the superior bargaining power of the digital labour platform.[24] They are the most active category of platform workers in demanding rights and striking against unfair changes in payment rates and unfair working conditions. Besides their visibility, the power of bike couriers, of location-based on-demand workers in general, stems from interaction with the customers. Their activity is performed in the 'real' economy, physically, in a geographically determined area, empowering them to defend their interests.

On the other hand, the lack of visibility of crowdworkers is enhanced by the fact that they are deprived of identity, often hidden under a code (as in the case of Amazon Mechanical Turk); they seem to be parts of the algorithm, not humans. In addition, crowdworkers perform placeless work and the transnational factor is an important obstacle to the conclusion and enforcement of collective agreements.

[23] *Digest of the Case Law of the European Committee of Social Rights* (December 2018) 98.
[24] Vandaele (n 9) 14.

There are also important difficulties in identifying the employer and/or getting the platforms involved in negotiations. Collective bargaining supposes the existence of two parties, the social partners, representing 'management and labour'. Platforms usually present themselves as simple intermediaries, even if some of them exert a significant degree of control on the workers and their working conditions, without formally undertaking the role of an employer.[25] Sometimes, the companies administrating the platforms are based in countries other than the one where work is performed (as in the case of Uber or Amazon Mechanical Turk) and there is no (or limited) human interaction between the worker and the platform, the tasks being assigned and evaluated through algorithms. Even if the company administrating the platform is identified, it usually escapes collective bargaining of the working conditions. In countries where industry-level collective bargaining prevails, digital labour platforms should either join existing employers' associations or establish their own associations. Such platforms refuse to do so, as they only consider themselves a 'tech success', 'marketplaces', simple intermediaries and not genuine employers.

As a result, trade unions' initiatives to bargain on the working conditions of platform workers are usually met with 'ignorance, unwillingness and resistance by the digital labour platforms'.[26] Nevertheless, traditional trade unions in Denmark, Sweden, Belgium, Italy and the UK have attempted to negotiate with the platforms' representatives and managed to conclude collective agreements.

Platform workers often lack organisational and material resources; they usually perform work for little money. Couriers are, in this case too, the 'algorithm breakers', in the sense that they have built coalitions with trade unions or other organisations in order to gain organisational power. Thus, protesting couriers were actively supported by unions in several countries (such as Austria, Belgium, France, Germany, Norway, the Netherlands, Spain, Switzerland, the UK).[27] Trade union involvement has led to several results, such as affiliating self-employed workers among their members (in France, Belgium, the Netherlands, Spain), incorporating delivery workers into the national collective agreement in the logistics sector (Italy).[28] In France, the Labour Code was amended in order to grant platform workers the right to form or join trade unions and to assert through it their collective interests.[29]

[25] See the observations submitted by Christian Poppe for Delivery Hero SE to SWD(2021) 143 final: 'Food delivery platforms are … marketplaces which connect restaurants and retail partners with consumers … Self-employed riders neither offer nor provide their labour through our platforms' (3 February 2021), available at: ec.europa.eu/info/law/better-regulation/have-your-say/initiatives/12483-Collective-bargaining-agreements-for-self-employed-scope-of-application-EU-competition-rules/F1577400_en.

[26] Vandaele (n 9) 22.

[27] Anne Dufresne, 'Assemblée européenne des livreur.e.s "Riders4Rights"' (25/26 octobre 2018) Bruxelles.

[28] José María Miranda Boto, 'Collective Bargaining and the Gig Economy: Actors' (2020) 2 *Hungarian Labour Law E-Journal*, available at: hllj.hu/letolt/2020_2_a/02_MirandaBoto_hllj_uj_2020_2.pdf, 8.

[29] Art L.7342-6 French Labour Code.

In this context, it is important to highlight that 'trade unions must be where members and potential members are'.[30] Therefore, for people using technological means when looking for a job and performing work, trade unions should also use technological means in order to find, recruit and organise them. For these purposes, it has proven to be important for trade unions to use Facebook or WhatsApp groups, social media in general as 'a natural hunting ground',[31] to share information on their websites and pages, to use messaging apps and (encrypted) chat groups, as these are some of the tools used by platform workers, that they find accessible and check regularly, in order to or when they perform work.

III. 'Smart' Trade Unions and 'Smart' Strategies

Trade unions face structural and institutional challenges in providing platform workers with the collective voice they need for a decent and sustainable working life. A genuine collective autonomy can be created by removing the highlighted legal and practical obstacles and, sometimes, this is not possible using the traditional strategies.

Various forms of collective representation can be identified, mainly among high-skilled crowdworkers and location-based on-demand platform workers, such as grassroots unions, union-affiliated guilds, 'traditional unions', labour market intermediaries as labour mutuals or quasi-unions and worker-led platform cooperatives. These structures follow different strategies in defending the interests of platform workers: grassroots unions and union-affiliated guilds try to mobilise, organise and represent on-demand platform workers, while worker-led platform cooperatives try to organise crowdworkers with high-skilled jobs or freelancers.[32] As the actors of collective representation are varied, we shall focus only on the 'old actors' – trade unions – as 'masters' of social dialogue and collective bargaining. In order to achieve these results, trade unions had to change in many cases their strategies, to attract platform workers (self-employed, more generally) and to integrate them into their structures. There were various initiatives, depending on the country, on the type of platform work, the legal framework and the trade union's experience in integrating self-employed workers. We shall focus on two different strategies involving 'smart' means (the use of technology): building online communities (in order to create a collective voice); and raising awareness and tackling platform reputation (as a tool for involving them in collective bargaining or other forms of workers' protection).

[30] Samuel Engblom, 'Atypical Work in the Digital Age – Outline of a Trade Union Strategy for the Gig Economy' in Mia Rönnmar and Jenny Julén Votinius (eds), *Festskrift Till Ann Numhauser-Henning* (Juristförlaget i Lund 2017) 225.

[31] ibid.

[32] Vandaele (n 9) 18.

A. Building Online Communities

Initially, the online presence of trade unions was rather limited. An analysis of the official Facebook pages of five trade union confederations in Europe and Brazil, carried out in 2018, has shown a small number of followers, a network restricted to organisations within the labour movement and a 'one-way' model of online communication. The need for trade unions to reach non-labour organisations and social media active grassroot groups, as well as to improve their digital communication strategy were highlighted.[33] On the other hand, many trade union confederations (more than 80) in the EU use YouTube actively; they have uploaded about 2,000 videos per year, of different lengths and popularity. Their message usually supports union activism, political campaigns or have an informative nature, about union activities or different professions.[34] By far, the highest number of videos were uploaded by Italian, followed by French, Spanish and Portuguese trade unions. Their popularity is measured by the number of views and 'likes'; videos with a political message, that mobilise for protest actions or inform about trade union activism and issues, are more popular than others.[35] The use of YouTube has a high potential in reaching out to new audiences, particularly among young people and videos can easily be disseminated. Professionally produced videos have a higher impact compared with posting on Facebook or Twitter, but producing videos is more costly in terms of time and resources.[36] Short and visually impacting messages or videos are easily read, viewed and shared, compared with long descriptive messages or videos.

Traditionally, trade unions use their institutional power resources in relation to the employers' associations and the state.[37] However, a particular challenge was linked to 'convincing' platform workers of the ability to represent their interests. Social media was essential for this purpose, playing an essential role in invigorating trade union campaigns and movements as it helps create or strengthen a sense of collective identity among workers,[38] particularly necessary in the case of platform workers, and it provides practical and emotional support.

The use of digital tools by trade unions has progressively developed and social media is now the main communication and coordination channel, the main

[33] Bia Carneiro, 'Trade unions and Facebook: the need to improve dialogue and expand network' (2018) 5 *ETUI Policy*, available at: *Brief* www.etui.org/sites/default/files/Trade%20unions%20Facebook%20Carneiro%20Policy%20Brief%202018.05%20Web.pdf.

[34] Jenny Jansson and Katrin Uba, 'The untapped possibilities of YouTube as a trade union tool' (2018) 7 *ETUI Policy Brief*, available at: www.etui.org/sites/default/files/Trade%20unions%20YouTube%20Jansson%20Uba%20Policy%20Brief%202018.07.pdf.

[35] ibid, 3–4.

[36] ibid, 2.

[37] Vandaele (n 9) 19–20.

[38] Vincent Pasquier and Alex J Wood, 'The power of social media as a labour campaigning tool: lessons from OUR Walmart and the Fight for 15' (2018) 10 *ETUI Policy Brief*, available at: www.etui.org/sites/default/files/Trade%20unions%20Social%20media%20Pasquier%20Wood%20Policy%20Brief%202018.10%20%281%29.pdf.

publication and organisation instrument.[39] Facebook, Twitter, WhatsApp play an important role in creating online communities and in building capacity. One of the possibilities taken into consideration by the EU is to stimulate social dialogue in platform work through communication channels that, according to the agreement of the social partners, would be embedded in the digital infrastructure of platforms. This would enable worker representatives to communicate directly with all platform workers and engage in union activism, in order to strengthen their ability to defend their rights;[40] this is the role played now by social media. The traditional workplace communication had to be replaced with online fora.

The use of social media was particularly useful in developing a sense of community among platform workers. For example, trade unions in Belgium got engaged with food delivery riders via support for the Riders Collective (Collectif des coursier-e-s/KoeriersKollectief). Membership to this collective is free and a 'like' on the Facebook page is enough to be considered a member. By liking the same page, trade unions had the opportunity to engage with riders.[41] Several other self-organised 'internet-based communities' (usually city-based guilds) benefited, in time, from counselling, logistics and other resources from the traditional trade unions (such as the Plataforma Riders X Derechos BCN in Spain, the German Deliverunion,[42] the Italian Deliverance Milano[43] and the Dutch Riders Union).[44] Very active on Facebook, Plataforma Riders X Derechos BCN – now a trade union section – is asking for labour rights, is developing solidarity around experiences of injustice, is raising awareness on unfair platform practices or, on the contrary, is advertising platforms that respect labour rights and express the workers' point of view on different legislative initiatives.[45]

Social media supports 'offline' collective actions and facilitates labour movement expansion. This is especially the case with Deliverunion and Deliverance Milano ('Riders, our strength is collective action'),[46] highlighting the need to organise on a metropolitan, national and transnational basis.

TurespuestasindicalYa is a website created by the Spanish trade union, UGT, presented as a 'union section through the internet' to help about two million workers who provide their services on digital platforms. It answers (not exclusively) platform workers' questions, and it provides a comparative approach of the rights

[39] In 2019, only one Romanian trade union (in the IT sector) had a Facebook page. In September 2021, about 50 trade unions two confederations (of employees) and five confederations (of employers) had such a page and were actively involved in communicating.

[40] Commission, 'Second-Phase Consultation of Social Partners Under Article 154 TFEU on Possible Action Addressing the Challenges Related to Working Conditions in Platform Work' (Analytical Document) SWD(2021) 143 final, 105 2021 (n 5).

[41] Vandaele, Piasna and Drahokoupil (n 3) 11.

[42] Supported by the structures of the Free Workers Union (FAU).

[43] 'Autonomous and self-convened union of the riders of Milan'.

[44] Vandaele (n 9) 20.

[45] Plataforma Riders X Derechos BCN – IAC: www.facebook.com/ridersxderechos/.

[46] Deliverance Milano (25 August 2021): www.facebook.com/deliverancemilano/posts/2865342210443472.

as employees or self-employed and tools to denounce abuses and to pass information. UGT also has a website, a Facebook page and uses WhatsApp as a channel of intense communication. *TurespuestasindicalYa* offers digital employment support to platform workers, combining an information, claim, organisation and complaint tool.[47] A similar tool is the CCOO's website *#PrecarityWar*.[48] German trade unions have also launched information campaigns online and on Facebook profiles.[49]

Trade unions' strategy of backing other actors ('independent unions') enables a coalition power and it helps in creating a community and gaining the visibility needed in order to influence public policy and engage in collective bargaining. On 26 October 2018, an 'International Declaration of Riders' was adopted in Brussels by food and other delivery couriers from 12 countries (Austria, Belgium, Finland, France, Germany, Italy, the Netherlands, Norway, Spain, Switzerland, the UK and Ireland)[50] and a Transnational Federation of Couriers was created.[51] On this occasion, the diversity of links – more or less formal – that exist between riders' collectives and trade unions has emerged. There are a variety of actors involved in the national struggle: collectives of independent workers without a union (Italy, Spain, Finland); collectives structurally linked to institutional unions (Norway, the Netherlands, Switzerland, Germany, Austria); or informally linked to these unions (Belgium, France); as well as linked to independent unions (the UK, Germany).[52] Since 2018, many trade unions got involved in platform workers' protection and there are numerous results, even if sometimes widely varying or limited. Overcoming the local dimension is an important step towards effective defence of platform workers' rights and is essential for raising awareness among trade unions and platform workers in Eastern European countries.

A Facebook page or a Twitter account are particularly useful for attracting young workers, fervent users of social media; short, high-impact posts are easy to create and are shared rapidly. However, in June 2020, Facebook was accused of blacklisting the 'unionise' term and associated terminology, while trying new features for 'Facebook Workplace' software. Facebook replied that the content moderation tool was at an early development and has eliminated it.[53]

[47] UGT, 'UGT presenta en Bruselas la plataforma "Tu Respuesta Sindical YA"' (23 January 2018), available at: www.ugt.es/ugt-presenta-en-bruselas-la-plataforma-tu-respuesta-sindical-ya.

[48] Sindicato CCOO Federación de Servicios de Comisiones Oberas: precaritywar.es/.

[49] www.ich-bin-mehr-wert.de from Ver.di.

[50] Alter Summit, 'Assemblée Transnationale des Coursiers #riders4rights', available at: www.alter-summit.eu/accueil/article/assemblee-transnationale-des-coursiers.

[51] Anne Dufresne, 'Coursiers de tous les pays, unissez-vous! La naissance de la Fédération Transnationale des Coursiers' (*Gresa*, 19 December 2018), available at: www.gresea.be/Coursiers-de-tous-les-pays-unissez-vous.

[52] ibid.

[53] Samuel Stolton, 'EU trade unions take stand against Facebook attempts to suppress "Unionise" term' (*Euroactive*, 12 June 2020), available at: www.euractiv.com/section/digital/news/eu-trade-unions-take-stand-against-facebook-attempts-to-suppress-unionise-term/; European Trade Union (Twitter, 12 June 2020), available at: twitter.com/etuc_ces/status/1271458340212793344?lang=en.

B. Raising Awareness and Tackling Platform Reputation

A particular challenge for trade unions is linked to raising awareness – of workers themselves, of platforms and of clients. In many cases, platform workers had to be informed and convinced that they can be effectively represented by trade unions. IG Metall, the Austrian Chamber of Labour, the Austrian Trade Union Confederation and the Swedish white-collar union Unionen have developed a joint project, FairCrowdWork, in order to strengthen workers' voices. Platform workers are provided with a list of trade unions defending their rights in Austria, Germany, Sweden, the UK and the United States.[54] These trade unions issued, in December 2016, the 'Frankfurt Paper on Platform-Based Work', including the right to organise and negotiate collective agreements, regardless of the employment status, aiming to ensure 'that platform businesses comply with relevant national laws and international conventions, rather than using technology to work around them'.[55]

The site also intends 'to beat platforms at their own game', as it offers ratings of working conditions on 12 online labour platforms based on paid surveys with workers.[56] It provides advice, information to anyone interested in crowdwork and legal information for crowdworkers (such as on fair pay and self-employment). Trade unions' involvement in this project is very complex as, on the one hand, it provides information and support to platform workers and, on the other, it raises awareness among platforms and shares good practices in terms of working conditions. Platforms use customers' ratings as an evaluative and disciplinary tool for workers; poor public ratings 'ruin' the workers' online credibility. The same way, crowdworkers are paid by trade unions to evaluate platforms. Tackling platform reputation (poor ratings might lead to fewer workers and clients) and 'advertising' platforms that respect decent working conditions are means to protect platform workers' rights. As a result of the good ratings, workers (and even clients) see the platform as being more reliable. This is a long, but effective process, given the specificities of crowdwork and its transnational dimensions; its effectiveness is enhanced by the clients' willingness to prevent abuse by using platforms that ensure proper working conditions and social protection.

A relatively similar tool is online forums, used by crowdworkers to express their opinions and criticise the different platforms they work for. One of the most famous such tools used by crowdworkers is TurkerNation and the Turkopticon initiative, working as a user-script that adds functionality to Amazon Mechanical Turk. The website allows 'turkers' to review clients ('requesters'), in order to gain

[54] Fair Crowd Work, 'Unions and worker organizations are defending the rights of crowd- and platform-workers and taking action to improve working conditions in several countries', available at: faircrowd.work/unions-for-platform-workers/.

[55] IG Metall, 'Frankfurt Paper on Platform-Based Work Proposals for platform operators, clients, policy makers, workers, and worker organizations' (Eurofound, 27 January 2021), available at: www.igmetall.de/download/20161214_Frankfurt_Paper_on_Platform_Based_Work_EN_b939ef89f7e-5f3a639cd6a1a930feffd8f55cecb.pdf. See also Brockmann in this volume (ch 7), pages 119 et seq.

[56] Fair Crowd Work, 'Platform Reviews', available at: faircrowd.work/platform-reviews/.

protection against the non-payment of the work performed, and to review tasks by indicating unclear, incomplete or underpaid tasks. As workers browse 'HITs' (gigs or tasks), Turkopticon places a button next to each requester, highlighting the ratings of requesters and the reports made against them.

Tackling platform reputation is very important for breaking the vicious circle of competition among platforms based on low labour costs. The same trade union who initiated FairCrowdWork has managed to involve platforms in adopting a voluntary code of conduct for paid crowdsourcing ('The Crowdsourcing Code of Conduct') initially signed by three German platforms.[57] A revised and extended version was signed by eight platforms, aiming for 'prosperous and fair cooperation between companies, clients and crowdworkers' and it is supported by the German Crowdsourcing Association (Deutscher Crowdsourcing Verband). The Code of Conduct includes 10 principles, one of the most important being 'fair payment'; the other principles refer to legal tasks, advice and support on legal situations, motivation and good work, respectful interaction, clear tasks and reasonable timing, freedom and flexibility, constructive feedback and open communication, regulated approval process and rework, data protection and privacy. The Code is a form of self-regulation which is particularly relevant from the perspective of platform–union collaboration. Its voluntary nature should not hinder the importance of an instrument that manages to protect workers who are difficult to identify, to recruit and to involve in active unionism. As crowdworkers work online, in a geographically dispersed area, often involving a transnational factor, it is more difficult to create 'typical' forms of trade union representation. Collective actions for crowdworkers are more likely to be put in practice online; however, the mere existence of a 'crowd' of workers, ready to take simple, repetitive tasks renders the effectiveness of a digital collective action (such as disconnection) rather illusory. The Code of Conduct is particularly important because it tackles the problem from the perspective of competition among platforms: it is not just the price that matters, but also the platform's 'reputation'. Platforms are undertaking to grant decent working conditions in return for an available quality workforce and good reputation, as reputation systems are more likely to affect competition among platforms. On the other hand, the Code of Conduct shows crowdworkers that there is hope for better working conditions. The German IG Metall trade union, the signatory platforms and the German Crowdsourcing Association in 2017 established an Ombuds Office,[58] with the role of enforcing the Code of Conduct and to resolve by consensus disputes between platform workers and a client or a signatory platform. The cases are submitted by workers via an online form if a previous attempt to solve the issue with the platform operator was unsuccessful.[59]

[57] See in more detail the contribution by Brockmann in this volume (ch 7), pages 121 et seq especially.

[58] It consists of a board of five people: a representative of the German Crowdsourcing Association; of the signatory platforms; a representative platform worker; a trade union representative; and a neutral chair.

[59] Janine Berg et al, *Digital labour platforms and the future of work: Towards decent work in the online world* (International Labour Office 2018) 99.

The digital tools that ensure the success of the platform also serve as a means of a rapid exchange of information and ideas among platform workers; the internet is an excellent tool for spreading best practices.[60] Such strategies are even more successful when clients/customers become aware of the precarity of platform workers and join their struggle for fair and decent working conditions.

A particular aspect of the strategy of tackling platforms' reputation consisted in raising customer awareness on the precarity of platform workers, in a form of civil involvement in preventing or banning abuses; extensive media coverage is extremely helpful. The image promoted by the food delivery companies is that of a 'cool, fresh and environmentally friendly' rider and, by attacking this image that brings profit for the company, a key element of the value chain is also attacked.[61]

In Bologna (Italy), Carta dei diritti fondamentali del lavoro digitale nel contesto urbano (the Charter of Fundamental Rights of Digital Work in an Urban Context) was signed in 2018 between the Riders Union Bologna, three main Italian trade union confederations (CGIL, CISL and UIL), the centre-left city council and the local food delivery platforms Sgnam and MyMenu, followed by Domino's Pizza. Minimum standards covering remuneration, working time, health and safety, but also a right to information, to form or to join a trade union and to collective action were undertaken voluntarily by the signatory platforms. However, as platforms like Deliveroo, Foodora and Just Eat have not signed the Charter, the mayor of Bologna has listed on the city's website both signatory and non-signatory platforms, calling on customers to boycott the non-signatory platforms.

Another important campaign was initiated by couriers aiming to improve their working conditions and of drivers working for platform companies in Finland (*justice4couriers*). A short-lived meme (*Bongo Cat 4 Couriers*) spread on Instagram and Facebook in 2018 establishing a day of action during which people were encouraged to give Foodora's app one-star reviews in order to support courier' struggle for rights. This modern form of collective action was meant to raise awareness of the precarity of couriers and to put pressure on the platform by tackling its reputation in order to improve working conditions. Another initiative in 2014 aimed at enhancing ethics in academic research[62] (*The Dynamo Guidelines for academic requesters on Amazon Mechanical Turk)*. The guidelines were signed by over 75 requesters, researchers at prestigious universities in the United States, Europe and Asia.[63] These campaigns were not initiated, nor supported by trade unions,[64] but they provide a good example of how informal, online campaigns may

[60] *Coworker* hosts and promotes workplace petition campaigns, in an attempt to 'create digital tools and communities for employees to share information, form collectives, and advocate for change'.

[61] Lorenzo Zamponi, 'Bargaining With the Algorithm' (*Jacobin*, 6 September 2018), available at: www.jacobinmag.com/2018/06/deliveroo-riders-strike-italy-labor-organizing.

[62] Hannah Johnston and Chris Land-Kazlauskas, *Organizing On-Demand: Representation, Voice, and Collective Bargaining in the Gig Economy* (International Labour Office 2019) 14–15.

[63] Berg et al (n 58) 97.

[64] Justice4couriers was also supported by Vapaa Syndikaatti – a free syndicate of anarchic views.

contribute to more formal representation and protection through the collective bargaining of platform workers.

Nowadays, people spend a lot of time online, on their phones. In particular, young people have a habit of searching on the internet for information, checking profiles and watching videos. In eastern European states it is rather unlikely that a platform worker would search for a trade union online. But a massively shared video (eg, of a cat playing drums loudly) asking for fair working condition would definitely draw attention. On the other hand, tackling platforms' reputation is vital in order to solve the lack of an interlocutor in collective bargaining, thus creating incentives for the platforms to negotiate.

IV. Conclusion: From 'Smart' Strategies to 'Smart' Content of Collective Agreements

The 'final mission' of trade unions consists in the collective representation of workers' interests and rights, collective bargaining and collective agreements, as essential regulatory instruments. Unlike 'typical' workers, for a proper exercise of their collective rights, platform workers need to be organised and to become aware of their existence.[65] Social networks, as well as the groups that can be created by using them, might prove to be a great space for trade union organisations, for workers' activism, for defending workers' rights. Users might exchange ideas and opinions about their workplaces and common challenges, they can be consulted, debate on important and/or controversial work-related issues even in cases where the direct consultation of workers is physically impossible because of different work schedules or locations. Social media, websites and apps replace traditional workplace communications between trade unions and platform workers, digitally proficient and almost permanently online.

There are important differences between European countries in terms of the collective representation of platform workers and of the means that are used in order to protect their interests. From this perspective, trade union traditions and mentalities are crucial: workers in countries with a strong tradition in this field being more active in defending their rights and in demanding decent working conditions. The chances to conclude a collective agreement seem to be higher when the platform is established in the same country as the trade union.[66] Despite the obstacles, collective bargaining agreements were concluded during the last few years for different categories of platform workers. Even if their scope can be considered relatively limited, they represent a major step towards decent work, adequate protection and effective collective bargaining, essential components of

[65] Miranda Boto (n 28) 2.
[66] Vandaele (n 9) 23.

the European social model. The first step is always the hardest. Platform workers are brought into the realm of labour law, ideally regardless of their employment status. On the other hand, collective agreements stand against the tendency of businesses to compete on labour costs.[67]

The next step has been already taken in Spain, with the Ley Rider. The contents of collective bargaining and agreements are different, since labour patterns have changed. Automatic management is essential in managing platform work, but also a source of abuses and violations of labour rights.[68] Therefore, in Spain platform workers' representatives have to be informed by the company of the parameters, rules and instructions on which the algorithms or artificial intelligence systems are based, affecting decision-making that may impact working conditions, access and maintenance of employment, including the preparation of profiles.

The use of the internet allows for a massive sharing of information, turning every national (or even local) victory in defending platform workers' rights into a major success, as it serves as a model and paves the way for another victory, in the same or in another country. Paradoxically, in a context of trade unionism, mobilising platform workers constitutes a revival with important consequences for collective bargaining.[69] According to the ILO, one of the criteria for decent work in the online economy consists specifically of platform workers' freedom of association and the right to collective bargaining.[70] Since social dialogue and the involvement of workers is one of the 20 principles of the European Pillar of Social Rights, it is striking that, in the twenty-first century, there are still large categories of workers who cannot enjoy the right to collective bargaining as an essential regulatory instrument. Despite the obstacles, trade unions in many European countries play their traditional role of collective bargaining and of concluding collective agreements, but they had to 'update' their role and strategies: 'We are just at the beginning of this work, but it has already taken on a diversity of forms, including innovative organising, technology development, new services, policymaking, public awareness campaigns, research, and dialogue with platform operators'.[71]

[67] Silvia Rainone and Nicola Countouris, 'Collective bargaining and self-employed workers. The need for a paradigm shift' (2021) 11 *ETUI Policy Brief* 4.

[68] Valerio De Stefano, '"*Negotiating the algorithm*": *Automation, artificial intelligence and labour protection*' (International Labour Office 2018); see especially in this volume ch 9 by Teresa Coelho Moreira, 'Algorithms, Discrimination and Collective Bargaining'.

[69] Miranda Boto (n 28) 2.

[70] Berg et al (n 58) 105–06.

[71] Fair Crowd Work, 'The Frankfurt Declaration on Platform-Based Work', available at: faircrowd.work/unions-for-crowdworkers/frankfurt-declaration/.

9

Algorithms, Discrimination and Collective Bargaining

TERESA COELHO MOREIRA

I. Introduction

We live in the age of the algorithm. Increasingly, the decisions that affect our lives are being made not by humans, but by mathematical models. In theory, this should lead to greater fairness and transparency because everyone is judged according to the same rules, and bias is eliminated. But, in reality, that does not happen. The models being used today are opaque, unregulated and incontestable, even when they are wrong. And, even more problematic, is that they reinforce discrimination.

One possible solution is to use collective bargaining to try to diminish this kind of discrimination, because it could try to influence business practices for the better and could be instrumental in both clarifying workers' rights and delineating employers' responsibilities under an employment contract. Social partners can play a significant role in advancing this situation.

The right to equality and the prohibition of discrimination is a universal right, recognised by the Universal Declaration of Human Rights, the United Nations Convention on the Elimination of All Forms of Discrimination against Women, the United Nations International Covenants on Human Rights, Civil and Political Rights and on Economic, Social and Cultural Rights, and by the Convention for the Protection of Human Rights and Fundamental Freedoms, to which Portugal is a signatory. In addition, Convention No 111 of the International Labour Organization prohibits discrimination in the field of employment and occupation.

Nowadays we are facing a true digital revolution, relating to the internet, cloud computing, 3D printing, automatisation, robotisation, working with collaborative robots or *cobots* and new ways of performing work. With this also comes the so-called digital work in the collaborative economy, on digital platforms, and a new type of worker.

In many parts of the world, technological innovations such as artificial intelligence, robotics and machine learning are already having an impact on many aspects of society in general and in labour relationships in particular. They allow us to communicate faster, to share information, to feel closer to one another. They have become an essential part of our everyday lives, providing us with unprecedented opportunities for advancement in areas ranging from education to political participation but they also show us many threats and problems.

The new ways of performing work may be further increasing gender inequality or other ways of discrimination as reconciling private and family life when on an on-call basis and on these ways of work can be very difficult and in many times a work–life balance is not achieved. In fact, it is women who continue to provide most of the care at the family level, while the most lucrative and best-paid activities belong to those who do not have these responsibilities, and may also lead to a widening gender pay gap in these new forms of work; in Portugal recent data showed that in the pandemic the number of women teleworking was greater than men.

As the European Economic and Social Committee pointed out:

> While gender equality depends on many factors, and teleworking has various economic and social impacts other than those regarding gender equality, this exploratory opinion specifically considers the links between teleworking and gender equality, as requested by the Portuguese Presidency. The objective is to find ways of making teleworking one of the engines for promoting gender equality and avoid exacerbating the unequal distribution of unpaid care and domestic work between women and men, as teleworking may involve both benefits and risks with respect to gender equality. The EESC emphasises the need for gender mainstreaming in policy making with the aim of helping to mitigate risks and grasp opportunities.[1]

And:

> In considering the gender dimension of teleworking, there are lessons to be drawn from the pandemic period. The pandemic highlights the importance of the role of women in the economy – as essential care workers, in most cases working 'on the frontlines'.[2]

Studies reveal that many existing structural gender inequalities in the labour market and society have been exacerbated by the pandemic and that 'women have been disproportionately impacted'.[3]

[1] Milena Angelova, 'Teleworking and gender equality – conditions so that teleworking does not exacerbate the unequal distribution of unpaid care and domestic work between women and men and for it to be an engine for promoting gender equality', Exploratory opinion at the request of the Portuguese Presidency (European Economic and Social Committee, 28 October 2020, adopted 24 March 2021), available at: www.eesc.europa.eu/en/our-work/opinions-information-reports/opinions/teleworking-and-gender-equality-conditions-so-teleworking-does-not-exacerbate-unequal-distribution-unpaid-care-and, para 2.3.

[2] Laura Turquet and Sandrine Koissy-Kpein, 'COVID-19 and gender: What do we know; what do we need to know?' (*UN Women*, 13 April 2020), available at: data.unwomen.org/features/covid-19-and-gender-what-do-we-know-what-do-we-need-know.

[3] Rosamund Shreeves, 'Achieving gender equality in the face of the pandemic and existing challenges' (European Parliament, 2021), available at: www.europarl.europa.eu/RegData/etudes/ATAG/2021/659440/EPRS_ATA(2021)659440_EN.pdf; European Institute for Gender Equality: eige.europa.eu/topics/health/covid-19-and-gender-equality.

Of course, the flexibility of the sharing economy can offer to both men and women the promise of gainful employment alongside family care, potentially even changing the normalised gendered roles of caretaking and breadwinning.[4]

However flexibility often does not rhyme with freedom and when work is done at home there is a clear blurring in the boundaries between work and private life and we are seeing this in this pandemic situation.[5]

The concept of AI, or at least the term, came up in a series of conferences that took place at Dartmouth College in 1956. At this time several scientists came together to try to teach machines how to solve problems that only humans could solve at that time. On the other hand, there is AI that is considered 'weak' and other 'strong'. Strong AI means that these systems have the same intellectual capacity as humans, or even exceed it. 'Weak' AI is focused on solving specific problems by using maths and computer science to evaluate and get systems to optimise. To achieve this goal, certain aspects of human intelligence are mapped and formally described, and systems are designed and stimulated to support human thinking. And the first type of AI has intrigued many throughout the ages. In 1950, Alan Turing posed the question: 'Can machines think?'[6]

So, as we can see AI is not a new phenomenon. It has been around for over 70 years. However, today, with the rise of digital technologies and the vast amount of data produced each day, AI has gained a new significance and an entirely new dimension: machine learning. Machine learning is an application of artificial intelligence that provides systems with the ability to automatically learn and improve from experience without being explicitly programmed. Machine learning focuses on the development of computer programs that can access data and use it to learn for themselves.[7]

And related to AI, we have the rise of the algorithms. Very important in this matter is the 'Proposal for a Regulation of the European Parliament and of the Council laying down harmonised rules on artificial intelligence (artificial intelligence act) and amending certain union legislative acts' of 21 April 2021, stating that:

> The obligations for ex ante testing, risk management and human oversight will also facilitate the respect of other fundamental rights by minimising the risk of erroneous or biased AI-assisted decisions in critical areas such as education and training, employment, important services, law enforcement and the judiciary. In case

[4] Teresa Coelho Moreira, 'Algorithms, Discrimination and Labour Law' [2020] *Anuário de Direitos Humanos* 2.

[5] In the same sense, Naomi Schoenbaum, 'Gender and the Sharing Economy' (2016) 43 *Fordham Urban Law Journal* 1023, 1024 et seq.

[6] Phoebe V Moore, 'OSH and the Future of Work: benefits and risks of artificial intelligence tools in workplaces' (European Agency for Safety and Health at Work, 5 July 2019), available at: osha.europa.eu/en/publications/osh-and-future-work-benefits-and-risks-artificial-intelligence-tools-workplaces/view.

[7] UNI, 'Top 10 principles for ethical artificial intelligence', available at: www.thefutureworldofwork.org/opinions/10-principles-for-ethical-ai/.

> infringements of fundamental rights still happen, effective redress for affected persons will be made possible by ensuring transparency and traceability of the AI systems coupled with strong ex post controls.

And:

> AI systems used in employment, workers' management and access to self-employment, notably for the recruitment and selection of persons, for making decisions on promotion and termination and for task allocation, monitoring or evaluation of persons in work-related contractual relationships, should also be classified as high-risk, since those systems may appreciably impact future career prospects and livelihoods of these persons.

II. Algorithmic Discrimination

As Cathy O'Neil advocates, we live in the age of the algorithm.[8] Increasingly, the decisions that affect our lives are being made not by humans, but by mathematical models. In theory, this should lead to greater fairness and transparency because everyone is judged according to the same rules, and bias is eliminated. But, in reality, that does not happen. Many of the models being used today are opaque, unregulated and uncontestable, even when they are wrong. And, even more problematic, is that they reinforce discrimination.

Theoretically it seems that the conceit of removing humans from the decision-making process will also eliminate human bias. The paradox, however, is that in some instances automated decision-making has served to replicate and amplify bias.[9]

The use of algorithms carries the promise of objectivity. People assume that algorithm outcomes are 'neutral'. This neutrality is, however, an illusion. Algorithms are not as unbiased as we think, and the risk of discrimination rises.

The profiling of human behaviour and the resulting data allow management to make judgements about who people are, as well as to predict their future behaviour. Computer-generated data are expected to be reliable and neutral and to help with forecasting.

Employees are increasingly selected and discarded, replaced and disposable in this 'profane referencing system'.[10] As Jeremias Adams-Prassl pointed out:

> Employees across the socio-economic spectrum, from factories and offices to universities and professional services firms, are increasingly managed by, or with

[8] Cathy O'Neil, *Weapons of Math Destruction – How Big Data Increases Inequality and Threatens Democracy* (Crown 2017).

[9] Ifeoma Ajunwa, 'The paradox of automation as anti-bias intervention' (2020) 41 *Cardozo Law Review* 1671.

[10] Pav Akhtar and Phoebe Moore, 'The psychosocial impacts of technological change in contemporary workplaces and trade union responses' (2016) 8(1–2) *International Journal of Labour Research* 101, 112.

> assistance from, algorithms. Start-ups and established software providers promise to automate employer functions across the life-cycle of the employment relationship, from hiring and managing workers through to firing them.

And,

> the Covid-19 Pandemic led to an explosion of the deployment of algorithmic management software, in both white collar and blue collar professions. As regards the former, with traditional control and management options quickly disappearing as work shifted from offices to the home, software solutions to monitor staff working remotely became increasingly popular. The potential for data collection and processing increased significantly: with nearly all staff interactions taking place through collaborative work software, information about workflows, interactions, and productivity could suddenly be collected at a comprehensive level.[11]

Decisions are increasingly made based on algorithms, posing a new problem for society, which is the development of a society based on a new type of black box – the 'black box society'[12] – given that most of them are opaque and lack transparency.[13] In this scenario, it is essential to remember that all types of control must comply with the principle of transparency, which is the employees' knowledge of the supervision and control, and is essential for the correct processing of personal data of individuals in general, and employees in particular, who should know how, when, where and how control is carried out. This right, moreover, is reinforced in the General Data Protection Regulation (GDPR), and has to apply to the control performed by the algorithms, thus moving from a black box society to a kind of transparent box society.[14]

[11] 'Algorithmic management and the EU social acquis: opening the black box' (January 2021) in 'A Thematic Working Paper for the Annual Conference of the European Centre of Expertise (ECE) in the field of labour law, employment and labour market policies: Exploring ways to improve working conditions of platform workers: The role of EU labour law' Session 2: Regulating and negotiating the 'black box' of algorithmic management. Directorate General for Employment, Social Affairs and Inclusion.

[12] As the European Commission pointed out in 'First Phase Consultation of Social Partners Under Article 154 TFEU on Possible Action Addressing the Challenges Related to Working Conditions in Platform Work' (Consultation Document) C(2021) 1127 final, 15–16: 'While algorithmic management can be a useful tool that helps achieve efficient solutions, it also raises new challenges as some decisions impacting the working lives of people are taken within so-called "black boxes" which may make them difficult to understand, analyse and question. These algorithms can carry for example gender, ethnical or other bias', adding that 'Because these algorithms often lack human oversight, they may lead to unaccountable and potentially discriminatory decisions or to a lack of predictability in work relationships'.

[13] See the Report of the United Nations High Commissioner for Human Rights, 'The right to Privacy in the Digital Age' (13 September 2021) UN Doc A/HRC/48/31, 6, saying that 'The decision-making processes of many AI systems are opaque. The complexity of the data environment, algorithms and models underlying the development and operation of AI systems, as well as the intentional secrecy of government and private actors are factors that undermine meaningful ways for the public to understand the effects of AI systems on human rights and society. Machine-learning systems add an important element of opacity; they can be capable of identifying patterns and developing prescriptions that are difficult or impossible to explain. This is often referred to as the 'black box' problem. The opacity makes it challenging to meaningfully scrutinize an AI system and can be an obstacle for effective accountability in cases where AI systems cause harm. Nevertheless, it is worth noting that these systems do not have to be entirely inscrutable'.

[14] With the same opinion, Report of the United Nations High Commissioner for Human Rights, ibid, 14: 'Promoting transparency should go further by including sustained efforts to overcome the

The implementation of programs capable of learning and adapting to perform functions that relate to people creates new ethical and regulatory challenges, since it increases the possibility of obtaining results other than those intended, or even totally unexpected ones. In addition, these results can cause harm to other actors, such as the discriminatory offences. The use of technology, with an emphasis on artificial intelligence, can cause unpredictable and uncontrollable consequences, so that often the only solution is to deactivate the system.[15]

We must remember that algorithms have become, in many cases, the new supervisors of workers, and in some cases there is an increase in sexism and other ways of discrimination, as none is neutral. Quite the opposite. They often reflect biases that exist in the real world and that also exist in programmers and clients. And in the case of the evaluations and ratings made, these are often the reflection of their prejudices. In reality, just as technological innovations can help us advance, they can also further deepen existing inequalities and biases.

Nowadays, algorithms make many important decisions for us, like our creditworthiness, best romantic prospects and whether we are qualified for a job. Employers are increasingly using them during the hiring process in the belief that they are both more convenient and less biased than humans. But that is not true. In fact, for example, automated hiring platforms have enabled discrimination against job applicants and other platforms have led to discrimination in the progression of workers.

When using algorithms, employers can process large amounts of data in order to obtain relevant information which can be used for automatic decision-making. For example, algorithms can speed up the application process by weeding out large numbers of resumes or by analysing video interviews and selecting the most suitable applicants. Employers can also use algorithms to assess the performance of employees or to choose which employee is eligible for a promotion or bonus. According to research, 40 per cent of the HR functions of international companies are currently using AI applications.[16]

Furthermore, algorithms are used by companies for distribution of work and rewards or to send people out. The use of algorithms can streamline these processes and may cut costs, since fewer people are needed for the recruitment and assessment of potential employees. However, the use of these algorithms is not without risk because they can discriminate against employees.

Algorithms are, in the end, human constructs: algorithms are invented, programmed and trained by humans. The choices made by humans while

"black box" problem described above. The development and systematic deployment of methodologies to make AI systems more explainable – often referred to as algorithmic transparency – is of utmost importance for ensuring adequate rights protections'.

[15] Eduardo Magrani, 'New perspectives on ethics and the laws of artificial intelligence' (2019) 8(3) *Internet Policy Review*, available at: policyreview.info/pdf/policyreview-2019-3-1420.pdf.

[16] PWC, 'Artificial Intelligence in HR: a No-brainer' (2018), available at: www.pwc.at/de/publikationen/verschiedenes/artificial-intelligence-in-hr-a-no-brainer.pdf.

programming and training an algorithm affect its operation and results. Thus, algorithms are not free of human inspiration. Additionally, algorithms are trained on historical data. If this training data is biased against certain individuals or groups, the algorithm will replicate the human bias and learn to discriminate against them.

The selection process of the training data is also important. Data that is outdated, incorrect, incomplete or unrepresentative, or wrong, may lead to machine learning mistakes and misinterpretations. Eventually, algorithms are only as good as the data they are trained on. This is also referred to as 'garbage in, garbage out' or 'discrimination in, discrimination out'.

However, we do not think we should be so pessimistic because technology, being neutral, can be used to improve women's working conditions or that of other workers and enable them to be heard and create their own space for discussion on these issues. Indeed, if technology is created initially through an approximation of human rights, incorporating this vision of defending equality transparency and sustainability, and prohibiting discrimination, it is considered that this situation could be greatly improved.

In fact, this New Digital World of Work does not need to be scary. With the right tools, equality-friendly technology, as a kind of Equality by Design and by Default,[17] and the necessary education, it is possible to adapt and work with machines and robots using algorithms.

This idea of equality by design and by default seems to be essential for tackling the discrimination that many continue to suffer even when they are working through digital platforms, and trying to make it easier to prove because this is very difficult in the virtual world. It is therefore argued that the concept of equality and the prohibition of discrimination, whether direct or indirect, as well as the rules on the burden of proof, must be reviewed in the face of this new cyber digital world of work.

We should then change attitudes from questioning who created the discrimination to how the discrimination happens and how the platforms provide it through the algorithms that are introduced and which reproduce many of the prejudices and stereotypes of real-world discrimination.

Of course, detecting algorithmic discrimination is not easy, especially since smart algorithms are increasingly complex. Algorithms, often described, as noted above, a 'black box': the input – for instance, applicants' resumes or a employees' performance – and the output of the algorithm – for instance, which applicant will be invited for a job interview or which employee is going to be promoted – are clear. However, how the algorithm came to this conclusion is highly opaque.

That is why we reinforce the idea that algorithms must be transparent and include the principle of equal treatment from the beginning of the process of building them.

[17] Like Art 25 of the GDPR that establishes privacy by design and by default.

In Portugal, the 'Green Paper on The Future of Work 2021', establishes this transparency and even responsibility in some cases not only of the provider, but the employer who buys it and uses it.

In these cases, the GDPR can help us and it is very important because it establishes in Recital 71

> the right not to be subject to a decision, which may include a measure, evaluating personal aspects relating to him or her which is based solely on automated processing and which produces legal effects concerning him or her or similarly significantly affects him or her, such as automatic refusal of an online credit application or e-recruiting practices without any human intervention. Such processing includes 'profiling' that consists of any form of automated processing of personal data evaluating the personal aspects relating to a natural person, in particular to analyse or predict aspects concerning the data subject's performance at work, economic situation, health, personal preferences or interests, reliability or behaviour, location or movements, where it produces legal effects concerning him or her or similarly significantly affects him or her.

Article 22 establishes some rights relating to:

> Automated individual decision-making, including profiling', and number 1 states that 'The data subject shall have the right not to be subject to a decision based solely on automated processing, including profiling, which produces legal effects concerning him or her or similarly significantly affects him or her.

We think that what the Article 29 Data Protection Working Party defended in the document 'Guidelines on Automated individual decision-making and Profiling for the purposes of Regulation 2016/679'[18] is very important in these kinds of decisions:

> The controller cannot avoid the Article 22 provisions by fabricating human involvement. For example, if someone routinely applies automatically generated profiles to individuals without any actual influence on the result, this would still be a decision based solely on automated processing.
>
> To qualify as human involvement, the controller must ensure that any oversight of the decision is meaningful, rather than just a token gesture. It should be carried out by someone who has the authority and competence to change the decision. As part of the analysis, they should consider all the relevant data.

There is already some case law regarding this topic.

On 11 March 2021, the Amsterdam District Court ruled in two cases regarding Uber – *Uber employment* and *Uber deactivation* – and one case regarding Ola. In the *Ola* judgment, the Court required Ola to explain the logic behind a fully automated decision in the sense of Article 22 of the GDPR. This was the first time that a court in the Netherlands recognised such a right and it was also the first time that a court anywhere in Europe recognised it.

In the *Ola* case the Court decided that the organisation must ensure that the victim of a fully automated decision can ask a human to reconsider the decision.

[18] Adopted on 3 October 2017 and last Revised and Adopted on 6 February 2018, 21.

In the *Uber employment* case, the Court stated, in paragraph 3.3, that the GDPR is key to avoiding 'the discriminatory consequences of profiling'. In the cases at issue, the drivers used the GDPR to contest the unfairness of a licence-removal decision and to expose the power that platform economy apps have over drivers.[19]

On the other hand, the Charter of Fundamental Rights stipulates in Article 23 that equality between women and men must be ensured in all areas, including employment, work and pay. Gender discrimination is a major concern when it comes to the design and use of AI and related technologies, as pointed out by the European Commission.[20]

On the development side, the European Economic and Social Committee[21] noted that the development of AI is taking place within a homogenous environment principally consisting of young white men. This results in cultural and gender disparities, which are being embedded in AI technologies. For example, training data are prone to manipulation, may be biased, reflect cultural, gender and other prejudices or preferences, and contain errors.[22] But even if they do not, with research correlation, like where people go, where people shop, where people eat, it is possible to know a lot of information about them and thus discriminate.

Disparities at the design and deployment stage are linked to the systematic disadvantages affecting women in the labour market and the potential lack of awareness of gender biases. A recent study showed that the increased use of industrial robots could widen the gender gap, despite both genders benefiting from increased automation, as the analysis indicated that men in medium- and high-skilled occupations would benefit disproportionally.[23]

The European Commission in its document of 8 April 2019 *Ethics Guidelines for Trustworthy AI*[24] established a number of very important requirements:

> Human agency and oversight: AI systems should empower human beings, allowing them to make informed decisions and fostering their fundamental rights. At the same time, proper oversight mechanisms need to be ensured, which can be achieved through human-in-the-loop, human-on-the-loop, and human-in-command approaches.
>
> Privacy and data governance: besides ensuring full respect for privacy and data protection, adequate data governance mechanisms must also be ensured, taking into account the quality and integrity of the data, and ensuring legitimised access to data.

[19] For more information, see Raphaël Gellert, Marvin van Bekkum and Frederik Zuiderveen Borgesius, 'The Ola & Uber judgments: for the first time a court recognises a GDPR right to an explanation for algorithmic decision-making' (*EU Law Analysis*, 28 April 2021), available at: eulawanalysis.blogspot.com/2021/04/the-ola-uber-judgments-for-first-time.html.

[20] Commission, 'White Paper On Artificial Intelligence – A European approach to excellence and trust' COM (2020) 65 final, 1.

[21] Catelijne Muller, 'Artificial intelligence – The consequences of artificial intelligence on the (digital) single market, production, consumption, employment and society (own-initiative opinion)' [2017] OJ C 288, 43.

[22] See for more developments, European Union Agency for Fundamental Rights, *Getting the future right – artificial intelligence and fundamental rights – Report* (Publications Office of the European Union 2020).

[23] Cevat Giray Aksoy, Berkay Ozcan and Julia Philipp, 'Robots and the Gender Pay Gap in Europe' (2020) IZA Discussion Paper No 13482.

[24] ec.europa.eu/digital-single-market/en/news/ethics-guidelines-trustworthy-ai.

> Transparency: the data, system and AI business models should be transparent. Traceability mechanisms can help achieving this. Moreover, AI systems and their decisions should be explained in a manner adapted to the stakeholder concerned. Humans need to be aware that they are interacting with an AI system, and must be informed of the system's capabilities and limitations.

Of the utmost importance is:

> Diversity, non-discrimination and fairness: unfair (algorithmic) bias must be avoided, as it could have multiple negative implications, from the marginalization of vulnerable groups, to the exacerbation of prejudice and discrimination. Fostering diversity, AI systems should be accessible to all, regardless of any disability, and involve relevant stakeholders throughout their entire life circle.

Finally, very important also and related to this issue is:

> Accountability: mechanisms should be put in place to ensure responsibility and accountability for AI systems and their outcomes. Auditability, which enables the assessment of algorithms, data and design processes plays a key role therein, especially in critical applications.

Moreover, adequate accessible redress should be ensured.

The ILO stated the same when defending that there should be a 'human-in-command' approach to artificial intelligence,

> that ensures that the final decisions affecting work are taken by human beings. An international governance system for digital labour platforms should be established to require platforms (and their clients) to respect certain minimum rights and protections. Technological advances also demand regulation of data use and algorithmic accountability in the world of work.[25]

Further that:

> The exercise of algorithmic management, surveillance and control, through sensors, wearables and other forms of monitoring, needs to be regulated to protect the dignity of workers. Labour is not a commodity; nor is it a robot.[26]

Another principle that is very important is the principle of transparency of the algorithm because we cannot live in a 'black box society' but in a transparent society in terms of using algorithms. Algorithms should not operate as black boxes but should be opened up for examination. And in Portugal, the use of covert surveillance or control is totally forbidden.

The GDPR can help here because it reinforces this principle and establishes in Article 88 that:

> Member States may, by law or by collective agreements, provide for more specific rules to ensure the protection of the rights and freedoms in respect of the processing of employees' personal data in the employment context, in particular for the purposes of

[25] ILO, *Work for a brighter future – Global Commission on the Future of Work* (International Labour Office 2019) 13.

[26] ibid, 43.

> the recruitment, the performance of the contract of employment, including discharge of obligations laid down by law or by collective agreements, management, planning and organisation of work, equality and diversity in the workplace, health and safety at work, protection of employer's or customer's property and for the purposes of the exercise and enjoyment, on an individual or collective basis, of rights and benefits related to employment, and for the purpose of the termination of the employment relationship.

Recital 39 establishes that:

> The principle of transparency requires that any information and communication relating to the processing of those personal data be easily accessible and easy to understand, and that clear and plain language be used. That principle concerns, in particular, information to the data subjects on the identity of the controller and the purposes of the processing and further information to ensure fair and transparent processing in respect of the natural persons concerned and their right to obtain confirmation and communication of personal data concerning them which are being processed. Natural persons should be made aware of risks, rules, safeguards and rights in relation to the processing of personal data and how to exercise their rights in relation to such processing. In particular, the specific purposes for which personal data are processed should be explicit and legitimate and determined at the time of the collection of the personal data.

Workers must have the right to demand transparency in the decisions and outcomes of AI systems as well as the underlying algorithms, establishing the right to appeal decisions made by AI/algorithms, and having them reviewed by a human being.

We always must remember that not everything that is technically possible is legally admissible. While developing and using machine learning algorithms, employers have to be aware of privacy laws. For this reason, employers should introduce a human control system and should always remain capable of explaining how a decision was made.

They should also ensure that the use of algorithms is not at the expense of equal treatment rights. After all, the use of algorithms in decision-making poses a risk to a worker's right to equality.

III. Algorithmic Discrimination and Collective Bargaining

In the face of this question of discrimination by algorithms, we can see some light ahead of us and use collective bargaining to try to diminish this kind of discrimination, because it could try to influence business practices for the better and could be instrumental in both clarifying workers' rights and delineating employers' responsibilities under an employment contract.

Through collective agreements reached by social partners, the parties could address both data input into automated hiring systems and the promotion of employees for example, and thereafter employees' control over the data created by these systems.

In reality, social partners can play a significant role in advancing this situation in a way that contributes to gender equality, promoting wellbeing at work and productivity, for example, through collective bargaining.[27] Social partners in all sectors could be able to act as spearheads on this issue, which is essential for human rights.

In Portugal, a very recent Law – Law No 17/2021 of 17 May establishing a Portuguese Charter of Human Rights in the Digital Age – recognised in Article 9, Nos 1 and 2 that

> the use of artificial intelligence must be guided by respect for fundamental rights, guaranteeing a fair balance between the principles of explainability, security, transparency and responsibility, which takes into account the circumstances of each specific case and establishes processes aimed at avoiding any prejudices and forms of discrimination.
>
> 2. Decisions with a significant impact on the recipients' sphere that are taken through the use of algorithms must be communicated to the interested parties, being subject to appeal and auditable, under the terms provided by law.

We think that is very interesting and can and should be use by social partners in collective agreements.

In the 'Green Paper on the Future of Work in Portugal 2021', one of the lines of reflection is to

> encourage, in particular, the regulation of the use of algorithms in the context of collective bargaining, involving the social partners and ensuring the treatment of the matter at the level of collective agreements, in order to ensure an adequate adequacy of AI and to reflect the needs specific to each sector.

Similarly, in the collective agreements, principles that minimise the new risks associated with the autonomous behaviour of AI, establishing requirements to ensure the protection of privacy and personal data, equality and non-discrimination, ethics, transparency and the explicability of systems based on algorithms, both in terms of the selection of job candidates and in terms of the execution of the employment contract and the inspection of the workers' professional activity, could be reinforced.

Another possibility is to regulate the use of algorithms, namely in the distribution of tasks, work organisation, performance evaluation and progression, particularly in the scope of work provided through digital platforms, which represents a redoubled gap between employer and worker, both physically and through a technological intermediation relationship, thus avoiding potential bias and discrimination.

In fact, social partners can establish in collective agreements the type of data that could be used in the hiring process and in the employment relationship having in mind all the legislation like the GDPR, and in the case of Portugal, Articles 14–22 of the Labour Code about Personality Rights, in particular Article 17

[27] See Angelova (n 1) 4.

that determines the kinds of questions that can be asked in the hiring process, and Article 19 about the type of medical examinations that can be made. In these collective agreements the partners could discuss what data would be processed by these automated systems, and set the standards for probative assessment criteria.

Likewise, in collective agreements the end uses of such data could be established, showing what the data will be collected for, and also as data-retention agreements, and agreements as to the control and portability of the data created by these automated systems.

In collective agreements there could be also a part about the consultation of the employees' unions on AI systems' implementation, development and deployment.

Similarly, another point that could be discussed in collective bargaining and be included in collective agreements, bearing in mind the principles about data protection, is the need to establish rules about the collecting, storing and – if necessary – destroying data obtained from human labour, ensuring that what remains is respectful of the human dignity of individual workers. It is necessary to control the use of the data collected and how these data are translated into managerial decisions concerning employees.[28]

It is interesting to take into account the answer of the European Trade Union Confederation on the First-phase consultation of social partners under Article 154 of the Treaty on the Functioning of the European Union (TFEU) on possible action addressing the challenges relating to working conditions in platform work as they emphasise the need for collective bargaining at different levels, one of them being 'at national and transnational level when relevant (rules for algorithm, GDPR, cross-border issues and workers representation in EWC, for e.g.' and 'in respect of the transparency of algorithmic management when its effects fall within the traditional scope of collective bargaining activities'.

It is also interesting to bear in mind the Spanish Law 9/2021, 12 May, that resulted from an agreement concluded by the Spanish government and social partners and that changed the 'Workers' Statute' – Estatuto de los Trabajadores – establishing on the right of information, Article 64.4(d), that 'Be informed by the company of the parameters, rules and instructions in those that are based on algorithms or artificial intelligence systems that affect the decision-making that may affect working conditions, access and maintenance of employment, including profiling'. This is applicable to trade unions so it is important and can be use also in collective agreements and may help to diminish the risk of unfair and discriminatory algorithmic decision-making.

The importance of collective agreements in these situations is also recognised in Article 88 of the GDPR, as already noted.

In this Article, collective agreement is considered an important source for ensuring fair and lawful data processing in the context of employment. It refers

[28] Valerio De Stefano, '"Negotiating the Algorithm": Automation, Artificial Intelligence and Labour Protection' (2019) 41 *Comparative Labor Law & Policy Journal* 15.

explicitly to data-processing for recruitment and management purposes, which means that collective agreements could provide for adequate safeguards when AI-enabled tools and algorithmic-management practices are implemented in workplaces. They could, for example, require information on how employers use workers' personal data and how data are processed by AI systems and could also ban the most intrusive applications of technology, including neuro-surveillance.[29]

In Portugal, the social partners were all in favour of discussing this issue as soon as possible.

IV. Conclusion

It is obvious that AI and algorithms are consistently exerting more influence on the way we think and organise ourselves in society and, consequently, the scientific and legal advances cannot detach themselves from the ethical and legal issues involved in this new scenario.

Governing AI, and specifically algorithms, with some ethical and mostly legal principles like fairness, reliability, security, privacy, data protection, inclusiveness, transparency and accountability, and by design and by default technique, is an important step to try to follow the pace of technological innovation, and at the same time try to guarantee the effectiveness of the law.

Direct or indirect discrimination through the use of algorithms that involve big data is considered one of the most pressing challenges in the use of AI-driven technologies. Bias and discrimination, including gender-based discrimination, in data-supported algorithmic decision-making can occur for several reasons and at many levels in AI systems. They are difficult to detect and mitigate. Often, the quality of the data and biases within it are the source of potential discrimination and unfair treatment. The discriminatory effects generated on certain groups are, in practice, very difficult for individuals to challenge. And so far, only a limited number of court cases have dealt with discrimination relating to AI systems.

So, it is essential to legislate on this matter but also leave to social partners and collective bargaining the possibility of the adoption of more concrete measures to ensure transparency and access to information, and to ensure the principles of human dignity, integrity, freedom, privacy and cultural and gender diversity, as well as fundamental human rights, respecting the right to equality and the prohibition of discrimination.

[29] See all this with more detail in Valerio De Stefano and Simon Taes, 'Algorithmic Management and Collective Bargaining' (2021) 10 *Foresight Brief*, available at: www.etui.org/sites/default/files/2021-05/Algorithmic%20management%20and%20collective%20bargaining-web-2021.pdf.

10

Protection of Gig Workers against Contract Termination: Not for Everyone?

JAKUB TOMŠEJ

I. Introduction

The area of termination of employment has always been in the spotlight of both legal theory and practice. Regardless of which country's legal system we choose to examine, European scholars would typically argue that the stability of an employment relationship represents one of its key features, and that one of the main purposes of employment law consists in the protection of workers against a sudden, unexpected loss of income, which is a natural result of termination of employment. Hence, the legal regulation of termination of employment shows a strong pattern of employee protection, be it in the form of exhaustive lists of termination reasons, in the regulation of notice periods and severance pay, in the protection against dismissal in certain life situations like pregnancy or sickness, or in the introduction of processes where employees can challenge unfair dismissals before courts.

The mutual relations in the gig economy seem to have grown from completely different foundations. It is commonly understood as an area of *freedom, autonomy and self-determination.*[1] It is flexibility, and not security, that is typically talked about the most, the modus operandi of the key players in this sector. Flexibility seems to be the key element not just in the relationship between the service providers and their clients, but in relation to their individual suppliers (business users).

There have been numerous discussions in relation to the position of these business users and their possible reclassification as employees. In several countries, courts have confirmed the allegation that the level of control exercised by some of the service providers over these 'suppliers' is significant enough to support such reclassification.

[1] James Gwartney, Robert Lawson and Joshua Hall, *Economic Freedom of the World: 2016 Annual Report* (Fraser Institute 2016).

This chapter intends to focus on only one particular aspect of this contractual relationship: termination of contract and potential measures to protect the workers against such termination. After a general outline of the topic, I will analyse publicly available terms and conditions of selected key players in the gig economy, and confront them with the applicable legislation, including the recently adopted EU Regulation No 2019/1150.

II. Termination of Employment in European Law

The regulation of the protection against dismissal on the European Union (EU) level is rather limited. Apart from Article 30 of the Charter of Fundamental Rights of the European Union, according to which every worker has the right to protection against unjustified dismissal,[2] Article 33 of the Charter provides for the right to protection from dismissal for a reason connected with maternity. Council Directive 92/85/EEC[3] prohibits the dismissal of pregnant employees and employees on maternity leave, with the exception of rare and strongly justified cases where the dismissal is not connected with their condition. This does not seem to trigger any major consequences for the area of gig economy as the number of workers falling within the protection category would be very small.

The International Labour Organization issued a Termination of Employment Convention (No 158) of 1982 which defines basic principles with regard to protection of employees. It has only been ratified by some of the EU Member States, but many of its principles do not seem controversial from the overall perspective of EU Member States: with the exception of some excluded categories (eg, workers on probation), the employment relationship may only be dissolved for a valid reason connected with the capacity or conduct of the worker or based on the operational requirements of the undertaking, establishment or service. Certain reasons (union membership, filing complaints, discriminatory reasons etc) are expressly prohibited. Workers need to be given an opportunity to defend themselves against the allegations raised in relation to their performance or conduct. Any worker who considers that his employment has been unjustifiably terminated shall be entitled to appeal against that termination to an impartial body (a court in the first place).

Even in EU countries that have not ratified the Convention, local laws would follow the principle that employers may only dismiss employees based on a reason expressly defined in local regulation. These reasons would follow the classification foreseen by the Convention and fall either within the category of change of operational requirements (ie, organisational changes, restructurings, redundancies etc); capacity issues (consisting in particular of unfitness to work for health reasons,

[2] See in more detail on Article 30 Erika Kovács, *Ein europäisches Grundrecht auf Kündigungsschutz: Art 30 GRC* (Manz 2022).

[3] Council Directive 92/85/EEC of 19 October 1992 on the introduction of measures to encourage improvements in the safety and health at work of pregnant workers and workers who have recently given birth or are breastfeeding [2018] OJ L347.

poor performance issues and other situations representing a 'general' fitness of the worker to the job); and conduct issues (consisting in particular of termination for breach of the employee's obligations that is usually classified and sanctioned using its gravity as the main criterion). Some countries may define other termination reasons or even leave some room for them to emerge without an express provision set in the law (eg, 'some other substantial reasons' defined by the UK law), but even in that case the law would expect employers to act reasonably and fairly.

In summary, the labour laws of European countries would give rise to the following minimum standards when it comes to contract termination:

1. A termination of employment due to changes in operational requirements needs to be based on a clear business justification why a certain role, department (or even entire legal entity) is no longer needed.
2. A termination of employment due to capacity or conduct issues must follow a process defined by the individual country's laws, during which the employee has the opportunity to provide her views and is given an option to improve (unless the case relates to serious misconduct that typically leads to termination of employment without any prior steps).
3. The social disadvantages resulting from termination of employment are usually mitigated by measures like notice period, payment in lieu of notice and/or severance.
4. Employees who believe they have been dismissed unfairly have an option to turn to a court (or another impartial body) and ask it to declare that the dismissal was unlawful. In many countries, the court would reinstate the employee in her previous role if the lawsuit is successful.

III. Findings from the Area of Gig Economy

In an effort to compare the general framework described above with the reality in the gig economy, I have selected three major players in the area of gig economy. As the purpose of this chapter is to analyse the existing patterns in the gig economy, and not to point fingers, I am not referring to their names (although I am aware it may not be difficult to guess them). My analysis only reflects publicly available documents that have been either posted on the company website, or are available to individuals who register themselves as service providers with the company.

The first company is active in the area of car-sharing services. In the terms and conditions it defines certain requirements that its drivers need to fulfil, with customer satisfaction being one of the priorities. The contract with drivers suggests that:

> Each Driver must maintain an average rating by Users that exceeds the minimum average acceptable rating established by XXXX for the Territory, as may be updated from time to time by XXXX in its sole discretion ('Minimum Average Rating'). If such Driver does not increase his or her average rating above the Minimum Average Rating within

> the time period allowed (if any), XXXX reserves the right to deactivate such Driver's access to the Driver App and the XXXX Services.

The contract does not describe any processes that would aim to investigate potential issues and give the drivers an opportunity to defend themselves. It only provides the following wording:

> XXXX retains the right to, at any time in XXXX's sole discretion, deactivate or otherwise restrict Customer or any Driver from accessing or using the Driver App or the XXXX Services in the event of a violation of this Agreement, a violation of a Driver Addendum, Customer's or any Driver's disparagement of XXXX or any of its Affiliates, Customer's or any Driver's act or omission that causes harm to XXXX's or its Affiliates' brand, reputation or business as determined by XXXX in its sole discretion. XXXX also retains the right to deactivate or otherwise restrict Customer or any Driver from accessing or using the Driver App or the XXXX Services for any other reason at the sole and reasonable discretion of XXXX.

While the measure described above seems to refer to a temporary suspension of the cooperation rather than a clear contract termination, the contract does not clarify the period for which such suspension can happen, and it seems likely that the provisions can also be used for a permanent deactivation of a driver's account.

The second company is a leading player in the area of delivery services. Its terms of use governing the relationship with the workers who carry out the deliveries contain a relatively detailed description of standards that must be followed by these workers. The following statement is contained in the contract:

> Failure to comply with section 3 (Acceptable Use) and/or 5 (Content Standards) in these Terms of Use constitutes a material breach of the Terms of Use, and may result in our taking all or any of the following actions:
>
> - immediate, temporary or permanent withdrawal of your right to use our Service;
> - immediate, temporary or permanent removal of any posting or material uploaded by you to our Service;
> - issuing of a warning to you;
> - legal action against you including proceedings for reimbursement of all costs (including, but not limited to, reasonable administrative and legal costs) resulting from the breach;
> - disclosure of such information to law enforcement authorities as we reasonably feel is necessary.
>
> The responses described in this clause are not limited, and we may take any other action we reasonably deem appropriate.

The third company operates a virtual crowdsourcing marketplace where companies can find suppliers to whom they can outsource their activities. The contract concluded with the individuals who provide these services states the following:

> We may terminate this Agreement, terminate or suspend your account and access to the Site, or remove any Task listings immediately without notice for any reason. Upon any termination or suspension of this Agreement, your right to use the Site will cease, and you will not be able to retrieve any information related to your account. If you are a

> Worker and we terminate this Agreement, then your account balance, less any amounts you owe us (including an amount determined by us to be adequate to cover charge-backs, refunds, adjustments, or other offsets we are entitled to take in connection with your account), may be withdrawn if all withdrawal-related authentication requirements have been fulfilled. However, if we terminate this Agreement for cause (eg, you have breached our Acceptable Use Policy), your remaining account balance (if any) may be forfeited.

In summary, none of the three contracts seem to provide its users with a level of comfort that would be comparable with the standards applicable for employees described above. On the contrary, all three contracts seem to provide an easy option for the company to terminate cooperation with an individual without having to justify a reason and without having to provide an option where the individual could defend herself. None of the provisions would provide for any monetary compensation – on the contrary, in one of the cases, termination for cause may even lead to the income of the individual being forfeited. While it is not precluded that a business user could file a lawsuit against the platform provider, it would typically happen in the jurisdiction of the platform provider, and it is unclear what type of claims the business user would be able to make.

IV. Fairness and Transparency Promoted by a New Regulation?

With regard to online platforms, it is necessary to mention that a new EU Regulation No 2019/1150 became effective on 12 July 2020.[4] The new Regulation introduces significant new obligations for online platform providers and strengthens the position of their users and suppliers. It has been argued that online platform providers can unilaterally dictate any rules of the game (terms and conditions governing the relationship with entrepreneurs) and some of their practices can harm the market environment and individual entrepreneurs. Moreover, as is clear from the activity of the European Commission[5] and the cases handled by European cartel authorities (eg, in Germany or Italy),[6] many suppliers have already faced a

[4] Council Regulation (EU) 2019/1150 of 20 June 2019 on promoting fairness and transparency for business users of online intermediation services [2018] OJ C 440.

[5] Commission, 'Commission Staff Working Document Impact Assessment: Accompanying the document Proposal for a Regulation of the European Parliament and of the Council on promoting fairness and transparency for business users of online intermediation services' (Staff Working Document) SWD(2018) 138 final.

[6] eg, entrepreneurs selling their goods on the Amazon Marketplace online platform have filed a number of complaints with the German Federal Cartel Office (Bundeskartelamt), claiming that Amazon favours its own goods over their goods. See Bundeskartellamt, 'The Bundeskartellamt obtains far-reaching improvements in the terms of business for sellers on Amazon's online marketplaces' (Bundeskartellamt, 17 July 2019), available at: www.bundeskartellamt.de/SharedDocs/Meldung/EN/Pressemitteilungen/2019/17_07_2019_Amazon.html.

sudden, unannounced unilateral change in the business conditions of online platform providers, as well as some of the aforementioned issues like an unjustified downgrade of their rating, blocking of their account or contract termination. At the same time, the opportunity to seek justice in court or out of court is often not used by business users, either due to fears of lengthy proceedings, often held in an unknown jurisdiction, or of possible retaliation by online platform providers (immediate account blocking or downgrading the user).[7]

As part of the Digital Single Market Strategy, the Commission has concluded that the relationship between business users and online platform providers, and in particular unfair contractual obligations, needs to be regulated on the level of the EU law.[8] Two years after the adoption of the Strategy, the relevant Regulation has therefore been adopted, which specifically regulates only these so-called P2B (ie, platform-to-business) relationships.

The aim of the Regulation is to ensure a fairer and more transparent environment on online platforms, while transparency is also intended to ensure a change of role of the online platforms. It is to 'serve as a gateway to the downstream market, and not as a guardian of that gate', as described by the European Parliament.[9]

The Regulation covers the activity of online intermediation services and online service engines.[10] Online intermediation services are defined as services that (i) constitute information society services within the meaning of point (b) of Article 1(1) of Directive (EU) 2015/1535; (ii) allow business users to offer goods or services to consumers, with a view to facilitating the initiating of direct transactions between those business users and consumers, irrespective of where those transactions are ultimately concluded; and (iii) are provided to business users on the basis of contractual relationships between the provider of those services and business users which offer goods or services to consumers.[11]

The Regulation contains several requirements relating to the terms and conditions of the platform. Besides other items that are not relevant for this chapter, providers of online intermediation services shall ensure that their terms and conditions set out the grounds for decisions to suspend or terminate or impose

[7] Recital 5 of Council Regulation (EU) 2019/1150.

[8] Commission, 'Digital Single Market: Commission calls for swift adoption of key proposals and maps upcoming actions' (European Commission, 10 May 2017), available at: ec.europa.eu/commission/presscorner/detail/en/IP_17_1232.

[9] European Parliament, 'Report on online platforms and the digital single market' (31 May 2017) P8_TA(2017)0272.

[10] These include online engines like Google Search. Section 2(5) of Regulation (EU) 2019/1150 defines them as a digital service that allows users to input queries in order to perform searches of, in principle all websites, or all websites in a particular language, on the basis of a query on any subject in the form of a keyword, voice request, phrase or other input, and returns results in any format in which information related to the requested content can be found. The likelihood a search engine would engage business users and could potentially terminate their contract is very low, hence this concept will not be further examined.

[11] s 1(1)(b) of Council Directive (EU) 2015/1535 of 9 September 2015 laying down a procedure for the provision of information in the field of technical regulations and of rules on Information Society services [2015] OJ L241.

any other kind of restriction upon, in whole or in part, the provision of their online intermediation services to business users.[12] For that purpose, the Regulation lays down requirements concerning the time limit, manner and content of notification of decisions about suspension or termination of contract.[13] The reasons for the decision must in most cases be provided on a durable medium. If the services of the online platform are only to be restricted or temporarily suspended for the business user, it is sufficient to notify the business user of this justification at the latest when such restriction or suspension becomes effective. On the other hand, in case of termination, any justification for termination must be provided at a minimum of 30 days in advance.[14] In terms of content, it is necessary to point out in the justification the specific actions of the business user that led to the termination. These must correlate with a termination reason that was defined in advance in the terms and conditions. A mere reference to a provision of the terms and conditions enabling termination due to breach of the terms without further specification will therefore not be sufficient.

The Regulation also covers the fact that suspension or termination may be unjustified. For this reason, it obliges online platform providers to provide for an internal system for handling the complaints of business users, in which the business user is given the opportunity to comment on the measure.[15] On top of that, platforms must appoint two mediators in the event of a dispute being resolved with the business user in the form of mediation.[16] However, these costlier obligations would only apply to large online platform providers (employing more than 50 people or with an annual turnover of more than €10 million).

A novelty that goes hand-in-hand with the internet environment in which disputes occur is the ability of the mediator to communicate with the parties remotely. The Regulation provides for an online mediation as a tool to reduce the overall costs associated with it (including the 'reasonable proportion of the total costs of the mediation' which is always borne by the platform provider). The above-mentioned internal system must introduce easy, free and transparent handling of complaints by business users. Complaints may be directed against the online platform provider for a reason of non-compliance with the obligations set in the Regulation, due to technical problems related to the provision of its services or as a response to any measures of the online platform provider that affect the complainant (eg, suspension or contract termination).

In addition, platform providers must regularly publish statistical data on the functioning and effectiveness of this system (such as number of complaints, results, average time taken to review a case). In practice, these statistics can help business users compare the platforms and choose the most suitable one they want

[12] Art 3(1)(c) of Regulation (EU) 2019/1150.
[13] Art 4 of Regulation (EU) 2019/1150.
[14] Certain exceptions from this rule are envisaged by Art 4(4) of Regulation (EU) 2019/1150.
[15] Art 11 of Regulation (EU) 2019/1150.
[16] Art 12 of Regulation (EU) 2019/1150.

to work for (using the number of complaints or the number of complaints resolved positively as criteria).

Finally, in legal proceedings against an online platform provider, organisations representing business users can take actions against platforms.[17] These organisations can file a lawsuit against an online platform provider for non-compliance with the Regulation with a view to bringing the infringement to an end. The purpose of this special procedural subjectivity is to protect business users from retaliation by online platform providers, as the proceedings are conducted on the basis of a lawsuit filed by this organisation, and not on behalf of a specific business user.

V. Applicability of the Regulation

The Impact Assessment Report suggests that the Regulation applies in particular to e-commerce marketplaces (eg, eBay or Amazon Marketplace), to online application purchase platforms (eg, Google Play, Apple App Store) and product price comparators (eg, Skyscanner, Google Shopping). The Regulation also applies to online platforms that facilitate the conclusion of a contract between a business user and a consumer, even if the contract itself may no longer be concluded within the online platform. An example might be Facebook (marketplace or individual pages), or various online platforms with offers of apartments for rent or purchase where entrepreneurs publish their offers.

However, in some cases, it may be difficult to establish whether some providers fall under the remit of the Regulation. Uber and Airbnb can be used as examples here. The Court of Justice of the European Union (CJEU) recently issued a ruling in the *Elite Taxi v Uber* dispute[18] where it addressed the question of whether Uber operates in the field of transport, online intermediation service, or information society services. Similarly in a recent Airbnb case,[19] the CJEU addressed the question of whether Airbnb provides a service within the meaning of Article 56 of the Treaty on the Functioning of the European Union and Directive 2006/123,[20] or information society services within the meaning of Directive 2000/31.[21] The latter assessment means that a Member State would have only limited options to restrict such services in the national law as the rules set out in Directive 2000/31 prevail.[22]

[17] Art 14 of Regulation (EU) 2019/1150.

[18] Case C-434/15 *Asociación Profesional Elite Taxi v Uber Systems Spain SL* [2017] ECLI:EU:C:2017:981.

[19] Case C-390/18 *Airbnb Ireland and others* [2019] ECLI:EU:C:2019:1112.

[20] Council Directive 2006/123/EC of 12 December 2006 on services in the internal market [2006] OJ L376.

[21] Art 2(a) of Council Directive 2000/31/EC of 8 June 2000 on certain legal aspects of information society services, in particular electronic commerce, in the Internal Market (Directive on electronic commerce) [2000] OJ L178.

[22] Art 2(a) of Directive 2000/31/EC refers to a definition contained in Article 1(2) of former Directive 98/48 which is no longer effective. As already mentioned above, that definition corresponds with the definition contained in the currently valid Directive 2015/1535.

Under the Directive, restrictions may be imposed only for predefined reasons that pass the test of proportionality and they must, with a few exceptions, be notified in advance to the Commission.[23]

After comprehensively assessing the activities of both companies, the CJEU found significant differences between the two entities. Specifically, it examined the question whether in the given cases, the business activities have the prevailing form of information society services, or the relevant sectoral services (accommodation, transport).[24] The latter (ie, transport services) would be the case for Uber: according to the CJEU, Uber provides an intermediary service by arranging contact between a non-professional driver using his own the vehicle and the person who needs to be relocated, but in addition has a significant influence over the transport service itself. Uber not only sets the maximum price for transport, but also controls drivers' behaviour and the quality of their vehicles. As a result, the dominant part of Uber services would fall under the area of transport rather than information society. On the contrary, the services of Airbnb have been found to meet the definition of information society services.

This unveils a significant loophole in the scope of application of the Regulation as there seem to be important players in the area of gig economy that will not fall under its remit. According to the CJEU decision, the activity of Uber does not fulfil the characteristics of an information society service. As a result, the protection offered by the Regulation cannot be offered to its business users. It should be noted that in this case the CJEU did not assess the provision of services by any entrepreneurs (ie, 'business users' in the terminology of the Regulation) but focused on non-professional drivers. Knowing that the application provides comparable levels of support and control for both professional and non-professional drivers, and notably influences their activity in the same level (quality, pricing etc), there is little room to argue that the CJEU would rule differently if it examined the relationship of Uber and its business users. Pieter Van Cleynenbreugel came to the same conclusion.[25] He also considers the intermediary service of Uber as a necessary precondition for the transport itself to happen, and refers to a previous CJEU judgment in the case of *Itevelesa*[26] where the CJEU also included under transport services, services which are inherently connected with transport, but which are not a direct performance of transport. In the *Itevelesa*, technical inspections of vehicles were excluded from the scope of Directive 2006/123 with the argument that it represents a transport service that is excluded from the scope of

[23] s 3(4)b) of Directive 2000/31/EC.

[24] Directive 2006/123/EC on internal market Services does not apply to transportation Services (Article 2(2)(d) of the Directive.

[25] Pieter van Cleynenbreugel, 'Will Deliveroo and Uber be captured by the proposed EU platform Regulation? You'd better watch out' (*European Law Blog*, 12 March 2019), available at: europeanlawblog.eu/2019/03/12/will-deliveroo-and-uber-be-captured-by-the-proposed-eu-platform-regulation-youd-better-watch-out/.

[26] Case C-168/14 *Grupo Itevelesa SL and others v OCA Inspección Técnica de Vehículos SA and Generalidad de Cataluña* [2015] ECLI:EU:C:2015:685.

the Directive. Similarly, in his opinion, taking into account the broad concept of transport services according to the interpretation of the CJEU, the Uber intermediary provided to professional drivers will qualify as a transport service, not as an information society service.

In view of the above, it seems that Uber would escape the application of the Regulation. A different conclusion could perhaps only be justified if we (for the purpose of the assessment of the application of the Regulation) separated the online intermediary service from other services provided by Uber, and argued that to the extent Uber provides these services, the Regulation applies. Such separation could be justified by the fact that the Regulation has a different purpose from other directives referring transport services. However, previous CJEU judgments make it relatively clear that the online intermediary services are deemed an integral part of its services. Only time will tell whether there is any room for such interpretations. Judicial interpretation is surely needed.

VI. Conclusions: Is Collective Bargaining the Answer?

The analysis has shown that workers at many online platforms may be in a vulnerable position where they are – among other issues – exposed to an unpredictable termination process that does not provide sufficient guarantees against such termination.

The Regulation seems to provide a potential answer to most of these concerns, but it may not be available to most of the individuals in question.

While the Regulation does not provide a level of protection comparable to the European standards defined by country laws for employees, it does deal with most of the crucial elements including an obligation to provide reasons for suspension or termination of contract, notify the business user in advance, and provide an option to make any statements before a decision is made.

Whether the Regulation has brought significant changes in the platform work sector remains unclear. Uber may be just an example of a platform provider that may find sufficient reasons to escape it. Obviously, this may create bizarre situations where providers who have always argued that they perform online intermediary services rather than any other services would now have to turn around and completely reverse their line of arguments. In any case, a year and a half has passed since the Regulation became effective, and major changes are not visible on the market.

As most of the Member States do not seem to envisage any regulation in the national law in near future, it appears that action taken by the business users themselves seems to be the only option to improve the situation. We have already seen several individual cases that have been filed to courts successfully, with a court issuing a decision that would reclassify a business user to a worker or award her with certain protection measures that are usually seen in employment law.

However, the number of such cases is still relatively low, and it is questionable to what extent a defeat in an individual case will convince the platform provider to change its policy. As a result, even in this area, collective action seems to be the most powerful tool.

A concept where business users who are not employees would unionise and claim rights that are usual in employment relationships may seem somehow unusual. On the other hand, it can be argued that it is in the nature of industrial actions to emerge out of darkness and claim rights that the legislation has not yet acknowledged. In many European countries, the status of trade unions and their entitlement to represent workers have only been acknowledged after a period where employees have fought hard to achieve that. From that point of view, it would appear as a logical development if individuals in positions of business users adopted a similar approach and started to gather to express their claims.

From a strategic point of view, it would seem logical for such a movement to first focus on the definition of their position. If it is expressly acknowledged that platform workers enjoy some sort of status similar to employees, this creates a solid foundation for further claims to strengthen their position. The change may, however, come in a less structured way. While most platform workers do not seem to be too emotional about the legal classification of their contractual relationship with a platform provider, insensitive cases of contract termination could be a trigger for platform workers to start claiming an arrangement that would offer some guarantees in that respect.

As detailed in other chapters, several European countries have already seen gig workers group to exercise their rights and claims in a coordinated manner, including some cases where workers of a certain platform started to strike against a certain effort of the platform. Many countries have laws that expressly permit individuals who do not enjoy the status of an employee to participate in collective actions.

While this may give rise to some optimism, it is obvious that in many European countries, local laws do not provide for a sufficient framework for such action to happen, and there are no movements in the local labour market that would make it probable for platform workers to follow this direction. This may not only be due to a relatively low number of platform workers in the country, but to a different historical and political context where the role of trade unions is lower. However, the developments at least in some countries seem to be promising. In history, it has often been collective actions that contributed the most to the development of workers' rights, and it seems likely that it could also be the appropriate solution for the near future.

11

The Personal Dimension of Collective Bargaining in the Gig Economy: The Spanish Perspective

DANIEL PÉREZ DEL PRADO

I. Introduction: The Gig Economy and Platform Work in Spain

In most of the countries where platform work is operating, it is quite a new phenomenon, emerging since the late 2000s or early 2010s. According to Eurofound, crowd employment is rising in 11 Member States, among a mix of large and small countries and geographic locations. Interestingly, among northern European countries, often linked to a high level of adoption of new technologies, only Denmark shows indicators to be included in the emerging group. Among the eastern European Member States, employment platforms have been established in the Czech Republic, Latvia and Lithuania. Southern countries are represented by Greece, Italy, Portugal and Spain, where the recent increase is explained by the financial and pandemic crisis, which has resulted in lack of liquidity and the need to find alternative (and cheap) ways of marketing one's services. The last group is formed by Belgium, Germany and the UK, now outside the EU.[1]

Despite the influence of the last two crises (and, in some cases, fuelled by them), the activity is increasing strongly. Since 2018, the sector has doubled its contribution to GVA.[2] But Spain is not only a country in which platforms are achieving fast and important development, but also a relevant increasement in terms of employment. The best way to assess the impact of the labour market is by focusing on the jobs they involve.

[1] Eurofound, *New Forms of Employment* (Publications Office of the European Union 2015).

[2] Adigital and Afi, 'La Contribución Económica de Las Plataformas Delivery En España' (2019), available at: www.adigital.org/media/publicacion_contribucion-economica-plataformas-delivery-espana.pdf.

Figure 1 shows the percentage of the working age population that corresponds to each of the four categories of platform workers across the countries participating in the COLLEEM I and II surveys.[3] These categories relate to the time they spend working for platforms and, consequently, it shows the type of income it represents.

Figure 1 Intensity and relevance of platform work – estimates combining information on income and hours worked

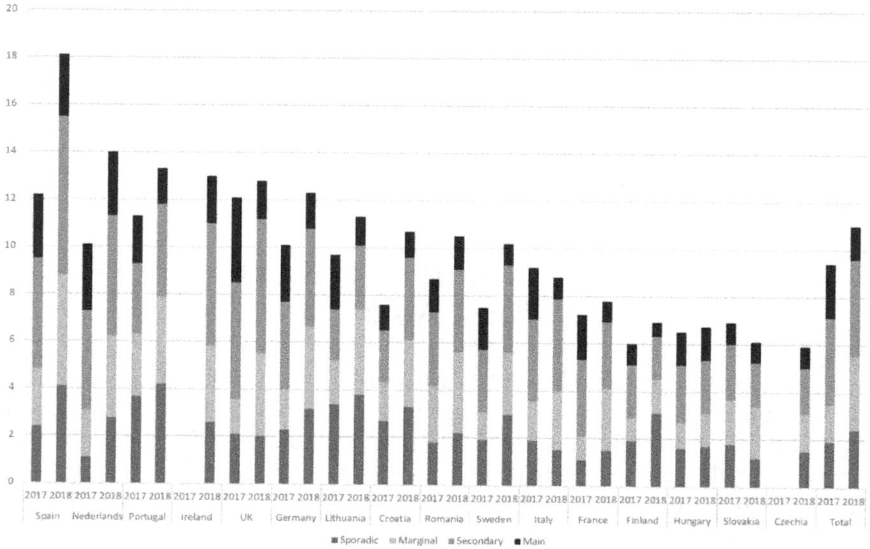

Source: Maria Cesira Urzi Brancati, Annarosa Pesole and Enrique Fernández-Macias, *New Evidence on Platform Workers in Europe* (EUR 29958 EN, Publications Office of the European Union, Luxembourg, 2020, doi:10.2760/459278 (online), JRC118570).

As can be seen, Spain forms with the Netherlands, Portugal, Ireland and the UK the group of countries which leads the share of the workforce who provide services to platforms. In particular, in 2018, Spain rocketed up to 18 per cent, more than four percentage points than the second one, the Netherlands, and more than five points above the average. Additionally, the country is the first in terms of secondary employment – 6.7 per cent versus an average of 4.1 per cent– and the second, after the Netherlands, if focused on main platform workers – 2.6 per cent compared with the Dutch share of 2.7 per cent and the average of 1.4 per cent.

As a consequence, in Spain, platform employment is not only relevant in terms of the proportion of the working population engaged in it, but also considering the financial importance for them, being the first or secondary source of income

[3] Maria Cesira Urzí Brancati, Annarosa Pesole and Enrique Fernández-Macías, *New Evidence on Platform Workers in Europe: Results from the Second COLLEEM Survey* (Publications Office of the European Union 2020).

for more than half of platform workers. This would be in line with the studies which show that platform workers would earn, on average, 1.4 times the Spanish minimum wage.[4]

As a consequence, regulating platform work is important, not only from the economic point of view, but from the social perspective. Nevertheless, regulation options vary depending on the legal classification of platform work. Obviously, the law will play a decisive role, but it requires a previous step which means taking a decision concerning which is the most appropriate legal framework to regulate this phenomenon or, more precisely, to answer the question about its employment status. Beyond the limits of the law, collective bargaining will freely regulate platform work when it is classified as a classical employment relationship. Despite this, even within the limits of self-employment there would be some room for self-regulation, as some forms of collective bargaining for self-employed persons are admitted in the Spanish legal system. In other words, if collective bargaining can intervene, it will depend on for whom and from whom it negotiates.

This chapter focuses on the personal dimension of the regulation of platform work in Spain as a key element for its regulation by collective bargaining. The following sections aim to analyse the different alternatives available concerning the employment status applicable to it and the judicial and legal steps taken so far. On this basis, it will complete the personal dimension of this phenomenon by pointing at the different actors involved in the regulatory reaction against the emergence of platform work. Finally, this research analysis will be closed by leaving some reflections concerning the short-term future.

II. The Personal Scope of Collective Bargaining in the Platform Economy: Bargaining for and by Whom

A. The Starting Point: Three Different Categories

Traditionally, Spanish regulation has set the limits of the employment relationship through three different notions which have emerged successively with the evolution of the labour market. As a consequence, the Spanish legal framework for the employment relationship could be described as an 'obtuse triangle'[5] because it is

[4] Adigital and Afi, 'Importancia Económica de Las Plataformas de Delivery y Perfil de Los Repartidores En España' (2020), available at: www.adigital.org/media/importancia-economica-de-las-plataformas-digitales-de-delivery-y-perfil-de-los-repartidores-en-espana.pdf?utm_medium=email&utm_campaign=200908GraciasPresentacionInformeDelivery&utm_content=200908GraciasPresentacionInformeDelivery+CID_85fca3d33ec8e9d1bc33e91d3d7a7885&utm_source=Email%20marketing%20software&utm_term=DESCARGAR%20INFORME.

[5] Daniel Pérez del Prado, 'Spain: Towards a New Architecture for Labour Law Institutions' in Mark de Vos (ed), *The Cambridge Handbook of Technological Disruption in Employment and Labour Law* (Cambridge University Press 2021, forthcoming).

formed by three elements but they do not have the same importance. As in this type of triangle in which one of its angles is bigger than the others, here the importance of the employment relationship, from a legal point of view, is not comparable to the others.

Hence, attention must be paid, first and logically, to the employment relationship, represented by the concept of the employee. In contrast to other legal systems (ie, Anglo-Saxon) this is a single concept which defines it as someone 'voluntarily rendering their services for compensation on behalf of another party, within the scope of the organisation and management of another, physical or legal person, called the employer or entrepreneur' (Article 1 Workers' Statute – Estatuto de los Trabajadores).

On this basis, from the Spanish labour law perspective, the employee and, as a consequence, the employment relationship is defined by the convergence of a number of elements. The classical classification distinguishes the following: (i) willingness, as labour law covers and protects those activities which are freely carried out by the employee, rejecting and prosecuting the different forms of forced labour; (ii) alterity, meaning that the employee works for another person, the employer; (iii) control, which is also included because the work must be developed under the instructions of the employer; and, finally (iv) remuneration, that is, the professional activity in exchange for a salary.[6] Other authors synthetise this definition in only three elements or 'coordinates': (i) objective coordinate, referred to as the development of a professional activity; (ii) space coordinate, under the coverage of the employment relationship; and (iii) time coordinate, where it takes place during a certain period of time.[7]

Whatever the approach, Spanish regulation defines the employment relationship quite similarly to other close legal systems. Indeed, this is quite similar to the definition provided by ILO Recommendation 198, including most of indicators mentioned in its paragraph 13, despite being organised in a different way:

> (a) the fact that the work: is carried out according to the instructions and under the control of another party; involves the integration of the worker in the organization of the enterprise; is performed solely or mainly for the benefit of another person; must be carried out personally by the worker; is carried out within specific working hours or at a workplace specified or agreed by the party requesting the work; is of a particular duration and has a certain continuity; requires the worker's availability; or involves the provision of tools, materials and machinery by the party requesting the work. (b) periodic payment of remuneration to the worker; the fact that such remuneration constitutes the worker's sole or principal source of income; provision of payment in kind, such as food, lodging or transport; recognition of entitlements such as weekly rest and annual holidays; payment by the party requesting the work for travel undertaken by the worker in order to carry out the work; or absence of financial risk for the worker.

[6] Manuel Alonso Olea and Maria Emilia Casas Baamonde, *Derecho del trabajo* (Civitas 2005).
[7] Jesús R Mercader Uguina, *Lecciones de Derecho Del Trabajo* (Tirant lo Blanch 2008).

Actually, Spanish courts frequently use these types of elements or indications when applying the multiple test as a methodological tool to determine if an employment relationship exists. Nevertheless, this is not an easy task in practical terms. As the Supreme Court recognises

> in the resolution of litigious cases, it frequently resorts, for the identification of these notes of the employment contract, to a set of indications or indicative facts of one and the others. These indications are sometimes common to the generality of the activities or jobs and, other times, specific of certain work or professional activities.[8]

The insufficiencies of the definition are not only detected by courts but assumed by the law when setting the so-called special employment relationship. These activities have their own regulation in order to provide a specific framework for some particularities. Except for these, the rest of its regulation is derived from the Workers' Statute. In other words, special employment relationships are regulated, primarily, by their own special regulation and, in a subsidiary and complementary way, by the common one. This category includes managers, household workers, convicts in penitentiary institutions, professional sportsmen and women, artists, sales agents, workers with disabilities, junior doctors in training and lawyers who work in law offices.

The second element to appear has been the concept of 'self-employment'. This is the opposite side of the coin, making the influence of the notion of employee crystal clear. According to the Self-Employment Statute – even in the name of the law it observes the weight of the traditional regulation, despite it having the merits of being the pioneer in Europe[9] – a self-employed person is defined as

> a natural person who regularly, personally, directly, on their own account and outside the scope of management and organization of another person, carries out an economic or professional activity for profit, whether or not they give employment to workers employed by someone else.[10]

Whereas in the employment relationship, the employee works for another person, here the self-employed person carries out his professional activity 'on their own account'. While in the first relationship the work is provided under the direction and control of the employer, in the second it is done 'outside the scope of management and organization of another person'. Finally, the employee works in exchange for a salary, but the self-employed person develops an economic or professional activity 'for profit'. The only genuine features of the definition are: (i) the requirement that the activity must be developed 'regularly, personally and directly', but it does not say too much regarding the limits of the notion, because the employment relationship is also carried out under the same circumstances; (ii) by a

[8] Supreme Court Resolution 24 January 2018, ECLI: ES:TS:2018:588.

[9] Frederic López i Mora, 'Un Año y Medio de Estatuto Del Trabajo Autónomo y Su Infradesarrollo: Y En Eso Llegó Una Gran Crisis Económica' (2008) 98 *REVESCO: Revista de estudios cooperativos* 89.

[10] Article 1 Self-Employment Statute (Estatuto del Trabajador Autónomo).

natural person, excluding the possibility of applying the figure to legal persons; and (iii) whether or not the self-employed person hire one or more employees, admitting the possibility of being employer.

Consequently, it is possible to affirm that the distinction between employment and self-employment is clearly dominated by the first one. Actually, the debate is frequently focused on the existence of an employment relationship because, otherwise, the legal relationship will be covered by a civil or commercial contract and the presence of self-employment admitted.[11] Hence, from a practical perspective, the definition does not add too much in a debate which is governed by the classical definition of employment relationship.

However, defining self-employment was not the only effort to delimitate it provided by the Self-Employment Statute. In order to also cover 'grey areas', the law introduced another definition, which is the third notion in the triangle described here. It is the so-called economically dependent self-employment -TRADE as per the Spanish acronym (*Trabajador Autónomo Económicamente Dependiente*)-. TRADEs are understood as those who usually, personally and directly carry out an economic or professional activity for lucrative purposes and for one client, from whom they receive, at least, 75 per cent of their income. Among the measures, these self-employed workers have the right to enjoy 18 days of holiday per year, the right of affiliation to trade union or employer's associations or to create specific professional associations and a sort of collective bargaining, whose result, the named 'agreements of professional interest', can benefit the associates of the signatory organisations.

The emergence of this notion has aroused great interest in light of its potential impact on traditional industrial relations and of the consequences for the design of social policies.[12] Nevertheless, it seems its introduction does not change too much in the Spanish labour market panorama. Despite the country having an intermediate position concerning self-employment among European countries – according to Eurostat, self-employment rate is around 15 per cent and remains quite stable-, TRADEs mean only 1.5 per cent of the whole workforce – 10 per cent of the self-employed – would be covered by an 'agreement of collective interest'[13] (*acuerdos de interés profesional*). As a consequence, it is possible to say

[11] Francisco Javier Gómez Abelleira, *Handbook on Spanish employment law* (Tecnos 2012).

[12] Colin C Williams and Frédéric Lapeyre, 'Dependent Self-Employment: Trends, Challenges and Policy Responses in the EU' (International Labour Office 2017); Colin C Williams and Ioana Alexandra Horodnic, 'Evaluating the Prevalence and Distribution of Dependent Self-Employment: Some Lessons from the European Working Conditions Survey' (2018) 49 *Industrial Relations Journal* 109; Concepción Román, Emilio Congregado and José María Millán, 'Dependent Self-Employment as a Way to Evade Employment Protection Legislation' (2011) 37 *Small Business Economics* 363; Werner Eichhorst et al, *Social Protection Rights of Economically Dependent Self-Employed Workers Based on a Study Conducted for the European Parliament under Contract IP/A/EMPL/FWC/2008-002/C1/SC8* (IZA 2013), available at: www.iza.org/en/webcontent/publications/reports/report_pdfs/iza_report_54.pdf.

[13] Patricia Nieto Rojas, 'Los acuerdos de interés profesional.: Balance tras diez años del estatuto del trabajo autónomo' (2018) 3 *Revista de información laboral* 161.

that TRADE's evolution is not a story of success, except for the traditional sectors in which it was previously consolidated.[14]

Anyway, the result of this evolution is regulation characterised by the convergence of the three mentioned categories, with different sources and very different guarantees concerning working conditions and social protection (see Table 1). This increasing regulatory effort does not achieve, however, the objective of solving the problems concerning professional classification. On the contrary, new regulations have been used in some sectors to avoid classical labour law protection.[15] Furthermore, the emergence of new technologies and business models related to the digitalisation of the economy has complicated the situation even more.

Table 1 Types of professional relationships and legal coverage

Type of relationship	Regulation	Rights
Employee	Workers Statute + Collective Agreements	All rights
Self-Employee	Self-Employee Statute	Some individual rights + Freedom of association
ED Self-Employee	Self-Employee Statute + Agreements of Professional Interest	Some individual rights + Freedom of association + special collective bargaining

Source: own elaboration.

B. The Judicial Debate and the Emergence of the 'Riders' Law'

Within this framework, the debate on platform work could be summarised, as in so many other discussions, in three different perspectives.[16]

First, the position of platforms, supported by some economists and lawyers, which requires specific regulation for platform work, which would be outside the prototypical confrontation between employment and self-employment and suggests the existence of a *tertium genus* which needs its own regulatory framework. In other words, from this point of view, the solution would crystallise in the creation of a fourth new category to be added to the three explained above.[17]

[14] Jesús Cruz Villalón, 'El trabajo autónomo económicamente dependiente en España' (2013) 98 *Documentación Laboral* 19, available at: idus.us.es/handle/11441/41506.

[15] Román, Congregado and Millán (n 12).

[16] Diego Álvarez Alonso, 'Plataformas Digitales y Relación de Trabajo' in J García Murcia (ed), *Nuevas tecnologías y protección de datos de carácter personal enlas relaciones de trabajo* (Gobierno de Asturias, Universidad de Oviedo 2019).

[17] Ángel Augusto Aguirre Forero, Angie Katherine Zamora Guaba, María Alejandra González Pinto, 'La prestación de servicios en plataformas digitales: nuevos indicios para una nueva realidad' in Adrián Todolí Signes and Macarena Hernández-Bejarano (eds), *Trabajo en plataformas digitales: innovación,*

This alternative would be inspired by French Law 206-1088 on labour, social dialogue, modernisation and the guarantee of professional itinerary (Loi n°. 2016-1088 du 8, août 2016, relative au travail, à la modernisation du dialogue social et à la sécurisation des parcours professionnels).

Second, the perspective close to trade unions' point of view, supported by most of the academy, which highlights that the platforms' business model would be based on a strategy focused on saving costs by avoiding (fraudulently) the application of labour and social security law. From this perspective, the debate would not be too different from others taken in the past and the solution would be the same one: revealing the abuse and applying the correct legal framework, that is, labour law.[18]

Finally, there is still room for a third intermediate position which is based on the idea that no new categories are needed, but simply the adaptation of the three that already exist. This point of view does not prejudice the classification of someone as employee, self-employed or economic dependent self-employed but suggests that, depending on the final accommodation according to the particular circumstances of the case, specific rules should be considered.[19]

Which option has been taken by the courts? Since 2018, several rulings analysed Deliveroo's, Take Eat Easy's and Glovo's models, to determine if riders who work for them (and who had been usually terminated previously) should be considered as employees, as self-employed or as economically dependent self-employed. Table 2 shows the courts' resolutions delivered from 2018 to October 2020,[20] distinguishing between first instances (light grey) and appeals (dark grey). According to its content, the following elements must be highlighted: (i) the discussion is monopolised by delivering platforms; (ii) despite the Supreme Court having the final word before its resolution, the debate was clearly inclined in favour of the

derecho y mercado (Aranzadi 2018); Alejandra Martínez Escribano, '¿Nuevos trabajadores? Economía colaborativa y Derecho del Trabajo. Repensando el Derecho del Trabajo: el impacto de la economía colaborativa' (2018) 1 *Derecho de las relaciones laborales* 48; César Otero Gurruchaga, 'El complicado encaje de los trabajadores de la economía colaborativa en el Derecho Laboral: Nuevos retos para las fronteras de la laboralidad' (2018) 1 *Derecho de las relaciones laborales* 61; Francisco Pérez de los Cobos y Orihuel, 'El trabajo en plataformas digitales' in Yolanda Sánchez-Urán Azaña and María Amparo Grau Ruiz (eds), *Nuevas tecnologías y derecho: retos y oportunidades planteadas por la inteligencia artificial y la robótica* (Juruá Editorial 2019); María Luz Rodríguez Fernández, *Plataformas digitales y mercado de trabajo* (Ministerio del Trabajo, Migraciones y Seguridad Social, Subdirección General de Información Administrativa y Publicaciones 2019).

[18] Cristóbal Molina Navarrete, 'Derecho y trabajo en la era digital: ¿"revolución industrial 4.0" o "economía sumergida 3.0"?', *El futuro del trabajo que queremos*, vol II (OIT 2017); Adrián Todoli Signes, *El Trabajo En La Era de La Economía Colaborativa* (Tirant lo Blanch 2017); Anna Ginès Fabrellas, 'Diez retos del trabajo en plataformas digitales para el ordenamiento jurídico-laboral español' (2018) *Estudios financieros. Revista de trabajo y seguridad social: Comentarios, casos prácticos : recursos humanos* 89; Francisco Trillo Párraga, 'El trabajo en plataformas virtuales: a propósito del caso Uber' in Adrián Todolí Signes and Macarena Hernández-Bejarano (eds), *Trabajo en plataformas digitales: innovación, derecho y mercado* (Aranzadi 2018); Antonio Pedro Baylos Grau, 'Los derechos digitales y la negociación colectiva' (2019) 9331 *Diario La Ley* 2.

[19] Álvarez Alonso (n 16).

[20] The moment at which the Supreme Court delivered its ruling, see below.

existence of an unemployment relationship; and (iii) this would not preclude other solutions for other types of platforms.

If focused on the details, the discussion was more open at the first instance level, in spite of a majority of these resolutions pointing towards the employment relationship than at the appeal stage, where the discussion clearly drove to this solution. The only judgment in favour of the existence of self-employment, STSJ Madrid 19-9-2019, was corrected by the following ones delivered by the same court and this position has been kept since then. Accordingly, it is possible to say that the appeal level court's opinion was practically unanimous.

The reasons provided by the courts to mostly adopt this particular option can be summarised according to the main factors that support the notion of the employment relationship.[21] On the one hand, the existence of subordination is justified because the company obtains the profits of the riders' activity and assumes the risks of that task. Additionally, the rider cannot lend his activity disconnected from the platform, owing to the fact that the platform is the essential intermediary between the rider and the client. Furthermore, the ownership of the vehicle and mobile phone cannot be considered as evidence of non-subordination.

The rider could not lend his work outside the digital platform in which it is integrated. If he decided to undertake this type of activity by himself as a true self-employed person, he would be doomed to fail and his chances of growing as an entrepreneur would be non-existent, because

> the success of these platforms is due to the technical support provided by ICT, which they use for their development and exploitation of a brand, in this case Glovo, which is advertised on social networks through Google-type search engines, a place where customers go when they need the purchase and delivery of the products that demand provides.[22]

In other words, the platform's business model uses the app as a technological tool, to interconnect subjects, so whoever is its owner determines the relationship and, as a consequence, can be considered as evidence in favour of the existence of an employment relationship.

On the other hand, the existence of dependence can be affirmed on the basis of a number of factors. It is true, as the company often highlights that riders enjoy a considerable margin of flexibility. For example, regarding working time, riders can choose the schedules and days on which they want to work, as well as the route or the number of orders they want to attend, without the company being able to impose any of these requirements. Nevertheless, riders do not have absolute freedom when rejecting or accepting the service. The rider enjoys some flexibility, but this is the obvious result of the platform's business model.

[21] COGENS Project, 'Collective Bargaining in the Gig Economy – Who and for Whom' (COGENS – Collective Bargaining and Gig Economy: New Perspective 2020) Spain's preliminary results of the project.

[22] SJS Madrid (nº 33) 11/02/2019.

As the SJS Madrid (nº 33) 11/02/2019 judgment explains:

> [T]he assertive faculty in the choice of each microtask is the logical consequence of the atomization of working time, because if the employer could always dispose of the dealer at his will, this would place him in a situation of permanent availability, which would constitute a state of personal servitude which would be contrary to the constitutional and EU conceptualisation of work as a right.

Furthermore, these freedoms do not provide any power to negotiate their working conditions, since companies have an enormous number of distributors willing to work. Consequently, when any rider refuses to carry out an assignment, he can be automatically substituted by another rider.

The final result is that the basic elements of the relationship, such as remuneration, are entirely determined according to parameters that the company establishes for each service.

Table 2 Spanish judgments since 2018 on platforms' legal relationship until the Supreme Court's Resolution in 2020

RULING	PLATFORM	CORE-EMPLOYEE	TRADE
SJS Barcelona (nº 11) 29/5/2018	TAKE EAT EASY	✓	
SJS Valencia (nº 6) 01/06/2018	DELIVEROO	✓	
SJS Madrid (nº 39) 3/9/2018	GLOVO		✓
SJS Madrid (nº 17) 11/01/2019	GLOVO	✓	✓
SJS Madrid (nº 33) 11/02/2019	GLOVO	✓	
SJS Gijón (nº 1) 20/02/2019	GLOVO	✓	
SJS Oviedo (nº 4) 25/02/2019	GLOVO		✓
SJS Madrid (nº 1) 3/4/2019	GLOVO	✓	
SJS Madrid (nº 1) 4/4/2019	GLOVO	✓	
SJS Barcelona (nº 24) 21/05/2019	GLOVO		✓
SJS Barcelona (nº 24) 29/05/2019	GLOVO		✓
SJS Valencia (nº 6) 10/6/2019	DELIVEROO	✓	
SJS Barcelona (nº 31) 11/06/2019	DELIVEROO	✓	
SJS Salamanca (nº 1) 14/06/2019	GLOVO		✓
SJS Madrid (nº 19) 22/7/2019	DELIVEROO		
SJS Barcelona (nº 29) 30/07/2019	GLOVO	✓	
SJS Vigo (nº 2) 12/11/2019	GLOVO		✓
SJS Barcelona (nº 3) 18/11/2019	GLOVO	✓	
SJS Zaragoza (nº 2) 27/4/2020	DELIVEROO	✓	

(continued)

Table 2 ***(Continued)***

RULING	PLATFORM	CORE-EMPLOYEE	TRADE
SJS Barcelona (nº 21) 7/9/2020	DELIVEROO	✓	
STSJ Asturias 29-07-2019	GLOVO	✓	
STSJ Madrid 19-09-2019	GLOVO		✓ (reviewed by the Supreme Court)
STSJ Madrid 27-11-2019	GLOVO	✓	
STSJ Madrid 18-12-2019	GLOVO	✓	
STSJ Madrid 17-1-2020	DELIVEROO	✓	
STSJ Madrid 3-2-2020	GLOVO	✓	
STSJ Castilla y León 17-2-2020	GLOVO	✓	
STSJ Cataluña 21-02-2020	GLOVO	✓	
STSJ Cataluña 7-5-2020	GLOVO	✓	
STSJ Cataluña 12-05-2020	GLOVO	✓	
STS Cataluña 16-06-2020	DELIVEROO	✓	
TOTAL		23	8
STS 23-09-2020	GLOVO	✓	

Source: own elaboration based on ignasibeltran.com. Light grey: first instance; dark grey: appeals. Black: Supreme Court Resolution. SJS: Sentencia de Juzgado de lo Social; STSJ: Sentencia de Tribunal Superior de Justicia. STS: Sentencia del Tribunal Supremo.

Regarding judgments excluding the existence of an employment relationship, it is interesting to highlight that five out of eight rulings stated that these riders are TRADES because they would not fulfil the two main features of the employment relationship, and additionally, they would comprehend the main elements of the economic dependent self-employed.

Hence, according to this minority position there is no employment relationship owed for two main reasons. On the one hand, there is no subordination because the rider would have almost absolute freedom to choose working time, place and route tasks, the rider has a direct relationship with the final clients if the rider accepts the task, and the rider provides his own bike and phone as the worker's tools. On the other hand, there would not be dependence because the company does not have any disciplinary tools to force riders to work in a case where one of them refuses tasks, which would be the only case in which the rider does not perform his duty.

Nevertheless, once the employment relationship has been excluded, the most common situation is being under the TRADE's coverage. It must be kept in mind that TRADEs develop economic or professional activities for one client, from whom they receive at least 75 per cent of their income and that, in Spain, around half of the platform employees work in this sector as their main or secondary activities.

Within these two positions, Spain's Supreme Court has inclined to the existence of an employment relationship for Glovo. Its Resolution of 25 September 2020 (ECLI: ES:TS:2020:2924) states that a rider is not completely free to decide when he works owing to the point system conditions on his activity; it is controlled by geolocation; his activity is determined by precise instructions on how to do the tasks, waiting time is paid; and the most important tool to develop the activity, the platform, belongs to the company. As mentioned above, this Resolution closes the judicial debate for the delivery sector, but not for others or even for other platforms.

Nevertheless, this is not the last milestone in the debate on platform work. The agreement[23] between the social partners and the government to regulate the delivery sector has become the first law in Europe regulating platform work, the so-called 'Riders' Law' or technically, Law 12/2021 of 28 September, which modifies the Workers' Statute, approved by Royal Legislative Decree 2/2015 of 23 October, to guarantee the labour rights of people dedicated to distribution in the field of digital platforms.[24]

Several reasons have been considered to initiate the social dialogue to regulate platform work. First, it was a compromise of both political parties in the coalition government (Socialist Party and Podemos). Second, the poor working conditions of these workers have been at the core of both political and social debate, putting pressure on political agents and social partners to find a solution. Third, the intense judicial debate also empowered the legislative path. Despite negotiations being initiated before the Supreme Court's judgment, the different resolutions delivered by lower courts highlighted the necessity of having an explicit legal framework. The Supreme Court's judgment gives the final support in favour of the employment relationship solution.

Nevertheless, according to the text of the proposed legislation the new law will include the following reforms:

On the one hand, it presumes, unless proven otherwise, the existence of an employment relationship for those who provide services in exchange for remuneration for delivery and distribution of products for employers who exercise the business powers of the organisation, direct and control indirectly or implicitly through a digital platform, or through the algorithmic management of the service or conditions of work. This means the explicit translation of the general

[23] Ministerio de Trabajo y Economía Social, 'El Gobierno y los interlocutores sociales alcanzan un acuerdo sobre los derechos laborales de las personas dedicadas al reparto a través de plataformas digitales' (10 March 2021), available at: prensa.mites.gob.es/WebPrensa/noticias/laboral/detalle/3958.

[24] Ley 12/2021, de 28 de septiembre, por la que se modifica el texto refundido de la Ley del Estatuto de los Trabajadores, aprobado por el Real Decreto Legislativo 2/2015, de 23 de octubre, para garantizar los derechos laborales de las personas dedicadas al reparto en el ámbito de plataformas digitales. Official Gacette 29 September 2021, nº 233.

presumption of Spanish employment law to this activity. However, this rule has opened another new debate among scholars concerning its legal nature, that is, whether it is a 'strong' presumption or '*quasi iure et de iure*' presumption (non-rebuttable) or a mere '*iuris tantum*' presumption (rebuttable).[25]

On the other hand, article 64 of the Workers' Statute (Spanish employment law) states that employees' representatives have the right, among others, 'to issue a report, prior to the execution by the employer of the decisions adopted by him, on … the implementation and review of work organization and control systems, time studies, establishment of bonus and incentive systems and job evaluation'. The new proposed wording adds a brief paragraph of special relevance at the end, which is 'included when they derive from mathematical calculations or algorithms'. As a consequence, workers' representatives will have the right not only to be informed, but consulted concerning this issue, as they can deliver a report on it.

Despite the trade unions' proposals being more detailed,[26] it is a great advance, as it does not only extend information and consultation on this issue, but requires collective bargaining to negotiate the details. In order words, it puts the algorithm into the object of negotiation.

III. Actors Involved in Collective Bargaining in the Platform Economy Context

But there are other subjects involved in the regulation of platform work. In this regard, it is possible to distinguish between the reaction of traditional actors and the emergence of new ones.

Starting with the last ones, according to some authors the rise of populism in Europe can be connected, among other factors, with increasing inequalities, poorer working conditions and weaker social protection.[27] Spain is not an exception. The variety of political parties has increased since 2008, including those at the extremes. The only difference was on the far Right. Despite economic crisis and fast eroding political trust, Spain had not seen any right-wing populist party obtain more than 1 per cent of the vote in national elections in recent years, which

[25] A good summary of each position can be found in Eduardo Rojo Torrecilla, 'Y Llegó La Norma Que Declara La Relación Laboral de "Las Personas Dedicadas al Reparto En El Ámbito de Las Plataformas Digitales". Primeras Notas y Comentarios al RDL 9/2021 de 11 de Mayo' (*El Blog de Eduardo Rojo*, 18 May 2021), available at: www.eduardorojotorrecilla.es/2021/05/y-llego-la-norma-que-declara-la.html.

[26] eg, 'all the information related to the parameters and decision-making rules used by the algorithms used by the company that may directly or indirectly affect the conditions of work and access and maintenance of employment'. Their proposal also included the creation of a platform register, in which must be included the 'g) Algorithm applied to the organization of the activity, which will include, as a minimum, the pseudo code or flow diagram used, as well as the reputation systems used, if any, and to whom they apply'.

[27] Paul Mason, *Postcapitalismo: Hacia un nuevo futuro* (Grupo Planeta Spain 2016).

created interest among scholars.[28] Nevertheless, this differential element disappeared at the end of 2019 with the emergence of the far right-wing party VOX. Hence, Spain can be included in the group of countries in which populism has a presence, as a new actor in the current political and social debate.

But focusing on labour law issues, most of the new subjects relate to the platform economy. Hence, owing to very poor working conditions, the primary absence of unions' reaction and the atmosphere of mistrust against them, new employees' associations emerge, such as 'riders x derechos' (riders for rights). Although they prefer to act as a 'collective' or association, their activities are quite close to those relating to classical trade unions. Nevertheless, as soon as the unions' strategy regarding platform workers changed, their influence weakened. Nowadays, most of the cases pending in courts are led by the traditional trade unions, UGT and CCOO. Something similar has happened on the employers' side. After a first period acting outside traditional employers' associations, CEOE and CEPYME, the strategy changed recently and, for example, Uber decided to join CEOE at the beginning of 2020. Other companies, such as Deliveroo, Cabify and Glovo are also part of it. However, the tensions derived from the negotiation of the Riders' Law broke the union of employers' action.

Concerning traditional actors, it must be highlighted how political parties and the government are launching different proposals to regulate a number of manifestations of the disruptive change. Moreover, the current progressive coalition government has rescued social dialogue as the way to analyse, debate and implement those reforms relating to social issues after a long period which coincided with the financial crisis, in which the legislative strategy was set unilaterally by the government.[29] Despite these efforts, legal or governmental reaction seems not to have arrived on time.

Actually, most of the dysfunction derived from digital change has been dealt with by courts implementing the traditional instruments they used to apply, adapting them to the new circumstances when necessary. The current debate on the existence of employment relationships under the activity provided by those who work for delivery platforms is the prototypical example and is explained below. Nevertheless, this is not the only case. The discussion on the impact of digitalisation on employment has gone further than the limits of scientific analysis to arrive in the courts' arena. The social judge of Las Palmas delivered a resolution in which

[28] Carmen González-Enríuez, 'The Spanish Exception: Unemployment, Inequality and Immigration, but No Right-Wing Populist Parties' (2017) Elcano Royal Institute Working Paper 3, available at: www.realinstitutoelcano.org/wps/wcm/connect/e9e0d7c1-7c71-4335-a2fb-15b219e62c5e/WP3-2017-GonzalezEnriquez-Spanish-Exception-unemployment-inequality-inmigration-no-right-wing-populist-parties.pdf?MOD=AJPERES&cacheid=1487009991261.

[29] Jesús R Mercader Uguina et al, 'DIADSE- Dialogue for Advancing Social Europe. Country Report: Spain' (DIADSE Project 2016), available at: aias-hsi.uva.nl/en/projects-a-z/diadse/reports/reports.html.

it declares that the substitution of an employee by a bot must be considered as unfair dismissal.[30]

Even the Labour Inspectorate has introduced control over the worst effects of digitalisation in its daily work. In particular, its Strategic Plan 2018–2020 states a line of action on 'activities developed by platforms'. This includes the creation of a specific operative procedure, specialised training for inspectors and the implementation of pilot programs with Autonomous Communities.

But focusing on industrial relations, it would be possible to see that Spanish social partners and collective bargaining would be dealing with the disruptive change in a very incipient way. Moreover, most of these actions have risen in the platforms' arena, as a consequence of the very poor working conditions of 'offline' workers – whereas 'online' workers would still be outside this movement, despite them being barely in a better situation.[31] Additionally, the pressure of the new agents mentioned above also played a very important role, compelling social partners, particularly trade unions, to make a move.

For instance, trade unions have launched their own platforms in order to provide legal advice for delivery workers: turespuestasindical.es (UGT), precaritywork.es (CCOO) and Deliveroo CNT's Union Branch. It is also remarkable that the actions supported by youth organisations such as RUGE (linked to UGT), focused on providing assistance to young workers and, particularly, those who work under very poor working conditions. Its campaigns are frequently directed to those activities in which the employment relationship is under discussion, as in the case of platform workers, internships or other forms of outsourcing. Additionally, its strategy, based on a high presence in social networks, is fresh and imaginative and different from traditional unions' action.

IV. Conclusions: The Following Steps

Platform work, as a technological, economic and social phenomenon, has increased notably in the last two decades. Since 2018, the sector has doubled its contribution to GVA, highlighting Spain as one of the countries in which platforms are achieving fast and important development and also a relevant increase in terms of employment. In Spain, platform employment is not only relevant in terms of the working population, but also considering the financial importance for them, being the first or secondary source of income for more than half of platform workers. As a consequence, regulating platform work is important, not only from

[30] Jesús R Mercader Uguina, 'Despido de Una Administrativa Cuyo Trabajo Ha Sido Sustituido Por Un Robot: ¿es Posible Poner Puertas al Campo?' (*El Foro de Labos*, 1 October 2019), available at: forodelabos.blogspot.com/2019/10/despido-de-una-administrativa-cuyo.html.

[31] Fernando Rocha, 'Strengthening the Decentralisation of Collective Bargaining in Spain. Between the Legal Changes and Real Developments' in Salvo Leonardi and Roberto Pedersini (eds), *Multi-employer bargaining under pressure: Decentralisation trends in five European countries* (ETUI 2018).

the economic point of view, but from the social perspective. This puts pressure on several actors about the importance of regulating it carefully.

The starting point is the subject which is the object of regulation, that is, the platform worker. The Spanish legal system provides three different categories, the employee, the self-employed person and the TRADE, with different sources and very different guarantees concerning working conditions and social protection for each. This varied regulatory effort does not achieve, however, the objective of solving the problems concerning professional classification. On the contrary, new regulation has been used in some sectors to avoid classical labour law protection. Furthermore, the emergence of new technologies and business models relating to the digitalisation of the economy which further the limits of the platform economy, has complicated the situation even more.

Nevertheless, some solutions have also emerged. After a very profound judicial and academic debate, Spain's Supreme Court inclined to the existence of an employment relationship. In its judgment of 25 September 2020 (ECLI: ES:TS:2020:2924) it stated that a rider is not completely free to decide when he works owing to the point system which conditions his activity; it is controlled by geolocation; his activity is determined by precise instruction on how to do the tasks, waiting time is paid; and the most important tool to develop the activity, the platform, belongs to the company. All these elements go in the same direction: riders are employees.

However, despite it being a great advance this resolution closes the judicial debate only for the delivery sector, but not for others and even for other platforms. The same conclusion can be achieved by the other main tool in the construction of legal solutions for the problems relating to the platform economy. The so-called 'Riders' Law' (Law 12/2021, of 28 September) which stated a presumption of employment relationship is only applicable to persons in the delivery sector.

As a consequence, the following steps aimed to discover if these solutions are applicable to other sectors within the platform economy and, if so, if they are a general solution or only applicable to some of them. This stage in the evolution of the regulation of platform work is shared with other European countries in which the debate is mature enough in delivery services or transport of persons but not in other areas.

Additionally, the European level can also provide useful solutions. In this sense, the proposal of a directive on platform work,[32] if successful, could set a common broad framework which permits all Member States to advance faster, besides finding common solutions for a shared problem.

But analysing the subjective approach of platform work also means focusing on other actors. Its development has involved both the appearance of new subjects and changes in the traditional ones.

Concerning the first ones, owing to very poor working conditions, the primary absence of unions' reaction and the atmosphere of mistrust against them, new employees' associations emerged, such as 'riders x derechos' (riders for rights).

[32] See in detail the contributions by Ratti (ch 3) and Brameshuber (ch 14) in this volume.

Despite their preference to act as a 'collective' or association, their activities are quite close to those related to classical trade unions. Nevertheless, as soon as a union's strategy regarding platform workers has changed, its influence has weakened. From the employers' side, after a first period acting outside the traditional employer associations, CEOE and CEPYME, the strategy changed recently and, for example, Uber decided to join CEOE at the beginning of 2020. Other companies, such as Deliveroo, Cabify or Glovo are also part of it. Only the tensions derived from the negotiation of the Riders' Law broke the union of employers' action.

Regarding traditional actors, it must be highlighted how social dialogue is being used as the way to analyse, debate and implement reforms related to platform work and digitalisation. However, despite the importance of this tool, social dialogue is not enough. Spanish social partners are dealing with the disruptive change by changing their traditional strategies. As a consequence, new imaginative tools have been developed, such as trade unions' own platforms to provide legal advice for delivery workers (turespuestasindical.es (UGT), precaritywork.es (CCOO)) or new related organisations such as RUGE (linked to UGT), focused on aiding young workers and, particularly, those who work under very poor working conditions. These kinds of adaptations must reach collective bargaining once the legal status becomes clearer. In other words, the debate is mature enough to make collective bargaining a new decisive instrument in the regulation of platform work.

12

The Shortcomings of the North American Collective Bargaining Model with Regard to Platform Workers: The Turkish Perspective

KÜBRA DOĞAN YENİSEY*

I. Introduction

Established institutions of labour law are facing profound technological challenges. Not a single day passes without news or discussion of digital labour platforms or AI-driven management systems. According to recent research, the number of digital platforms globally has risen fivefold since 2010.[1] Freelance, consulting and project-based work are increasing, as is remote working. In some countries, we can already observe the impacts of technological changes on the labour market: for instance, 11 per cent of the European Union (EU) workforce has already provided services through platforms.[2] Both in developing and developed countries, a sizeable majority of workers would like to do more online work.[3] In Turkey, although relevant data are not yet available, the new forms of work are noteworthy, particularly in the courier sector.

I share the concern of Nicolas Schmit, the European Commissioner for Jobs and Social Rights, that if there is no regulation protecting the rights of platform workers, businesses will try to outsource increasing numbers of activities to

* I would like to thank İstanbul Bilgi University for the financial support for the editing of this chapter.

[1] ILO, *World Employment and Social Outlook 2021: The role of digital labour platforms in transforming the world of work* (International Labour Office 2021).

[2] Commission, *Questions and Answers: First stage social partners consultation on improving the working conditions in platform work* (24 February 2021), available at: ec.europa.eu/commission/ presscorner/detail/ en/qanda_21_656; see also Ursula Huws et al, *The Platformisation of Work in Europe, Results from Research in 13 European Countries* (FEPS 2019).

[3] ILO, *World Employment and Social Outlook 2021* (n 1).

platforms, resulting in the platformisation of economies.[4] Both crowdwork and work on-demand via apps enable extensive outsourcing to individuals rather than businesses.[5] This development would lead to a large proportion of the population working in the grey zone between employee and self-employed status. The legal status of platform workers varies according to the type of platform, terms and conditions and national legislation.[6] In a world where 'technology enables work to be outsourced globally, and that work can be performed remotely from any location',[7] platformisation may increase pressure on unions or bring another wave of de-unionisation in countries where trade unions are weak and there is no strong corporatist tradition. In terms of union organisation, recalling the effects of outsourcing practices in the 1980s, this development poses risks not only to those who work through platforms, but to those recruited as employees.

Key features of the Turkish labour market include an informal economy and high unemployment. Judicial organs and labour inspectorates have been fighting against sham employment practices, which are likely to apply to at least some forms of platform work in the near future. However, the importance of new job opportunities brought by platforms cannot be underestimated for a large unemployed population.[8] Thus, Turkey's labour market seems likely to become profoundly heterogeneous, in the sense that those working under similar working conditions would have different legal statuses, including employees based in a workplace or working remotely, platform workers, and solo-independent workers with their own workplaces. The binary division of employment law and social security regulations seems to have drawbacks with regard to protecting fundamental rights at work.[9]

There is no doubting the necessity to develop a model enabling the representation of platform workers. Article 2 of ILO Convention No 87 protects the right of 'workers and employers, without distinction whatsoever, … to establish and, subject only to the rules of the organisation concerned, to join organisations of their own choosing without previous authorisation'. Self-employed workers may also join trade unions in Turkey. Under Article 1 paragraph 4 of Act No 6356 on Trade Unions and Collective Agreements, within the meaning of the right to establish and join trade unions,

> a natural person who carries out his professional activities independently for a fee, apart from an employment contract and in accordance with a transport contract, contract for

[4] Nicolas Schmit, 'The role of digital labour platforms in transforming the world of work', available at: www.youtube.com/watch?v=2SqixGASxhg.

[5] Valerio De Stefano, 'The rise of the "just-in-time workforce": on-demand work, crowdwork and labour protection in the "gig-economy"' (International Labour Office 2016) 4.

[6] See, eg, Valerio De Stefano et al, 'Platform Work and the Employment Relationship' (2021) ILO Working Paper.

[7] ILO, *World Employment and Social Outlook 2021* (n 1) 73.

[8] For positive impacts of online labour in developing countries, see Richard Heeks, 'Decent Work and the Digital Gig Economy: A Developing Country Perspective on Employment Impacts and Standards in Online Outsourcing, Crowdwork, etc' (Centre for Development Informatics Global Development Institute, SEED 2017) 8–10.

[9] See, eg, De Stefano (n 5).

> service, contract of agency, brokerage contract, publishing contract and partners in an ordinary partnership shall also be considered as workers.

Employees and self-employed workers can organise in the same trade union.

Although platform workers should enjoy a collective voice and the right to collective bargaining, the question of 'how' they exercise these rights is left obscure. In many legal systems, the right to collective bargaining is only granted to employees. Turkey is no exception in this regard, reserving collective bargaining rights exclusively for those with an employment contract. Self-employed workers cannot benefit from collective agreements with an *erga omnes* effect. Thus, the binary between subordinated employment and self-employment plays a crucial role in determining collective rights under Turkey's current system.[10] In addition, bargaining rights for the self-employed are subject to the scrutiny of competition law.

In a report prepared for the European Parliament, experts recommend the extension of collective bargaining rights to platform workers, underlining that policy development should be sensitive to national systems and the variety of platform work.[11] Even if the fundamental principles are the same, there is no compulsion to shape a representation model for platform workers that confers similar bargaining structure to those of employees. A special labour law may be developed for those who work offline through a specific platform, including rights to fair representation and collective bargaining.[12] However, it would not be surprising if different collective bargaining models for employees and platform workers were to coexist – despite numerous legal and practical problems in terms of negotiation – for instance, concerning the negotiating counterparty, level of bargaining and bargaining unit.

It is necessary to develop a model which considers the heterogeneity and particularity of the platform economy, provides strong protection for platform workers' collective rights, and is in harmony with the existing collective representation model applicable to employees. However, my intention in this chapter is not to comprehensively analyse such a system but to identify one segment of the challenges facing platform workers. Specifically, this chapter examines whether Turkey's existing collective representation model can cover the needs of platform workers. I believe that, depending on its characteristics, the legal structure of a collective bargaining model may facilitate or complicate collective representation of this new group of workers. Structural issues become more significant when we consider workplaces in which platform workers provide services alongside the traditional workforce. This chapter investigates the extent to which the Turkish model offers solutions for the active exercise of platform workers' rights.

[10] On the employment status of platform workers, see, eg, De Stefano et al (n 6). See for more examples of this binary divide the contribution by Brameshuber (ch 14) in this volume, pages 237 et seq.

[11] European Parliament, 'Directorate General for Internal Policies: Policy Department A: Economic and Scientific Policy. The Social Protection of Workers in the Platform Economy, study for the EMPL Committee' (2017) IP/A/EMPL/2016-11, 106.

[12] Adrián Todoli-Signes, 'The "gig economy": employee, self-employed or the need for a special employment regulation?' (2017) 23 *Transfer* 193, 205.

II. Heterogeneity of Platforms and Collective Representation Models

A. An Overview of Existing Models

Platforms are classified with reference to business models, key participants, the nature of tasks and other factors.[13] Based on two distinct patterns of how platform work is organised ('crowdwork and work-on-demand via apps'),[14] Johnston shows how a geographic perspective can enhance platform workers' collective organising.[15] Therefore, I will take as a base the division between online web-based platforms and location-based platforms.[16] Examples of the former include freelance platforms, content-based platforms, competitive programming platforms and micro-task platforms; examples of the latter include taxi and delivery platforms. Location-based platforms provide a better known structure for collective bargaining, whereas online web-based platforms (depending on their business model) seem to create more challenges in terms of collective organising.[17]

A general overview shows that platform workers may establish their own mechanisms to review clients and tasks and distribute information about pay and other matters, or they may join a trade union or establish an association to provide some degree of voice.[18] Grassroots organisations could emerge, or existing unions could support platform workers.[19]

Three basic models are identifiable among existing organisations:[20] first, forums and groupings help platform workers to communicate with one another and distribute news, but do not engage in negotiating working conditions on their behalf.[21] Examples include online forums and groupings (eg, Upwork Community forums), off-platform social media groups, specific portals including discussion forums (eg, TurkerNation, WeAreDynamo), and client/task rating systems (eg, Turkopticon).

[13] See eg, Debra Howcroft and Birgitta Bergvall Kareborn, 'A Typology of Crowdwork Platforms' (2019) 33 *Work, Employment and Society* 21; Florian A Schmidt, *Digital Labour Markets in the Platform Economy, Mapping the Political Challenges of Crowd Work and Gig Work* (Friedrich-Ebert Stiftung 2017) 6–7.

[14] De Stefano (n 5) 2–6.

[15] Hannah Johnston, 'Labour geographies of the platform economy: Understanding collective organizing strategies in the context of digitally mediated work' (2020) 159 *International Labour Review* 25.

[16] ILO, *World Employment and Social Outlook 2021* (n 1) 74–77.

[17] On challenges in terms of collective representation of platform workers, see Johnston (n 15) 25–41; Howcroft and Bergvall Kareborn (n 13) 31–33.

[18] Andrew Steward and Jim Stanford, 'Regulating Work in the Gig Economy: What are the Options?' (2017) 28 *Economic & Labour Relations Review* 420, 428.

[19] De Stefano (n 5) 8.

[20] Zachary Kilhoffer, Karolien Lenaerts and Miroslav Beblavy, 'The Platform Economy and Industrial Relations: Applying the Old Freamework to the New Reality' (CEPS Research Report, 7 August 20217), available at: www.ceps.eu/ceps-publications/platform-economy-and-industrial-relations-applying-old-framework-new-reality/, 28–31.

[21] Heeks (n 8) 15.

Second, platform workers organise in unions and associations for self-employed workers, such as the All India Gig Workers Union (India), App Drivers & Couriers Union (UK), FreiArbeiterinen-und Arbeiter-Union (Germany), Independent Workers' Union of Great Britain (UK), Indian Federation of App-based Transport Workers (India), National Union of Professional App-based Workers (Nigeria), SIRAApps (Mexico), Union Syndicale des Chauffeurs Privés (Belgium) and United Freelancers (Belgium).[22] In Turkey, motorcycle couriers are currently organised under an association but not a union, while homeworkers, including those providing services through a platform, are organised in a union.[23]

Third, existing trade unions support platform workers. Examples include ABVV BTB (Belgium), Gewerkschaft-Nahrung-Genuss Geststaetten (Germany), GMB Union (UK), IG Metall (Germany), National Union of Public Service and Allied Workers (South Africa), Transport Workers Union (Australia), Unions NSW (Australia) and ver.di (Germany).[24]

Collective agreements for platform workers' working conditions exist at the sector level as well as the firm level. In some cases, existing sectoral agreements also apply to platform workers; in others, platform-specific agreements are concluded.[25] Nordic countries took the lead in instituting collective agreements for platform workers. In particular, the companies Hilfr and Foodora implemented agreements containing innovative clauses.[26] In the United Kingdom, Uber has signed a deal to recognise the GMB trade union for its private hire drivers: drivers will not become members automatically but can sign up to take part in collective bargaining.[27]

In summary, the above overview shows that in terms of collective labour rights, the main tendency is to apply the existing framework for employees to the new reality. In countries with strong union movements and robust and flexible bargaining systems,[28] legal and practical barriers are progressively being overcome.[29] However, in countries with weaker union movements, mutual-aid groupings and associations address pressing needs and physical risks, enable information sharing,

[22] Examples retrieved from Fairwork, 'Unions & Workers' Associations': fair.work/en/fw/unions/#continue.

[23] Motosikletli Kuryeler Derneği and Ev Eksenli Çalışanlar Sendikası.

[24] Examples retrieved from Fairwork (n 22).

[25] For different national examples of collective agreements, see Zachary Kilhoffer et al, *Study to Gather Evidence on the Working Conditions of Platform Workers*, VT/2018/032 (European Commission 2020) 118–21.

[26] Anna Ilsøe and Kristin Jesnes, 'Collective Agreements for Platforms and Workers – Two Cases from the Nordic Countries in Kristin Jesnes and Sigurd M Nordli Oppegaard (eds), *Platform Work in the Nordic Models: Issues, Cases and Responses* (Nordic Council of Ministers 2020).

[27] Sarah Butler, 'Uber agrees union recognition deal with GMB' *Guardian* (26 May 2021), available at: www.theguardian.com/business/2021/may/26/uber-agrees-historic-deal-allowing-drivers-to-join-gmb-union.

[28] Guy Mundlak, *Organizing Matters, Two Logics of Trade Union Representation* (Edward Elgar Publishing 2020).

[29] ILO, *World Employment and Social Outlook 2021* (n 1) 213.

and offer a sense of community. Regarding wages and working conditions, the Indonesian example shows us grassroots organisations based on the mutual aid logic and traditional trade unions may have differences in values and structure, therefore the need for articulation between labour organisations and organisations for platform workers evokes.[30]

B. Comparing the North American and Turkish Collective Bargaining Models

The Turkish model of collective bargaining shares the same fundamental principles as the North American model of collective representation used in the United States and Canada. The principle of exclusive representation is the distinguishing feature of this model. Under this principle, the representative union has authority to represent all employees in the bargaining unit, regardless of their trade union membership or consent; moreover, designation of a trade union as representative is determined by the majority of employees working in the bargaining unit.[31] Unlike in the North American model, there are no secret ballot elections to designate the representative union; instead, membership is proof of having a majority under Turkish law. Requiring the union to have as votes or as members the majority of employees at the plant level is considered a democratic justification for exclusive representativeness. Therefore, determination of the bargaining unit has crucial importance in this system.

A bargaining unit comprises a group of employees who constitute a community of interests in the sense of sharing the same terms and working conditions. In the North American model, the shop floor is the primary bargaining unit in which the common interests of employees are developed. The union that is party to a collective agreement represents the employees working in this unit. Delineation of the bargaining unit affects the group of people within which the majority determines the representative union.

In the United States, section 9, paragraph (b) of the National Labor Relations Act provides that:

> (b) The [National Labor] Board shall decide in each case whether, in order to assure to employees the fullest freedom in exercising the rights guaranteed by this Act, the unit appropriate for the purposes of collective bargaining shall be the employer unit, craft unit, plant unit, or subdivision thereof.

[30] See the example of Indonesia: Michele Ford and Vivian Honan, 'The Limits of Mutual Aid: Emerging Forms of Collectivity among App-based Transport Workers in Indonesia' (2019) 61(4) *Journal of Industrial Relations* 1.

[31] Clyde W Summers, 'Exclusive Representation: A Comparative Inquiry into Unique American Principle' (1998) 20 *Comparative Labor Law & Policy Journal* 47.

Similarly, Article 27(1) of the Canada Labour Code states that:

> Where a trade union applies under section 24 for certification as the bargaining agent for a unit that the trade union considers appropriate for collective bargaining, the [Canada Industrial Relations] Board shall determine the unit that, in the opinion of the Board, is appropriate for collective bargaining.[32]

In both cases, the law delegates to the responsible board the power to determine the appropriate unit for collective bargaining. The factors to be considered include communities of interests, group homogeneity, the employer's administrative or territorial divisions, geographical and physical proximity, functional integration, history of bargaining, employee interchange, integration of operations, and centralisation of the control of employees.[33]

Under Turkish law, the workplace is the lowest level of representation and the smallest mandatory bargaining unit. If an employer has several workplaces in the same branch of activity (industry), only one collective agreement – an enterprise collective agreement – shall be made under Article 3, paragraph 1-d of Act No 6356 on Trade Unions and Collective Agreements. One unique feature of the Turkish system is its mandatory character. Act No 6356 on Trade Unions and Collective Agreements restricts the discretionary power of the certification authority (the Ministry of Labour and Social Security) by giving reference to the legal definition of 'workplace' in Article 2 of Labour Act No 4857 (Article 3, paragraph 3 of Act No 6356). Accordingly, the Ministry of Labour and Social Security has no right to determine the competent trade union for collective bargaining, and is only granted declaratory authority. If the representativeness of a trade union is challenged with respect to which units are included in the workplace, the labour courts have authority to resolve this dispute.

Under Turkish law, the concept of 'workplace', derived from German law, is defined as 'the unit wherein the employees and material and immaterial elements are organised with a view to ensuring the production of goods and services by the employer' (Article 2 of Labour Act No 4857).[34] It is 'an organisational unit composed of the main part, managerially and objectively dependent units, facilities and all kinds of vehicles in the pursuit of producing goods and services' (Article 2, paragraph 4 of Labour Act No 4857). Therefore, different production units could be considered affiliated parts of a workplace if they serve production of the same goods and there is managerial unity. As under the North American model, geographical and physical proximity, functional integration, employee interchange, integration of operations, and the documentation of

[32] Government of Canada, 'Canada Labour Code': laws-lois.justice.gc.ca/eng/acts/L-2/page-7.html.

[33] See John E Abodeely, *The NLRB and the Appropriate Bargaining Unit* (University of Pennsylvania Press 1971); Walter L Daykin, 'Determination of Appropriate Bargaining Unit by the NLRB: Principles, Rules, and Policies' (1958) 27 *Fordham Law Review* 218, 220–22.

[34] For the translation of Labour Act No. 4857 see: www.ilo.org/dyn/natlex/docs/ ELECTRONIC/ 64083/ 77276/%20F75317864/TUR64083%20English.pdf.

employees' personnel affairs such as payrolls and paid leave are also considered in determining if an affiliated unit is separate from or part of another workplace.[35] However, unlike in the North American model, Turkish law offers no possibility of having different bargaining units or subdivisions in a workplace: the principle of one collective agreement per workplace/enterprise is strictly applied.

III. Designation of Bargaining Unit and Platform Workers

While discussing collective bargaining rights for platform workers, it is important to consider possible interactions between the respective collective agreement models for platform workers and employees, supposing that platform workers are not classified as employees. As self-employed persons and employees in Turkey may organise in the same trade union, it would be possible for both groups to be covered by the same collective agreement. However, the business model of the platform, either location-based or online web-based, seems to play a role in the platform workers' bargaining strategies. Johnston shows that location-based platform workers have adopted a greater variety of collective organising strategies and achieved better terms and conditions of work, when compared with crowdworkers. When the latter group is able to establish new regulatory spaces, such as multi-employer enterprise agreements, or when regulatory efforts place a larger focus on the work relationship rather than the workplace, they succeed.[36] In the same line of thinking, my main argument is that a bargaining structure based on the single worksite, single employer approach, together with the majority rule, entails structural difficulties for establishing solidarity between platform workers and employees working in the same bargaining unit. The main challenge seems to concern how a bargaining unit can be designated in a dematerialised, unstable and competitive network.

A. Geographical Proximity and Dematerialisation of Production

The workplace is the lowest level eligible for representation and the smallest bargaining unit in which employees' common interests are developed. The big factories of the twentieth century came to symbolise the organisation of industrial

[35] See, eg, Kübra Doğan Yenisey, *İş Hukukunda İşyeri ve İşletme, Alman ve Fransız Hukuklarıyla Karşılaştırmalı Bir İnceleme* (Legal Yayınları 2007) 332–36.
[36] Johnston (n 15) 35–40.

labour,[37] as well as physical togetherness, cooperation and solidarity. The outsourcing of some parts of production to third parties caused an important break in this model and left the workplace fissured, as identified by Weil.[38] As information and communication technologies enable employees to perform their work outside the employer's premises, the relationship between 'work' and 'place' has also been severed.

On location-based platforms, services are delivered physically, so there is still geographical proximity between workers and customers. However, on web-based platforms production is totally dematerialised and surveilled by algorithms. Therefore, technology enables a scaleable workforce that is dispersed in multiple jurisdictions, isolated and highly mobile,[39] which complicates our understanding of a unit that contains the idea of demarcation. With work increasingly divided into tasks, workers lose their overview of the total work process in which they are engaged and the extent of their contributions.[40] Platforms enable 'an extreme fissurisation of businesses' organisation',[41] causing the multiplication of competing centres of interest. At present, good examples of collective action among physically dispersed workers are found in the delivery and transport sectors, both operating on location-based platforms and involving workers operating on the routes of the same city.[42]

B. Stability

Employee representation mechanisms require a stable unit, such as a factory, shop, or office, facilitating unionisation and union activity. In some legal systems, such as in Germany under the German Work Constitution Act (Betriebsverfassungsgesetz), the criteria for a 'workplace' include temporal continuity.[43]

However, as Prassl and Risak explain, crowdwork provides a way to combine different incentives, such as increasing flexibility for employers or customers and reducing the cost of unproductive time, while still maintaining control over the production process. To achieve these objectives, the crowd should include a large

[37] Massimo D'Antona, 'Labour Law at the Century's End: An Identity Crisis?' in Joanne Conaghan, Richard Michael Fischl and Karl Klare (eds), *Labour Law in an Era of Globalization, Transformative Practices and Possibilities* (Oxford University Press 2002) 34.

[38] David Weil, *The Fissured Workplace: Why Work Became So Bad for So Many and What Can Be Done To Improve It* (Harvard University Press 2014).

[39] Hannah Johnston and Chris Land-Kazlauskas, *Organizing On-Demand: Representation, Voice, and Collective Bargaining in the Gig Economy* (International Labour Office 2019) 23–24.

[40] Juliet Webster, 'Microworkers of the Gig Economy: Separate and Precarious' (2016) 25 *New Labour Forum* 56, 58–59.

[41] De Stefano (n 5) 8.

[42] Arianna Tassinari and Vincenzo Maccorone, 'The Mobilisation of Gig Economy Couriers in Italy: Some Lessons for Trade Union Movement' (2017) 23 *Transfer* 353.

[43] Reinhard Richardi and Frank Maschmann in Reinhard Richardi (ed), *Betriebsverfassungsgesetz mit Wahlordnung*, vol 16 (CH Beck 2018) § 1, paras 40–41.

number of individuals, ensuring that available individuals can be reached when needed and rates can be kept low by maintaining adequate competition among them.[44] It should be borne in mind, though, that despite all the mechanisms pressuring individuals to be active members of the platform, it is the service provider who decides whether to work by logging into the app.

Therefore, the stability of ties between the workplace community and platform worker and also among platform workers presents another challenge in determining who belongs to the bargaining unit and shares common interests. If a country's industrial relations system enables social partners to cover all those working in an industry or for the same platform company, then the system may create its own solutions. Thus, first company-level agreement signed in Denmark was negotiated by the platform Hilfr.[45] Collective agreement for Foodora couriers in Norway or Uber drivers in UK were also negotiated by the platform companies. However, if a trade union needs to represent a certain percentage of employees/workers in the bargaining unit to be authorised to conclude a collective agreement, then it is important to determine which workers constitute the bargaining unit.

C. Solidarity and Competitive Logic

The presumption that physical togetherness induces solidarity and common interests is quite debatable today. Experiences during the pandemic have taught us that social togetherness and physical proximity are different concepts, with technology making it possible to identify and bundle common interests among people based far from one another. In recent years, sociologists have recognised digital solidarity as a new form of solidarity.[46]

Stalder argues that weak networks, in the sense of 'groups held together by casual and limited social interaction', are the most important new social forms.[47] Social networks are used to engage with or remake the world in accordance with personal preferences. This form of sociability is becoming ever more dominant in personal lives. Therefore, there is no need to have physical contact in order to defend a common interest. However, these social ties are considered weak in network sociology because they are based on sporadic and limited interactions on a platform between individuals separated by large physical distances. While digital networks seem to be becoming an essential element in reconstituting solidarity, it is questionable whether this collectivity is limited to connectivity. Indeed, Stalder argues that new forms of solidarity mostly concern participation but not representation.[48]

[44] Jeremias Prassl and Martin Risak, 'Uber, Taskrabbit, & Co: Platforms as Employers? Rethinking the Legal Analysis of Crowdwork' (2016) 37 *Comparative Labor Law & Policy Journal* 619, 625

[45] See Ilsøe and Jesnes (n 26) 53–59.

[46] Felix Stalder, *Digital Solidarity* (PML and Mute Books 2013).

[47] ibid, 43 ff.

[48] ibid, 54 f.

It is also arguable that remoteness is problematic with respect to the organisation of employees working at a distance from the plant. However, unlike remote working employees we should not underestimate the competitive logic behind the operation of platforms. Some platforms allow an employer to handpick workers from an undesignated group of people, and it is difficult to identify to whom the job will be awarded. Workers on the platform share neither common workplaces nor the same terms and working conditions, and tasks are generally assigned to the lowest bidders, requiring workers to compete with one another. They also have no contact with other workers or with customers while working.[49] Like micro-tasking, assigning jobs via smartphone apps also has the same competitive logic.[50] For all these reasons, the business model of the platform causes structural disadvantages for workers.[51]

D. Majority Rule and Platform Workers

Under the North American model, the trade union reaching the minimal membership threshold or receiving the majority of votes gains exclusive bargaining agent status. If platform workers were to enjoy the same bargaining rights as employees do, the fundamental question arises of whether they would be counted in the bargaining unit, which means increasing the majority threshold for a representative union. Without a majority, a trade union would lose authority to engage in collective bargaining, thus precluding collective representation for not only platform workers but also employees. Therefore, bargaining structure based on a single worksite and majority rule would not incentivise trade unions to support platform workers. In addition, a single workplace structure may empower an employer in negotiations with a union, as the threat of outsourcing more activities to platforms would also raise the number of members needed to retain a majority.

Another option could be separating bargaining units for employees and platform workers, which would require a legislative intervention under Turkish law. It may also create tension between employees and platform workers in the same workplace. Meanwhile, this would not solve the problem of how to determine the bargaining unit for platform workers. Also, it would be difficult to unionise among platform workers, particularly crowdworkers, competing with one another on a plant level.

The structural bargaining powers of platform workers may change this picture and rebalance the power distribution between employer and union. Vandaele finds that there are two components of platform workers' structural bargaining power, in the absence of any regulation recognising their bargaining rights. The

[49] Webster (n 40) 15–16.

[50] Alex J Wood et al, 'Good Gig, Bad Gig: Autonomy and Algorithmic Control in the Global Gig Economy' (2019) 33 *Work, Employment and Society* 56, 65–66, 68–70; Schmidt (n 13) 15–16; Johnston and Land-Kazlauskas (n 39) 3–4.

[51] Also see Howcroft and Bergvall Kareborn (n 13) 32.

first component is workplace bargaining power, which refers to workers' capacity to disrupt business through direct action by taking advantage of their strategic position. The second component is marketplace bargaining power, which stems from employers' needs for workers' skills, the unemployment rate in the market and to what extent workers can live from non-wage income sources.[52] Considering geographical location and skill levels, Vandaele's analysis shows that low-skilled micro crowdworkers have basically no bargaining power as they deliver their work through online apps, and lack workplace bargaining power as they are geographically spread across the globe. For high-skilled freelancers working via online web-based platforms, the ability to set higher prices in the local labour market does not extend to the global level due to fierce competition, so their marketplace bargaining power is quite low. Finally, workers on offline location-based platforms in the delivery and transport sectors have some degree of workplace bargaining power through their interaction with customers.[53] There is little evidence so far of platform workers seeking to strengthen their positions through collective action or solidarity.[54] Similarly, the findings of a recent study in Turkey show that freelancers have no expectation from the trade union movement in terms of representation as they have neither a fixed workplace nor a fixed working schedule.[55]

Therefore, in addition to their ambiguous employment status, platform workers have little bargaining power with which to address imbalances arising from the plant-level bargaining structure. A bargaining structure based on a single worksite and majority rule would put unions operating at the enterprise level in the difficult situation of seeking to fight for the rights of platform workers, which are intrinsically tied to employees' interests, without increasing the number of required members to reach the threshold. This analysis confirms that the gig economy is well suited for regulation through sectoral bargaining and extension mechanisms.[56]

IV. Conclusions

The growing expansion of the gig economy foreshadows a company workforce in which some workers perform tasks remotely via platforms alongside employees who work at the plant. Platform work could be used as a new form of outsourcing

[52] Kurt Vandaele, *Will trade unions survive in the platform economy? Emerging patterns of platform workers' collective voice and representation in Europe* (ETUI 2018) 10–11.

[53] ibid, 10–14.

[54] Mark Graham, I Hjorth and Vili Lehdonvirta, 'Digital Labour and Development: Impacts of Global Digital Labour Platforms and the Gig Economy on Worker Livelihoods' (2017) 23 *Transfer* 135, 140–45.

[55] Serpil Cigdem and Ismail Koç, 'Digital Platform Workers and New Organisational Models, International Non-Governmental Organisations Conference – NGO' 19, 1–3 November 2019, Bandırma – Turkey, available at: www.researchgate.net/publication/337010581_Dijital_Platform_Calisanlari_ve_Orgutlenme_Modelleri.

[56] Johnston and Land-Kazlauskas (n 39).

in this increasingly digitalised world. The main assumption of the COGENS project that collective rights will be reinvented to protect the interests of platform workers leads us to consider which models may enable the exercise of their collective rights.

This chapter argues that the collective bargaining model of a national system may facilitate or complicate this reinvention process. A bargaining structure based on the single worksite, single employer approach, together with the majority rule, presents structural difficulties likely to preclude solidarity between platform workers and employees working in the same bargaining unit. Such a decentralised model would not likely incentivise unions to actively support platform workers. Even if platform workers and employees could engage with the same trade union, the crucial points to resolve are how the bargaining unit is designated and which workforce members are counted in determining the majority threshold. This may be an opportunity to rethink existing bargaining models, and for Turkey specifically to introduce industry-level collective bargaining into the industrial relations system.

13

Extending the Personal Scope of Collective Bargaining as a Chance for Gig Workers? The Polish Case

MARTA KOZAK-MAŚNICKA AND ŁUKASZ PISARCZYK

I. Opening Remarks

Despite the heritage of the communist system and problems of the transformation period,[1] the Polish economy is characterised by high dynamics and flexibility. Even the pandemic crisis and a series of lockdowns have not caused a serious economic slowdown. The Polish labour market, one of the largest in the European Union (EU), is still growing. In the second quarter of 2021 the population of employed aged 15–89 comprised 16,597,000 people; 85 per cent of women and 76 per cent of men are engaged under an employment relationship regulated by the Polish Labour Code).[2] It means that several million people work outside the employment relationship (mainly civil law contracts or self-employment).[3] Poland, a country of emigration for centuries, attracts millions of foreign workers. There are around one million foreigners mostly from Ukraine and Belarus,[4] 725,000 of them are registered for pension and disability insurance as employees, as self-employed or civil law contractors.[5] The economy and labour market have been adapting to the

[1] See more Michał Seweryński, *Polish Labour Law from Communism to Democracy* (Dom Wydawniczy ABC 1999); Ludwik Florek 'Labour Law' in Stanislaw Frankowski (ed), *Introduction to Polish Law* (Kluwer Law International 2005).

[2] The Law of 26 June 1974 – Labour Code, Journal of Laws 2020, item 1320 as amended (the Labour Code).

[3] Statistics Poland, 'Labour force survey in Poland – quarter 2/2021', available at: stat.gov.pl/en/topics/labour-market/working-unemployed-economically-inactive-by-lfs/labour-force-survey-in-poland-ii-quarter-2021,2,42.html.

[4] Statistics Poland, 'The foreign population in Poland during the COVID-19 pandemic' (Statistics Poland, 29 June 2020), available at: stat.gov.pl/en/experimental-statistics/human-capital/the-foreign-population-in-poland-during-the-covid-19-pandemic,10,1.html.

[5] Social Insurance Institution in Poland, 'Cudzoziemcy w polskim systemie ubezpieczeń społecznych' (Foreigners in the Polish social security system) (Zakład Ubezpieczeń Społecznych 2021), available at: www.zus.pl/documents/10182/2322024/Cudzoziemcy+w+polskim+systemie+ubezpiecze%C5%84+spo%C5%82ecznych+-+wydanie+2021_v2.pdf/235779ba-d43e-6dcf-4540-6352eeef697f.

latest trends and phenomena. One of the best examples is the development of the gig economy and employment through digital platforms.

However, the legal position of gig workers remains highly unclear. Some of their problems are similar to those in other countries. The fundamental question concerns their employment status, including the right to bargain collectively. Global problems are strengthened by two specific features of the Polish labour market: dynamic (even uncontrolled) development of non-employee employment and a deep crisis of collective bargaining.

II. The Development of the Gig Economy in Poland

The scale of the gig economy is not as large as in Western Europe or in the United States.[6] The gig economy in Poland is still a relatively new but rapidly increasing market. Gig employment in direct services is developing mainly in big cities. The most common are peer-to-peer ridesharing apps such as Uber or Bolt (formerly Taxify) as well as food delivery apps, including Pyszne, UberEats, Glovo or Wolt. There are also cleaning and childcare platforms: Pozamiatane and Pomocedomowe. The importance of crowdworking is also gradually increasing. The best-known crowdwork platforms are Useme and Oferia, virtual marketplaces that allows users to publish offers and jobs to be done in spheres such as programming, marketing or translation. There is also a platform that offers legal services (SpecPrawnik).

Empirical research conducted on the Polish market shows that most platforms have a high degree of control over the conducted activities, requiring availability within specific time frames and sanctioning workers, even in the case of crowdworkers[7] (eg, the inability to renegotiate bids when a client has obscured the real content of a job; the necessity to overcontribute to tasks to maintain good reviews).[8] In 2018, 11 per cent of Poles (aged 18–65) had experience with platform work, but only 4 per cent of Poles work this way on a regular basis, so there is still a big potential for expanding this market.[9] There are no exact data about the scale of platform work in Poland and it is hard to estimate it, due to the huge diversity of this phenomenon.

One characteristic of the Polish labour market is that gig work is not the only (or basic) form of work for a large group of workers but an additional form.

[6] Eurofound, *New Forms of Employment: 2020 Update* (Publications Office of the European Union 2020) 8–9.

[7] See more about dichotomous classifications of gig economy (crowdwork and work on-demand via apps); Valerio De Stefano, 'The Rise of the "Just-in-Time Workforce": On-Demand Work, Crowdwork and Labour Protection in the "Gig-Economy"' (2016) 37 *Comparative Labor Law & Policy Journal* 471.

[8] Karol Muszyński, Valeria Pulignano, Markieta Domecka and Adam Mrozowicki, 'Coping with precarity during COVID-19: A study of platform work in Poland' (2021) *International Labour Review* 28, available at: doi.org/10.1111/ilr.12224.

[9] Dominik Owczarek, *Don't GIG up! Extending social protection to GIG workers in Poland. State of the art report* (Institute of Public Affairs 2018) 5.

For most of those who work via platforms regularly, it was an extra job, done occasionally (71 per cent of respondents).[10] It is part of a broader phenomenon of having more than one job (eg, full-time plus part-time work) which is caused by the level of remuneration that is still lower than in the countries of Western Europe. Moreover, the majority of gig workers working off-site (car drivers, bike deliverers) are foreigners (mainly from Ukraine and Belarus but increasingly from Asian countries). Many of them do not speak Polish well and do not know the local realities, which makes their position particularly vulnerable. Due to the system of permissions, some of them stay in Poland for a relatively short time. Lack of knowledge of local regulations and the complicated procedure for legalisation of their stay and work are the main reasons why foreigners often work illegally, without any contract or social insurance.[11] For example, people from the former USSR countries, who often work as Uber or Bolt drivers, do not have the means to buy a car that meets the platform's requirements and to open a business, so they rent a car from a so-called fleet partner, who charges an additional fee for rental.[12] In this case, the driver does not run his own business, does not own the equipment (car) to perform the services and has no direct relationship with the platform because the fleet partner is the intermediary. Moreover, the fleet partner charges an additional commission and may also establish additional provisions introducing an element of economic dependence between the parties. This example shows that in the gig economy, depending on the model used by a particular platform, relations are much more complicated than in the employee–employer model. However, a gig worker may not only be economically dependent on the employing entity, but more exposed to the risk of exploitation in comparison with ordinary workers as a result of staying outside the sphere of typical employment.

The Covid-19 pandemic will accelerate and deepen the processes of digitisation of the economy.[13] During the Covid-19 pandemic gig workers had to cope with increased fluctuations of demand, while some platforms have practically ceased to operate and lost clients (cleaning, care), others have experienced an increase in demand for the offered services (eg, food delivery).[14] Some people lost their source of income due to Covid-19 and found employment on a platform. While in regular employment relationships the business risk is typically associated with employer, in platform work, platforms shift the risk to workers.[15] Therefore, fluctuations of

[10] Dominik Owczarek, *New forms of work in Poland* (Institute of Public Affairs 2018) 69.

[11] See further, Izabella Florczak and Marcin Wujczyk, 'Precarious work of migrant workers. The example of Ukrainians in Poland in the light of regulations of (R)ESC' (2018) 1 *Hungarian Labour Law E-Journal* 5, available at: hllj.hu/letolt/2018_1_a/A_03_Florzak_Wujczyk_hllj_2018_1.pdf.

[12] Information on fleet partners on the Uber, available at: www.uber.com/en-pl/blog/lista-partnerow.

[13] OECD (2020), 'Digital Transformation in the Age of COVID-19: Building Resilience and Bridging Divides, Digital Economy, Outlook 2020 Supplement' (OECD 2020), available at: www.oecd.org/digital/digital-economy-outlook-covid.pdf.

[14] ETUI contributors (16 March 2021) 'Creative labour in the era of Covid-19' (ETUI, The European Trade Union Institute) 6, available at: www.etui.org/publications/creative-labour-era-covid-19.

[15] Jeremias Prassl, *Humans as a Service: The Promise and Perils of Work in the Gig Economy* (Oxford University Press 2018) 85–86.

demand for specific services have led to higher competition, increasing working time instability and extending work intensification. Even in highly demanded services like food delivery, platform workers have experienced serious income fluctuations (platforms were known to have changed the pay structure even up to four times during the two months of lockdown).[16] Ensuring even basic labour rights for gig workers would minimise the negative impact of the pandemic on platform work.

III. Abuse of the Non-Employee Status and the Crisis of Collective Bargaining

Although they work in conditions similar to the employment relationship, many workers are either formally employed on the basis of civil law contracts or treated as self-employed (formal entrepreneurs). National legal systems may develop various forms of counteracting abuses, for instance: (1) the assumption that an employment relationship exists, for example, in the case of legal relationships of a specific duration; (2) the possibility for labour inspectors to reclassify the contract; and (3) the right to have the contract reclassified by a court.[17] Polish law provides that a civil law contract comprising the terms and conditions similar to those of the employment relationship may be transformed into an employment contract.[18] The transformation is carried out by a labour court. The procedure may be initiated either by the worker or by labour inspectors (in practice, they exercise this right very rarely). The court should apply the employment test taking into account the features of employment. Under the employment relationship, work is performed personally and for remuneration, the relationship is of a permanent nature, characterised by employee subordination: the employee performs work based on the employer's guidelines, at a place and time determined by the employer. Finally, it is the employer who bears the risk connected with the employment.[19] If these features prevail, the legal relationship should be treated as an employment relationship irrespective of the name given to the contract. However, this mechanism turns out to be ineffective in practice. Moreover, the scale of abuse is enormous, incomparable with most other countries.

As a result, millions of workers (in various sectors, not only in the gig economy) are deprived of protection arising from labour law. The content of their

[16] Muszyński et al (n 8).

[17] The first solution may be perceived to be rigid yet efficient. Efficiency is also guaranteed by the labour inspectorate. However, it may lead to a collision with the right to fair trial. Judicial determination of the employment relationship is a good systemic solution but, in practice, it sometimes turns out to be insufficient. The legislation should develop mechanisms to support its efficiency.

[18] Article 22 § 1^1 of the Labour Code.

[19] See further, Bolesław Maciej Ćwiertniak in Krzysztof Wojciech Baran et al (eds), *Outline of Polish Labour Law System* (Wolters Kluwer Polska 2016) 122 ff.

employment relationship can be shaped freely, according to the rules arising from civil law (freedom of contracts). In recent years, a few pieces of protective legislation for non-employees have been adopted (eg, anti-discrimination regulation)[20] while some standards already existed (eg, health and safety in the workplace).[21] The most important example is the minimum hourly rate determined in proportion to the statutory minimum wage for employees.[22]

Another striking phenomenon is the decline of collective bargaining.[23] Since the beginning of its economic and political transformation, Poland has not yet developed a system of multi-establishment collective agreements. Nowadays they are, in fact, non-existent. In total, they cover only 200,000 workers (out of several million potential beneficiaries). Company-level collective agreements cover around 12.5 per cent of employees.[24] Although in 2019 Polish law recognised the full trade union-related rights of workers (non-employees) who meet certain criteria, in practice they are not covered by collective bargaining. Moreover, Polish law has not established a common non-union form of representation of employees (workers). Work councils operate in a relatively small group of companies.

As a result, the interests of a growing group of workers (including gig workers) in Poland are secured neither by statutory standards nor by collective agreements.[25] To a large extent, this results from the collective bargaining model and its current situation.

IV. Legal Status of Gig Workers

There are no special rules concerning the employment status of gig workers. It is worth mentioning that the legal qualification of platform workers was discussed during the meeting of the Parliamentary Team for the Future of Work.[26] Nonetheless there is no legislative work in progress regarding the legal status of platform work. As a result it is unlikely that special regulations for gig workers will be adopted in Poland shortly.

[20] Act of 3 December 2010 on the implementation of certain provisions of the European Union concerning equal treatment, Journal of Laws 2020, item 2156.

[21] Article 304, 304[1] of the Labour Code. The broad formula of worker protection in this field was recognised in the 1990s.

[22] Act of 10 October 2002 on the Minimum Wage, Journal of Laws 2020, item 2207.

[23] See further, Lukasz Pisarczyk, 'The Crisis of the Collective Bargaining System in Poland' (2019) 35 *International Journal of Comparative Labour Law and Industrial Relations* 57.

[24] *Układy zbiorowe mają przyszłość!*, available at: www.solidarnosc.org.pl/bbial/solidarnosc/uklady-zbiorowe-pracy-maja-przyszlosc/.

[25] However, the development of new technologies is also perceived as an opportunity for social dialogue: Andrzej Marian Świątkowski, *Elektroniczne technologie zatrudnienia ery postindustrialnej* (Wydawnictwo Naukowe Akademii Ignatianum w Krakowie 2019) 51–53.

[26] Official site of the Team for the Future of Work in the Polish Parliament: available at: www.sejm.gov.pl/Sejm9.nsf/agent.xsp?symbol=ZESPOL&Zesp=648. The Team has discussed, inter alia, the problem of platform work.

At least some gig workers, who perform direct services (eg, drivers, deliverers, cleaning service, caretakers), could be engaged as employees. Usually, the basic criteria of employee status, including work for one main client and a kind of subordination, are met. Consequently, there are no legal obstacles to concluding an employment contract. This practice, however, is rather rare. Employers avoid the employment relationship for two main (and quite unsurprising) reasons. First, the employment relationship generates higher costs of employment (special employee rights, social insurance contributions). Second, it creates a less flexible legal bond between parties. Labour law requires periods of notice that vary from two weeks to three months (depending on seniority).[27] Moreover, the termination of the contract concluded for an indefinite period must be justified and consulted with a trade union that represents the employee.[28] The position of crowdworkers (working online) is usually different. By using the platform as a tool to find jobs, they may have a larger number of clients. In such cases there is no entity that could be potentially viewed as an employer. However, there are also exceptions: the platform operator takes over the role of a quasi-employer.[29]

Those who perform work for a larger number of customers usually enjoy the legal status of self-employed. Theoretically, at least in some cases, they may also provide services as natural persons (not being entrepreneurs) concluding contracts regulated by the Civil Code.[30] For many reasons though, including taxes and social insurance, this might be an inconvenient solution.

The situation of those who depend on one main contractor is different. Despite the existing legal possibility they are not hired as employees. Also in their case, the most popular form is business contracts. Formally, they operate as entrepreneurs. However, in practice they work on the basis of one main contract (client) directly or indirectly. This creates a more formal and stable relationship. Gig workers become economically dependent (and in some cases also subordinate). As a result, their business status might be challenged. In 2019, the government planned to adopt the so-called 'entrepreneur test' to verify the legal status of the self-employed. It was raised that some of them abuse the status of entrepreneurs to enjoy tax preferences. The idea of a stronger protection returns in the recent political programme, Polish Deal, adopted by the government.[31] Its adoption could significantly limit the number of self-employed. The results of the programme, that came into force on 1st January 2022, remains, however, unclear. The self-employment rate in Poland is one of the highest in Europe (20.6 per cent of employment in 2020).[32] It is not recognised by official statistics how many of them are run by gig workers, but platform work has certainly grown in popularity in the Polish labour market.

[27] Art 36 of the Labour Code.

[28] Art 30(4) and Art 38 of the Labour Code.

[29] Jeremias Prassl and Martin Risak, 'Uber, Taskrabbit, & Co: Platforms as Employers? Rethinking the Legal Analysis of Crowdwork' (2016) 37 *Comparative Labor Law & Policy Journal* 604.

[30] The Law of 23 April 1964 – Civil Code, Journal of Laws 2020, item 1740, as amended.

[31] Polski Ład, available at: www.gov.pl/web/polski-lad.

[32] OECD Data, 'Self-employment rate' (OECD 2021), available at: data.oecd.org/emp/self-employment-rate.htm#indicator-chart.

Gig workers who do not enjoy the formal status of entrepreneurs are usually engaged on the basis of civil law contracts (eg a contract for services). They are neither entrepreneurs nor employees. They perform work on the basis of civil law contracts. They do not enjoy labour law protection. Over recent years, they have been covered by some basic protective standards (eg a minimum hourly rate).

In numerous cases the actual position of gig workers meets the criteria of the employment relationship. It concerns, first, a large group of those working on-site. They perform permanent and paid work in conditions of subordination. The level of their dependency on the employer is sometimes (similar to gig workers in other countries) relatively high. Unfortunately, a deficient system of protection against abuse in civil law contracts fails in the case of gig workers whose situation is non-standard (hardly recognised in the Polish labour market), and the market position (eg, due to a large number of foreigners) is particularly weak. Although they frequently perform work like employees, they are not governed by labour law. The situation could be improved by the imposition of new rules protecting them against abusive use of the non-employee status. One of the proposals is to grant labour inspectors the right to requalify civil law (business) contracts into employment contracts. It would not concern gig workers only (all non-employees who perform work in conditions similar to employees), but gig workers could be a group of beneficiaries. As employees they would enjoy the full protection under the applicable law; also, their position in collective relationships could improve. As discussed over recent years, another option, leading to similar results, would be the liberalisation of the employee status (eg, by adopting the criterion of dependency instead of subordination).[33] A broader approach to the employment relationship will lead to an automatic enlargement of the personal scope of collective agreements. Although it could slightly improve the situation, it would not solve the main problem – inefficiency of the mechanism protecting gig workers against abuse.

Compared with other countries, the problem of the legal status of gig workers is not only of a legal nature, but (probably mainly) of a factual character. No legal obstacles to requalifying civil law (business) contracts of some gig workers into employment contracts have been identified. However, like other non-employees they do not initiate any legal procedures to obtain the employee status. Consequently, the result of such a procedure remains unclear. At least in some cases, gig workers meet the criteria of the employment relationship.

There is a clear interaction between the legal status of gig workers and the need for their collective protection. After obtaining employee status, they would enjoy the whole body of labour law protection. Polish labour law guarantees a relatively high standard of statutory protection[34] (subject to some exceptions, eg,

[33] Zbigniew Góral and Katarzyna Bomba, 'The Future of Labour Law in Poland: selected issues' (2016) 23 *Studies on Labour Law and Social Policy* 6.

[34] See further, eg, Zbigniew Hajn and Leszek Mitrus, 'Poland' in Roger Blanpain (ed), *International Encyclopaedia of Laws: Labour Law and Industrial Relations* (Wolters Kluwer 2016).

severance payments). Poland has ratified the majority of key ILO Conventions and the European Social Charter as well as having implemented the majority of EU standards. Moreover, the communist regime developed employment standards as an element of a centrally planned economy and in order to justify the then existing economic and social system. Of course, the level of remuneration even in the employment relationship remains lower than in Western European countries,[35] yet it is an economic rather than a legal issue – from the legal point of view, the remuneration is well secured (payments for periods of non-performance of work, limitations concerning deductions from remuneration).[36] As a result, gig worker employees would enjoy a body of standards that guarantee fundamental rights and restore equilibrium between the parties. Then there is no need to establish collective standards in this area. From a different perspective, statutory standards limit the room for collective bargaining. An example is the adoption of the minimum hourly rate for some employees.

V. Collective Status of Gig Workers

When analysing the collective status of gig workers, it should be assumed that they are not employees but either workers engaged on the basis of civil law contracts or self-employed (entrepreneurs). There are no special provisions concerning the collective rights of gig workers. They are treated as other workers (non-employees).

Over recent years, Polish collective labour law has undergone a deep reconstruction. Until the end of 2018, trade union rights were guaranteed to employees only (with a few exceptions). This limitation was regarded as inconsistent with international standards. In 2015, the Polish Constitutional Court declared that it was a breach of the Polish Constitution.[37] According to the Court, trade union rights guaranteed by the Constitution cannot be limited to employees only.[38] All working people that meet specific criteria should have the right to form and join trade unions. As a result, in 2018 the Law on Trade Unions[39] was amended. The amendment came into force on 1 January 2019. The law recognised the full trade union rights of a specific category of workers called 'workers performing paid work'.

[35] Eurostat Statistics, 'Wages and labour costs' (Eurostat Statistics, March 2021), available at: ec.europa.eu/eurostat/statistics-explained/index.php?title=Wages_and_labour_costs#Gross_wages.2Fearnings.

[36] Articles 80, 81, 84–91 of the Labour Code.

[37] Polish Constitutional Court 02.06.2015, K 1/13, published in: OTK-A 2015, no 6, item 80.

[38] According to the Court, the right to form and join trade unions cannot be dependent on the legal form of employment (and limited to the employment contract only). This right should be granted to anyone who performs work in person and with remuneration, and has interests that can be represented by trade unions.

[39] Journal of Laws 2019, item 263, as amended.

This category covers those workers who are in paid employment, who do not employ other persons and who have employment-related interests that can be represented by trade unions. The law does not determine the level of remuneration. Consequently, workers with a low number of working hours are also covered by the guarantees. The law does not preclude any group of people performing paid work. It means that collective rights have been recognised in the case of both workers and self-employed people. The problem of interference with competition law (so important from the perspective of EU law) has not been broadly discussed. One can assume that a potential conflict may be eliminated by the criterion of 'rights and interests that can be represented by trade unions'. On the one hand, this may be quite general and vague, but on the other, flexible enough to be used by the courts evaluating the position of protected workers.

In order to apply labour rights in the field of collective labour law in the given situation, gig workers should be qualified as performing paid work. In other words, they should meet the following criteria: (i) they should provide paid work for another person or entity; (ii) they should do it on a basis different from the employment relationship; (iii) they should not hire other people for this type of work; and (iv) they should demonstrate rights and interests relating to the performance of work that can be represented by the trade union.

The above-mentioned criteria will also be verified in the case of gig workers. One can assume that those working on-site and for one principal contractor, as a rule, meet the requirements arising from the law. Consequently, they may be represented by trade unions and benefit from the system of collective bargaining. The situation of true entrepreneurs (eg, crowdworkers) seems to be more complicated. The prerequisites for recognising their collective rights are the performance of paid work (that constitutes an element of their professional activity) and not employing other workers. A criterion that may limit their collective status is the criterion of having rights and interests that can be represented by trade unions. This criterion must be seen in a broader perspective – the role of trade unions: free associations representing working people. On the one hand, it may justify the distinction between working people and entrepreneurs. On the other hand, one should not overlook the real position of the self-employed. As a result, many cases (the majority), due to their factual position,[40] meet the criteria determined by the law to enjoy collective rights, including the right to collective bargaining.

This problem appears when collective rights are confronted with economic freedoms and competition law. Collective agreements entered into within the framework of collective bargaining and intended to improve employment and working conditions must, by virtue of their nature and purpose, be treated as an exception to Article 101(1) of the Treaty on the Functioning of the European

[40] See further, Joanna Unterschütz, 'Praca w ramach platform i aplikacji cyfrowych – wyzwania dla zbiorowego prawa pracy, cz. 1' (2017) 8 *Monitor Prawa Pracy* 461.

Union (TFEU).[41] However, the judgments do not specify the personal scope of the collective agreements. In the *Albany* case the Court of Justice of the European Union (CJEU) referred to agreements concluded in the context of collective negotiations between management and labour. In the *FNV* case there are references to collective bargaining between employers and employees.[42] For this purpose, the CJEU decided to define the concept of employee that may differ from definitions adopted in the Member States. According to the CJEU, the essential feature of the employment relationship is that for a certain period of time one person performs services for and under the direction of another person in return for which the person performing the services receives remuneration.[43] It implies a rather narrow approach to the concept of employee. The CJEU adopted a bipartite division of workers and the self-employed, and the latter category is excluded from the scope of collective bargaining.[44] Only when self-employed service providers who are members of one of the contracting employees' organisations and perform for an employer, under a works or service contract, the same activity as that employer's employed workers, are they 'false self-employed'; in other words, service providers in a situation comparable to that of those workers. Then a provision of a collective labour agreement which sets minimum fees for those self-employed service providers does not fall within the scope of Article 101(1) TFEU. It does not lead to the enlargement of the personal scope of collective agreements. It is a mere attempt to eliminate abuse.

The bipartite division on workers and the self-employed seems to be a far-reaching simplification. It neglects the real market position of a large category of the self-employed. First, the self-employed can perform the same activities as employees.[45] Second, in many cases they perform work personally, without any form of support from other persons. Third, for the majority of the self-employed the work that they perform constitutes their basic level of income. Fourth, their market position is usually weak (weaker than the position of contractors for whom they work). Workers (who are not independent contractors) often find themselves in precarious and insecure situations, often even in worse situations than regular workers, also due to the fact that individually they can have a weak bargaining position and, additionally, are usually not unionised and not engaged in collective bargaining. Instead of freedom and autonomy they may experience dependency and subordination.[46]

[41] See, eg, Case C-67/96 *Albany International BV v Stichting Bedrijfspensioenfonds Textielindustrie* [1999] ECLI:EU:C:1999:430, para 60.

[42] Judgment in *FNV* EU:C:2014:2411, para 24 et seq.

[43] The classification of a 'self-employed person' under national law does not prevent that person from being classified as an employee within the meaning of EU law if that person's independence is merely notional, thereby disguising an employment relationship (see, to that effect, Case C-256/01 *Debra Allonby v Accrington & Rossendale College and Others* [2004] ECLI:EU:C:2004:18, para 71).

[44] Compare Mark Freedland and Nicola Kountouris, 'Some Reflections on the "Personal Scope" of Collective Labour Law' (2017) 46 *Industrial Law Journal* 52, 60.

[45] Case C-413/13 *FNV Kunsten Informatie en Media v Staat der Nederlanden* [2014] ECLI:EU:C:2014:2411, para 27.

[46] Prassl, *Humans as a Service* (n 15) 52 ff.

Consequently, instead of restricting the right to collective bargaining and impeding its effective implementation in practice, the state should promote it for all categories of workers, including self-employed workers who are in need of such protection. The majority decision in the European Committe of Social Rights' case *ICTU v Ireland* rightly says in the preliminary considerations that 'where providers of labour have no substantial influence on the content of contractual conditions, they must be given the possibility of improving the power imbalance through collective bargaining'.[47]

The lack of dependency does not significantly change their market position. Paradoxically, they may need support even more than dependent workers. To summarise, although numerous people are formally self-employed, they are in fact working people. In practice, their position is relatively close to the position of other workers (even employees). Because of their bargaining power as well as the real social position, they usually need collective representation. The lack of representation may lead to imbalance and negative social consequences such as underestimating the level of their remuneration and limiting the level of income, which influences the possibilities of personal development for workers (in this case the self-employed) and their families. The formally self-employed should be protected, if not against specific employers, then against the consequences of market functioning. From this perspective, a collective agreement can be perceived as an instrument of social inclusion. At the same time, the courts, in specific cases, should have appropriate instruments to exclude the right to bargain collectively if it is not justified by the position of the self-employed and could lead to a conflict with competition law. In such cases the law should ensure the right balance between competition law and social protection. The need for protection for the solo self-employed has been finally recognised in approval of the content of a draft for a Communication from the Commission 'Guidelines on the application of EU competition law to collective agreements regarding the working conditions of solo self-employed persons' (released on 9 December 2021).[48] The Commission admits that some categories of solo self-employed are in a position comparable to workers since they are unable to influence significantly their working conditions (economically dependent, working side-by-side with workers and, last but not least, working through digital working platforms). Consequently, collective agreements concluded for these groups of self-employed fall outside the scope of Article 101 TFEU (regardless of whether they could be classified as false self-employed).

The conditions adopted by Polish law (performing work/service personally, having collective interests that can be represented by trade unions) may turn out to be a practical tool to extend the protection to the self-employed who should be represented by trade unions. Thanks to this criterion the courts may evaluate the

[47] European Committee of Social Rights, *Irish Congress of Trade Unions (ICTU) v Ireland* (8 August 2016) C 123/2016, Case No 1, 38. See in detail on this case the contributions by Kresal (ch 4) and Brameshuber (ch 14) in this volume.

[48] Available at: /ec.europa.eu/info/law/better-regulation/have-your-say/initiatives/12483-Collective-bargaining-agreements-for-self-employed-scope-of-application-EU-competition-rules_en. See in detail the contribution by Brameshuber (ch 14) in this volume, pages 245 et seq.

bargaining position of specific groups of gig workers: the self-employed, and the need of their collective representation. Theoretically, in some cases it could lead to a conflict with EU competition law. Practically, one could expect the future development towards recognising collective rights of the self-employed, including those performing work via digital platforms – even if they are not false entrepreneurs. To summarise, in many cases gig workers may be treated as a group having common interests connected with work that can be represented by trade unions. Collective bargaining may play an important part in shaping their conditions of work and achieving social equilibrium.[49] The adopted solution may be also sufficient for the application of future EU standards (as outlined by the Commission). However, it is too early for a full assessment.

VI. Collective Procedures

In recognition of the freedom of association of the self-employed Polish law consequently extended the personal scope of the two main collective procedures: collective bargaining aimed at concluding collective agreements, and collective disputes.[50] In both cases, the regulations concerning employees apply mutatis mutandis to workers performing paid work. It formally opens the way to collective shaping of employment conditions.

Polish law recognises two types of collective agreement: company-level collective agreements and multi-company collective agreements. Company-level agreements are concluded for either one employer or a group of employers that constitute a part of a larger entity (usually a legal person). The scope of the application of multi-company collective agreements depends on the decision of the social partners. However, they are limited to employers who are members of the organisation that has concluded the agreement. The law provides for the extension procedure (so-called generalisation). Yet, the procedure has never been used in practice. As regards workers, collective agreements apply to all those employed by the employer, irrespective of their trade union membership, unless otherwise provided for in the agreement. The collective disputes procedure creates a legal framework for a strike. It supplements the typical collective bargaining. To summarise, trade unions may bargain collectively and organise strikes for the benefit of gig workers who are workers performing paid work. Consequently, those workers can be covered by collective agreements concluded as a result of those procedures.

[49] See further, Unterschütz (n 40).

[50] See further, Krzysztof Wojciech Baran in Krzysztof Wojciech Baran et al (eds), *Outline of Polish Labour Law System* (Wolters Kluwer Polska 2016) 89 and 425 ff.

VII. The Reality of Collective Bargaining for Gig Workers

Unfortunately, the theoretical possibilities have not been put into practice. The vast majority of existing collective agreements cover employees only. And even worse, after the amendment of the Law on Trade Unions, no significant change in the practice of the social partners has been observed. However, there have been some attempts to bargain for non-employees. This remark is valid for all non-employees, especially gig workers. In September 2021, the first trade union of the self-employed was registered, but it is nationwide in nature, and it is unclear whether it will also represent those employed in the gig economy.[51] In Poland there are no serious platform worker initiatives, which led to protests and strikes in Belgium, Italy and the United Kingdom.[52] The collapse of multi-company negotiations prevented the creation of a general framework for the whole category, for example, taxi drivers or food deliverers (as was the case in Denmark or Italy).[53] For example, drivers for such platforms as Uber or Bolt would have a common interest in negotiating how the platform algorithm sets the taxi fare or even more – basic employment rights like paid leave, insurance etc. In social media there are groups of Uber/Bolt drivers, where they exchange experiences. It is unlikely that such forms of remote contact may turn into a form of trade union in the future. Moreover, in the case of crowdworkers it can be difficult to identify a partner to negotiate with, and potential counterparties (entities operating the platforms) are rather reluctant to be involved in the negotiations.

There is no tradition of regional or local initiatives (such as the Bologna Charter). At the same time, it is difficult to initiate company-level negotiations for specific companies or establishments. The power of trade unions is insufficient to force strong companies to enter into collective bargaining for atypical workers. In some cases it is difficult to identify the real employer. According to the functional concept of employer[54] or purposive approach to labour law,[55] identification of the employer even if more than two parties are engaged in an employment relationship in platform work, will be possible. However, due to the crisis of collective bargaining in Poland the possibility for non-employees to bargain collectively is mainly theoretical.

[51] Grażyna J Leśniak, 'Jest pierwszy związek zawodowy samozatrudnionych' (*prawo.pl*, 17 September 2021), available at: www.prawo.pl/kadry/jest-pierwszy-zwiazek-zawodowy-samozatrudnionych,510673.html.

[52] Eurofound, *Employment and working conditions of selected types of platform work* (Publications Office of the European Union 2018) 53–57.

[53] Eurofound, 'The Danish trade union 3F' (Eurofound, 09 April 2021), available at: www.eurofound.europa.eu/data/platform-economy/initiatives/the-danish-trade-union-3f; National Collective Agreement for the Discipline of the Activity of Delivery of Goods on Behalf of Third Parties Carried out by Self-Employed Workers, so called Riders, available at: www.bollettinoadapt.it/wp-content/uploads/2020/09/CCNL-Rider-09_09_2020-def.docx.pdf.

[54] Jeremias Prassl, *The Concept of the Employer* (Oxford University Press 2015).

[55] Guy Davidov, *A Purposive Approach to Labour Law* (Oxford University Press 2016).

Collective bargaining for gig workers cannot really be an exception. The huge differentiation between platform workers is a great challenge to organising them in trade unions and allowing them to participate in collective bargaining, so platform workers are vulnerable while claiming their rights.[56] The rise and development of the gig economy forced the social partners to reflect on the need for, and forms of, collective representation in this sphere. Unfortunately, trade unions have not been able to propose a comprehensive and clear idea of representation. In some groups (eg, Uber drivers), there were attempts to encourage their members to join trade unions and to put pressure on employers. These initiatives have been far from successful. Gig workers are represented to a small extent. Therefore, it is not surprising that there are no major collective bargaining initiatives. Multi-company bargaining, that could be an opportunity for employees, is practically impossible. The multi-employer dialogue is non-existent at the moment. One cannot expect negotiations to be launched in the gig economy. There are more opportunities for bargaining at the enterprise level. However, this would require more initiatives and pressure from the trade unions. The impression is that the trade unions currently do not know what they can do for the workers. The situation is exacerbated by the employment structure in the gig economy. It is home to the most vulnerable groups (those entering the labour market, migrant workers) who do not know how to seek protection and who are not a priority for the trade unions (which themselves are undergoing an identity crisis).

There are no other movements of gig workers that could be an alternative to trade unions or enhance trade union activity. After all, gig workers are not represented by any elected bodies. First, the practical importance of the elected representatives remains very limited. The establishment of a work council is not obligatory. It depends on the employee's initiative. As a result, the procedures were initiated in only a few companies (it also reflects the lack of interest in collective activity). Second, work councils are created and composed of employees only. In such a situation, their commitment to non-employees (including gig workers) may remain limited. Third, the law does not recognise the right of work councils to bargain collectively (information and consultation only). There are no forms of elected representation at multi-company level. At the same time, employers are not interested in launching a social dialogue.

As a result, no major autonomous initiative should be expected. Theoretically, the state could play a role. First, the legislation may determine the legal status of gig workers (or some groups of gig workers). Second, the state may encourage social dialogue. However, in both spheres, the state takes a rather passive stance. Unfortunately there is no coherent concept of worker protection. Besides, the issue is quite delicate. Any intervention is likely to give rise to social discontent, and current governments have a clear populist trait. Steps are taken to bring political gain.

[56] Owczarek, *Don't GIG up!* (n 9).

The gig worker situation does not arouse much public interest. Moreover, stronger protection of a group in which migrant workers play an important role would mean a change in the current policy and a potential conflict with part of the electorate. It should therefore be expected that the state will not intervene as long as it is not necessary. The reaction may be inspired by social pressure. This was the case in the past, when the government was forced by strong groups (eg, taxi drivers) to cover platform workers, including Uber, by regulations relating to the transport market (formal requirements, licences, etc).[57] New regulations introducing, for example, the obligation for platform drivers to have taxi licences have not caused such platforms to go out of business (contrary to taxi drivers' expectations); they are still more competitive than traditional taxi corporations.

VIII. Conclusions

Polish law can be treated as an illustration of Otto Kahn-Freund's thesis that the efficiency of the law depends on the real power of the labour law actors rather than legal solutions.[58] A relatively modern and flexible legal framework has not been filled with an appropriate content yet. Theoretically, numerous gig workers meet the criteria of employees. In practice, the majority of them lack the power and determination to request the reclassification of their contracts. As a result, they miss the statutory protection. Collective bargaining offers them a chance to change the situation. Since the turn of 2018 and 2019, various groups of gig workers have enjoyed full trade union rights. Theoretically, they could benefit from the standards arising from collective agreements. Practically, the system of collective bargaining has collapsed. Quite symbolic is the lack of multi-company collective agreements. Negotiations for non-employees are non-existent. The abolition of legal obstacles in the use of collective rights by a large number of non-employees, including gig workers, should clearly be assessed positively (also from the perspective of international and constitutional standards). However, one cannot expect that gig workers, whose actual position is particularly vulnerable, will be an exception. There is no clear and comprehensive strategy from the trade unions towards the gig economy. Without structural changes, social dialogue, possible from the legal point of view, will not play any bigger practical role for gig workers.

[57] *TVN24 News* in English, 'Only licensed drivers in Poland. 'Lex Uber' becomes effective' (*TVN24*, 1 January 2020), available at: tvn24.pl/tvn24-news-in-english/polands-law-regulating-uber-like-companies-becomes-effective-ra997117-2982072.

[58] Paul Davies and Mark Freedland, *Kahn-Freund's Labour and the Law*, 3rd edn (Stevens & Sons 1983) 21 ff.

14

(A Fundamental Right to) Collective Bargaining for Economically Dependent, Employee-Like Workers

ELISABETH BRAMESHUBER*

I. Introduction

Persons in the gig economy work under different statuses in the different Member States, sometimes as self-employed, sometimes as persons with an 'in-between status', sometimes as employees. Whether collective bargaining agreements can be concluded for gig workers is not necessarily linked to the status of employee (any more). As the Commission's platform workers consultation document from February 2021 shows, 'Some trade unions have opened their membership to non-standard workers and the self-employed … A few innovative collective agreements have also recently been signed between unions and digital platforms, but they remain very limited'.[1]

The underlying legal questions are: Can non-employees organise? Can collective bargaining agreements be concluded for non-employees? What are the potential legal obstacles at European Union (EU) level? Are there any differences as regards the legal and the factual situation in the Member States?

This chapter first focuses on Article 101 of the Treaty on the Functioning of the European Union (TFEU) and the respective Court of Justice of the European Union (CJEU) case law. By juxtaposing it to the fundamental right to bargain collectively, as guaranteed by Article 28 of the EU Charter of Fundamental Rights (CFR) or Article 11 of the European Convention on Human Rights (ECHR),

* The author is extremely grateful to those colleagues of the COGENS project who contributed to this chapter by providing her with the in-depth knowledge about the legal and factual situation in their respective countries. Parts of this contribution strongly rely on the author's contribution to the *Festschrift für Franz Marhold*, published by Manz in 2020.

[1] Commission, 'First Phase Consultation of Social Partners Under Article 154 TFEU on Possible Action Addressing the Challenges Related to Working Conditions in Platform Work' (Consultation Document) C(2021) 1127 final, 21.

reference points for possible future litigation are given. In some Member States there actually exists the possibility to bargain collectively for this third category of working persons.[2] Thus, irrespective of an apparent reluctance of trade unions and employers' organisations to introduce a so-called 'third category' for people working through platforms,[3] and irrespective of the Commission's decision not to create a 'third' employment status at EU level,[4] future references to the CJEU seem more likely than not.

The second part of this contribution investigates the different jurisdictions of the countries represented in the project. It analyses the factual and the legal situation as regards collective bargaining for non-employees, and categorises the agreements especially with respect to their personal scope and the effects they have.

The final part analyses the situation in the light of the Commission's initiative on collective bargaining agreements for the self-employed[5] and the respective draft Guidelines on the application of EU competition law to collective agreements regarding the working conditions of solo self-employed persons, including their Annex (hereinafter: Draft Guidelines), open for public consultation until 24 February 2022.[6] Furthermore, the Commission's second stage consultation of social partners on improving the working conditions in platform work[7] and the Commission's subsequent proposal for a Directive on improving working conditions in platform work (hereinafter: Proposal for a Platform Work Directive),[8] are analysed briefly in light of the aforementioned questions of collective bargaining for 'third-category working persons'. By arguing that a 'model' definition of those persons should take into account their economic dependence, above all, and by suggesting that such a definition could be made by an agreement under Article 155, paragraph 2, first alternative TFEU, this chapter strives to accommodate the Court's case law as well as the Commission's initiatives in this field.

II. The Legal Situation at EU Level

Traditionally, collective bargaining agreements are concluded to regulate the employment relationship. Thus, on the side of labour the personal scope is

[2] *cf* s 12a German Tarifvertragsgesetz – Law on Collective Bargaining Agreements (TVG).

[3] Commission, 'Second-Phase Consultation of Social Partners Under Article 154 TFEU on Possible Action Addressing the Challenges Related to Working Conditions in Platform Work (Consultation Document) Commission C(2021) 4230 final, 3.

[4] ibid, 21.

[5] Commission, 'Collective bargaining agreements for self-employed – scope of application of EU competition rules' (Inception Impact Assessment) Ares(2021)102652.

[6] Communication from the Commission – Approval of the content of a draft Communication from the Commission for Guidelines on the application of EU competition law to collective agreements regarding the working conditions of solo self-employed persons, C(2021) 8838 final, and the respective Annex (Draft Guidelines).

[7] Commission, C(2021) 4230 final (n 3).

[8] COM(2021) 762 final.

restricted to employees. Independent workers were usually excluded from collective bargaining under specific formulae, except in some countries such as Germany. Yet, a teleological interpretation of Article 28 CFR also allows for a differentiated outcome.

A. Competition Law as a Restriction to Collective Bargaining Agreements

In line with its former case law,[9] the CJEU states, in *FNV Kunsten*, that only those collective bargaining agreements which are negotiated between 'management and labour' do not infringe EU competition law.[10] However, the Court also held in *FNV Kunsten* that collective bargaining agreements for 'service providers in a situation comparable to that of … workers' do not fall within the scope of Article 101 TFEU.[11] Furthermore, a service provider can lose his status of an undertaking

> if he does not determine independently his own conduct on the market, but is entirely dependent on his principal, because he does not bear any of the financial or commercial risks arising out of the latter's activity and operates as an auxiliary within the principal's undertaking.[12]

This seems to allow for an interpretation in favour of concluding collective bargaining agreements for 'service providers comparable to workers' without infringing EU competition law. Yet, uncertainties remain as to which service providers are actually comparable. The Commission's initiative on collective bargaining agreements for the self-employed[13] and its Draft Guidelines[14] engage in detecting which persons could be included in the notion of 'comparable service-providers'.[15]

B. The Fundamental Right to Collective Bargaining According to Article 28 CFR and Article 11 ECHR

From a fundamental rights point of view, Article 28 CFR is central. Article 28 CFR provides for a fundamental right of employees' and employers' organisations to collective bargaining. Therefore, it allows for provisions in the Member States promoting the conclusion of collective bargaining agreements by, at the same time, limiting competition between companies and therefore setting limits to

[9] Case C-67/96 *Albany International BV v Stichting Bedrijfspensioenfonds Textielindustrie* [1999] ECLI:EU:C:1999:430.
[10] Case C-413/13 *FNV Kunsten Informatie en Media v Staat der Nederlanden* [2014] ECLI:EU:C:2014:2411, para 22.
[11] ibid, para 42.
[12] ibid, para 33. See also Annex to C(2021) 8838 final, 9 (n 6).
[13] Commission, Ares(2021)102652 (n 5).
[14] C(2021) 8838 final (n 6).
[15] See in detail below, section III.

competition law.[16] Yet, the personal scope of Article 28 CFR is unclear. According to some, those fundamental rights guaranteed in the Charter's chapter on solidarity apply only to those persons fulfilling 'the'[17] autonomous definition of worker provided for by EU law.[18] Others argue that generally speaking, economically dependent employee-like workers should also benefit from the Charter's social fundamental rights.[19] Up until now, there has been no case law on that question.

Regarding the personal scope of Article 28 CFR, recourse to Article 11 ECHR and the European Court of Human Rights (ECtHR) case law[20] is not helpful either since the latter is ambiguous. Although the wording of Article 11 ECHR does not explicitly refer to employees but to 'all people',[21] there is ECtHR case law where the Court has recognised that freedom of association also applies to the self-employed.[22] Furthermore, the ECtHR increasingly relies on International Labour Organization (ILO) instruments and conventions, and their interpretation by the competent bodies, to determine what is covered by Article 11 ECHR. The ILO Committee on Freedom of Association assumes that freedom of association has a broad personal scope of application. Freedom of association is not conditional on the existence of an employment relationship, but also applies to 'self-employed workers in general'.[23] With respect to ILO Convention 98, the Committee of Experts on the Application of Conventions and Recommendations has concluded that the right to collective bargaining provided for under Article 4 should also apply to the 'self-employed',[24] even though the Convention itself refers to 'workers' organizations'.

In *Păstorul cel Bun v Romania*, the ECtHR ruled with regard to the right to form a trade union under Article 11 ECHR that the obligations of the service

[16] Claudia Schubert in Martin Franzen, Inken Gallner and Hartmut Oetker (eds), *Kommentar zum Europäischen Arbeitsrecht*, 2nd edn (CH Beck 2018); Art 28 CFR, para 2; Hans D Jarass, *Charta der Grundrechte der Europäischen Union unter Einbeziehung der sonstigen Grundrechtsregelungen*, 3rd edn (CH Beck 2016); Art 28 CFR, paras 2, 4, 18.

[17] See, for a differentiated view on the notion of worker in the EU, Martin Risak and Thomas Dullinger, *The concept of 'worker' in EU law. Status quo and potential for change* (ETUI aisbl 2018).

[18] eg, Claudia Schubert in Martin Franzen, Inken Gallner and Hartmut Oetker (eds), *Kommentar zum Europäischen Arbeitsrecht*, 3rd edn (CH Beck 2019); Art 28 CFR, para 17; Art 27 CFR, para 19. Also referring to employment relationships, Michael Holoubek in Jürgen Schwarze et al, *EU-Kommentar*, 4th edn (Facultas, Helbing & Lichtenhahn, Nomos 2019); Art 28 CFR, para 13.

[19] Johannes Heuschmid in Wolfgang Däubler (ed), *Arbeitskampfrecht*, 4th edn (Nomos 2016) § 11, para 34.

[20] See Art 52(3), Art 53 CFR for the question of interpreting the Charter's rights in parallel to their corresponding Convention rights; see, eg, Schubert (n 18); Art 28 CFR, para 9 with further references.

[21] See also *Hendy*, as referred to by the High Court of Justice, *Independent Workers Union v Roofoods Ltd t/a Deliveroo*, Case No: CO/810/2018, para 26.

[22] *Vörður Ólafsson v Island* App no 20161/06 (ECtHR, 27 April 2010) para 54; in fact, it was about the negative freedom of association of a carpenter.

[23] Nicola Countouris and Valerio De Stefano, *New Trade Union Strategies for New Forms of Employment* (ETUC 2019) 20.

[24] International Labour Conference, *Giving globalization a human face. General Survey on the fundamental Conventions concerning rights at work in light of the ILO Declaration on Social Justice for a Fair Globalization, 2008, Report III (Part 1B)* (International Labour Office 2012) para 209.

provider must correspond to those obligations typically found in an employment relationship in order for Article 11 ECHR to apply.[25] Using the criteria applicable under the relevant international conventions, the ECtHR concluded that such an employment relationship is primarily dependent on the following factors: 'performance of work' and 'remuneration'.[26] However, it is unclear which '*facts relating to the performance of work*' are to be taken into account.

Likewise, a clear conclusion cannot be drawn from the CJEU's case law. Whereas some have concluded on the basis of the *FNV Kunsten* case that only ('hidden') employees profit from the guarantees enshrined in Article 28 CFR,[27] it could also follow from the judgment that all those who are in a comparable situation to employees fall within the scope of Article 28 CFR.[28] With regard to associations representing self-employed persons, it is argued that they are not covered by Article 28 CFR.[29] However, taking into account that independence and freedom are maintained with respect to other parties,[30] there is no reason in principle why protection cannot be granted to associations of economically dependent employee-like workers whose status is comparable to that of employees, especially in view of the purpose of collective bargaining[31] – primarily, compensating for a structural imbalance of power, affording protection to the structurally weaker party to the contract, and the cartelisation of working conditions. Any possible 'double representation' by trade unions – we should consider the possibility that a person whose status is comparable to that of an employee may also employ a few workers[32] – is unproblematic in view of the trade unions' relative freedom with respect to other parties.[33] The European Committee of Social Rights (ECSR)[34] is clearly in favour of the possibility, which is afforded even to 'self-employed workers', of exercising the right to negotiate and conclude collective agreements.[35]

[25] *Sindicatul 'Păstorul cel Bun' v Romania* App No 2330/09 (ECtHR, 9 July 2013) para 141.

[26] ibid, para 142, referring to ILO Employment Relationship Recommendation 2006 No 198 (15 June 2006).

[27] eg, Schubert (n 18); Art 28 CFR, para 18.

[28] eg, Johannes Heuschmid and Daniel Hlava, 'Anm zu EuGH C-413/13' [2015] *AuR* 193, 194 et seq. See also, Abbo Junker, 'Die Gewährleistung der Tarifautonomie im europäischen Recht' (2015) 46 *ZfA* 267, 284.

[29] Schubert (n 18); Art 28 CFR, para 20.

[30] ibid, Art 28 CFR, para 21.

[31] See also Countouris and De Stefano (n 23) 20.

[32] eg, s 12a(1) lit 1 TVG: 'Employee-like workers need to carry out work "*essentially (im wesentlichen)*" without employing others'.

[33] Manfred Löwisch and Volker Rieble, *Tarifvertragsgesetz: Kommentar*, 4th edn (Franz Vahlen 2017) § 12a, para 11.

[34] According to the Charter's explanations, Art 28 is based on Art 6 of the revised European Social Charter (RESC). Thus, the latter needs to be respected when interpreting Art 28, including the ECSR's opinions; Schubert (n 18); Art 28 CFR, para 8; Countouris and De Stefano (n 23) 53.

[35] European Committee of Social Rights, *Irish Congress of Trade Unions (ICTU) v Ireland* (8 August 2016) C 123/2016, Case No 1, paras 35–40, 95.

C. Solving the Tensions between Article 101 TFEU and Article 28 CFR with Regard to Collective Bargaining Agreements for Certain Non-Employees

Industry or sector-specific collective agreements,[36] which also prohibit any deviations to the detriment of employees, are necessarily associated with certain restrictive effects on competition: this only starts from a certain (wage) level.[37] As a matter of principle, such agreements would have to be inadmissible and thus null and void pursuant to Article 101 TFEU. However, the social policy objectives pursued by collective agreements would be '*seriously compromised*' as a result.[38] Collective agreements concluded between social partners, which aim to improve employment and working conditions, therefore, do not fall under Article 101 TFEU due to their nature and subject matter.[39]

This is in line with the prevailing opinion that Article 28 CFR constitutes a sectoral derogation from Article 101 TFEU.[40] It is necessary in order to ensure the sound operation of collective bargaining autonomy and thus to safeguard the right to collective bargaining under Article 28 CFR.[41] To put it more bluntly, it would not be possible to exercise the fundamental right to collective bargaining if this sectoral derogation did not exist. However, the sectoral derogation only applies to the extent that collective agreements and bargaining are protected.[42] As a result, it must apply to all working conditions that are regulated in collective agreements and that accordingly lead to cartelisation, too, and thus to an exclusion of competition. This must apply to all those matters in respect of which a market exists, ie, the basis for determining labour costs. This therefore includes any minimum terms and conditions of employment in respect of which there is a competitive situation.[43] However, the burden of proving the existence of a sectoral derogation lies with the parties to the collective agreement.[44]

[36] *cf Albany* (n 9) para 63 – the Court refers to (a system of) collective agreements that applies to '*all workers in that sector*' and that '*contributes directly to improving one of their working conditions*'.

[37] Robert Rebhahn and Michael Reiner in Jürgen Schwarze et al, *EU-Kommentar*, 4th edn (Facultas, Helbing & Lichtenhahn, Nomos 2019); Art 151 AEUV, para 22.

[38] *Albany* (n 9) paras 54, 59.

[39] ibid, para 60.

[40] Explicitly Schubert (n 18); Art 28 CFR, para 7; Holoubek (n 18); Art 28 CFR, para 23. Maximilian Fuchs, Franz Marhold and Michael Friedrich, *Europäisches Arbeitsrecht*, 6th edn (Verlag Österreich 2020) 512.

[41] Schubert (n 18); Art 28 CFR, paras 65, 86.

[42] ibid, Art 28 CFR, para 85. See also Rudolf Mosler, 'Das unionsrechtliche Kartellverbot und seine Bedeutung für das Arbeitsrecht und das Sozialversicherungsrecht' (2016) 30 *Wirtschaftliche Blätter* 774, 776.

[43] Mosler, 'Das unionsrechtliche Kartellverbot und seine Bedeutung für das Arbeitsrecht und das Sozialversicherungsrecht' (n 42) 775.

[44] See also the Dutch Competition Authority's opinion, cited by Countouris and De Stefano (n 23) 45, 54.

i. Teleological Approach

Collective agreements are justified by the fact that, generally speaking, the person who is 'only' offering his work performance is in a comparably weaker negotiating position.[45] Although there are also a (small) number of instruments available under general civil law that can be employed in an attempt to redress a blatant imbalance of interests,[46] these instruments do not resolve a structural imbalance that may exist within a group of individuals. It is helpful to remind ourselves of the purpose of collective bargaining,[47] also in terms of the personal scope of application of the fundamental right in question. In a nutshell, this should therefore be a right enjoyed by all those persons for whom there is an imbalance of power between them and their contract partner, the consequence of which is that freedom of contract alone cannot guarantee that a contract will be well balanced.[48]

Specifically, this would include those service providers who, due to their economic dependence and weaker bargaining position, are likely to have working conditions imposed on them without guaranteeing their means of subsistence. Section 12a of the German Collective Bargaining Act also refers to this need for social protection. This need is assumed to exist if the degree of – economic – dependence reaches a level that generally only occurs in an employment relationship and the services rendered are comparable to those rendered by an employee in terms of their social character.[49] According to the German Federal Labour Court (Bundesarbeitsgericht), in order to define the 'need for social protection', it is necessary to determine whether there is a '*typical need*' to '*utilize the labour force to safeguard one's economic existence*'. Such a need may not exist if the person has other sources of income.[50] However, this may also find expression in the fact that (mainly) the person only acts for another person and also does not offer his services competitively on the market as an undertaking, but rather in exchange for the remuneration that the contract partner deems economically viable. On the contrary, it cannot hinge on a possible obligation to follow instructions or personal dependence – especially given the purpose of the prohibition of cartels[51];[52]

[45] *ICTU* (n 35) para 38.

[46] eg, s 879 Abs 4 oder, s 934 of the Austrian Civil Code – Allgemeines Bürgerliches Gesetzbuch, ABGB), allowing for redress in case of a contract being *contra bonos mores* or in case the imbalance exceeds 50% of the other party's contributions' worth (*laesio enormis*).

[47] Schubert (n 18); Art 28 CFR, para 85; Fuchs, Marhold and Friedrich (n 40) 457 et seq. Note, employers also benefit from collective bargaining agreements, taking into account their cartelising function.

[48] *cf ICTU* (n 35) para 38. For a teleological approach also Risak and Dullinger (n 17) 45 et seq.

[49] Martin Franzen in Rudi Müller-Glöge, Ulrich Preis and Ingrid Schmidt (eds), *Erfurter Kommentar zum Arbeitsrecht*, 22nd edn (CH Beck 2022) § 12a TVG, para 5 with further references.

[50] BAG 4 AZR 106/90 AP TVG § 12a Nr 1.

[51] Konrad Grillberger, 'Tarifvertrag für Selbständige und Kartellverbot' (2015) 3 *DRdA* 162, 167; see also, Mosler, 'Das unionsrechtliche Kartellverbot und seine Bedeutung für das Arbeitsrecht und das Sozialversicherungsrecht' (n 42) 778.

[52] Clearly *ICTU* (n 35) para 38.

for this, the person should indeed act in a largely personal capacity.[53] Further criteria include, for example, the absence of operating resources and/or employees, and restrictions on whether it is also permissible to act on behalf of other persons.[54]

Admittedly, it is necessary to explore the extent to which a fundamental right to collective bargaining is subject to restrictions in terms of content for persons whose status is comparable to that of employees. If one consistently focuses on the need for protection and thus on the comparability of the situation in which employees find themselves, collective agreements should be concluded for persons whose status is comparable to that of employees in those areas only in which such comparability actually exists.[55] The difficulty of making objectively justifiable comparisons is illustrated by the simple example of the personal scope of application of the Austrian Holiday Entitlement Act (UrlG) and the German Federal Holiday Entitlement Act (BUrlG): the former does not apply to economically dependent employees whose status is comparable to that of employees, whereas the latter does apply pursuant to section 2.

ii. The Comparability of Situation as Anchor

As already pointed out, however, the Court's *FNV Kunsten* judgment can also be interpreted to the effect that economically dependent employees whose status is comparable to that of employees are covered by the sectoral derogation from the prohibition of cartels,[56] in spite of the fact that they do not fulfil the Lawrie Blum criteria, because, according to the CJEU, a service provider loses his status as an undertaking if he

> does not determine independently his own conduct on the market, but is entirely dependent on his principal, because he does not bear any of the financial or commercial risks arising out of the latter's activity and operates as an auxiliary within the principal's undertaking.[57]

It is also argued in the literature that the criterion of work performed on the 'instructions' of another party should be interpreted broadly because the 'false self-employed' would otherwise only then be covered if they actually fulfilled the same requirements as employees.[58]

[53] See, for the typological criteria that apply in Austria, Robert Rebhahn in Matthias Neumayr and Gert P Reissner, *Zeller Kommentar zum Arbeitsrecht*, 3rd edn (MANZ 2018) § 1151 ABGB, para 125 with further references.

[54] Risak and Dullinger (n 17) 46 f.

[55] *cf* Rudolf Mosler, 'Ist das ArbVG noch aktuell? – Kollektive Rechtsgestaltung' (2014) 5a *DRdA* 511, 514.

[56] Countouris and De Stefano (n 23) 49; Draft Guidelines C(2021) 8838 final, 21 (n 6).

[57] *FNV Kunsten* (n 10) para 33. See also Mosler, 'Das unionsrechtliche Kartellverbot und seine Bedeutung für das Arbeitsrecht und das Sozialversicherungsrecht' (n 42) 778; and Countouris and De Stefano (n 23) 49.

[58] Countouris and De Stefano (n 23) 48.

The judgment is also open to a teleological interpretation in that it is a question of comparability between employees and other service providers in connection with the derogation for collective agreements from the prohibition of cartels because, according to the CJEU, service providers must be 'in a situation comparable to that of employees'.[59] The interests of employees on the one hand and persons comparable to them on the other can be the only criterion for comparability with regard to collective agreements. In other words, collective agreements both for employees and for comparable persons must serve the same purpose.[60]

Thus, there are good reasons for making collective agreements for persons whose status is comparable to that of employees exempt from the prohibition of cartels; however, the CJEU has not explicitly given an opinion on this issue. However, a recent decision issued by the ECSR could point the way forward for future proceedings. The ECSR is of the view that competition law regulations (at the national level) that prohibit in any case both the negotiation and conclusion of collective agreements by economically dependent persons whose status is comparable to that of employees are not necessary in a democratic society; *ergo*, they are not necessary to safeguard undistorted competition. In the opinion of the ECSR, the conclusion of collective agreements on the subject of remuneration for services rendered by economically dependent employees whose status is comparable to that of employees would have an influence on competition that would not differ significantly from that which collective pay agreements for employees have on competition.[61] Consequently, it was held that there had been no infringement of competition law. In addition, with regard to Article 101 TFEU, the ECSR notes that it is unlikely that the implementation of rights under the revised European Social Charter (RESC) will be affected by Article 101 TFEU given that Article 101 TFEU does not prohibit the right to collective bargaining per se and in view of the fact that it would also exclude certain categories of the 'self-employed' from its scope of application. However, the ECSR could not assess the risk of an application of Union law.[62]

Both including economically dependent persons whose status is comparable to that of employees in the scope of protection of Article 28 CFR and restricting the definition of 'undertaking' in Article 101 TFEU, and the reliance on comparability and the principle of equality,[63] are predicated on the same idea: these persons whose status is comparable to that of employees are likewise in need of the same protection as comparable employees with regard to remuneration; often, they are also in competition with them.[64] If they offer their services at a lower price, this will give

[59] *FNV Kunsten* (n 10) para 42. See also Mosler, 'Das unionsrechtliche Kartellverbot und seine Bedeutung für das Arbeitsrecht und das Sozialversicherungsrecht' (n 42) 778.

[60] Compare Elias Felten, *Koalitionsfreiheit und Arbeitsverfassungsgesetz* (MANZ 2015) 262.

[61] *ICTU* (n 35) paras 100 ff.

[62] ibid, para 115.

[63] *In extenso*, Schubert (n 18); Art 28 CFR, paras 90 ff.

[64] For bike couriers, eg, Andreas Danzer, 'Umfrage: Foodora und die Zufriedenheit der Mitarbeiter' *Der Standard* (22 July 2018), available at: bit.ly/2G4pdp5.

rise to a downward spiral of competition compared with employees, even though a single market exists.[65] To prevent this distortion of competition, it is therefore also necessary to make it possible for persons whose status is comparable to that of employees to conclude collective agreements,[66] at least in those instances where they share a market with employees. However, it is striking that the CJEU does not consider the latter reasoning in *FNV Kunsten*, even though it was endorsed in the Opinion of Advocate General Wahl. This could be due, amongst other things, to the fact that placing greater emphasis on protections against or the avoidance of social dumping (which, according to the case law of the CJEU, may even be an overriding reason in the public interest that can provide justification for a restriction of fundamental freedoms)[67] could break up the case law on restrictions of competition, which has so far been based primarily on aspects of an economic nature. In other words, if protections against social dumping are admissible as a legitimate justification for restrictions of competition, this raises the question (which goes far beyond the points of interest raised here) of what other interests should be permitted to restrict competition.

However, even if a sectoral derogation is rejected for collective agreements for employees whose status is comparable to that of employees, this does not automatically result in an infringement of Article 101 TFEU in every case. Under competition law, what generally matters is that competition is restricted to an appreciable extent.[68] Therefore, where there has not been a restrictive effect on competition if only one cost factor for a service is cartelised and if as a result the final costs are only marginally affected, this does not – as a rule – constitute a violation of Article 101(1) TFEU.[69] There would be no incompatibility with Article 101(1) TFEU if only those working conditions were to be cartelised in collective agreements for persons whose status is comparable to that of employees that, as a result, do not have any restrictive effect on competition. Only very recently, the CJEU ruled in connection with the establishment of minimum fees by a professional association of lawyers that a national regulation prohibiting the undercutting of this minimum fee officially decreed and determined by the professional association may affect competition in the internal market within the meaning of Article 101(1) TFEU[70] unless it can be ensured that the tariffs 'are

[65] See also the Opinion of AG Wahl in Case C-413/13 *FNV Kunsten Informatie en Media v Staat der Nederlanden* [2014] EU:C:2014:2215, Opinion paras 76 f.

[66] Schubert (n 18); Art 28 CFR, para 92; Mosler, 'Das unionsrechtliche Kartellverbot und seine Bedeutung für das Arbeitsrecht und das Sozialversicherungsrecht' (n 42) 778. AG Wahl, *FNV Kunsten* (n 65) paras 74 ff; Countouris and De Stefano (n 23) 50.

[67] eg, Case C-577/10 *European Commission v Kingdom of Belgium* [2012] EU:C:2012:814, para 45.

[68] Denied by the Court in Joined Cases C-180/98 to C-184/98 *Pavlov and Others* [2000] ECLI:EU:C:2000:428, paras 90 ff, 95, 97.

[69] See the Irish Competition law referred to by Countouris and De Stefano (n 23) 50.

[70] Joined Cases C-427/16 and C-428/16 *CHEZ Elektro Bulgaria AD v Yordan Kotsev and others* [2017] ECLI:EU:C:2017:890 para 51.

fair and justified in accordance with the general interest'.[71] An infringement of Article 101(1) TFEU therefore does not necessarily exist as the objectives associated with such a regulation must also be taken into account and it must be verified whether the conditions restricting competition are necessarily related to the pursuit of these objectives.[72] On the other hand, the CJEU does not specify which objectives may be legitimate. However, it could be argued on the basis of more recent CJEU case law that the Court of Justice does not in every case oppose taking account of social policy objectives, and thus also the promotion of social protection in general.[73]

III. Collective Bargaining Rights for Non-Employees at National Level

Persons working in the gig economy can often be classed as so-called **e**conomically **d**ependent, **e**mployee-like **w**orkers. In the following, the acronym 'EDEW' is used. Of course, this definition is not a uniform one to be found in all Member States,[74] nor is it an EU-wide definition. The preliminary assumption when assessing the situation in the different countries, which shall be displayed in this section, was that specific collective bargaining rights might exist or that collective bargaining agreements have been concluded for persons who

- work primarily for one other person and/or
- do not offer their services on the market, and
- who work in person (no/limited possibility of substitution).[75]

[71] ibid, para 46.
[72] ibid, para 53.
[73] See the recourse to Art 3(2) TEU and Art 9 TFEU, Case C-201/15 *Anonymi Geniki Etairia Tsimenton Iraklis (AGET Iraklis) v Ypourgos Ergasias, Koinonikis Asfalisis kai Koinonikis Allilengyis* [2016] ECLI:EU:C:2016:972, paras 76, 78. See also Countouris and De Stefano (n 23) 53.
[74] See, eg, for a different definition, the Italian Statute of Self-employment and Smart Work, Law No 81 from 6 June 2017, according to which independent contractors, who constantly have to *refer to the market* to offer their services mainly by personal and self-organised work, but who might be in a position of weakness as regards competition with other service providers and who might be in a weak bargaining position as regards their working conditions, are granted specific protection. A status of economic dependency is also deemed to occur when 'an undertaking is capable of causing an excessive imbalance in its commercial relations with another company'. Another decisive factor for assessing whether a person is economically dependent is 'the real possibility for the dependent party to find satisfactory alternatives on the market'; Maurizio Del Conte and Elena Gramano, 'Looking to the Other Side of the Bench: The New Legal Status of Independent Contractors under the Italian Legal System' (2018) 39 *Comparative Labor Law & Policy Journal* 579, 600, 602.
[75] These criteria are also mentioned by Rebhahn and Reiner (n 37); Art 153 TFEU, para 12; and Rebhahn (n 53) § 1151 ABGB, para 123.

A. Formal Recognition of a Third Category Guaranteeing Also (Some) Collective Labour Rights

Examples of such a status which is not limited to specific branches can be found in France, Germany, Italy, the Netherlands, Poland, Spain and the UK. In Austria, however, special collective agreements that differ from collective bargaining agreements concluded under the Labour Constitution Act can be concluded for certain economically dependent journalists falling under the scope of the Law for Journalists (§§ 16 et seq) and for certain economically dependent persons performing manual work at home under the so-called 'Heimarbeitsgesetz' (§§ 43 et seq).[76]

In France, independent workers (so-called auto-entrepreneurs, to whom labour law, generally speaking, does not apply)[77] have the right to constitute a trade union, to be a member of a trade union and to have a union represent their interests, and to take collective action in defence of their interests. These rights are guaranteed by the Act of 8 August 2016 on work, modernisation of social dialogue and securing of career paths (the El Khomri Act).

In Germany, collective bargaining agreements can be concluded not only for employees but also, according to § 12a TVG, for independent workers who are economically dependent and in need of social protection comparable to an employee. These independent workers need to fulfil the following criteria:

- Works for someone else on the basis of a civil law contract ('Dienst- or Werkvertrag');
- Personally perform the contractual duties essentially without the support of own employees; and
- (a) Work predominantly for one employer or (b) earns more than half[78] of his or her total revenues from that particular employer.

In Italy, it is possible to conclude collective bargaining agreements applicable to independent contractors, which is a heterogenous category. In principle they should be solo self-employed persons, but the relevant feature is that they do not organise their activity by themselves but have to fit into someone else's organisation. Article 39 of the Italian Constitution, recognising the right to collective bargaining, is invoked as the legal basis. It is said to have a wide scope of application and can be interpreted as comprising collective bargaining agreements for the self-employed.

[76] Mosler, 'Das unionsrechtliche Kartellverbot und seine Bedeutung für das Arbeitsrecht und das Sozialversicherungsrecht' (n 42) 777.

[77] Exemptions exist for journalists and some artists, ie, to them, some labour laws apply.

[78] This part is lower for persons performing artistic, writing or journalist services to a third of their total revenues, *cf* Art 12a(3).

In the Netherlands, collective bargaining agreements can be extended/declared applicable to contracts for services/providers of services.

In Spain, collective agreements which do not have the same legal effects as those concluded for employees, can be concluded for so-called TRADE, ie, economically dependent self-employed. Furthermore, TRADE enjoy the right of affiliation to trade unions or employers' associations, and they have the right to create specific professional associations. A TRADE is a person who is not subordinated and who is not bound by disciplinary duties.[79] Furthermore, a TRADE obtains at least 75 per cent of their professional income from the same (natural or legal) person called a 'client'. A TRADE's activity must be different from the client's other workers (ie, clearly differentiated from the worker's tasks), TRADEs must have their own material and productive infrastructure, their own organisational criteria (even if TRADEs can receive technical indications from their client) and must accept the risk of their own professional activity. In addition, TRADEs have the possibility to outsource their services. The legal basis is the self-employed statute and Agreements of Professional Interest (Acuerdo de Interés Profesional).

In Poland, workers who engage on the basis of civil law contracts (regulated by the Civil Code) have the right to form and join trade unions. They can be covered by collective agreements and represented within the procedure of resolving collective disputes. They are excluded from some special collective procedures that are strictly connected with the content of the employment relationship. The prerequisites for enjoying the mentioned collective rights are

- performance of paid work;
- performance in person (without employing any other person);
- having collective interests.

In the UK, workers[80] and employees have the right to form collective bargaining units, to the minimum wage or to holiday pay. On the contrary, independent contractors do not enjoy these rights. The legal basis is the Trade Union and Labour Relations (Consolidation) Act 1992, Schedule A1, which specifically uses the 'worker' (rather than 'employee') category. Collective Bargaining is at the employer level. In practice, there is ongoing litigation whether EDEW are workers.

[79] More specifically, the lack of subordination is being understood as absolute freedom to choose working times, places, routes, and tasks. The rider has a direct relationship with the final customer in case the rider accepts the task. In addition, the rider provides his own bike and phone as work tools. As regards dependence, the company does not have disciplinary power in the case where the rider refuses a task. The company is not able to withdraw from the contract except in the case where the rider does not perform his duty.

[80] See, for the difference between workers and employees, Government of the United Kingdom, 'Employment Status', available at: www.gov.uk/employment-status/employee.

The UKSC said yes in *Uber*; but the Central Arbitration Committee (CAC) found in *Independent Workers' Union of Great Britain v RooFoods Ltd (t/a Deliveroo)*[81] that riders were *not* workers because of genuine substitution rights.[82]

B. Examples of Countries where a Specific Status, Sometimes Designed for the Platform Economy Especially, Exists, but where Collective Labour Rights Do Not Apply

In Austria, EDEW enjoy some basic protection as regards equal treatment, employees' liability or maternity protection. Furthermore, EDEW enjoy the same social security protection as employees. A similar assessment can be made for Hungary, where independent contractors enjoy some basic labour rights (equal treatment, social security affiliation and health and safety protection); and Portugal,[83] where rights of personality, equality and discrimination and occupational safety and health, but also on work-related accidents apply to situations in which the provider of the work is to be considered economically dependent on the beneficiary of the activity.

In Belgium, the status of 'independent worker from the collaborative economy' (synonym to the status of 'platform worker', created by the law of July 2016) basically creates some tax and social security contributions exemptions. The law of 1968 on collective labour law does not apply to these platform workers, ie, that any agreement concluded for these persons does not have the effect of a 'real' collective bargaining agreement but might entail effect under civil law, thus effects of purely contractual nature. Yet, some uncertainties remain as to whether labour law in general (including collective rights) applies to these 'platform workers': in its judgment of 23 April 2020, the Constitutional Court annulled the law of 18 July 2018 (creating extra ad hoc statuses) on grounds that shed some doubt about the constitutionality of a completely labour law-free platform worker status.

In Romania, a legal definition for 'independent workers' exists insofar as a person is qualified as such, if four out of seven criteria, specified by law, are fulfilled.

The Slovenian law ZDR-1 (from 2013, Article 213) also provides for a legal definition of economically dependent persons: these are self-employed persons who on the basis of a civil law contract perform work in person, independently and for remuneration for a longer period of time in circumstances of economic

[81] *Independent Workers' Union of Great Britain v RooFoods Ltd (t/a Deliveroo)* [2018] IRLR 84 (CAC) (not workers for purposes of s 296 of the Trade Union and Labour Relations (Consolidation) Act 1992. Moreover, the union's subsequent judicial review application which had received permission to proceed in part was subsequently rejected in *R (on the application of Independent Workers Union of Great Britain) v Central Arbitration Committee* [2018] EWHC 3342 (Admin).

[82] See, in more detail, ch 5 by Adams-Prassl, Laulom and Maneiro Vázquez in this volume.

[83] See Art 10 of the Labour Code.

dependency and do not employ workers. Economic dependency means that a person obtains at least 80 per cent of her annual income from the same contracting authority. They enjoy limited labour protection, including assurance of payment for contractually agreed work appropriate for the type, scope and quality of the work undertaken, taking into consideration the collective agreement and the general acts binding the contracting authority. This means that the level of remuneration of the collective bargaining agreement in the respective sector needs to be respected. However, since the application of these rules depends on the EDEW's official demand for protection, there is no evidence of actual application of these rules.[84] No collective bargaining agreement exists for this group of persons, with one exception, namely for professional journalists.[85]

C. Collective Bargaining Agreements Can be Concluded for or Apply to EDEW

Although the general rule in Austria is that traditional collective bargaining agreements can be concluded for employees only, there is one exception, namely for journalists: there is a collective bargaining agreement, concluded according to the Labour Constitution Act, between the (free) association of Austrian papers and media (Österreichischer Zeitschriften- und Fachmedienverband ÖZV) and the Austrian Trade Union Federation. Its personal scope of application encompasses employees and all freelancers employed by members of the association who provide their journalistic services to the respective employer not only on a part-time basis. Yet, there are differences as regards the material scope of application: to employees, all regulations regarding wages, working time, holidays etc, apply. To freelancers, only some very specific rules regarding their wages apply.

In Germany, collective bargaining agreements can be concluded for independent workers who are economically dependent and in need of social protection comparable to an employee, according to § 12a TVG.[86] These collective bargaining agreements have the same effects as those concluded for employees. Note, though, that it is a barely used possibility; in practice, collective bargaining agreements concluded under the framework of § 12a TVG exist for some special groups of freelancers in the public broadcasting sector. Up until now, no such collective bargaining agreement has been concluded in the gig economy.

As already pointed out, in Italy, there exists the possibility to conclude collective bargaining agreements applicable to independent contractors, which is a heterogeneous category.[87] These collective bargaining agreements have, as in Germany, the

[84] Kresal, BCLR 2021, 229, with further references.

[85] See below, section III.D.

[86] See also above, section II.A.

[87] Above, section II.A.

same effect as those concluded for employees. Up until now, several such collective agreements have been concluded.[88]

In the Netherlands, collective bargaining agreements can *concern* contracts for services (meaning that they can be declared applicable to contracts for services).[89] The two contracting parties need to be employers or their representative organisations on the one side, and trade unions on the other. Thus, the members of the association on the employees' side must be employees in the sense of the law, meaning they need to work on the basis of an employment contract. According to the law, though, these 'traditional' collective bargaining agreements, concluded by the traditional players, can include or refer to persons who are not employees (note, that no difference is made whether these persons are economically dependent, employee-like, or self-employed) and therefore apply to them ('kan tevens betrekking hebben op'). However, following the CJEU's *FNV Kunsten* case,[90] such agreements are deemed to be contrary to Article 101 TFEU. In the light of the approach followed in this chapter, this is puzzling as the Court in its case law only holds that collective bargaining is prohibited for the self-employed; the Court does not refer to a 'third' category like EDEW. On the contrary, it can be deduced from the *FNV Kunsten* case that collective bargaining agreements concluded for service providers in a situation comparable to that of workers are exempt from Article 101 TFEU.[91] To conclude, under Dutch law declaring collective bargaining agreements applicable to EDEW would be possible since the wording of the provision is unclear. It only states that the agreement can be extended, without referring to specific categories of workers. Yet, since the Court's *FNV Kunsten* case, the provision is a dead letter.

The situation in Slovenia is special and can be compared to some extent to the one in Austria, as there is a Collective Agreement for Professional Journalists (KPPN) concluded in 1991 by different associations of employers and the Slovenian Union of Journalists (on the side of workers). According to its Article 2, this Collective Agreement is (from the beginning) also valid for freelance journalists. In 2005, the commission competent for the interpretation of a collective agreement accepted an interpretation accompanying this Collective Agreement regarding the scope of rights that apply to a freelance journalist. The validity of the KPPN was never questioned. As regards other working persons, the situation is unclear from a legal point of view. The legal basis for collective bargaining agreements (generally speaking) is Article 2 of the Slovenian Collective Agreements Act (Zakon o kolektivnih pogodbah; ZKolP). According to this Act, collective

[88] See the specific section of the CNEL website (National Council for Economics and Labour), available at: www.cnel.it/Archivio-Contratti under the specific link parasub-autonomi.

[89] Art 1(2) of the law concerning Collective Agreements (Wet CAO). See also Draft Guidelines C(2021) 8838 final, 15 (n 6), according to which these Guidelines also cover this very case where solo self-employed persons wish to be covered by an existing collective agreement.

[90] *FNV Kunsten* (n 10).

[91] See in detail, above section I.A.

agreements are concluded by trade unions or associations of trade unions on the workers' side and by associations of employers on the employers' side. However, there is no definition of the word 'worker', which gives space to interpretation. Thus, it is not surprising that there were at least attempts to conclude collective bargaining agreements for the self-employed, in fact in the cultural sector at branch level. Yet, it failed.[92]

In the UK, the situation is quite mixed and fluid. There is one much-touted agreement[93] but its precise legal status is unclear, not least given the questionable tax implications. The agreement was concluded between one employer, Hermes (the leading consumer delivery company), and the GMB Union (Britain's general trade union). According to this agreement, couriers can choose to become 'self-employed plus', which provides a number of benefits such as holiday pay (pro-rata up to 28 days), and individually negotiated pay rates that allow couriers to earn at least £8.55 per hour over the year. In addition, those self-employed plus couriers who join the GMB Union will benefit from full GMB representation. Apparently, though, self-employed plus cannot earn premium rates any more (which is only possible for 'real' self-employed). Another union, the Independent Workers' Union of Great Britain (IWGB) has also been successful with smaller employers.[94] The IWGB is recognised by the CAC for collective bargaining on behalf of couriers[95] at National Health Service (NHS) provider The Doctor's Laboratory (TDL). Note, though, that at least in 2018, it was stated that these couriers were workers and not independent contractors.

D. Possibility to Conclude Special Agreements without the Same Effect (No *erga omnes* Effect, Especially)

The most prominent example thereof is the Spanish so-called Professional Interest Agreement (Acuerdo de Interés Profesional) that can be concluded for TRADE.[96] In fact, several such Professional Interest Agreements actually exist: UPTA, the main self-employed association, offered a mediation service to Deliveroo in order to sign such a Professional Interest Agreement in which Deliveroo's riders were recognised as TRADEs, as long as these riders consented to affiliate to the UPTA and gave the green light to the Agreement. A Professional Interest Agreement was

[92] Kresal (n 84) 228.

[93] GMB Union, 'Hermes and GMB in groundbreaking gig economy deal' (4 February 2019), available at: www.gmb.org.uk/news/hermes-gmb-groundbreaking-gig-economy-deal accessed 27 October 2021.

[94] iwgb.org.uk/post/5aa707360af09/iwgb-wins-first-ever-union-rec.

[95] The couriers who form part of the collective bargaining unit work for TDL carry pathology samples to their laboratories, but also take blood to hospitals for emergency transfusions. Over 100 couriers work at TDL.

[96] See in detail, above section II.A.

also signed amongst Deliveroo and Asoriders (Riders Autonomous Association) with the aim of mediating at national level between all digital delivery workers and digital platforms in order to jointly achieve improved conditions for riders. As regards the material scope of these agreements, basically anything can be regulated by them, including fees.

In France, the ordinance of 21 April 2021 organises a representation of certain platform workers (bike delivery drivers, chauffeurs) at branch level.[97] The aim is to enable a '*social dialogue*' in the sector. The organisations representing these workers (trade unions or associations) will take part in a vote organised every four years, in order to measure their audience. Depending on the results of the vote, each organisation will be able to designate a certain number of representatives. A 'Platforms Social Relations Authority' is created which is competent to organise the conditions of social dialogue in the sector and to support the representatives of platform workers in the development of social dialogue. For the time being, consultation remains at the sectoral level, and not at the platform level. Collective bargaining is not directly envisaged, but the ordinance sets out the conditions that could lead to it, particularly concerning the actors. Furthermore, a non-mandatory 'Charte' can be adopted for platforms guaranteeing some social protection.

An alternative form of protecting employment conditions, which was no collective bargaining agreement according to the law, was concluded in the Netherlands, where one trade union negotiated with an employer's organisation in the restaurant sector. As a result, working conditions for freelancers, ie, persons who were not working on employment contracts and who were considered self-employed, improved (higher revenues, right to training and instruction and rules concerning invalidity insurances and civil liability). This 'bargaining' took place for the whole restaurant sector. Yet, it was a relatively small agreement and has since been discontinued after pressure from the trade union.

IV. Action at EU Level (Required)

The picture mapped in the second part of this chapter is diverse. Most strikingly, some countries (eg, Germany and Italy generally speaking, Austria and Slovenia for a specific group of working persons only) allow for collective bargaining for non-employees. In fact, collective bargaining agreements with the same effect as those for employees have already been concluded for non-employees. As already argued in the first section of this chapter, collective bargaining agreements concluded for working persons in a situation similar to those of employees, when

[97] Note, the general rules on representativity and more specifically on 'audience' cannot be fulfilled by organisations representing independent workers, since elections which are mandatory for creating 'audience' concern just companies with employees (and not those with independent workers). Thus, one prerequisite for actually concluding collective bargaining agreements is missing.

it comes to economic dependence, should be exempt from Article 101 TFEU. Yet, uncertainties remain as regards the personal scope of this exemption. This is displayed by the Commission's initiative on collective bargaining agreements for the self-employed and the Draft Guidelines.[98] Potential EU action in this field could provide for a common definition of this exemption. In the light of the first two sections of this chapter, the Commission's initiative and its Draft Guidelines shall be critically assessed. Prima facie completely independently discussed from this first question is the question of EU action addressing the challenges relating to working conditions in platform work.[99] Yet, as is argued in the final section of the chapter (section III.C), an EU framework agreement concluded according to Article 155 paragraphs 1 and 2 (first alternative) TFEU could actually bring together these two – only apparently – distinct topics, providing for legal certainty and at the same time giving the floor to social partners at national level, and therefore also strengthening social partnership.[100]

A. The Commission's Initiative on Collective Bargaining Agreements for the Self-Employed and its Respective Draft Guidelines

The Commission's DG Comp initiative's objective is to

> ensure that EU competition law does not stand in the way of initiatives to improve working conditions through collective agreements for **solo self-employed** where they choose to conclude such agreements, while guaranteeing that consumers and SMEs continue to benefit from competitive prices and innovative business models, including in the digital economy.[101]

In other words, collective bargaining for solo self-employed persons should be possible without the risk of violating EU competition law. Collective bargaining agreements concluded for some groups of solo self-employed persons would therefore be exempt from EU competition law.[102] According to the initiative and the Draft Guidelines, the exemption should be valid for those collective bargaining agreements (only) that aim at improving working conditions, including fees, and not for agreements concerning trading conditions (eg, such as prices charged). Furthermore, the Commission states that it 'will not intervene against certain other categories of collective agreements',[103] and that any other 'collective

[98] Commission, Ares(2021)102652 (n 5).

[99] Commission, C(2021) 4230 final (n 3).

[100] See in the same light the Commission's, 'Proposal for a Directive of the European Parliament and of the Council on adequate minimum wages in the European Union' COM (2020) 682 final.

[101] Commission, Ares(2021)102652 (n 5) (emphasis added).

[102] See also Draft Guidelines C(2021) 8838 final, 10 (n 6).

[103] Draft Guidelines C(2021) 8838 final, 10 (n 6). See, in detail, para 32 et seq of the Draft Guidelines.

agreements concluded by self-employed persons that are not covered by these Guidelines do not automatically infringe Article 101 TFEU, but require an individual assessment'.[104]

The initiative acknowledges that the self-employed are categorised as undertakings in the framework of Article 101 TFEU, leading to a possible breach of competition law when collective bargaining agreements are concluded for these persons. Yet, it also recognises that 'boundaries between employment and self-employment are increasingly blurred'. As a result, 'individuals may sometimes not have clarity about their employment status, and thus about their access to collective bargaining'. Since this situation might have a 'chilling effect' preventing collective bargaining out of fear of EU competition rules, action at EU level may be needed, on the basis of Article 103(2)(c) TFEU. Consequently, the Commission presented the Draft Guidelines in December 2021.

While the initiative also recognises that collective bargaining for certain non-employees actually exists at Member State level (see, eg, Germany, Italy), it argues that obstacles stemming from competition law can only be removed at EU level. Yet, uncertainties remain as regards the initiative's and the Draft Guidelines' personal scope.

i. Personal Scope

The initiative's and the Draft Guidelines' focus lies on exempting collective bargaining agreements for those self-employed from competition law who do not employ another person, ie, who are solo self-employed and who are either economically dependent or in a situation of weak bargaining power against their counterparties. Apparently, those self-employed not employing others are 'at a higher risk of precariousness compared to those with employees', according to a 2016 study carried out for the European Parliament.[105]

The four[106] presented policy options as well as the Draft Guidelines then further differentiate between certain groups of the solo self-employed to be covered by the EU's action. Option 1 comprises all solo self-employed persons providing their own labour through digital labour platforms, apparently because evidence shows that these persons are more likely to have little bargaining power.[107] Option 2 focuses on the same group but adds that services could also be offered to

[104] Draft Guidelines C(2021) 8838 final, 13 (n 6).

[105] Andrea Broughton et al, 'Precarious Employment in Europe: Patterns, Trends and Policy Strategies' (European Parliament 2016), available at: www.europarl.europa.eu/RegData/etudes/STUD/2016/587285/IPOL_STU(2016)587285_EN.pdf.

[106] The Commission let go of the exemptions provided for by Option 3 in the Draft Guidelines. Thus, this Option is not dealt with in detail hereafter.

[107] Zachary Kilhoffer et al, 'Study to gather evidence on the working conditions of platform workers, VT/2018/032' (European Commission, 13 March 2020), available at: ec.europa.eu/social/main.jsp?catId=89&furtherNews=yes&langId=en&newsId=9582.

'professional customers of a certain minimum size'. Thus, this option also covers traditional professions in the offline economy, as long as they are not covered by other specific competition law provisions included in sectoral instruments. In this way, freelancers and independent contractors, amongst others, would be covered. The threshold to be applied could be the one used for SME (250 – 50 – 10 employees; thresholds as regards annual turnover/balance sheets). The Draft Guidelines reflect this Option: The Commission states that it will not intervene against collective bargaining agreements of solo self-employed persons who are not in a situation comparable to that of workers, but which are negotiated or concluded with a counterparty 'whose annual aggregate turnover exceeds EUR 2 million or whose staff headcount is equal or more than 10 persons or with several counterparties which jointly exceed one of these thresholds'.[108] In this case, an imbalance in bargaining power is considered to exist.[109]

Option 4 covers 'all solo self-employed providing their own labour through digital labour platforms or to professional customers of any size'. Therefore, Option 4 provides for the widest scope of application. Apparently (only?) in this scenario, the bargaining counterpart (ie, the 'employer's side') could jointly negotiate with organised solo self-employed persons.

The Draft Guidelines further concretise and narrow down the personal scope of collective bargaining agreements falling outside the scope of Article 101 TFEU. The focal point is the comparability of situations. According to the Commission, the following solo self-employed persons are in a situation comparable to that of workers:

- Economically dependent solo self-employed persons, who provide their services exclusively or predominantly to one counterparty, and who, as a result, do not determine their conduct independently on the market and are largely dependent on their counterparty, forming an integral part of its business.[110] Economic dependence is deemed to exist where the solo self-employed person earns at least 50% of his/her total annual work-related income from a single counterparty.[111]
- Solo self-employed persons performing the same or similar tasks 'side-by-side' with workers for the same counterparty, who, according to the Commission, provide their services under the direction of their counterparty and do not bear the commercial risks of the counterparty's activity or enjoy any independence as regards the performance of the economic activity concerned.[112]

[108] Draft Guidelines C(2021) 8838 final, 35 (n 6).
[109] Note that the same is deemed true for collective agreements negotiated or concluded with one or more counterparties which represent the whole sector or industry.
[110] Draft Guidelines C(2021) 8838 final, 24 (n 6).
[111] ibid, 25.
[112] ibid, 26.

- Solo self-employed persons working through digital labour platforms. Their dependence allegedly stems from their customer outreach, and from 'take it or leave it' work offers with little or no scope to negotiate their working conditions, including their remuneration.[113]

ii. Assessment

From a legal perspective, some differentiations made between the initial four policy options are problematic, first and foremost the one between persons covered by Option 1 and Option 2: exempting only persons working in the platform economy (Option 1) would be hard to argue against the principle of equality, in case other persons (identified under Option 2) are in a same position of 'bargaining weakness'. Furthermore, it is not clear why joint negotiations on the side of the counterpart are possible only in Option 4 and not in Option 2.

The Draft Guidelines' reference to the criterion of 'comparability of situation' can be positively assessed, above all because it is in line with the Court's case law. Yet, the devil is in the detail. Although the Draft Guidelines refer to the Court's line of arguing when assessing when a person is in a situation of economic dependence,[114] additional reference is then being made to a total annual work-related income of **at least 50 per cent**[115] that is earned from a single counterparty. In short: is a solo self-employed person only in those cases in a situation of economic dependence where she earns at least 50 per cent of her total annual work-related income from a single counterparty, or can other criteria replace this income-related threshold criterion? The critique is twofold: first, the analysis of collective bargaining agreements has shown, for example, that different thresholds apply in the Member States.[116] Second, according to the national examples, other criteria can be decisive, too. In Germany, for example, not only exceeding the threshold (of 50 per cent) is decisive, but **alternatively**[117] also the fact that a person predominantly works for one employer only. In Italy, the relevant feature is that the self-employed do not organise their activity by themselves but have to fit into someone else's organisation.[118]

A closer look at the Draft Guidelines also, most interestingly, reveals an apparent twofold approach that the Commission applies: on the one hand, it advocates that collective bargaining agreements concluded for the economically dependent solo self-employed should actually be exempt from Article 101 TFEU. By doing so, one could argue that it, first, concretises the Court's case law, apparently being rather confident that the Court would also follow this line of argumentation. On the

[113] ibid, 28.
[114] ibid, 24.
[115] Emphasis added.
[116] See above, section III.C.
[117] Emphasis added.
[118] See, for further examples, above section III.A.

other hand, the Draft Guidelines reflect existing practices, sometimes even provided for by the legislators at national or EU level: apparently, at least from the Commission's point of view, some of these practices cannot be brought in line with the exemption from Article 101 TFEU. Nevertheless – and this could be interpreted as giving leeway to social partners' autonomy in the Member States – the Commission is not going to intervene against those collective bargaining agreements concluded for the solo self-employed that 'aim to correct a clear imbalance in the bargaining power'[119] or, briefly speaking, are concluded following (other?) 'social objectives', if so provided by the national legislator.[120] Uncertainties remain, though, as to how to determine the 'social objectives' that the Commission refers to.

Above all, however, the big question is why the initiative and the Draft Guidelines focus on solo self-employed persons only. In other words, why is the criterion 'not employing another person', the decisive one? This needs to be critically assessed particularly in the light of the CJEU's case law. It follows from the Court's decisions in *Albany* and in *FNV Kunsten*, that rather a teleological approach, taking into account the weakness in bargaining resulting from economic dependency, above all, should have been considered. According to the Court, this dependency stems from the fact that the service provider 'does not bear any of the financial or commercial risks arising out of the latter's activity and operates as an auxiliary within the principal's undertaking'.[121]

Although it needs to be acknowledged that the 'solo self-employed' might often actually be in a 'situation comparable to that of … workers',[122] and although this criterion is a rather easy one to apply in practice, the Member State traditions show that other criteria could also be applied. In Germany, Slovenia and Spain (additional) reference is being made to a certain amount of earnings; in Italy, the competition on the market is taken into account. To conclude, a teleological approach focusing on the actual economic dependency might be a more sound path. The Draft Guidelines can be regarded as a first step towards such a teleological approach. Yet, they still apply to the solo self-employed only. Although the Commission acknowledges that some self-employed persons who are not in a situation comparable to that of workers might still be in a weak bargaining position vis-a-vis their counterparties, and although it thus acknowledges that it will not intervene against collective bargaining agreements aiming at correcting the imbalance in the bargaining power,[123] this, still, applies to solo self-employed persons only.

[119] Draft Guidelines C(2021) 8838 final, 32 (n 6). See also (11) of the Draft Guidelines: The Guidelines do not wish to affect the competences of the Member States or social partners as regards the organisation of collective negotiations in the framework of labour law.

[120] Draft Guidelines C(2021) 8838 final, 36 (n 6). The Commission aims not to intervene against collective bargaining agreements concluded on the basis of what the Copyright Directive 2019/790 provides for, either. See in more detail para 37 et seq of the Draft Guidelines.

[121] *FNV Kunsten* (n 10) para 33.

[122] ibid, para 42.

[123] Draft Guidelines C(2021) 8838 final, 32 (n 6).

B. The Commission's Initiative on Platform Work and its Respective Proposal for a Platform Work Directive

The Commission initiative on platform work and the Proposal for a Platform Work Directive aim to ensure working conditions that are in line with the high standards guaranteed in the EU, amongst others in the fields of social protection and fair income.

Yet, neither the consultation that preceded the Proposal for a Platform Work Directive nor the Proposal itself address the topic of convergence of collective bargaining rights for platform workers with EU competition law. Rather,

> the Commission would like to consult the social partners on collective bargaining aspects in platform work that go beyond the competition law dimension … such aspects could for example support social partners' coverage of platform work, facilitate contacts between people working through platforms, and promote social dialogue.[124]

The Commission's approach is therefore rather a policy-oriented one: 'Social partners' coverage of platform work could be supported and social dialogue promoted. Opportunities for people working through platforms to discuss, share experiences and opinions, could be established and actively encouraged, including the rating of digital labour platforms'. Information and consultation rights could also be considered for persons working through platforms; unionisation and participation of platforms in employers' organisations could be encouraged.[125]

The two main findings from the first-phase consultation document are that the self-employed enjoy hardly any (labour) protection under the EU legal framework and that there is a 'patchwork of regulatory requirements across Member States' as regards working conditions for people working through platforms. Since digital labour platforms are often transnational, working cross-borders, a common EU approach is deemed most appropriate.[126] Yet, the Proposal for a Platform Work Directive applies to workers only,[127] except of its provisions on Algorithmic Management relating to the processing of personal data by automated systems, which apply to the self-employed, too.[128]

If social dialogue shall in fact be promoted, the question is, though, why an EU framework agreement concluded according to Article 155, paragraphs 1 and 2 TFEU was not presented as a policy option. The answer might be found in the second-phase consultation:[129] (at least) the traditional trade unions and employers' organisations at EU level seem reluctant, since they also oppose the introduction of a so-called 'third category' for people working through platforms.[130] Yet, since

[124] Commission, C(2021) 1127 final (n 1).
[125] ibid, 28.
[126] ibid, 26.
[127] See, eg, Recital 19 or Article 2(4) of the proposed Directive.
[128] See, above all, Recital 16 and Articles 6, 7, 8 and 10 of the proposed Directive.
[129] Commission, C(2021) 4230 final (n 3).
[130] ibid, 3.

the Commission wanted to know from social partners at EU level whether they would consider initiating a dialogue under Article 155 TFEU,[131] the possibilities such an agreement could offer shall be discussed in the following.

C. (Collective Bargaining) Agreements Concluded by the Social Partners at EU Level as a Policy Solution

According to Article 155, paragraphs 1 and 2 first alternative TFEU, the dialogue between management and labour at EU level may lead to contractual relations, including agreements. These agreements shall, under the first alternative of paragraph 2, be implemented in accordance with the procedures and practices specific to management and labour and the Member States.

As regards the (legal) nature of these agreements, Protocol No 27 of the Amsterdam Treaty states that 'implementation' means that the content of the agreements will be developed 'by collective bargaining according to the rules of each Member State'.[132] Yet, it also means that Member States are not obliged to apply these agreements directly or to implement them, nor are they obliged to 'amend national legislation in force to facilitate their implementation'. Whether, and if so how, agreements concluded under Article 155, paragraph 2 first alternative TFEU are implemented, is therefore completely up to management and labour and the Member States. Rebhahn argues that since Member States are not obliged to implement such agreements, these agreements, although concluded by social partners at EU level, are not part of EU law. As a result, such an agreement cannot provide for any specific effect (eg, *erga omnes* effect),[133] nor is the CJEU competent for its interpretation.[134] Furthermore, it is stressed that Article 155 TFEU does not provide for a basis for transnational collective bargaining agreements.[135]

Therefore, in the context of working conditions for workers in the gig economy, such an agreement could in fact be concluded. Prior agreements which did not fall under the scope of Article 155, paragraph 2, *second* alternative TFEU[136] and which therefore required implementation by the social partners or the Members States are the agreement on telework (2002) or the agreement on work-related stress (2004).[137] Most interestingly, the Commission stresses that it follows from

[131] See also Commission, *Questions and Answers: First stage social partners consultation on improving the working conditions in platform work* (24 February 2021), available at: ec.europa.eu/commission/presscorner/detail/en/qanda_21_656; Commission, C(2021) 4230 final, 27 (n 3).

[132] EC Treaty of Amsterdam (as amended) Declarations adopted by the Conference, 136.

[133] Robert Rebhahn in Jürgen Schwarze et al, *EU-Kommentar*, 4th edn (Facultas, Helbing & Lichtenhahn, Nomos 2019); Art 155, para 10.

[134] ibid, Art 155, para 11.

[135] ibid, Art 155, para 10.

[136] Such as, eg, the framework agreement on fixed-term contracts which led to the adoption of Directive 1999/70/EC, or the framework agreement on part-time work which led to the adoption of Directive 1997/81/EC.

[137] Commission, 'Partnership for change in an enlarged Europe – Enhancing the contribution of European social dialogue' (Communication) COM (2004) 557 final, 10.

the wording of Article 155, paragraph 2, first alternative TFEU that the contracting parties, ie, the social partners at EU level, are actually obliged to cater for implementation of the agreement by their members in the Member States.[138]

Particularly in light of the Commission's contentious proposal on a Directive for adequate minimum wages[139] it is important to note that agreements under Article 155, paragraph 2, first alternative TFEU are not bound by Article 153 TFEU as regards their content. For example, in other words such an agreement could in fact also provide for a minimum wage (relative to the national average wage).[140]

Thus, such an agreement could actually act as template for collective bargaining agreements for gig workers in the Member States. First, it could define its personal scope of application, creating an intermediate category of working persons, between employees *stricto sensu* and self-employed, for whom collective bargaining agreements could be concluded or to whom such agreements could be applied without infringing EU competition law. In this way, the two Commission initiatives on working persons in the platform economy could be aligned. Furthermore, it could enlist topics that could be regulated by collective bargaining agreements in the Member States. As regards the minimum floor of rights to be guaranteed, the rights guaranteed by the Posting of Workers Directive could be taken as template, for example.

V. Résumé

Collective bargaining agreements for certain groups of non-employees exist at national level. Whereas the definitions of those persons benefiting from these bargaining agreements differ, the aim seems to be clear: to protect those who are economically dependent from their contracting partner. A reading of the CJEU's case law in the light of this goal allows for arguing that any such agreement is – already now – exempt from Article 101 TFEU. Nevertheless, action at EU level could provide for more legal certainty. In spite of the fact that social partners oppose creating a third category of working persons, they could take the floor and create a model collective bargaining agreement under the framework of Article 155, paragraph 2, first alternative TFEU, securing minimum working conditions for persons who are traditionally not protected by collective bargaining agreements.

[138] ibid, 12.
[139] COM (2020) 682 final (n 100).
[140] EC Treaty of Amsterdam (n 131); Art 155, para 11.

INDEX

Note: Alphabetical arrangement is word-by-word, where a group of letters followed by a space is filed before the same group of letters followed by a letter, eg 'digital work will appear before 'digitalisation'. In determining alphabetical arrangement, initial articles and prepositions are ignored.

Printed in the USA
CPSIA information can be obtained
at www.ICGtesting.com
LVHW0[illegible]038190923
758532LV00005B/15[illegible]

9 781509 956197